WILLIAM FAULKNER

THE CRITICAL HERITAGE

Edited by
JOHN BASSETT
Department of English
Wayne State University, Michigan

ROUTLEDGE & KEGAN PAUL: LONDON AND BOSTON

First published in 1975
by Routledge & Kegan Paul Ltd
Broadway House, 68–74 Carter Lane,
London EC4V 5EL and
9 Park Street,
Boston, Mass. 02108, USA
Set in 'Monotype' Bembo
and printed in Great Britain by
W & J Mackay Limited, Chatham

ISBN 0 7100 8124 3

Printed in Great Britain
by W & J Mackay Limited, Chatham

FOR KAY

General Editor's Preface

The reception given to a writer by his contemporaries and near-contemporaries is evidence of considerable value to the student of literature. On one side we learn a great deal about the state of criticism at large and in particular about the development of critical attitudes towards a single writer; at the same time, through private comments in letters, journals or marginalia, we gain an insight upon the tastes and literary thought of individual readers of the period. Evidence of this kind helps us to understand the writer's historical situation, the nature of his immediate reading-public, and his response to these pressures.

The separate volumes in the *Critical Heritage Series* present a record of this early criticism. Clearly, for many of the highly productive and lengthily reviewed nineteenth- and twentieth-century writers, there exists an enormous body of material; and in these cases the volume editors have made a selection of the most important views, significant for their intrinsic critical worth or for their representative quality—perhaps even registering incomprehension!

For earlier writers, notably pre-eighteenth century, the materials are much scarcer and the historical period has been extended, sometimes far beyond the writer's lifetime, in order to show the inception and growth of critical views which were initially slow to appear.

In each volume the documents are headed by an Introduction, discussing the material assembled and relating the early stages of the author's reception to what we have come to identify as the critical tradition. The volumes will make available much material which would otherwise be difficult of access and it is hoped that the modern reader will be thereby helped towards an informed understanding of the ways in which literature has been read and judged.

B.C.S.

General Editor's Preface

Contents

CONTENTS

Acknowledgments

Over the last few years Howard Horsford and Thomas Inge have provided assistance indispensable to the completion of this project. Staffs at the Wayne State University Library, the Alderman Library at the University of Virginia, the Library of Congress Newspaper Room, and Random House have been very helpful.

For permission to reprint, and for answering queries, acknowledgment is due to Brandt & Brandt, © 1935, 1939, 1940, 1942, 1951, 1958, by Conrad Aiken, reprinted by permission; London Express News and Feature Services for Richard Aldington; Walter Allen and *New Statesman and Nation*; New Orleans *Times-Picayune* for Julia K. Wetherill Baker; the estate of the late H. E. Bates; Warren Beck, this essay will appear in *Essays on Faulkner*, by Warren Beck (to be published by the University of Wisconsin Press in 1974), and is included here by special permission; London Express News and Feature Services for Arnold Bennett; *Canadian Forum* and Earle Birney; *Saturday Review* for Thomas Boyd, © 1926 by Saturday Review Co., used with permission; Kay Boyle and A. Watkins, Inc.; James Burnham; *Saturday Review* for Henry Seidel Canby, © 1931 by Saturday Review Co., used with permission; *Kenyon Review* for Richard Chase; *New Statesman and Nation* for Cyril Connolly; Malcolm Cowley, 'Poe in Mississippi' © 1936 by Editorial Publications; 'William Faulkner's Legend of the South' © 1945 renewed 1973 by Malcolm Cowley; Mrs Donald Davidson and the Nashville *Tennessean*; *Saturday Review* for Bernard De Voto, © 1936 by Saturday Review Co., used with permission; F. W. Dupee; Ralph Ellison, reprinted by permission of William Morris, Inc., on behalf of author, © 1953 by Ralph Ellison reprinted from *Shadow and Act*, by Ralph Ellison, by permission of Random House, Inc.; James T. Farrell; Leslie A. Fiedler, reprinted from *Commentary* by permission, copyright © 1950 by the American Jewish Committee; Mrs Cornelia Fitts and Norman Holmes Pearson for Dudley Fitts; R. W. Flint, reprinted by permission from *Hudson Review*, copyright © 1954 by The Hudson Review, Inc.; Maxwell Geismar, copyright 1947, © 1961 by Maxwell Geismar, reprinted by permission of Houghton Mifflin Company; Charles I. Glicksberg and *Arizona Quarterly*; *Observer* Foreign News Service for Gerald Gould; Graham Greene and Laurence Pollinger Ltd, reprinted by permission of Monica McCall, IFA © 1937, 1965 by Graham Greene; Horace Gregory; Harlan Hatcher; Lillian Hellman; Russell & Volkening Inc. for Granville Hicks; Richard Hughes, reprinted by permission of Harold Ober Associates Incorporated © 1930 by Richard Hughes; F. R. Leavis; *Daily Telegraph & Morning Post* for C. Day Lewis; John Lydenberg and *American Literature*, reprinted by permission of the publisher, copyright 1952, Duke University Press, Durham, North Carolina; Lady Lilian Mackenzie and the Society of Authors as agent for the Estate of the late Sir Compton Mackenzie; Abbott C. Martin and the Nashville *Tennessean*; T. S. Matthews, copyright © by *American Spectator*, 1936, reprinted by permission of the author and Cyrilly Abels, Literary Agent; New Orleans *Times-Picayune* for John McClure; Faber & Faber Ltd for Edwin Muir; The New York Times Company, © 1926/1929/1930, reprinted by permission; *Commercial Appeal*, Memphis, Tenn., the Nashville *Banner*, *Kenyon Review* for George Marion O'Donnell; A. P. Watt & Son and *Spectator* © 1935 for Sean O'Faolain; Philip Rahv; *American Mercury* for Burton Rascoe; *Nation* for Philip Blair Rice; Mrs Marjorie Ellis and the Estate of Kenneth Roberts; Dwight Macdonald for Delmore Schwartz; Providence *Sunday Journal* © 1929 for Winfield Townley Scott; Henry Nash Smith, the Dallas *News*, and *Southwest Review*; Paula Snelling, reprinted from *From the Mountain*, edited by Helen White, by permission of Memphis State University Press © 1973; Benjamin T. Spencer and *Sewanee Review*; *American Mercury* for Laurence Stallings; Wallace Stegner; Jean Stewart Pace and *Cambridge Review*; *Spectator* © 1931 for L. A. G. Strong; Frank Swinnerton; *Times Literary Supplement*, reproduced by permission; Lionel Trilling and *Nation*; *Nation* for William Troy; Milton Waldman; A. C. Ward and Methuen & Co. Ltd; Robert Penn Warren, reprinted by permission of William Morris Agency, Inc., on behalf of author, © 1934, 1941, 1946 by Robert Penn Warren; Eudora Welty, reprinted by permission from *Hudson Review*, copyright © 1949 by The Hudson Review, Inc.; Dame Rebecca West and the *Daily Telegraph & Morning Post*; Linda Jean Aldrich and the Estate of Philip Wheelwright; Farrar, Straus & Giroux, Inc., reprinted with permission from *Classics and Commercials* by Edmund Wilson, copyright 1948, 1950 by Edmund Wilson.

Grateful acknowledgment is extended to Random House, Inc.,

Chatto & Windus Ltd, and Curtis Brown Ltd for use of copyrighted material from the works of William Faulkner.

It has proved difficult in certain cases to locate the proprietors of copyright material. However all possible care has been taken to trace ownership of the selections included and to make full acknowledgment for their use.

Introduction

A volume on William Faulkner in this series poses three small problems. The relationship of commentary on a modern writer to broader cultural and intellectual patterns of his century has not assumed quite the clarity that similar relationships have for Austen or Carlyle or Dickens. Second, immediate responses to modern literature, especially fiction, do not reflect prevailing critical attitudes. The term 'criticism' covers several levels of commentary—journalistic reviews and feature articles; interpretive analyses found in quarterlies and books; scholarship; and formal aesthetics.[1] Most commentary on a contemporary novelist, though a portion of this may come from the pens of professional critics and scholars, falls into the category of journalism. Thus a gap—sometimes large—between what is representative and typical among attitudes toward a given writer and what we can define as the critical mainstream of the same period. Among the main currents of criticism in the 1930s were the Marxist or quasi-Marxist commentary amplified by the Depression; the more formalistic essays sponsored by, among others, such Southern writers as Ransom, Tate, and Warren; and psychological biography and criticism. Though all show up in early Faulkner criticism, they are not dominant factors, not only because the Marxists often ignored Faulkner and the New Critics dealt more often with poetry than with fiction, but also because most commentary on Faulkner was being written by newspaper and magazine reviewers not part of a critical school, or by literary historians in academia who by and large rejected him for morbidity or obscurity, or by men of letters either praising or dispraising him but not on Marxist or 'New' or in any strict sense psychological grounds. The two dominant issues in Faulkner commentary of the 1930s being his obscurity and his morbidity, it can better be explained as a manifestation of first the difficulty even good critics had learning to read the modernistic work of Joyce, Eliot, Pound, Proust, and Woolf, and second the squeamishness and repulsion many 'Humanists' expressed toward a school of fiction they considered the ultimate extension of Naturalism. Yet a third complication in arranging a volume on an author still publishing prolifically for fifteen years after World War II is the great swell of critical-scholarly publishing after the war, especially in America, where the wave of doctoral students and scholars has flooded journals and publishers with their output. It has affected all authors living and dead, of course; but since Faulkner was writing novels up until 1962 it falls within the parameters of his 'critical heritage.' Because so many collections now available anthologize the best post-war criticisms on Faulkner, it seemed wise to emphasize here the cross-currents of critical response prior to 1950, when he received the Nobel Prize. Therefore only a handful of reviews and articles represent the plethora of more recent Faulkner studies. Similarly the exclusion of foreign criticism must be noted. The at times very incisive French commentary that began in the 1930s would justify a separate volume in itself. The Japanese, ever since Faulkner's visit in the 1950s, have studied his work avidly and written on it prolifically, a body of work calling for a separate and serious inter-cultural study. Still, despite minor problems and the necessity of certain lacunae, there is no other American prose writer of this century whose own 'critical heritage' reveals so much about literary, cultural, and social attitudes of his age. The context for this volume, to be sure, would consist in the record of comparable responses to Hemingway, Dos Passos, and West, Joyce, Woolf, and Powell, as well as modern attitudes toward writers of the past century. But with the quantity of significant fiction Faulkner wrote, covering five different decades by the way, and the multiplicity of matters in that fiction that invite commentary of so many different sorts, there is no better starting place for a review of twentieth-century literary attitudes than the reaction to William Faulkner.[2]

THE 1920S

Outside Mississippi his first recognition was that by Sherwood Anderson in New Orleans, where Faulkner, one of several writers frequenting the Vieux Carre in the mid-1920s and coming under Anderson's influence, was publishing occasional pieces in the *Double Dealer* and *Times-Picayune*. Whether or not Anderson actually read the manuscript of Faulkner's first novel, he recommended it to Horace Liveright, who, not long after issuing Hemingway's *In our Time*, published both *Soldiers' Pay* and *Mosquitoes*. During that same period Faulkner's close friend Phil Stone arranged for a small Boston press to print *The Marble Faun*, a long poem with clear echoes of Swinburne and the English Decadents. It elicited two long reviews in Southern papers by Miss Monte Cooper and John McClure, the latter an acquaintance of Faulkner in New Orleans. Each pointed out faulty metaphors, tiresome repetitions, rhythmic flaws, and Swinburnean archaisms; each also considered the poetry ample evidence of a promising literary future.[3] Faulkner, however, had already turned away from a poetic discipleship to Tennyson, Swinburne, and poets of the 1890s, toward the genre in which he would be endlessly experimental while keeping ties to many elements in the Western literary tradition.

His first novels, considering their structural weaknesses and stylistic superfluities, were sympathetically received. Cautiously encouraging American reviewers called *Soldiers' Pay*, *Mosquitoes*, and *Sartoris* promising if somewhat undisciplined products of post-war malaise and stylistic experimentalism. Limited in number, both because Faulkner was not an established writer and because many newspapers did not institute review sections until the 1930s, the reviews none the less were written by figures notable or soon to become so, such as Conrad Aiken, Donald Davidson, Lillian Hellman, and Henry Nash Smith. Davidson (No. 2) judged *Soldiers' Pay* superior to John Dos Passos's *Three Soldiers*, 'because it digs deeper into human nature,' and faulted the next novels only for inconsequential subject matter. Another Southerner, McClure, also spoke highly of *Soldiers' Pay*; but though a case can be made for Faulkner's most fervent early advocates having been Southerners, from the beginning his appeal was intersectional—no less sympathetic were reviews in the *New York Times* and *Post*. In the *Post* (3 April) E. C. Beckwith wrote that among novels on this theme, 'for originality of design and beauty of writing, this book stands alone.' It was Faulkner's style, as we might expect, the general theme having been worked by others, that aroused the most commentary. Thomas Boyd (No. 5), author of the more naturalistic war novel *Through the Wheat*, differed with Beckwith, McClure, and Davidson: the 'impressionistic manner,' he wrote, was 'honest but slap-dash.' Concurring were Louis Kronenberger, Lawrence S. Morris, and Larry Barretto, with whose *A Conqueror Passes* Boyd coincidentally compared *Soldiers' Pay* unfavorably; they emphasized the book's lack of discipline and literary echoes. Hints of Swinburne, Keats, Wilde, and Huxley indicated to some reviewers he might become faddish or cultish. Others picked up Joycean echoes, surprising at first because it is Faulkner's major novels that seem to owe more to Joyce. It is uncertain how much Joyce he had read at this time, but Joyce's was a name in the air, and any writer having either a clever way with words or an interest in psychological themes was liable to find himself compared with the Irish novelist, as is confirmed by a look at reviews of Aiken or Cummings or Ludwig Lewisohn. Then again a conscious literary quality pervades Joyce's work as it does Faulkner's early books. In this fiction he was affecting a rather hazy, unreal atmosphere like that of his poetry.

When *Mosquitoes* appeared a year later, reviewers again pointed to the stylistic horseplay and Joycean passages, though with surprisingly little comment on the concern with theoretical aesthetics that links it with *Portrait of the Artist as a Young Man*. Ruth Suckow (No. 11) feared that 'the worst result of too resolute a determination to be sophisticated is the rawness of the amateurishness that shows through the fissures when the gloss cracks.' Elinor Wylie, though bothered by 'Joycean passages and bursts of purple lyricism,' was pleased that here was a book revealing 'an urbanity in fiction which we can well afford and which the author himself shows promise of one day attaining.'[4] Comparing Faulkner with Aldous Huxley rather than Joyce, John McGinnis (Dallas *News*, 15 May) called *Mosquitoes* 'a Huxleyan comedy; for it recalls *Those Barren Leaves* unmistakably,' and Lillian Hellman (No. 9) related its satiric brilliance to *Antic Hay*. Sherwood Anderson, satirized in this novel as he had been burlesqued the year before by Hemingway in *Torrents of Spring*, did not review *Mosquitoes*; but another writer with an interest in psychological themes and technical ingenuity did—Conrad Aiken. That very year Aiken published *The Blue Voyage*, his stream-of-consciousness novel of a self-conscious man on a transatlantic voyage, a book with links back to Joyce and Woolf and forward to Faulkner's first major books. In his generally favorable review (No. 8) Aiken criticized Faulkner for 'a desire to shock, a desire to see how naughty he can be, and how very, very sophisticated he can appear, . . . an ungoverned appetite for purple passages,' and such structural weaknesses as those which result from an inadequate integration of Gordon and Fairchild into the story. Surprisingly he called the dialogue 'as good, in its way, as Mr. Hemingway's' only one year after calling the dialogue in *The Sun Also Rises* unsurpassed in contemporary fiction.[5] Several reviewers did praise the conversations, which probably do not equal Hemingway's, and they do show Faulkner could play the witty games of the 1920s.

Then he left behind this material and in his next novel began to construct the most important imaginary county in American literature—Yoknapatawpha. Most remarkable about the reception of *Sartoris*, published only eight months before *The Sound and the Fury* and in a slightly abbreviated form by Harcourt Brace, was the book's general neglect. Weakly publicized, it sold fewer than two thousand copies, and, so far as extensive research authorizes generalization, elicited fewer reviews than any other Faulkner novel. The handful of reviewers generally agreed on such matters as the book's structural weaknesses and stylistic virtuosity. The two most similar comments, in fact, come from strange bedfellows indeed, the Agrarian Davidson and the Marxist Bernard Smith. The former lamented that 'he has not found a theme or a character that really comes up to the possibilities of his style and his perception. For his style is a major style, not a trifling one; and his perception ought not to be lavished on weak or inconsequent persons.' Smith was upset that 'his is a talent wasted on a thoroughly unimportant theme.'[6] Beneath the surface, of course, the comments were not the same, for while Davidson referred to the author's failure to find a psychologically satisfying protagonist, even as Henry James felt Emma Bovary was not a sufficiently sensitive or intelligent character for Flaubert's genius, Smith meant simply that the romantic fare of decayed Southern gentility was not suitable for any writer of talent. Both critics saw that in *Sartoris* Faulkner had not fulfilled his potential. Yoknapatawpha was a brilliant discovery, but in this work he was still shedding the post-war malaise of *Soldiers' Pay*, still learning the process of composition, the mechanics of structure. By 1929, after as he said deciding to write according to his own bent rather than to follow the tastes of readers, writers, and publishers, he both found his matter and achieved independence and genius in his manner.

As original and difficult as Faulkner's first masterpiece was for readers of the late 1920s, the uncertainty and confusion in the reviews is not surprising. The number of favorable reviews is. *The Sound and the Fury* appeared in the fall of 1929, about the same time as *A Farewell To Arms* and *Look Homeward, Angel.* Of the three Hemingway's novel was the most widely covered and became a best seller, while Faulkner's was the least widely covered and sold fewer than three thousand copies.[7] The less famous novelist from Mississippi was writing about people strange to most Northern readers and in a style baffling to anyone nurtured on traditional prose fiction. Dudley Fitts (No. 18), calling the work a memorable 'experiment in prose atonality' and the prose beautiful, still found the method impractical, because the 'deliberate obscurity of the opening pages repels rather than invites; and when the reader perseveres, he struggles out at the other end of Benjy's maunderings with no clearer idea of what has happened, or may be expected to happen, than he had when he entered.' At least one potential reviewer admitted he could not finish the novel, and we can only guess how many others simply decided not to bother with *The Sound and the Fury* on their review page.[8] Accompanying the book was a brief pamphlet-introduction by Evelyn Scott (No. 14), who had just published her own ambitiously experimental novel on the South, *The Wave*. In the kind of comment rarely found before Faulkner spoke at the 1950 Nobel Prize ceremonies, she called the book 'an exaltation of faith in mankind.' An unwavering pessimism and despair as to surface facts, she said in describing Faulkner's essential humanism, is nevertheless overcome by 'the reassertion of humanity in defeat that is, in the subjective sense, a triumph.' In responding to that, Lionel Trilling rejected the 'transcendental significance' with which she tried to credit the novel. Denying that the tragic emotions were as well drawn as those in *A Farewell To Arms* or even those in Edward Dahlberg's *Bottom Dogs*, he suggested that the new modern techniques were not as good for raising the pity and terror requisite for tragedy as they were for comedy and satire.[9] Still, despite three or four unfavorable reviews, at least a dozen critics, including Southerners Lyle Saxon, Abbott Martin, Julia K. Wetherill Baker, and Henry Nash Smith, and Northerners Ted Robinson, Harry Hansen, and reviewers for *Scribner's* and the *New York Times*, were sympathetic to the novel, especially what they called its tragic dimension. With the method they were less successful, making the usual shoptalk shorthand comparisons with Joyce, for example, and then trying to unravel the plot.

By October 1930, when *As I Lay Dying* came out, Faulkner's name, if not a household word, was at least known to many critics and reviewers, who spoke of him no longer as a neophyte, or new voice in fiction, but as one either continuing his development in fruitful ways or floundering after several attempts, in either case as a writer known to the literary world. None of the reviews were decisively negative; most were quite favorable, and perhaps surprisingly it was especially newspaper reviewers scattered around the country who found merit in *As I Lay Dying*—Mrs Baker in New Orleans, Morgen Morgan in Wilmington, North Carolina, Ted Robinson in Cleveland, John Leek in Oklahoma City, Margaret Cheney Dawson in New York. All through the 1930s a substantial portion of Faulkner's support came from such weekly reviewers. Others in 1930 began to object to his subject matter. Such mean 'low' people as the Bundrens, said the *New*

York Times (No. 21), are 'more amenable to the method Ring Lardner has used on his ballplayers. . . . We should be the last to deny any novelist the right to poke his nose into any human territory,' but should a mind of such 'a high order' dip so 'close to trash'? Edith H. Walton regretted that Faulkner had lavished 'his talents on material which is so grotesque and so essentially insignificant.'[10] They complained that Faulkner was still concerned only with idiots and degenerates, as if the whole cast of *As I Lay Dying* were literary offspring of Benjy Compson. Almost no one recognized the book's humor or the comic vision behind the most bizarre and catastrophic events in the journey. More commented on the book's method, the mixture of styles and the relationships between various monologues, though it posed much less a problem than had *The Sound and the Fury*. Though reviewers seem to have been ill at ease dealing with fiction that could not be fitted into the two traditional categories of the Romance or Realism, some were at least receptive to Faulkner's originality.

Fortunately, Harrison Smith (Cape & Smith) having recognized his ability, Faulkner no longer had to worry about publishers' addresses. Then, shortly after the modest critical success of *The Sound and the Fury*, magazines gave indirect evidence of his stature by accepting his short stories, in some cases stories previously turned down. In April 1930 *Forum* printed 'A Rose for Emily', and within the next fifteen months eight more of his tales appeared in journals like *Scribner's*, *Saturday Evening Post*, and *American Mercury*. Then in the fall of 1931, at the same time his first collection, *These Thirteen*, appeared, *Harper's* printed three new tales. Around 1930 he also elicited some response from abroad. Arnold Bennett before his death wrote two articles, a review of *Soldiers' Pay* (No. 7) and a briefer comment on *The Sound and the Fury*, both in the *Evening Standard* and the latter the first published comment on Faulkner in England. To Bennett, whom Faulkner coincidentally once called the only writer who started out to be a second-rate novelist and succeeded, the difficulties and ambiguities of *The Sound and the Fury* were merely the products of a youthful stage of eccentricity.[11] 'None of the arrived American stars can surpass him in style when he is at his best.' Bennett had learned of Faulkner from Richard Hughes, who both recommended to Chatto & Windus that they publish the British editions and wrote two sympathetic introductions.[12] He, Frank Swinnerton, and L. A. G. Strong, though like Bennett admitting they were skeptical about unusually difficult books, affirmed that the complex technique of *The Sound and the Fury* was absolutely necessary. Other Britons were not so sure. Howard Marshall (*Daily Telegraph*, 21 April) called the Compsons' story 'most tedious and obscure,' the experience having been lost in the 'amorphous incoherence of impressionism.' Gerald Gould (*Observer*, 19 April), who ironically was one of very few critics ever praised by Faulkner, refused even to finish the book, rejecting it as incomprehensible, and found *Soldiers' Pay* not 'in the least moving; but one cannot be moved except by reality; and in this book . . . there appears nothing real at all.'[13] Though such comments would become more typical of his British reception in the mid-1930s, his early novels attracted substantial praise; nor was it long before the plaudits from France added to his international reputation.

THE 1930S

In 1931 *Sanctuary* increased Faulkner's notoriety if it did not improve his reputation or greatly increase his following. It did sell slightly better than his earlier novels, well enough for Modern Library to market an inexpensive reprint the following year; and by and large the reviews were more sympathetic than the retrospective attitudes of literary historians later in the decade. But it was this book that justified to a number of readers their notion that the American novel was going to a 'school of cruelty,' that first-rate talents had stooped to the hard-boiled mode of fiction. Not surprisingly, there was a further shift away from concern with Faulkner's technical experimentation—a more conventional style was welcome—and toward more concern with the choice of subject matter, his obsession with cruelty, lust, degeneracy. Noteworthy among such reviews, both because it revealed a typical concern and because it showed more reflection than the rest, is Henry Seidel Canby's 'The Cult of Cruelty' (No. 26). Formerly a teacher at Yale, Canby in the 1920s helped establish both *Saturday Review of Literature* and the Book-of-the-Month Club. Troubled by a sordidness and brutality in even the best fiction of the age, he described Faulkner 'as a prime example of American sadism because he is so clearly a writer of power, and no mere experimenter with nervous emotion.' This bifurcated response common to readers clutching at 'New Humanism' in the post-war world was more acutely evident in a review by Alan Reynolds Thompson in *Bookman* (April 1931). Denying that such brutality has any justification in aesthetic theory and insisting 'the novelist should practise somewhat the same restraint in his imagination as is expected of him in his conduct,' Thompson still could praise the book for its brilliant fusion of the cinematic qualities of expressionism, the vividness of imagism, and the intensity of Conrad, with a classically controlled plot. Thompson's ambivalent review, moreover, is about the least favorable American review of all. In Britain such a presentation of, as one said, 'terrors and brutalities, giving flesh and circumstantiality to nightmare doings perpetrated by creatures almost too sick or too depraved to be called human' disgusted several critics.[14] Even more favorable readers like L. A. G. Strong and Helen Fletcher were reluctant to soil their journals' reputations by recommending the story to English families. Repudiating it as 'a rewriting in the coarsest terms of *High Wind in Jamaica*,' Rebecca West (No. 29) charged that the only 'new contribution to literature' which Faulkner has made was in the 'filth and hideousness' of the Memphis passages. Some Americans, however, considered it his best novel. A reviewer in *Forum* wrote: 'From the point of view of style, organization, and emotional force, it is the best novel William Faulkner has written.' Praise of this order is likely to seem excessive now to readers no longer dismayed by the demands of *The Sound and the Fury*. Whether or not shocked by the central events in *Sanctuary*, they are in any case likely to respond more fully to the more moving implications of the fables in *The Sound and the Fury* or *As I Lay Dying* or *Light in August* or *Absalom, Absalom!* Having felt in 1929, however, the frustrations readers experience upon reading a very rich poem for the first time and only superficially comprehending the orchestration of *The Sound and the Fury*, reviewers were able with *Sanctuary* to exercise their more conventional apprehensions.

A year and a half later *Light in August* demonstrated Faulkner's genius in yet another direction. For some of his critics like New York reviewers J. Donald Adams and Margaret Cheney Dawson it was his most solid achievement, to the latter 'a broader, stouter work than anything he has done before. It counts less upon the disembodied emotions, and it is packed, bursting with a mass of detail which explores every phase in the lives of its characters.'[15] Canby (*Saturday Review of Literature*, 8 October) called it 'a novel of extraordinary force and insight, incredibly rich in character studies, intensely vivid, rising sometimes to poetry, and filled with that spirit of compassion which saves those who look at life too closely from hardness and despair.' Vague encomiums, to be sure, but indicative of the book's favorable reception. Seven years before his more famous article on 'Faulkner's Mythology' and while an undergraduate, George Marion O'Donnell (No. 35) praised Faulkner's dramatic power, mature vision, and broad outlook. Even to James T. Farrell (No. 34), a quite different novelist, it was 'his sheer ability to write powerfully that carries many readers through the consistently melodramatic and sensational parts.' While calling him 'technically . . . the master of almost all American writers who fit under such a loose and general category as "realists",' Farrell also suggested that Faulkner had been overpraised. Anti-Faulkner sentiment, in fact, was festering among a substantial and varied group. In England, where two-thirds of the reviewers praised *Light in August*, F. R. Leavis (No. 38) deprecated the book's structure and technique, the modern methods and technical 'Gertrude-Steinian' tricks, and called Faulkner's moral vision sentimental and melodramatic. Compton Mackenzie, upset by trends in modern writing, predicted Faulkner's collapse, because 'writing like that is the result of weakness masquerading as strength.'[16] In America eight or nine reviewers expressed an anti-Faulkner sentiment that by the mid-1930s would dominate Faulkner criticism. To Barry Bingham, a Louisville journalist (*Courier Journal*, 20 November), 'Faulkner has managed only to produce a rambling, inchoate, and slipshod novel that cannot be redeemed by occasional patches of good writing. . . . He plays with inversions of narrative style that were objectionable in Conrad and intolerable in Faulkner.' Faulting Faulkner for 'a lack of power,' Dorothy Van Doren (*Nation*, 26 October) offered unwittingly as criticism what could seem a praise: 'Mr. Faulkner writes with a kind of understatement, as if a charge of dynamite that was somehow smokeless and noiseless had been set off under one's feet. The resulting explosion is no less disastrous; but there is no fuss.' Alvah Bessie (*Scribner's*, December) argued that there had been 'little behind this intricate façade; his distinctly unusual imagination has applied itself only to gymnastic exercises; his photographic eye has acutely observed and meticulously recorded the appearances of things without troubling with what lay beneath the surface.'

Charges of melodrama, moreover, accompanied a continued unrest, even among his supporters, over Faulkner's nihilism and despair, which some related to his personal life. For example, Joseph Henry Jackson, literary editor of the San Francisco *Chronicle* (19 October), suggested: 'It is clear that the wound in his spirit has not yet healed. He still strikes out blindly (powerfully, too) against the fate that seems to him to exercise a peculiar malignance toward the weak.' In general, however, American reviewers considered *Light in August* a success. It was the only novel he published in the four-year period between *Sanctuary* and

Pylon; but he did appear regularly in print, not only in magazines but also in several volumes of collected poems and stories—*These Thirteen*, *Salmagundi*, *A Green Bough*, and *Dr. Martino*. At the same time he was the subject of an occasional article in journals and was mentioned in surveys of American literature. Fellow Southerners Louis Cochran, A. Wigfall Green, Phil Stone, and Bill Hudson all wrote articles on Faulkner's background, though he would commonly tell outsiders prying into his personal life that he had been born of a Negro slave and an alligator or at best what he sent *Forum*, when it requested information on his life (May 1930): 'Born male and single at early age in Mississippi. Quit school after five years in seventh grade. Got job in Grandfather's bank and learned medicinal value of his liquor. Grandfather thought janitor did it. Hard on janitor.'

Early in 1931 James Burnham, who with Philip Wheelwright was then editing *Symposium*, wrote a perceptive article on the themes of human inarticulateness and the failure of communication in Faulkner's work (No. 25). The same year a curious and ironic pamphlet, *The Pseudo-Realists*, written under the pseudonym Junius Junior and printed by the Outsider Press in New York, compared *Sanctuary* with Ben Hecht's *A Jew in Love*. The character Horace Benbow and the author Ben Hecht were pseudo-realists, men who sought to escape from facing reality directly. Author Faulkner, on the other hand, deserved praise for facing reality squarely and writing about it so well. There was more favorable commentary. The Canadian scholar Pelham Edgar, in *The Art of the Novel* (No. 40), called him a leading American writer; and Joseph Warren Beach, one of very few American academics to laud Faulkner, called him 'one of the greatest literary talents of the day.'[17] Aubrey Starke, in *Colophon* (No. 46), surveyed his accomplishment up to 1934 and printed one of the earliest bibliographies. Interesting in a different way is Laurence Bell's 'Faulkner in Moronia' (No. 45), a defense of his hero against Hemingway fans who scoffed at him, New Humanists and journals like *American Spectator* which deplored him, and other ridiculers. It is less important for what it says than for what it indicates about hostility to Faulkner in America. At one level this came out in satires and parodies. One by Corey Ford, 'Popeye the Pooh', was in good fun, since Ford considered *Sanctuary* 'one of the outstanding books of 1931.'[18] Others, like those occasionally printed in *American Spectator* (No. 52), were more biting.

At another level the criticism was more explicit. In 1932 the British scholar A. C. Ward (No. 33), who called his technical devices failures, complained of the untransmuted pathological factor in Faulkner's fiction. Although Canby the previous year had put Faulkner in 'The School of Cruelty,' he appears in retrospect to have been a sympathetic reader, bothered by post-war cynicism and disillusionment but feeling 'in these new American writers a sense of power, a scope, a conscious skill in the transcription of fresh and unrecorded life.'[19] Still it was Faulkner's subject matter and moral vision, rather than his experimental methods, that fostered the first wave of hostile criticism. A mixture of genteel squeamishness, effete New Humanism, and frustrated searching for something more positive during the Great Depression, the syndrome became more common toward mid-decade, when the difficulties of *Pylon* and *Absalom, Absalom!* provided a second reason for rejecting Faulkner. Earlier in the decade his primary detractors were such scourges of gentility as Alan Reynolds Thompson in *Bookman* and Robert Linn in *American Spectator*. Thompson, despite his distaste for the 'cult of cruelty,' was rather restrained; but Linn attacked Faulkner for atheism, morbidity, lack of virtue, and yellow journalism, then lashed out at his audience: 'And we, the people, pray to the Almighty Dollar and He sent his only begotten son, the half-fannied Faulkner, to be our lord and master of materialistic prose. Let us resign ourselves. Faulkner's writing may smell as bad as some of his corpses. But perhaps it is our noses which are not attuned to the exquisite perfume of a dead body.'[20] Rarely was the commentary itself so ungenteel. College professors writing the literary histories of the day, men like Harry Hartwick and Percy Boynton, disdained Faulkner for his nihilism and technical dilettantism. Searching for writers with nobler visions, Hartwick, in *The Foreground of Modern Fiction* (1934), concluded that 'Faulkner's volumes, both in prose and verse, are singularly void of philosophy.' Faulkner was a dead end, more a 'symptom of our neurotic age' than a novelist with any roots that 'go far down into life . . . and the incidents of his novels have no moral momentum for carrying them over from the concrete into the abstract, from fact into symbol.' To the slightly more sympathetic Harlan Hatcher (No. 53), Faulkner's work also represented, despite its power, an unhealthy branch of American literature, that of shock and cruelty, one that would soon burn itself out. Cultural historian Herbert Muller, describing him as a member of the 'realistic' school who had not come to terms with life, minimized his fiction as 'an experience of limited value: one that, like a Grand Guignol melodrama, does little to sensitize and organize the normal responses to life.' Though admitting Faulkner's technical mastery of his materials,

Muller insisted that he confused 'material . . . with meaning, technique with value, eccentricity with originality. The fascinating work of William Faulkner lacks a spiritual center.'[21]

Though reviewers regularly pointed to Faulkner's pathological concerns, little explicitly Freudian criticism appeared during this period. Dr Lawrence Kubie, a New York neurologist, in a series on the 'literature of horror' for *Saturday Review of Literature*, did use *Sanctuary* (20 October 1934) to exemplify the relationship between art and neurosis, and the function of impotence and horror in modern fiction. Outside of a few letters in response, however, it did not generate any further work on Faulkner. Marxist criticism poses a different problem. Since so many of the period's literary critics leaned to the left, to include all their comments under the rubric 'Marxist criticism' would render the category so broad as to be meaningless. In V. F. Calverton's *Modern Quarterly* Oakley Johnson quite favorably reviewed *Sanctuary*, and several years later Calverton himself found merit in *The Unvanquished* and *The Wild Palms*. The more doctrinaire *New Masses*, though it rarely included Faulkner in general discussions of art and the novel, did regularly review his books. In 1932 referring to Faulkner's novels, Philip Rahv (August, p. 10), probably the brightest of the young men writing for Michael Gold's journal, wrote: 'The impotence of bourgeois literature is best evidenced by the utter lack of katharsis within it: it is no longer capable of its traditional static signification. In its place it substitutes disgust, or simply a series of shocks attendant upon the exhibition of various *naturalia*.' The next year Granville Hicks, in *The Great Tradition*, argued that Faulkner was not 'interested in representative men and women' but only in criminal violence and insanity that cannot lead him to any constructive analysis.' Two years earlier Hicks had written a somewhat more sympathetic feature on Faulkner in *Bookman* (No. 30), outside of Burnham's 'Trying to Say' the first article-length appraisal of Faulkner's fiction. Though critical of Faulkner's despair, his lack of social and moral direction, Hicks did not then question his ability or deny the merit of his achievement. By 1933 more committed to his politics Hicks insisted that such burning hatred required a social theme to serve as an outlet. With a writer available like John Dos Passos, not a Marxist but 'headed in the right direction,' Faulkner could be put aside. Three years later the British Marxist Philip Henderson, in *The Novel Today*, drew on Hicks's arguments to repudiate the Mississippi novelist. But such testaments are rare, and are no more than a counterpart of the literary histories examined above.

Simply stated, Faulkner's moral and political vision to various groups of readers was unsatisfactory; literature was to some a superstructure, erected upon a base of either Marxism or genteel respectability. That does not describe the basic assumptions of most of his serious readers, however, be they parlor pink or Agrarian green, small town journalist or fellow writer.

Defining the attitude of Faulkner's fellow writers toward him, of course, is complicated by the looseness of the term 'writer,' but most of the public comments by American writers were favorable. His genius for experimentation, says Malcolm Cowley, is what impressed writers; that Faulkner refused to lapse into writing books by formula made him an honorable model to follow: 'He simply *was* what we vaguely thought of becoming. That is one reason—though his work is the principal reason—why he was admired by writers of his own generation at a time when his books as well as his actions confused the American public.'[22] Which writers is not clear though his list of reviewers had included or would include Aiken, Farrell, Scott, Wallace Stegner, and Stephen Vincent Benet. Henry Miller spoke of him as Miller's only possible rival in America; and Ernest Hemingway always respected him, more than once admitting Faulkner was the better writer. Southern writers, especially those associated with the Fugitive-Agrarian group, also admired his work, Robert Penn Warren in 1934 concluded an article on T. S. Stribling by illustrating the reasons for Faulkner's superiority (No. 43). John Crowe Ransom, though disliking *Pylon*, called him 'the most exciting figure in our contemporary literature,' one who produced successful 'atmosphere and characterizations with almost a new minimum of machinery!' Allen Tate and Andrew Lytle very likely respected his work, though our evidence comes from articles written several years later. Donald Davidson had sympathetically reviewed his apprentice work and in 1938 called Faulkner 'our most notable single example of a novelist whose sensibility is alive to all the dimensions and possibilities of his subject, and who keeps, nevertheless, full control of that sensibility.'[23] One older novelist, Ellen Glasgow, despite respect for his talent, feared he was an escapist from the real South in the opposite direction from Thomas Nelson Page: 'Gothic tales have their place, but after all, why do all mushrooms have to be toadstools?'[24] But Hamilton Basso defended him against her jibes;[25] and Thomas Wolfe spoke of Faulkner as a writer 'whose talent could play over all of life. . . . He has extensive knowledge of all types of humanity. . . . I doubt that a man of that imaginative and inventive power can be held down—as people have indicated—or restricted to one type of story.'[26]

American writers—Southern and Northern alike—were generally more laudatory than their British contemporaries. Although British reviewers occasionally mentioned the high regard in which he was held in literary circles, the published evidence indicates admiration was often tempered with serious reservations. Bennett, Hughes, Strong, Swinnerton, and Richard Aldington had all written favorably; but Mackenzie, Greene, Garnett, O'Faolain, and Day Lewis were at best ambivalent, not denying Faulkner's ability but doubting that he had harnessed it or could control it within first-rate fiction. Rebecca West and Edwin Muir had even less respect for his work; and Wyndham Lewis, who to be sure had little use for most modern fiction, satirized Faulkner as a melodramatic moralist, a 'moralist with a corn-cob,' with a style as sloppy as Sherwood Anderson at his worst.[27] Perhaps the differences between the English and American traditions in the novel explain the lukewarm response, but then much of this commentary did appear in the mid-1930s, which was also the low point in Faulkner criticism in America.

Pylon (1935) and *Absalom, Absalom!* (1936), unorthodox in both matter and manner, were more harshly received than any of his other novels. Though reviewers were about as favorable toward *Pylon* as toward Thomas Wolfe's *Of Time and the River*, at least twenty called it a total failure. Some complained of its frenzied style, others of the degenerate characters and unpalatable subject matter. Though William Troy (No. 49) called it the best Faulkner had written—the subject matter was the most appropriate he had found for his perennial romantic themes of flight and bravado—Ransom (Nashville *Banner*) and Ben Ray Redman (*Saturday Review*) feared he might be finished as a writer, and George Marion O'Donnell (*Direction*), sensing a steady decline over the previous five years, asked Faulkner to return to Yoknapatawpha, the roots of his strength. Even Malcolm Cowley (*Nation*), in his first review of Faulkner, lamented the 'air of unnecessary horror and violence,' but still praised his handling of myths of contemporary life and his resonant lyricism. Though remarkably almost no one pointed to the book's humor, several discussed its social commentary, usually in terms of Faulkner's anti-modernism or anti-urbanism. Granville Hicks, in a *New Masses* review dated (14 May) the day after he was fired from Rensselaer Institute apparently for his communist activities and affiliations, did reject the book as another example of the failures of bourgeois literature and the writer as one with no sense of significance beyond the sensationalism of extraordinary and abnormal physical stimuli; but C. Jane-Mansfield (*New York Sun*, 27 March) argued that Faulkner had 'at last produced a novel of social rather than unsocial significance. . . . If he could just cram all of his thoughts into readable words, into sound English, what a havoc of overwrought social consciousness might ensue.'

Pylon is minor Faulkner, a respite from the more demanding labors of *Absalom, Absalom!*, which a year and a half later perplexed reviewers even more. One of Faulkner's most difficult works, it was so demanding on reviewers with but limited time to prepare their copy that few sensed the relationship between the stories of Sutpen and Quentin, and fewer still discerned that method became theme. There was no dearth of favorable commentary—George Marion O'Donnell, William Troy, Wallace Stegner, and Henry Nash Smith were four to recognize early its importance. Malcolm Cowley (No. 57), though finding fault with the occasionally strained style and pretentious diction, again praised Faulkner's lyricism. But the style and method baffled most reviewers. Not only people like Clifton Fadiman who regularly disparaged Faulkner but also such an accomplished cultural historian as Bernard De Voto called the book a failure, a failure due to the author's faulty understanding of the primitive consciousness he was trying to convey. Faulkner, said De Voto (No. 56), was a mystic who, in a futile attempt to compensate for his failure, substituted a kind of witchcraft-mysticism for the ordinary human concerns of the serious novelist. A proponent of American realism, De Voto found Faulkner's powerful style too frequently mere rhetorical bombast, his convoluted techniques mere tricks to cover incomprehension. Expressing a disdain of fictional experimentalism common to reviews in the Depression, Dorothea Mann (Boston *Transcript*, 31 October) argued that 'stylist' should be considered a term of opprobrium. 'Where genuine literary style really exists it is so simple, so natural, so fitted to the subject matter that it is possible to be quite unconscious of it.' Any verbal structure not transparent was ornamentation smacking of decadence, an attitude quite different from the perplexed but not hostile response to *The Sound and the Fury* in the late 1920s. The same impatience was exhibited by a reviewer for *American Spectator* (February–March): 'Insofar as he indulges in mumbo-jumbo or pseudo-mysticism, just so far does he forfeit his right to a permanent place in literature. . . . In his attempt to achieve either a lyrical effect or some sort of mystic grandeur, Faulkner displays for words an almost surgical morbidity. . . . Such devices should draw only the contempt of an honest writer, for they give him a means whereby he can perpetrate bad writing and slovenly thinking under the guise of profundity.' Similar responses were proportionately even more common in England, among a corps of reviewers including H. E. Bates, Graham Greene, and C. Day Lewis, but again the book's method accounts for much of this;[28] and in both countries it did call forth compliments as Faulkner's greatest work, not only from the better known critics mentioned above but also from weekly reviewers in local newspapers.

Although in the fall of 1936 *Absalom, Absalom!* (in England February 1937) received more negative reviews than any of Faulkner's novels theretofore, sixteen months later *The Unvanquished* brought him more favorable notices than any earlier book. The reasons are clear. The collection of Civil War stories has a more lucid style and conventional chronological pattern. Though many of the critics were writing about Faulkner for the first time, some had reviewed *Absalom* and sighed with relief when they opened and began *The Unvanquished*. It appealed to readers suckled on the historical fiction of Kenneth Roberts and Hervey Allen, the Southern romances of Margaret Mitchell and Marjorie Kinnan Rawlings. Faulkner did not catch those ladies on the best-seller lists, but several reviewers made a point of the book's superiority to both *Gone With the Wind* and *Action at Aquila*. The whole issue of the writer and his region was central to the commentary since he seemed to be returning to the world of *Sartoris*, to what Baylor University librarian William Stanley Hoole (Dallas *News*, 27 February) called the 'moonlight and mimosa' setting of the Old South, a string quartet softly playing in the background and slaves singing in the cottonfields. Actually, however, though a handful of critics like Fadiman, Kronenberger, De Voto, Hicks, and Earle Birney disparaged Faulkner for cavalier romanticism, *The Unvanquished* hardly depends on 'milktoast romanticism' or, as Kronenberger (*Nation*, 19 February) said, the worship or fondling of 'a faded gray uniform with epaulets, a sword put up in its tired scabbard.' In most cases reviewers admitted here was a lighter side of Faulkner, then recognized the book's serious aspects. In *Partisan Review* (June) Helen Neville defined its theme as the uprooting and demoralization of a people fighting for their honor and values. For Alfred Kazin it was the latest illustration that 'Faulkner's love and hatred for his region are so inextricably meshed that his passion is the struggle of the will against itself.'[29] Despite the handful of dissenting comments, Faulkner had gained a solidly favorable majority of reviewers, a majority he was never again to lose, not even in the case of the rather bleak *Wild Palms.*

That novel posed a more complex formal problem—Faulkner's method of alternating chapters in two different stories to achieve a counterpoint. Some reviewers advised their readers to skip every other chapter so as to finish one story before starting another. A few of the less sympathetic critics even accused Faulkner of deliberately frustrating the reader's attempts to enjoy the story by frequently interrupting it. Others, like Wallace Stegner and Edwin Berry Burgum, praised the device, even found it necessary in light of the main tale's relentless gloom. In general the distinction between those who disparaged and those who recommended the book was the distinction between 'style' and 'power,' the former pejorative the latter honorific, and often manifested in musical terminology (inspired by both the publishers' blurb and Faulkner's appeal to the aural sense) as in Hoole's depiction of Faulkner as a powerful but diabolic musician, 'like a mighty ogrish phantasme who sits before the steps of a universal console and bleeds fateful music from the organ of the spheres, . . . the discordant music of the doomed.'[30] Ralph Thompson of the *New York Times* (19 January), on the other hand, complained that 'the elaborate inversions, delayed modifiers, banked-up adjectives and quaint turns of phrase . . . come to somewhat more than the traffic will bear.' Some reviewers also found the subject matter repulsive, as they had years before *Sanctuary* and *Light in August.* Fadiman (*New Yorker*, 21 January) debunked the man 'who provides monsters for all literate American homes, . . . the only living writer who could retell "Snow White and the Seven Dwarfs" using for characters only Grumpy and the Witch.' William McFee (*New York Sun*, 23 January) discarded him as a writer now working only for 'a cult who nourish their imaginations on the blood of werewolves, who regard literature as a sort of Voodoo devil worship and who relish the gory details of unnatural crimes.' Most who made such remarks did so, however, amid generally favorable articles, also as they had done with *Sanctuary* and *Light in August.* Even John Chamberlain, no Faulkner apologist, admitted (*Harper's*, February): 'He leaves you with a far better sense of the horrible depths that lurk beneath contemporary surfaces than you could ever get from the soberly realistic writers who are concerned with what they fancy as the cold truth.' Alfred Kazin (*New York Herald Tribune*, 22 January) advised his readers not to pin Faulkner down as a realist, rather to read him as one who picks up where the realists leave off and explores 'the limitless spaces of the heart's weariness and abnegation, . . . the innermost patterns of atmosphere.'

The insistence on physical verisimilitude so prevalent among proponents of Realism and Naturalism during the early and mid-1930s now somewhat muted, reviewers were more tolerant of non-realistic methods, which after the war would dominate American fiction. This whole question of how to read Faulkner lay beneath the crosscurrents of the criticism. Was he a naturalist? To Alan Reynolds Thompson, Robert Linn, Harry Hartwick, Harlan Hatcher, Percy Boynton, and Ellen Glasgow, among others, he had been an ultimate and unhealthy extension of naturalism; but for the Marxists he was hardly advancing the cause of socialist realism. Was he a symbolist, perhaps another Axel in flight from the crucial issues of the day? Was he perhaps an allegorist? At a time when the homiletic fiction of Lloyd Douglas (*Disputed Passage*) returned to the best-seller lists, when John Steinbeck's *The Grapes of Wrath* offered sympathy for a dislocated and uprooted generation, when at the top of the non-fiction lists stood such diverse figures as Vincent Sheean and Adolf Hitler, it was hardly surprising to find reviewers allegorizing the ineffable Faulkner. To Albert Guerard (Boston *Transcript*, 28 January) 'Old Man' was 'clearly intended to be an allegorical study of man's struggle against the incalculable and mysterious in nature.' To Chamberlain it was 'a highly charged political allegory' of the modern world set against nature. In an irony unintended but especially suitable for the year of Stalin's pact with Hitler, Edwin Berry Burgum on the one hand found in the convict's heroism, in contrast with 'the neurotic instability of the educated middle-class doctor,' the 'virtues of the proletarian,' and Malcolm Cowley on the other argued that 'Faulkner is saying that some people fight and die to create their own precarious world, whereas others will perform deeds of physical courage, even heroism, in order to escape from the need for moral effort. The tall convict is the ideal soldier for a fascist army.'[31] 1939 was also the year in which George Marion O'Donnell published his allegorical interpretation of Faulkner in terms of the Sartoris–Snopes conflict; and only a year later Random House published *The Hamlet*, a work that seemed to reinforce O'Donnell's thesis.

Despite this attention in review sections, Faulkner's popular appeal was very limited, as attested to by surveys as well as sales, one survey among Georgia readers showing that either *Gone With the Wind*, *Green Light*, or *Magnificent Obsession* could account for more readers than all the works of Caldwell, Faulkner, Wolfe, and Kenneth Burke combined.[32] Thus the long stretches in Hollywood writing scripts. Still, in January 1939 the National Institute of Arts and Letters admitted him to membership, and in the next four years his work received substantial commentary, much of it favorable. During those same years that had seen so little favorable commentary on Faulkner, moreover, readers in a Europe arming for war had turned toward his work. As early as 1931 Maurice Coindreau had introduced him to French readers by means of a short article in *La Nouvelle Revue Française* and translations of two short stories. In the next few years a half dozen of his books appeared in French, most translated by Coindreau, and created substantial interest in and support for Faulkner right up to the Vichy period. Valery Larbaud and André Malraux, who wrote prefaces for *As I Lay Dying* and *Sanctuary* respectively, were fascinated by his situations and characters, his horror and intensity, often achieved by means of the absurd. For years French commentary was more astute than American or British. René Liebowitz perceptively analyzed Faulkner's mastery of the Greek sense of tragedy and his successful synthesis, in his best novels, of all the disparate components of a story.[33] Maurice LeBreton studied the relationship between psychological themes and technique.[34] In an essay-review of *The Sound and the Fury* in 1939 Jean-Paul Sartre evaluated the problems in Faulkner's metaphysics, the metaphysics of a despairing existentialist using his remarkable ability to dramatize man's suffocation in a decaying world. Faulkner's heroes were imprisoned in time.[35] This whole issue of Faulkner's handling of Time as method and theme continued at the center of French criticism, the only criticism until the late 1950s that could effectively bring an existential perspective, often overstressed to be sure, to Faulkner's fiction.

In the late 1930s Sartre, like many others, considered Dos Passos America's best writer, but Faulkner's French reputation was secure. His books seem to have sold relatively well in France, though nowhere near as well as *The Grapes of Wrath* or *For Whom the Bell Tolls.* His appeal was to a certain extent limited, as in the United States and England, to a sensitive and articulate minority; but there was not in France as in America and Britain a large group of outspoken critics hostile to his writing. In Germany, where the more romantic Thomas Wolfe was the favorite, Faulkner was a close second.[36] Two of his stories appeared in 1935, and then Ernst Rowohlt Verlag published *Light in August*, *Pylon*, and *Absalom, Absalom!* By and large, despite restrictions imposed by the Third Reich and a lack of popular success and although there were no more German translations until the 1950s, Faulkner's novels were read and praised by German critics. Spanish criticism had begun in 1933 with Lino Novas Calvo's attempt to explicate Faulkner's fiction psychologically.[37] The same year Antonio Marichalar, though lamenting his needless obscurity, recommended Faulkner for his emotional realism. The article appeared as a foreword to Calvo's translation of *Sanctuary*, which was poorly received in Spain and Spanish America. Perhaps as a result it had no immediate successors in Spain, although Jorge Luis Borges translated *The Wild Palms* in Argentina shortly after its appearance in America. In fact, almost the only significant Spanish criticism of Faulkner by the end of the decade was coming out of Argentina, from a group centering around the periodical *Sur*, and his influence is more clearly seen in the work of a writer like Gabriel Garcia Marquez than in anything coming out of Spain. In Italy Emilio Cecchi and Cesar Pavese helped introduce Faulkner between 1934 and the war. Only two stories were published in the Soviet Union, which generally ignored Faulkner while paying substantial attention to Dreiser, Dos Passos, and Steinbeck.[38] Still Faulkner, largely because of French enthusiasm, had achieved a firm position in European literary circles, and after the war some of the most imaginative critical essays would come from the continent.

THE 1940S

By March 1940, when *The Hamlet* appeared, Faulkner could count on sensitive reviews from numerous critics like Stegner, Cowley, Warren, and O'Donnell, all of whom described the novel with regard for its narrative strength and humor. O'Donnell, of course, did relate it to his Sartoris–Snopes allegorical scheme; to Cowley it suggested a Southern legend, a struggle between the old aristocracy and the new bankers, and mutations in and challenges to 'a traditional code of ethics';[39] and Warren (No. 75) raised questions about structure. He also admonished not only those squeamish reviewers who claimed Faulkner's work was 'morally reprehensible, that he invites us "to let our virgin fancies wallow in the sloughs of Zolaism,"' but also more sympathetic reviewers, like Cowley and O'Donnell, who overemphasized parts of a Faulkner novel without examining their relationship to the whole. Prior to Warren's article Burton Rascoe had also written a rejoinder (No. 73) to two New York reviewers, Clifton Fadiman and Milton

Rugoff. For many years a 'New York critic' himself, Rascoe belittled 'what passes for intellectual accoutrements in the quasi-intellectual circles of New York.' They were oblivious to Faulkner's humor, his tall tales, the whole tradition of frontier and southern humor out of which he wrote. Rascoe himself was a little hasty both in his conservative zeal to deny the importance of the social criticism he felt many liberal critics were distorting and in his tendency to diminish Faulkner's seriousness; but, as many reviewers, both friendly and unfriendly, continued to portray Faulkner as primarily a purveyor of bizarre abnormalities and demonic violence, his corrective was basically sound. Kronenberger (*Nation*, 13 April) called *The Hamlet* an exploration into the 'most polluted streams and malarial swamps of the subhuman spirit,' a book without any contrasting values to its puny grotesques; and Fadiman (*New Yorker*, 6 April) continued to dismiss Faulkner as merely the provider of idiots and horrors for literate American families. Even former admirers of Faulkner's work like Frank Swinnerton and Paula Snelling suggested that he had lost intellectual and artistic control over his material, that he had become more a symptom and symbol of than an analyst of the South's problems. A few sympathetic readers like Warren and Desmond Hawkins also fretted that the novel's loose structure indicated he might be losing interest in the problems of form with which he had worked so brilliantly before, but then concluded that the present loose effect was appropriate for the particular demands of the material. On the whole sympathetic reviewers, many of whom did have that reservation about his pessimism, were numerous enough to indicate that his reputation was not in decline.

Neither ought we to conclude, merely on the basis of numbers of reviews, that something had happened by 1942 when *Go Down, Moses* was issued. Since it was originally billed as a collection of stories, some newspapers with limited space would have routinely omitted it; and with the United States well into the war, many book-review sections had been abbreviated and others were laying a heavy emphasis on books dealing with the war or war fiction. The best-seller lists of this period are replete with everything from *See Here, Private Hargrove* to *Victory Through Air Power*. Other fiction received less space than before. Despite fewer reviews, however, *Go Down, Moses* was quite favorably received. Of more than forty American reviewers, only a half dozen were negative (quite the opposite was true in Britain, where very few were favorable), though several were dismayed by the fourth section of 'The Bear.' Horace Gregory was one of those admiring the prose, which he said demanded attention in American literature beside Hawthorne's and Melville's.[40] William Abrahams, in the Boston *Globe* (6 May), called Faulkner our great unread genius: 'It is time . . . to recognize that the faults, if such they be, are characteristic portions of a work that, when all is said against it, remains as valuable and imposing as anything produced in this country in recent years.'

Go Down, Moses was Faulkner's last novel until 1948, the longest gap in his entire publishing career. With the exception of a brief period in the mid-1930s the plaudits had outweighed the attacks over a period of fifteen years, and during this time he had built an impressive record. Had he written none of the seven novels that came out after the war, he would still be the best modern American novelist. There is every reason to expect that had he continued to publish during the 1940s, an appreciative audience would have awaited his books. Between 1939 and 1942 a dozen significant essays on Faulkner had appeared in critical journals and as chapters of literary histories, some concerned with matters of style and method, others with social issues and Faulkner's South. Some of the old misconceptions survived, indeed would survive after the war; but the considered interpretations by O'Donnell, Aiken, Warren Beck, and Joseph Warren Beach brought together the best of the earlier criticism, established some new parameters for Faulkner studies, and signified a more general acceptance of his work as a major accomplishment in American literature. Whether or not a turning point in Faulkner criticism, this material provided useful points of departure for those critics after the war who began to fill scholarly and critical journals with exegeses of the Yoknapatawpha novels.

The first of those items tying theme to method was Aiken's examination in November 1939 (No. 71) of Faulkner's 'hypertrophy of form,' his sacrifice of verisimilitude for other effects, and his use of long sentences to retain a sense of the moment. Two years later Beck analyzed the relationship between the involuted sentences and the uncertainty, the ambiguity of knowledge in the stories.[41] O'Donnell's article, 'Faulkner's Mythology,' appeared some six months before Aiken's in the first volume of *Kenyon Review*, a quarterly which not only helped raise the general level of criticism in America—O'Donnell's contribution appeared along with writings by R. P. Blackmur, William Empson, Kenneth Burke, Lionel Trilling, Allen Tate, Philip Rahv, and Philip Wheelwright—but also published several important articles on Faulkner after the war. Repudiating the position of most of the literary historians that Faulkner represented an unhealthy trend or a dead-end of modern literature, O'Donnell (No. 69) argued that he was really a rather traditional moralist. Though ironically the thesis echoes the unsympathetic barbs of Wyndham Lewis five years earlier, to O'Donnell he was not a clumsy and mawkish satirist armed with a corn-cob, but rather a mythmaker developing around 'Sartoris' and 'Snopes' the conflict between traditionalism and the anti-traditional world in which it was immersed. Myth criticism was first explored seriously in the 1930s; but O'Donnell, a graduate student under Donald Davidson in the late 1930s, applied it more in the sense of 'legend' or 'allegory.' In effect he both described a thematic pattern which explained the interweavings and reappearances of characters and scenes in Faulkner's work that Starke had pointed to five years before and that others like Kay Boyle had mentioned in passing (No. 63), and justified Faulkner's fiction within a context of Arnoldian humanism.

Dissatisfied with O'Donnell's thesis, a whole series of critics in the next few years described Faulkner as a frustrated romantic, a pessimistic nihilist, a frantic virtuoso, or a reactionary primitivist, all stances foreshadowed in the reviews of the 1930s. Beck, in a pair of probing articles on 'Faulkner's Point of View' (No. 77) and 'Faulkner and the South' (*Antioch Review*, Spring 1941), rebuked critics who considered Faulkner either a decadent romantic or a melodramatic sensationalist; but unlike O'Donnell perceiving beneath Faulkner's apocalyptic vision a pessimistic idealism, the melancholy of a Hamlet, Beck argued that Faulkner, though distressed by the modern world, was not fooled by the myth of Sartoris. Maxwell Geismar (No. 79), however, said that he was. In *Writers in Crisis*, a survey of American fiction from the cynical disillusionment of the 1920s to a social affirmation in the 1930s, Geismar called him an unreconstructed rebel, defiant of modern civilization, denying humanity, discontented with his own life, so that 'in his total rejection of the modern South, portraying it only in terms of its bestiality, Faulkner is held by the historical southern myth as surely as that great-grandfather of his.' In attacking the modern, commercial spirit of the New South, moreover, said Geismar, Faulkner had continued to lay the blame on the Negro and the Female as the South's curses. Oscar Cargill (*Intellectual America*, 1941), of New York University, somewhat incongruously called him not only a sentimental apologist for everything the Sartorises do but also a primitivist. Both theses, not unlike the more sympathetic arguments of O'Donnell and Beck, implied a rejection of the present and a return to one past or another as a model. The young poet Delmore Schwartz (No. 78), who was not impressed by Faulkner's clumsy diction or mystifying devices but considered him comparable to Shakespeare in inventive imagination, feared he had reached the point where he could maintain his old values, which were the values of the Old South, only 'by imagining them being violated by the most hideous crimes.' Drawing on a common theme of earlier criticism that Faulkner like Erskine Caldwell was part of the school of 'Southern Gothic,' Joseph Warren Beach described him as a romantic cynic, morbidly and complacently pessimistic, 'a second Edgar Allan Poe.' Beach, however, though imperceptient with regard to Faulkner's complex methods, was generally sympathetic; his two chapters in *American Fiction, 1920–1940* (1941) comprise the only substantial favorable discussion of Faulkner in a literary history prior to the 1950s.

Significant in a different way was a chapter by Alfred Kazin in *On Native Grounds* (1942), his study of modern American prose. In 'The Rhetoric and the Agony' Kazin outlined Faulkner's 'ferocious misanthropy' and argued that his 'monotonal despair has always seemed the ironic negation of his extraordinary imaginative vitality.' A confused Southerner, he had turned in frustration to an involuted style and agonizing plots as compensation for his imaginative and artistic failure. By the early 1950s Kazin was clearly in Faulkner's corner, as was in fact Schwartz, whose earlier article is much like Kazin's in attitude. Even in the 1950s, however, Kazin was troubled by Faulkner's verbal excesses, his frequently frenzied prose, the weaknesses that are inseparable from the strengths. With a kind of integrity in a period when Faulkner has been canonized and it has become unfashionable to point out weaknesses, he has maintained discriminating reservations. Though his psychological explanation of 1942 was unsatisfactory because he had not fully considered the function of certain devices, his recognition that the context of naturalism is insufficient for viewing Faulkner, that the polyphonic rhetoric of the novels makes Faulkner himself always a dominant presence, and that it in turn may conceal intellectual failures, is important.

At either end of such sharply differentiated summaries of Faulkner's fiction, or more specifically his view of man, were comments by Robert Lind and Cleanth Brooks. To Lind, 'His work reveals no indication of sympathy, hope or salvation for the degenerate Southerners he has taken as his theme. . . . His work is the crowning illustration in modern fiction of a warped and ultimately sterile artistic and social attitude, made all the more fearful by the fact that it plainly shows a complete despair for mankind.'[42] In Brooks's eyes, 'a real concern for moral values, and a real interest in the land and its people, coalesce into a work which is not the less important for the fact that it carries no liberal slogans and propagandizes for no immediate program.'[43] Today most Faulknerians accept Brooks's version not Lind's; but for years most readers found Faulkner's view of human experience one of the bleakest and 'Faulkner's essential humanism' at best a moot point. A decade earlier it had been asserted by Evelyn Scott, denied by Alan Reynolds Thompson; a decade later it would be denied by Edith Hamilton, reaffirmed by Charles R. Anderson. In the 1960s Martin Green denied Faulkner's furious rhetoric provided any meaningful humanistic perspective, but Joseph Gold published a whole book describing the essential humanism of his novels.

Since anthologists by the 1940s were beginning to include Faulkner as a matter of course, college students were reading his stories now and then; but his sales were no better than before, and with the gradual wartime disappearance of his books from print, his audience must have declined. According to his own correspondence, he was in financial straits at this time.[44] Although Stanley Kunitz allotted him four columns in his new *Twentieth Century Authors*, a journal in the South, the *Southern Literary Messenger*, ignored him for the three years of its existence. Although a teacher at Lawrence College, Warren Beck, claimed that reading his best novels let one 'experience that catharsis of pity and terror which comes only of great literature,' a teacher at Washington and Lee College, James S. Moffatt, included not one of them in a list of the fifty greatest Southern books.[45] Although a special exhibition at Yale prompted the publication of a Faulkner bibliography in 1942, the very works listed were going out of print and the author himself seemed to disappear from the literary world for several years.[46] According to both Cowley and Granville Hicks, his fellow writers continued to esteem him highly, but his popular following remained limited.[47] *Sanctuary* alone had sold more than a few thousand copies. Only *A Green Bough* and *The Hamlet* were in the New York Public Library.[48] All his books were out of print, so Cowley tells us, by 1945.[49] The plates had even been melted down during the war. *Who's Who* gave him short shrift. Booksellers, librarians, publishers apparently had little interest in him; and certain that his stories had no market value, Viking rebuffed Cowley's proposal for a *Portable Faulkner*.[50] The writer himself had stopped publishing not only books but also short stories, and did not reappear in print until right after the war, when, with 'An Error in Chemistry,' he won *second* prize in the *Ellery Queen Mystery Magazine* Short Story Contest.[51]

Several articles during this period included brief deprecatory references to Faulkner. According to Marjorie Brace, in the Yoknapatawpha novels 'excitement and violence are substituted for meaning and reflection; a kind of rape of poetic emotion occurs, and a drama is created that is purely fraudulent.'[52] Diana Trilling (*Harper's*, May 1944) dismissed him as 'essentially a virtuoso,' and J. Donald Adams (*The Shape of Books To Come*, 1945) called his fiction 'fundamentally meaningless because there is no interaction in it between good and evil, to the end that the mystery of human life is absent from his writing.' The actual hiatus in serious Faulkner criticism lasted only a year or two if that, however, and seems to have been more a slowdown caused by the war than a real decline of interest. In 1943 the British writer Norman Nicholson (*Man and Literature*) extended the notion that Faulkner was a primitivist (three years later, in *The New Spirit*, he described him as a fatalist akin to the Jacobean dramatists); and the American scholar Harry Modean Campbell (*Sewanee Review*) analyzed Faulkner's method in *The Sound and the Fury* and *As I Lay Dying*. By 1945 Cowley had begun a series of articles on the fiction. He broke up an introduction he was preparing for a *Portable Faulkner*, in order to get Faulkner back in print and to that end convince Viking Press that such a volume would be marketable.[53] Faulkner was consciously creating in novel after novel, argued Cowley, a legend of the South, a synthetic mythology. Although he attributed more conscious intent to Faulkner than is likely and played down the integrity of individual novels for the sake of the larger pattern, he did succeed in putting Faulkner back in print in 1946; and the success of this volume prompted Random House to reissue some of the novels. His preface, moreover, replaced O'Donnell's article as the point of reference for future critics. It was a watershed in Faulkner criticism. Cowley refined the myth-saga-legend thesis, assimilated earlier critical attitudes, and provided a thesis against which the formalists and other interpreters of the next two decades could play off their own readings. The two-part essay-review Warren wrote that summer for *New Republic* (No. 83), in fact, combines with the preface to form almost too neat a fulcrum in Faulkner criticism.[54] Warren evaluated Faulkner's achievement not in terms of the novels' regional implications, though he paid tribute to Cowley's accomplishment, but in terms of their universality and the formal integrity of individual works. He then advised his readers: 'The study of Faulkner is the most challenging single task in contemporary American literature for criticism to undertake.'

Much of the commentary of the next few years, however, was an extension of that of the 1930s and early 1940s. The war over and literary as well as political matters returning to normality, Faulkner momentarily resumed his place as a controversial talent to be kicked back and forth among benign and malign critics. One situation, however, was different. With the end of the war came a whole new generation into the academic world, a generation raised during the Depression and bringing to their profession not only new energy and attitudes but also new standards by which to measure their success. Along with an enthusiasm over new ways of looking at their world—its history, society, and culture—grew a new emphasis on publication as a concrete way to measure each other's achievement, more by indirection than by intention, for the scholarly publication explosion was the necessary concomitant of the desire of academicians to communicate their findings and ideas to each other, to test them, and resultingly to test themselves in the academic marketplace. Along with new professors, of course, trooped the graduate students in larger numbers than ever before, numbers that would increase geometrically by the 1960s, students who would very shortly join the faculties. Among this new group interest in William Faulkner steadily grew, and the main contributions to not only Faulkner scholarship but also Faulkner criticism from then on came from American universities. It seems quite likely that without the war's intervention, especially in light of the flurry of interest in Faulkner between 1939 and 1942, some of this would have appeared several years earlier. At the same time two other factors contributed to this Faulkner boom—the acceptance of modern literature as a legitimate area of study in colleges and the ascendance of the New Criticism. The former had grown out of a rebellion against academic conservatism several years earlier. The latter provided a corrective to the tendency to read Faulkner's work as a single entity, and in many cases long needed clarifications of method and theme that contributed to appreciation of the novels. Despite the simplistic summaries of 'New Criticism' characteristic of later reactions using its weakest manifestations as whipping boys, the advent of a serious criticism that began with close attention to verbal facts was a necessary prelude to accurate appreciation of modernistic fiction and poetry.

In the meantime, however, criticism did continue in two of the old patterns—Faulkner's stylistic excesses cancelled the virtues of his imagination, to leave mere experimental raconteurism; and Faulkner was a tormented puritan whose pathological subject matter too often led to solipsism rather than meaningful reflection on the modern world. In one of the first post-war anthologies, W. Tasker Witham (*Living American Literature*, 1947) introduced Faulkner as a purveyor of perversions, convincing in his portrayals to be sure, but nevertheless a sensationalist who discovered with *Sanctuary* that the American public would buy tales of abnormality. In *The Novel and the World's Dilemma* (1947) Edwin Berry Burgum, only a few years before his dismissal from New York University for his Marxist activities, described those tales as 'patterns of American decadence,' products of a once promising talent that after *The Sound and the Fury* declined into mere experimental raconteurism without motivation or structure or commitment. George Snell, in a 1946 article later incorporated into *The Shapers of American Fiction* (1947), agreed that Faulkner was a man of great talent whose books fail because his difficult style is unendurable over several hundred pages, that his 'fury,' which he could not leash, carried him into unrestrained writing. Vincent Hopper, in 'Faulkner's Paradise Lost' (*Virginia Quarterly Review*, 1947), described Faulkner as a bitter but romantic Puritan, rebelling against man's animal nature and trying to escape into a never-never world, a Puritan engaged constantly in a struggle against nature which manifests itself in an abnormal sensitivity to the physical world: 'He shakes a Byronic fist at heaven or laughs sardonically in a Byronic–early Hemingway manner.'

If criticism was falling back into some of the same patterns, at least Faulkner himself was back writing again, publishing stories, and serving briefly as a visiting lecturer at the University of Mississippi (where in 1947 the faculty voted against awarding him an honorary degree). The same year, in a New York poll, he had been left off a list of the ten best modern American writers;[55] and Jean-Paul Sartre, visiting eastern colleges in America, was shocked to find so many students who had never heard his name.[56] But in 1948 *Intruder in the Dust* sold better than any of his earlier works, and the next year was made into a movie by M-G-M in Oxford, Mississippi, itself. Magazines printed photographic specials on Faulkner's country. On 23 November 1949, he was elected to membership in the American Academy of Arts and Letters; that in a way indicated his acceptance by the literary establishment, as his gradually increasing sales marked a wider readership.

THE NOBEL PRIZE

The years just preceding and following Faulkner's recognition by the Swedish Academy, 1948 to 1952 or thereabouts, witnessed the most significant transition in Faulkner studies. Not only did university scholar-critics make him a most favored subject and turn their attention toward the intricacies of his novels, but also the timely subject matter of *Intruder in the Dust* and its modest success as a movie, the republication of his earlier novels and stories especially in cheap paperback editions, and the Nobel Prize brought Faulkner a wider audience. *Intruder* is Faulkner's most obviously socially conscious book, and at a time when the term 'civil rights' was beginning to polarize American citizens, any novel about an attempted lynching was topical and potentially controversial among both Southerners and Northern liberals. Outside of a handful of attacks on what was called the book's needlessly convoluted and obfuscating style, in fact, the unfavorable comments came from those to whom the story was just an excuse for Faulkner to preach his political views, to sermonize through the figure of Gavin Stevens, to spread ideas that were irresponsible, ridiculous, or just carelessly considered. Whether or not Gavin's verbiage represents Faulkner or a part of Faulkner, it bothered several reviewers, not always because it was boring. Cowley regretted both that an otherwise good story was overshadowed by Stevens' sermons, and that the sermons themselves were fraught with contradictions. By presenting Gavin's position without a contrasting point of view, Faulkner was neglecting the racism which had for years prevented changes in the South. Liberal and radical reviewers agreed, at times more caustically. In communist newspapers David Carpenter (*Daily Worker*, 6 October) and Gertrude Martin (Chicago *Defender*, 23 October) called it a bigoted, escapist work. In *Masses and Mainstream* (November) Barbara Giles, after praising *The Sound and the Fury* for its dissection of ruling class psychology, rebuked Faulkner for surrendering to Southern pride. But less doctrinaire reviewers like Charles Glicksberg, Sterling North, Hugh Gloster, Jacques Barzun, and Elizabeth Hardwick also deplored Faulkner's reactionary parochialism, Miss Hardwick claiming in *Partisan Review* (October) that he had falsified an excellent dramatization of 'the moral dilemma of the decent guilt-ridden Southerner' by means of states-rights pamphleteering. Even such defenders of the book as Paolo Milano, Robert Bunker, and Frances Neel Cheney found its politics troublesome or embarrassing. Conversely a number of Southern reviewers defended the book on somewhat similar grounds. The majority of those who praised the novel, however, and this was an overwhelming majority of reviewers in Britain and America, did so because Faulkner was a first-rate writer, because his prose was resonant, because he told a good story, or because his characters—especially Lucas and Chick—were vivid and real.

Outside the reviews—and to the list of these must be added scores of favorable comments on *Collected Stories* (1950) and even *Knight's Gambit* (1949)—the growing body of Faulkner criticism assumed a Janus aspect during this period; old approaches were reevaluated, new approaches were explored. Three important articles reconsidered the effect of Faulkner's vision on his method. John Arthos (*Accent*, Autumn 1948) outlined a conflict between his impulse toward humor and comic dénouement and the tragic violence of Southern history. Feeling like Alfred Kazin that Faulkner's own voice was always a dominant presence, he showed that the violent more frequently than the comic controlled it. Charles Glicksberg (No. 90), while concurring that the author's vision was bleak, advanced the view that he was the most detached of authors, that his perspective was that of the scientific naturalist, unattached to and unaffected by the pains of his characters; but that because he frequently imposed a romantic psychopathological point of view onto this naturalistic world, he produced an exaggerated Freudian nightmare, the grief of sin but no hope of redemption.[57] W. M. Frohock (*Southwest Review*, Summer 1949), denying that naturalism helped explain the fiction very well, argued that the violence in Faulkner's world was invariably symbolic. It is Glicksberg's description of Faulkner's naturalism that has generally been ignored by later critics, who have pursued symbolic or mythic patterns in Faulkner's fiction. Part of the problem is semantic: 'naturalism' can be both a way of looking at the world and a category of novels. Perhaps the ghost of Émile Zola makes us conflate positivism and the 'slice of life'; but, as conversely the symbolic method was exploited by American writers with such diverse world-views as Emerson, Thoreau, Hawthorne, and Melville, there is no reason why the 'naturalist' cannot employ diverse fictional methods. Glicksberg and Arthos did not make the mistake made by Hopper and Geismar and Kazin, or later Edith Hamilton, of seeing the sound and fury as the rantings of either a twisted Puritan or a talent out of control; and they differed on the extent to which Faulkner was involved in or detached from the dilemmas of his characters. But from then on most general inquiries into the relationship between vision and method depended on close consideration of the purposes of and intentions behind particular methods.

To some it was Faulkner himself who was changing directions. One set of articles—by Tom Greet, Russell Roth, Catherine Cater, and Dayton Kohler—emphasized the gradual brightening in Faulkner's vision by 1948, in Greet's terms the dialectic between the Sartoris ideal and Ike McCaslin's escapism that is synthesized in Gavin Stevens.[58] It was not in such overviews, however, that the major insights appeared. They arose out of essays on individual novels, at times exploring meaning in a pattern of symbol or image and interpreting Faulkner as more the symbolist than the naturalist, at times studying closely narrative voice, style, and tone to provide a more careful reading of Faulkner's intentions and achievement. *Kenyon Review* in the fall of 1948 published two contributions to the new Faulkner criticism, Richard Chase's study of symbolic patterns in *Light in August* and Lawrence Bowling's analysis of Benjy's section as *The Sound and the Fury* in miniature. Then in both the summer of 1949 and fall of 1950 *Perspective*, a new quarterly coming out of the University of Louisville under the direction of Jarvis and Mona Thurston, published special issues on Faulkner. Harry Modean Campbell wrote a general study of Faulkner's structural devices, and Ruel Foster drew on Freud and Kenneth Burke to demonstrate the importance of unconscious elements in the fiction, or Faulkner's concern with 'the surrealistic, subconscious, dream aspect of life.' Seven of the nine critical articles, however, were on individual novels, the best of them being Olga Westland [Vickery]'s interpretation of *As I Lay Dying* in terms of the interplay of seriousness and farce and the use of two different styles. Also evident in both issues—and many of the articles were by graduate students—was the new vogue of myth criticism for which Faulkner was fertile ground. Edgar Whan looked at Gothic myth in *Absalom, Absalom!*; Sumner Powell described a pattern of Christian myth in *The Sound and the Fury*; and Phyllis Hirshleifer evaluated Joe Christmas as both isolato and Christ figure. At times the analyses were misdirected, as when Powell, while rooting around for evidence that Benjy is a Christ figure and that Faulkner is criticizing America for neglecting Christianity, lost sight of the main lines of *The Sound and the Fury*. Perhaps, as Harry Modean Campbell suggested, this kind of excessive symbol hunting resulted from the influence of Chase's 'The Stone and the Crucifixion: Faulkner's *Light in August*.' More likely it was no more than the natural corollary of post-war graduate study and some of the new approaches to literature then being taught and tested.[59]

By this time his books were being reprinted in paperback editions, were selling in corner drugstores, and were being used in college courses. 'Some professors and librarians' told Malcolm Cowley that Faulkner's work was 'more studied in the colleges than that of any other living author.'[60] Late in 1949 he won the O. Henry Award for 'A Courtship,' and then in April 1950 was announced winner of the quinquennial Howells Medal of the American Academy of Arts and Letters. Not only was his stature in America growing, but at a conference in New York of the Institute of International Education (August 1949) some sixty delegates and guests affirmed that he was 'rated abroad as this country's finest author.'[61] Marcel Aymé in 1950 said that the French people, 'not merely . . . intellectual snobs,' loved him for 'his gift for raising up a tragic world with the atmosphere of such singular poetry.'[62] The intellectuals and critics also loved him; and although almost none of the significant criticism on Faulkner was coming from England at this time, the French continued to explore his use of Time and his existentialist affinities.[63]

By 1950 Faulkner was not a surprising choice for the Nobel Prize. It was a measure of his international reputation. Not among all groups, however, for a handful of editorials indicated quite the opposite. The widely read *New York Times* editorial was laudatory but defensive. Voicing a common fear that the world might consider Faulkner's pictures of Mississippi degenerates as an accurate description of life in these United States, the editors (11 November) reminded their readers that 'incest and fear may be common practice in Faulkner's "Jefferson, Miss." but they are not elsewhere in the United States.' Elsewhere editors were not so decorous. In Detroit the *Free Press* (13 November), calling the award scandalous, labeled Faulkner 'the father of this school of Southern defamation. . . . His thousands of disciples, with nothing to recommend them but possession of a typewriter and some slight knowledge of Freud,' were 'fifth columnists, the biggest money maker for New York publishers.' The Knight newspaper rallied its Southern brethren: 'Oil up the old musket ye sons of Dixie! Start Shooting! In defense, suh, of the honor of the South.' Down the road in Toledo (1 December), *Blade* editor Grove Patterson repudiated the selection on the simple grounds that Faulkner could not write; he could not be read or understood. Meanwhile back in Faulkner's own state, Major Frederick Sullens, publisher of the Jackson *Daily News*, who had throughout the shooting and showing of the movie of *Intruder in the Dust* excoriated Faulkner, reprinted both those editorials (19 November, 10 December) and called Faulkner 'an exemplar of the garbage can school of writing.' These items were no trepresentative; most editorials were favorable. Still, novelists rarely attract that kind of public attack, especially at awards time. In the Cold War, with the stage set for McCarthyism, Americans were more defensive than usual about portrayals of their country being propagated abroad.

THE 1950S AND AFTER

These comments, of course, were not by literary editors. They had spoken quite favorably in late summer when the *Collected Stories* came out, and would incorporate their attitudes toward Faulkner's new prize in reviews of his next book, *Requiem for a Nun*. Though rarely considered major Faulkner these days, that book was quite well received in 1951, not as well as the *Stories* or *Intruder* but at least as well as Hemingway's latest effort, *Across the River and Into the Trees*. Once a writer has been elevated onto a pedestal, some reviewers think twice before belittling his most recent product. In Faulkner's case, moreover, several Southern reviewers had adopted him as their most favored native son. Jesse Hill Ford, Paul Flowers, Robert Richards, Cecil Abernathy, John Chapman, Lee Cheney Jessup—reviewers from Florida to Texas—lauded *Requiem*. Only one sour note came from the South. James Aswell, in the Houston *Chronicle* (30 September) complained that Faulkner was beginning to write like 'an awkward amateur'; the situations, characters, and prose were a total failure; and 'the tragic worst of the Faulkner catastrophe is that the callow ideologues of the pinko press, bereft of a hero now that Uncle Joe is naughty-naughty-don't-touch, will think this chaotic mess is great stuff. They'll praise it and cause it to be imitated; and they still run the Reviewers' Cartel.' Most reviews revolved around the question of whether the dramatic or narrative sections were better, the increasing role of Gavin Stevens in Faulkner's fiction, and the relationship between the more dramatic early Faulkner and the more explicit recent Faulkner. To Cowley *Requiem* illustrated the dilemma of the two Faulkners, the one explicitly concerned with defending human dignity, the other unregenerate and scampish but the greater novelist.[64] British reviewers—Walter Allen, Simon Raven, Nancy Spain, John Betjeman among others—were almost unanimously unfavorable; but very few in either country, outside of those almost never in Faulkner's corner like Fadiman, Geismar, and Orville Prescott, suggested the work necessitated a reappraisal of the earlier work of a now overrated author.

The response to *Requiem* represented only a part of the attention paid to Faulkner in the months and years immediately following the award in Stockholm. He won more prizes, including the National Book Award, and travelled outside the country as a representative of American writers, a service he continued later in the decade, often at President Eisenhower's request. The popular press began to give him broader coverage, often to his chagrin when it infringed on his privacy or dwelt on his personal life.[65] More considered criticism continued in two main streams throughout this period, attempts to define his moral or social vision and formalistic exegesis. The two works which demanded rigorous attention to complex fictional methods, *The Sound and the Fury* and *Absalom, Absalom!*, were the most frequent subjects for explication. By the time Olga Vickery's thorough study of the former appeared in December 1954, the first article ever on Faulkner in *PMLA*, at least ten noteworthy articles had preceded it, four of them in a special issue of *English Institute Essays*. Few modern novels were more suited to criticism of the day than *Absalom, Absalom!* Not only is it complex, but its method becomes its theme.[66] Curiously each of the first four critics to explore the work at this time examined it from the bias of one of the perspectives within the novel. Whan, like Rosa, had emphasized Gothic myth. Walter Sullivan (*South Atlantic Quarterly*, October 1951), like Mr Compson, described the story as Greek tragedy. Cleanth Brooks (*Sewanee Review*, Fall 1951) argued that Sutpen's innocence was an important condition of the action, a view in large part depending on Sutpen's own version of his past. Richard Poirier focused on the role of Quentin and Shreve, the perpetually necessary act of reconstructing and reinterpreting the past.[67] More importantly, the articles, especially Poirier's and also Brooks's, the first fruit of what has now become a quarter century of intense study of Faulkner's fiction by one of the best modern critics, helped bring to light the major issues and problems in a rich but difficult work. 'The Bear' elicited nearly as many studies, but almost invariably mythic or archetypal. Along with all this commentary on form and method, and articles on Faulkner's South and themes, came the first half-dozen books: extra-literary materials by Robert Coughlan and Ward Miner, an important and influential critical anthology edited by Frederick Hoffman and Olga

Vickery, and interpretations by Harry Modean Campbell and Ruel Foster, Irving Howe, and William Van O'Connor.[68]

Faulkner studies had certainly come into fashion; and certainly those sympathetic readers who knew that a novel over which he had labored nine years would soon be available eagerly awaited *A Fable*. It attracted more immediate attention than anything he had written. Faulkner studies in academia flourishing, it was subjected to instant exegesis. By the end of 1955 *A Fable* was the subject of five long articles; and it had been reviewed by more than two hundred persons, in almost every review section in America and England. Faulkner's new seriousness and affirmation, in Ralph McGill's terms (Atlanta *Constitution*, 10 August) his 'cry for compassion,' appealed to many. Sterling North (*New York World-Telegram and Sun*, 2 August) suggested that it was his best in over twenty years; though Faulkner did not deserve the Nobel Prize for Literature he did merit the Peace Prize. Despite scores of favorable responses, others saw all the noble and ignoble sentiments of *A Fable* as the mark not of a humanist matured but of a talent diminished. Whereas its defenders read it as the crowning accomplishment of a career, its debunkers read it as a more erudite but less successful retelling of Humphrey Cobb's 1935 anti-war novel, *Paths of Glory*. Though Delmore Schwartz, Warren Beck, Carvel Collins, and Carlos Baker were very favorable, Cowley still regretted the 'new Faulkner,' and according to Randall Stewart the unrealized allegorical characters failed to engage the reader's sympathies.[69] Irving Howe (*Reporter*, 14 September) argued that the book's themes would thrive within a simpler structure, and even denied that the book was optimistic. Norman Podhoretz, Leslie Fiedler, Philip Blair Rice, V. S. Pritchett, and other English reviewers examined intellectual failures in the book's plan and its political naïveté. Fiedler (*New Republic*, 23 August) regretted that a public role had been forced on Faulkner to the extent that the conflict between his ideas on the one hand and his myth-making and style on the other had resulted in a furious immobility that brought failure in both narrative and characterization as well as sentimentality in meaning.

Even among his defenders there was often a feeling that he should return to the source of his finest achievement, Yoknapatawpha, that the fabulous county still had fertile soil that had lain fallow long enough. And, in fact, although during the last eight years of his life Faulkner was out of Lafayette County more than ever before, what with his jaunts around the world for President Eisenhower and his annual sojourns in

Charlottesville, he never again strayed from Yoknapatawpha, unless it was to revisit Mr Binford's brothel in Memphis or to release Mink Snopes from Parchman, or briefly and anomalously to transport V. K. Ratliff to New York City. In the spring of 1957, simultaneous with the opening of a special Faulkner exhibition at Princeton, and while the author himself was in residence at the University of Virginia, his readers resumed the story of the Snopeses. *The Town*, though very readable for half a dozen marvelous tales within it, lacked the richness of *The Hamlet*. Faulkner had mortgaged Jefferson to Gavin Stevens, and even the once lovable Ratliff was getting to sound like the county attorney. The material on Gavin and Linda and a Eula hardly recognizable to readers of *The Hamlet* was inferior. Both *The Town* and *The Mansion*, whose strength is in the story of Mink's revenge, were well and widely reviewed, though the sheer numbers of favorable reviews again indicate his standing as a literary figure rather than a nearly unanimous acclaim from professional critics. Podhoretz, for example, noted a discrepancy between what Faulkner seemed to be trying to say about Snopesism, the deeper realities and meanings that were supposed to be implicit in the narrative, and the rather weak dramatizations of character and conflict which he provided.[70] Alfred Kazin complained that 'Snopes,' no longer a myth or grotesquely rich comic character, had become merely a symbol, a weak rubber stamp, just a trademark like a comic strip character.[71] Those like Arthur Mizener, Andrew Lytle, Steven Marcus, and George P. Elliott who, on the other hand, judged *The Town* not according to the very high standards of Faulkner's major fiction but with respect for its comic impulse and narratives, pointed to the consistent and exciting Faulknerian humor as the measure of the book's achievement. Invariably such reviewers linked the book with American folk humor, Mark Twain, and the frontier tradition. Returns on *The Mansion* were similar. Reviewers complained of both the sections on Linda and Faulkner's frequent backtracking over familiar material. Charles Anderson complained that the Snopes story had fallen off steadily in novelty and significance, and questioned whether Faulkner should have bothered to go back to it. Cowley, who considered *The Town* 'Faulkner's dullest work in thirty years,' called *The Mansion* a better book, more dramatic because of Mink's story, but still the work of a less powerful writer.[72] Among those agreeing, with different emphases, were Anthony West, D. W. Harding, Benjamin DeMott, Frederick Hoffman, and Irving Howe. But the sole owner and proprietor of Yoknapatawpha County still had tucked away in his imagination one of the fine comic tales in American literature.

Few claim for *The Reivers* the status of a major masterpiece, but few claim it is not great fun. Dropping the pretensions of his novels of the 1950s, leaving behind both General Gragnon and Gavin Stevens, Faulkner returned to the archetype of the boy's initiation which had served him well in the past. When the book appeared, a few sophisticated reviewers like Terry Southern, George Plimpton, Leslie Fiedler, and Stanley Hyman patronized it as at best a boy's book, in Fiedler's terms 'a surrender to sententious banality' in an 'attempt to recapture the authentic folk sources' that had been the strength of his early fiction, or in Hyman's 'a redoing of "The Bear" as farce' and melodrama, not even a good boy's book.[73] Plimpton and especially Southern regretted the heavy-handedness with which Faulkner handled the story, the 'ingratiating silliness' that required it to be marketed on the children's shelf, next to *Tom Sawyer* not *Huckleberry Finn*. Most reviewers made the same comparison more charitably: Lucius's story was worthy of Twain at his best; and as social comedy it was a hilarious and meaningful dramatization of manners and character. In general *The Reivers* was joyously received in both America and Britain. The British reviews appeared two months after Faulkner's death. Therefore they often took the form of an extended eulogy, some of the most thoughtful of which were by V. S. Pritchett, Julian Mitchell, and the reviewer for *TLS*. In the United States, news of his death followed short upon the final reviews. Dozens of newspapers in all parts of the country carried editorials, with only one or two reminding readers that his fiction had been distasteful and impenetrable. Rarely do writers on their death receive so much editorial attention; in America only Frost and Hemingway matched it. In addition writers like Eudora Welty, Allen Tate, and John Dos Passos wrote longer personal responses. Praise came from friends, from public figures, even from the White House, where President Kennedy said that Faulkner was the first American since Henry James to leave behind him 'such a vast and enduring monument to the strength of American literature.'[74]

Faulkner's death had little effect on either the quantity or content of criticism directed toward his work. Occasionally a noted author's fiction—Henry James is a case in point—experiences a brief upsurge of popularity after his death, then goes into eclipse, and finally is resurrected and placed in proper perspective. Faulkner's best work, however, had in a way already been resurrected in the late 1940s and established in the front rank of American fiction. By the 1960s it was no longer 'contemporary.' To young writers and critics the novels were part of a literary tradition that stretched back to James and Twain, Hawthorne and Melville. Scholars took for granted their merit in the same way they might assume the validity of studying Dickens or Hardy or Austen. Between 1959 and 1969 such scholars wrote hundreds of articles and forty books, countless master's theses and eighty doctoral dissertations on Faulkner. This proliferation actually goes back to the mid-1950s, when annual *PMLA* bibliographies began to list more items on him than on any other living writer, English or American.[75] *The Sound and the Fury*, *Absalom, Absalom!*, *The Hamlet*, and 'The Bear' received substantial attention; but it was *Light in August* that inspired the most commentary, much of it concerned in one way or another with Joe Christmas as Christ figure or with religious or mythic patterns. At least three factors were involved. In the first place, both myth critics and their students as well as theologians began to discover Christian archetypes in Faulkner's fiction. Second, in the emerging Afro-American struggle, an at least putative Negro whose life in any way paralleled the Nazarene's, and who suffered and died, was sure to be singled out for attention. Third, the most noticeable shift in general Faulkner criticism during this period was away from discussion of his Southern saga, of his legendary history, toward consideration of his philosophical and religious attitudes, his view of Man. The basis for such a shift, outside of such inviting material as Joe Christmas and Benjy Compson, was the explicit nature of Faulkner's fictional and non-fictional utterances since 1950, his Nobel Prize speech, *Requiem for a Nun*, and *A Fable*.[76] Meanwhile essays on Faulkner and his South temporarily became less common at a time when he had returned to his fictional county and was more outspoken than ever on Civil Rights and Southern progress. It was a time when, John Faulkner (*My Brother Bill*) tells us, the author frequently provoked family and friends with defenses of school integration. When Faulkner protested the proceedings in the well publicized rape trial of Willie McGee, a Negro, one Mississippi district attorney suggested that the novelist had either been 'seduced by his own fictitious imaginations or has aligned himself with the Communists.'[77] A Mississippi newspaper editor insisted that 'he does not know how to write, that something is wrong when a man with a sixth-grade education wins the Nobel Prize, that the prize must have been given by Negrophiles who pay with praise rather than money.'[78] When *The Sound and the Fury* was adapted for television in 1955, a columnist in the Jackson (Mississippi) *Clarion-Ledger* wrote: 'Another black eye and kick in the teeth for Mississippi is coming up tonight over a nationwide television network reaching millions. . . . Our Oxford genius has gained fame and fortune writing unkind things about his native Mississippi.'[79] Almost at the same time such a posture was justified by Westbrook Pegler, writing from Rome, where Faulkner had recently visited, that the novelist was 'one of those misanthropic Southerners who depict Southern life, morals and character in disgusting terms, . . . an author whose writing to the extent of my contact is as filthy as anything ever scrawled on any wall in any language.'[80] It was a period in which, trying to take what seemed to him a progressive, humane approach, Faulkner alienated all sides. In a most unfortunate interview in 1956 with British correspondent Russell Howe, he was quoted as saying that, if necessary to defend Mississippi from Northern agitators he might even go into the street to shoot Negroes, a statement he immediately denied having made and repudiated.[81] Despite attacks from a number of liberals for at the very least unrealistic conservatism, Faulkner did support integration and equal rights in the South in a period when it could be unhealthy to do so.

The whole topic related to Faulkner as citizen rather than to Faulkner as novelist, and to be sure he had in less than a decade become a much better known public figure. Still his most sympathetic audience was in universities, not all of it concentrating on Christ figures. As American literature was being re-evaluated in terms of American Adams and Virgin Lands, literary historians had to integrate Faulkner into that tradition. Then during the late 1950s and early 1960s, as Faulkner's own career came to a close, a decade of serious critical study culminated in several important books, notably those by Olga Vickery and Cleanth Brooks.

The main lines of Faulkner criticism in the 1960s were drawn in the 1950s, and the last decade or so has seen the continuation of varied and eclectic approaches: (1) Faulkner and the South, Faulkner and the Negro, Faulkner and Southwestern humor; (2) Faulkner and modernism, time and fatalism, existentialist affinities; (3) style, methods, mythic patterns, narrative voices. Though the mind boggles at the amount of repetitiousness in what is published, most noticeable in recent years has been an increase in scholarship—biography, genesis of the works, source studies, local history, textual work, and bibliography. Faulkner would have shuddered at this sort of attention; but to readers of the future interested in both his fiction and larger cultural patterns it can be of great use.

As we review a half-century of criticism leading up to all this, it still appears that Faulkner's difficulty and innovativeness, more than anything else, precluded more widespread approval before World War II, as similar qualities have limited more recently the readership of Pynchon and Hawkes. His style combines the rhetorical extravagance of the Renaissance and the nineteenth century with the rhetorical discontinuity of modernism, and filters them through the alembics of a Mississippi drawl and the common ramble of everyday speech. To some his original methods and involuted style, if comprehended at all, seemed mere technical virtuosity. He did have support among writers and critics, several of whom considered him the most exciting literary figure of the day. Faulkner criticism is not analogous to Melville criticism, though he may have regretted being generally identified as 'the author of *Sanctuary*' as Melville did being known only as 'the author of *Typee*' or 'the man who lived among the cannibals.' Faulkner was not our great unread genius, nor were his masterpieces so misread as Thoreau's *Walden* had been a century earlier. In the cases of Thoreau and Melville there was not only a gap in world view between on the one hand the ideal of progress so basic to even the people most likely to offer sensible criticism of *Moby Dick* and *Walden* and on the other the profound questioning of that ideal that lay beneath both books, but also the absence of a critical discipline that could adequately interpret those works. Men of letters may have been no less intelligent then than now, but the kind of complex symbolic and metaphorical forms the respective writers used were much more amenable to twentieth-century critical developments than to the historical and the impressionistic methods of their own age. The works of Poe and Hawthorne are too; but it was possible to find other approaches to their tales, whereas *Walden* was too easily reduced to mere social and botanical commentary by a freak in the woods, and *Moby Dick* ignored as an overcontrived whaling romance with more encyclopedic knowledge of whales than any reader ever wanted. Faulkner, however, was a writer whose view of the world and method were more in line with those of the best men of letters in his age. Oh, he was not popular; few first-rate writers have been. Nor was he accepted in academia for years; but then modern fiction was being taught there very rarely, and the best scholarship being done there was in earlier periods of literature. His appeal in certain circles, moreover, was limited on one side by what seemed a repugnant moral vision and on another by an inappropriate political vision. The Marxists, despite their significance, hardly delayed his acceptance; indeed, they were hardly of a mind in their attitude toward him, and hardly in a position to name the literary establishment. But the squeamishness or impercipience of genteel or neo-humanist critics probably had more effect. They emphasized the horror and nausea of his fiction, but, as Warren complained in 1940, too rarely asked their purpose in individual works. Although today Faulkner's critics must go beyond the formal qualities of his novels, it was Warren and others insisting on close readings whose lessons turned our attention away from Faulkner as an unfortunate curiosity in American intellectual history and toward 'understanding fiction.' Serious study of Faulkner dates, in effect, from the beginnings of serious study of modern literature—the late 1940s. The first important work on Joyce, Lawrence, Yeats, Hemingway, Eliot, and Stevens was also done, with as in Faulkner's case a few noteworthy exceptions, shortly after the war. Ironically his complex, very rich style and his modern, quasi-existential vision have helped bring him even more attention ever since. Like any other major writer Faulkner will have ups and downs as long as men read books; but if readers maintain the openness of imagination that has characterized his admirers ever since Richard Hughes, Evelyn Scott, Arnold Bennett, and Donald Davidson introduced him to the reading public, it is unlikely that the best of Yoknapatawpha will remain out of favor for long periods of time.

NOTES

1 More or less these are the categories listed by Stanley Hyman in his useful study of modern criticism, *The Armed Vision* (New York, 1948). None of the major critics he discusses, by the way, wrote significantly on Faulkner.

2 The most thorough listing of Faulkner criticism is John Bassett, *William Faulkner: An Annotated Checklist of Criticism* (New York, 1972). The best essay on the present state of Faulkner criticism is that by James B. Meriwether in J. R. Bryer, ed., *Sixteen Modern American Authors* (Durham, North Carolina, 1974). Because Joseph Blotner's comprehensive *Faulkner: A Biography* (New York, 1974) includes many comments on Faulkner by friends, acquaintances, and fellow writers, I have omitted this material from the anthology. For information on the publication and sale of Faulkner's novels see Blotner's biography, and William Van O'Connor, *The Tangled Fire of William Faulkner* (Minneapolis, 1954).

3 McClure's review (No. 1) was in the *Times-Picayune*; Cooper's was in the Memphis *Commercial Appeal*, 5 April 1925, iii, 10.

4 *New Republic*, 20 July 1927, li, 236.

5 *New York Herald Tribune Books*, 31 October 1926, 4.

6 Smith, *New York Sun*, 5 February 1929, 10; Davidson, Nashville *Tennessean*, 14 April 1929, magazine, 7. In 1966 Thomas Inge reprinted all three of Davidson's early reviews in *Georgia Review*.

7 Meriwether provides facts about the book's publication in *Papers of the Bibliographical Society of America* (1962), lvi, 285–316. The *New York Sun* (26 October 1929, 26) omitted it from a list of the season's thirty-six best novels, and later (7 December, 26) from a list of the year's twenty-six best novels.

8 Philadelphia *Inquirer*, 30 November 1929, 18.

9 *Symposium*, January 1930, i, 106–14.

10 *New York Sun*, 7 November 1930, 31.

11 Faulkner's comment appears in John Mason Brown, *The Worlds of Robert Sherwood* (New York, 1965), 284.

12 For a more complete discussion see Hughes's article 'Faulkner and Bennett,' *Encounter*, September 1963, 59–61. Bennett's note on *The Sound and the Fury* clinched Chatto & Windus's decision to publish Faulkner.

13 *Observer*, 13 July 1930, 6. Faulkner's comment on Gould appeared in 'On Criticism,' *Double Dealer*, January–February 1925, vii, 83–4.

14 *Times Literary Supplement*, 24 September 1931, 732.

15 *New York Herald Tribune Books*, 9 October 1932, 3. Adams's review was in the *New York Times Book Review* the same day.

16 *Daily Mail*, 9 February 1933, 4.

17 *The Twentieth Century Novel* (New York, 1932), 520–1.

18 *In the Worst Possible Taste* (New York, 1932), 84–99.

19 *Seven Years' Harvest* (New York, 1936), 15.

20 *American Spectator*, November 1933, 1.

21 *Modern Fiction* (New York, 1937), 406. Also see Percy Boynton, *America in Contemporary Fiction* (Chicago, 1940); Camille McCole, *Lucifer at Large* (New York, 1937); H. E. Luccock, *American Mirror* (New York, 1940); Jay B. Hubbell, *American Life in Literature* (New York, 1936).

22 Malcolm Cowley, *The Faulkner–Cowley File* (New York, 1966), 157–8. He also mentions Hemingway's attitude. For further comments on Hemingway and Faulkner see Carlos Baker, *Ernest Hemingway: A Life Story* (New York, 1969); and William Van O'Connor, 'Faulkner's One-Sided "Dialogue" with Hemingway,' *College English*, December 1962, xxiv, 208–15. On Miller see *Letters to Anais Nin* (London, 1965).

23 'The South Today,' Dallas *Times Herald*, 17 July 1938, i, 6. Ransom's favorable comments appeared in *Virginia Quarterly Review*, April 1935, xi, 197–8, his unfavorable review of *Pylon* in Nashville *Banner*, 24 March 1935, magazine, 8. In 1945 Tate called Faulkner 'the most powerful and original novelist

in the United States' (*Virginia Quarterly Review*, xxi, 272). A similar comment appears in *American Harvest* (New York, 1942), an anthology he edited with John Peale Bishop: 'Faulkner combines Flaubertian discipline with Southern eloquence and is one of the most powerful and original writers in America' (534).

24 Letter to Irita Van Doren, 8 September 1933, printed in Blair Rouse, ed., *Letters of Ellen Glasgow* (New York, 1958), 143; and 'Heroes and Monsters,' *Saturday Review of Literature*, 10 November 1934, xii, 272.

25 *New Republic*, 19 June 1935, lxxxiii, 161–3.

26 Interview with May Cameron, printed in *Press Time*, a collection of interviews published by the *New York Post* (New York, 1936), 248.

27 *Life and Letters*, June 1934, x, 312–28; included in *Men Without Art* (London, 1934).

28 Five English reviewers found the prose intolerably exasperating. Seven or eight appreciated the book's merit. J. D. Beresford (*Manchester Guardian*, 19 February 1937) said it would reward anyone with sufficient knowledge and patience.

29 Alfred Kazin, *New York Herald Tribune Books*, 20 February 1938, 5.

30 Dallas *Morning News*, 22 January 1939, iii, 15.

31 Burgum, *New Masses*, 7 February 1939, 23–4; Cowley, *New Republic*, 25 January 1939, xcvii, 349.

32 *Pseudopodia*, Winter 1937, 13–14, 18–19.

33 *Cahiers du Sud*, November 1940, xvii, 502–8. The most complete survey of early Faulkner criticism in France is S. D. Woodworth, *William Faulkner en France* (Paris, 1959).

34 *Études Anglaises*, September 1937, i, 418–38.

35 *La Nouvelle Revue Française*, June 1939, lii, 1057–61; (July 1939), liii, 147–51.

36 W. W. Pusey, 'William Faulkner's Works in Germany to 1940,' *Germanic Review*, October 1955, xxx, 211–26; and L. M. Price, *The Reception of U.S. Literature in Germany* (Chapel Hill, 1966).

37 Arnold Chapman, *The Spanish-American Reception of United States Fiction, 1920–1940* (Berkeley, 1966).

38 Deming B. Brown, *Soviet Attitudes Toward American Writing* (Princeton, 1962). On translations in Europe also see James B. Meriwether, *The Literary Career of William Faulkner* (Princeton, 1961).

39 *New Republic*, 15 April 1940, cii, 510.

40 *New York Times Book Review*, 10 May 1942, 4.

41 'William Faulkner's Style,' *American Prefaces*, Spring 1941, vi, 195–211.

42 *Sewanee Review*, January–March 1939, xlvii, 45.

43 *Saturday Review of Literature*, 19 September 1942, 30.

44 Michael Millgate, *The Achievement of William Faulkner* (New York, 1966), 43.

45 Beck, *Antioch Review*, Spring 1941, i, 94; Moffatt, *Southern Literary Messenger*, October 1940, ii, 574.

46 Robert W. Daniel, ed., *A Catalogue of the Writings of William Faulkner* (New Haven, 1942).

47 *The Faulkner–Cowley File*, 10; Hicks, 'Our Novelists' Shifting Reputations,' *College English*, January 1951, xii, 187–93. Alan Swallow also said that Faulkner's reputation had reached a high point among the same group at the end of the war (*Faulkner Studies*, Spring 1952, i, 2).

48 *The Faulkner–Cowley File*, 5–6; and 'William Faulkner's Human Comedy,' *New York Times Book Review*, 29 October 1944, 4.

49 *The Faulkner–Cowley File*, 5.

50 Ibid., 20.

51 *The Queen's Awards, 1946* (Boston, 1946). Queen himself (themselves) called Faulkner's 'the most distinguished writing' of all 838 entries.

52 'Thematic Problems of the American Novelist,' *Accent*, Autumn 1945, vi, 44–53.

53 Cowley also wrote three such articles on Hemingway in 1944 and edited *The Portable Hemingway* (New York, 1945).

54 On 5 May Caroline Gordon reviewed *The Portable Faulkner* on the front page of the *New York Times Book Review*; never before had the *Times* given such prominence to a book by Faulkner. Few newspapers covered the book, which, moreover, was not published in England.

55 Robert Pick, 'Old-World Views on New-World Writing,' *Saturday Review of Literature*, 20 August 1949, 7–8, 35–8. In 1947 *Sanctuary* was seized by Philadelphia policemen, spurred on by the local clergy, as 'obscene, blasphemous, and un-American' (*New York Times Book Review*, 7 November 1948, 8).

56 *Atlantic Monthly*, August 1946, 115.

57 Glicksberg in the last decade has continued to explore Faulkner's work as naturalistic tragedy, especially in *Modern Literature and the Death of God* (The Hague, 1966), in which he repudiates the notions of both Faulkner's Christian leanings and Faulkner's hopeful humanism, and in *The Sexual Revolution in Modern Literature* (The Hague, 1971).

58 'Toward the Light: The Thematic Unity of Faulkner's "Cycle,"' *Carolina Quarterly*, Autumn 1950, iii, 38–44. Compare Russell Roth, 'William Faulkner: The Pattern of Pilgrimage,' *Perspective*, Summer 1949, ii, 246–54. According to Roth the development towards optimism culminated in *Go Down, Moses*.

59 Campbell, *Western Review*, Summer 1952, xvi, 320–1.

60 *The Faulkner–Cowley File*, 128.

61 *New York Times*, 30 August 1949, 25.

62 *New York Times Book Review*, 17 December 1950, 4.

63 Notable are Jean Pouillon, *Temps et roman* (Paris, 1946), 238–60; Maurice Coindreau, *Aperçus de litterature americaine* (Paris, 1946), 111–46; and Claude-Edmonde Magny, *L'Âge du roman americain* (Paris, 1948), 196–243.

64 *New York Herald Tribune Books*, 30 September 1951, 1, 14.

65 The most notorious were two by Robert Coughlan in *Life* (28 September and 5 October 1953) which emphasized Faulkner's drinking habits.
66 Just as important were a series of general articles on form and method, especially R. W. Flint, 'Faulkner as Elegist,' *Hudson Review*, Summer 1954; Karl Zink, 'William Faulkner: Form as Experience,' *South Atlantic Quarterly*, July 1954; and Zink, 'Flux and the Frozen Moment,' *PMLA*, June 1956.
67 Printed for the first time in F. J. Hoffman and O. W. Vickery, ed., *William Faulkner: Two Decades of Criticism* (East Lansing, Michigan, 1951).
68 In 1951 a group of students in Denver, under Alan Swallow, began *Faulkner Studies*, a quarterly which soon moved to the University of Minnesota. Though it lasted only three years, before becoming *Critique*, and is little more than a footnote in Faulkner's critical heritage, the journal does suggest the fashion into which study of Faulkner had come.
69 Cowley, *New York Herald Tribune Books*, 1 August 1954, 1, 8; Stewart, Providence *Sunday Journal*, 1 August 1954, vi, 8.
70 *New Yorker*, 1 June 1957, 110, 113–16.
71 *New York Times Book Review*, 5 May 1957, 1, 24.
72 *New York Times Book Review*, 15 November 1959, 1; Anderson's review appeared the same day in the Baltimore *Sun*.
73 Hyman, *New Leader*, 9 July 1962, 18–19; Fiedler, *Manchester Guardian*, 28 September 1962, 6; Southern, *Nation*, 9 June 1962, cxciv, 519–21; Plimpton, *New York Herald Tribune Books*, 27 May 1962, 1.
74 *New York Times*, 7 July 1962, 7.
75 Randall Stewart, *Modern Age*, Winter 1962, vi, 82.
76 During this period significant articles on *Light in August* were written by Kazin, Chase, John Longley, and Ilse Dusoir Lind, as well as, emphasizing Christian patterns, Beekman Cottrell and C. Hugh Holman. Exploring Christian materials in the rest of Faulkner's fiction were Ernest Sandeen, Edwin A. Penick, Hyatt Waggoner, Randall Stewart, Amos N. Wilder, Joseph Blotner, Ward Miner, and William R. Mueller.
77 Floyd Watkins, 'William Faulkner in His Own Country,' *Emory University Quarterly*, December 1959, xv, 229.
78 Ibid., 228.
79 Ibid., 230–1.
80 Richmond *Times-Dispatch*, 5 October 1955, 16.
81 The interview was printed in the *Times* on 4 March and in the *Reporter* on 22 March. Faulkner's response appeared in the *Reporter* on 19 April. Charles D. Peavy reviewed the whole incident in *College Language Association Journal*, December 1967, xi, 117–23.

Note on the Text

Except for the silent correction of errors of fact or spelling errors, texts have been printed exactly as originally published. Deletions are shown by . . . or indicated by comments in square brackets.

Numbered footnotes are the addition of the present editor.

THE MARBLE FAUN

Boston, December 1924

1. John McClure, review, New Orleans *Times-Picayune*

25 January 1925, magazine, 6

McClure (1893–1956), who knew Faulkner in New Orleans, was book editor of this newspaper and an editor of *Double Dealer*. This is most likely the first book review ever written on Faulkner.

It is doubtful if there are a dozen thoroughly successful long poems in English. When a young poet attempts sustained production, he is, under Lloyd's or anybody's average, predestined to failure. The most he can hope for, even if his name is Keats, is to fail with honor. Mr. William Faulkner, a Southern poet from whom we shall hear a great deal in future, has failed, it seems to this reviewer, but with real honor.

The Marble Faun, by William Faulkner, with a preface by Phil Stone, although not a completely successful work, is a book of verse rich in promise, and successful in part:

> The candled flames of roses here
> Gutter gold in this still air

is a couplet of fine poetry if this reviewer ever saw one. And *The Marble Faun* contains scores of excellent passages. The book, with all its immaturity, proves that Mr. Faulkner is a born poet, with remarkable ability.

This poem was written when its author was barely of voting age. It is the forerunner of a more mature volume of shorter poems which will be brought out this year. That volume of later work should contain some genuinely excellent, sustained productions. The excellences of *The Marble Faun* are sporadic: charming couplets or passages sandwiched between stretches of creditable but not remarkable verse. The general effect of the poem is vague. It is a prophetic book rather than a chronicle of past performance. Mr. Faulkner possesses to an exceptional degree imagination, emotion, a creative impulse in diction and a keen sense of rhythm and form—all attributes demanded of a fine poet. The deficiencies of *The Marble Faun* are deficiencies of youth—diffuseness and overexuberance, impatient simile and metaphor which sometimes miss the mark, and a general galloping technique which runs away with the author every now and then. Immaturity is almost the only indictment which can be brought against the work.

To say that *The Marble Faun* is a long poem is in a way incorrect. It is a series of fairly short poems, natural episodes, but it is bound into a whole by prologue, epilogue and thread of argument, and is apparently intended to achieve unity of effect. Mr. Stone in his preface refers to the work as a book of 'poems.' This is correct, literally, but the work is stronger when viewed as a whole, as one imagines Mr. Faulkner conceived it, when he wrote it in April, May and June of 1919.

[quotes from preface by Phil Stone]

Nobody but the poet himself ever understands all the overtones and implications in a piece of imaginative verse. *The Marble Faun*, it seems —if it must be interpreted—is an excursion into direct experience. The marble faun, with its

carven eyes'
Bent to the unchanging skies,

this creature of cold stone which 'cannot break its marble bonds,' yearns to know the warm and infinitely varied life of nature. Through the necromancy of the imagination, it tours the forbidden worlds of life and motion, becoming not merely a spectator but a pulsing part of the natural scene. When we recall the not too remote similarity of flesh and marble—even though few of us are statues in a palace of art, we are all automatons in a droll waxworks—it becomes evident that Mr. Faulkner's poem is full of food for meditation.

[quotes from poem]

This reviewer believes that Mr. Faulkner promises fine things. He is soon off for Europe. His new book of poems will appear shortly.

Those who wish to keep in touch with the development of Southern poetry will do well to acquire *The Marble Faun*, and the new book when it appears.[1] One day they may be glad to have recognized a fine poet at his first appearance.

Mr. Faulkner, who served with the British Royal Air Forces, has taken a flier at nearly everything in his time (he is only 27 now). He has been in turn an undergraduate, house painter, tramp, day laborer, dishwasher in various New England cities, clerk in a New York book shop, bank clerk and postal clerk.

1 The second book of poems, *A Green Bough*, was not published until 1933, though most of them were written in the 1920s.

SOLDIERS' PAY

New York, April 1926
London, June 1930

2. Donald Davidson, review, Nashville *Tennessean*

11 April 1926, magazine, 6

Davidson (1893–1968) was one of the Fugitive poets at Vanderbilt in the early 1920s, and shortly thereafter contributed to the Agrarian movement and its manifesto, *I'll Take My Stand*. He taught for many years at Vanderbilt, and between 1924 and 1930 edited the book review section for the *Tennessean*.

William Faulkner is a Southerner, and lives at Oxford, Mississippi. That is all I know of him, biographically speaking, except that he has contributed to *The Double Dealer*, that New Orleans magazine which has succeeded in disclosing to the world many young writers of talent lying hidden in this part of the United States.

However, it is unnecessary to know anything about William Faulkner. He reveals himself quite clearly in his novel, *Soldiers' Pay*, as a sensitive, observant person with a fine power of objectifying his own and other people's emotions, and of clarifying characters so that they possess the 'real life' within themselves which it is one of the functions of art to present. Furthermore, he is an artist in language, a sort of poet turned into prose; he does not write prose as Dreiser does, as if he were washing dishes; nor like Sinclair Lewis, who goes at words with a hammer and saw. Take this bit of description:

> Solemnly the clock on the courthouse, staring its four bland faces across the town, like a kind and sleepless god, dropped eleven measured bells of golden sound. Silence carried them away, silence and dark that passing along the street

like a watchman, snatched scraps of light from windows, palming them as a pickpocket palms snatched handkerchiefs. A belated car passed swiftly.

Soldiers' Pay, then, is such a book as John Dos Passos might have written if he had not visualized life as such a mixture of harsh planes, intersecting in viciously haphazard ways. And *Soldiers' Pay*, which deals with post-war people in a Southern town, is superior to John Dos Passos' *Soldiers Three*, that much-talked-about war book, because it digs deeper into human nature.

Mr. Faulkner's title indicates the irony which he discovers in the post-war situation, that irony familiar to returned soldiers, who came back, sometimes much broken and changed, to discover life moving as casually as ever in its old grooves, and people as much untouched by the war as by a polar exploration. Such a discovery makes a man turn a little grim and bitter, but life goes on, with formidable fructifying and budding. People must still live, love, eat, dance, go to the movies, and therefore it is better not to remain grim and bitter. It is better to crack a joke, light a cigarette, and go about one's business. That is about what William Faulkner puts into his book.

[summarizes story]

It is, all in all, a powerful book, done with careful artistry and with great warmth of feeling. Mr. Faulkner is, as might be suspected, distinctly a 'modern,' and has used rather judiciously the special devices which Joyce and others have contributed to the technique of the novel. He has certain faults, such as a too insistent repetition of efforts which have an air of smartness rather than of fine art; he is too fond of phrases such as 'faint lust'; he has too much of the current mania for depicting people 'en deshabille'; he over-emphasizes sensuousness, as many moderns do. But he also has a sense of humor, is fairly equable, and avoids the nervous distortion which gives to so many modern novels an effect very much like that of the modern paintings and statues regularly reproduced in the *Dial*. His book will baffle and perplex some people who read it. Or at least they will say they are baffled and perplexed, largely because they are disturbed at the very core of their being. Nevertheless, it is an interesting and even an exciting book for persons who read with discrimination. Mr. Faulkner will perhaps do better books later, but meanwhile he is to be congratulated on a fine initial performance, for *Soldiers' Pay* is, so far as I know, his first novel. And I realize even as I write, that I have not halfway conveyed the flavor of it.

3. Unsigned review, *New York Times Book Review*

11 April 1926, 8

This novel by William Faulkner tells an old story—as old as the Greeks—and older—as old as war and its folly. It is concerned with the aftermath of war, with the returned soldier, who is forever found to be among the spoils. Its disenchanted emotional travail has been a recurring universal constant. This tinctured saturation of despair, high spirit, hope and conscious unrest, Tennyson realized in his finest poem, when he set down the nostalgia of the war-worn Ulysses, setting sail again, after his long years of returning from Troy, for far-off places beyond the sunset. William Faulkner has recreated the modern return of yesterday—from another Troy—and the gropings of these latest casuals to find a satisfying point of view, place in life, for lives already out of joint with the changed times.

The war decidedly divided the present age into two distinct periods, before the war and afterward. It has divided the people into those who went into service and those who didn't. Those who went lived a lifetime in several lusty years, and those of them who came back had a severe readjustment to perform. They were bitter, hard-boiled, or madly, determinedly gay, to be made dazed, mute, inarticulate and tacit, before a gap in life that seemed impossible to span with common understanding. *Soldiers' Pay*, however, isn't a tricked-out plea for neglected heroes. It's the feelings and adventures of striking and arresting war-hardened individuals after war is over. It relentlessly sets down an objective recital of irreconcilable factors of civilization meeting in an impasse of futility and irony, and probes the conscious and unconscious for the motives behind the individual actors caught in this blind alley of life. It is a novel without heroics or heroes. It has the gusto and mockery of more spacious days. It brings back the language and habits of people who lived fast and hard, with death ever near at hand. Here we have the release, the return and crowded memories.

Soldiers' Pay hasn't the conventional plot form. It employs a more direct approach to life by use of the episodic and elliptical pattern of modern experimental fiction. By this means Mr. Faulkner has been able to set off his characters in sharp contrasts. He evokes with fine selection, avoiding the dreary piling-up of details of naturalism—the high moments of life and the strong resurgent memories of his casuals, giving the transition that has brought them to their present status of disillusion. Brutalized for violence, they have been left without parts to play. The endless stream of life, meanwhile, has moved on in its constant flux of seasons and new people. The workaday world is now alien. A generation in its prime has been warped from the natural order of living. To pick up where they left off is impossible, for the old days have gone with the changing times.

[summarizes story]

This novel of transmuted life is poignant with beauty as well as a penetrating irony. There is a sensuous regard for the feeling of life that is quite Hellenic. The picture of the dying man—returned to a world that is flowering with its natural loveliness—utterly destroyed so as to be unconscious of it, has in its varied aspect a more austere quality than mere pathos. It doesn't touch the heights of tragedy. But it does strike a note of deepfelt distress that is more akin to us all. About the events of *Soldiers' Pay*, humor plays its part. Discordantly, as in life, it sounds the cap and bells in distressful scenes. A deft hand has woven this narrative of mixed and frustrated emotions and has set it down with hard intelligence as well as consummate pity. This book rings true. It is the opinion of this reviewer that it belongs among such excellent conceptions of war and man as are to be found in *What Price Glory* and C. E. Montague's *Disenchantment*.

4. John McClure, review, New Orleans *Times-Picayune*

11 April 1926, magazine, 4

William Faulkner in *Soldiers' Pay* has written a corking first novel on this theme of the return of the hero. Mr. Faulkner is already well known to readers of the *Times-Picayune* through his tales and sketches. He was known to observant critics as a poet of great promise, but nobody expected him to produce a novel. He has fooled us all, and most pleasurably. *Soldiers' Pay* was written in New Orleans last spring, and a few Orleanians have read it in manuscript. It is a striking piece of work and should, if Mr. Faulkner continues to write fiction, be the precursor of even finer things. Both in promise and in accomplishment it is probably the most noteworthy first novel of the year.

[summarizes story]

Viewed as a whole, the novel has the great merit of unity in design. It is formal in conception as tragedy ought to be. Its deficiencies—they are not serious—arise from a somewhat incoherent development of the theme, rather random motivation, and the author's tendency to get it over with in a series of spurts rather than in steady progression. The dialogue, always delightful, is not always convincing, and the action sometimes less so. As might be expected of a lyrical poet, there is more emotion and symbolical truth than objective accuracy in the novel. In many instances in which a character says or does something that one believes he would not actually say or do, one feels that there is nevertheless a symbolic truth in the by-play—that something of this sort is what the character would like to do and, if he lacked inhibitions, would do. In point of style, *Soldiers' Pay* is admirable. This reviewer can think of none of the younger novelists, and few of the older, who write as well as Mr. Faulkner.

There is something hazardous in the way all these people got together, and Januarius Jones undoubtedly dropped from the moon. The random method of assemblage is a technical deficiency. Mrs. Powers and Joe Gilligan, for no reason but human pity, take up with

Mahon on the train. They don't know each other and they don't know him, but they go home with him and settle down with the old man in the rectory. A little difficult to accept as fact, though symbolically appropriate. In this little Georgia town we find, too, a veteran who saw Mrs. Powers' husband killed in France, and the cowardly youth who shot him down was a native of the village. This, too, seems very, very far-fetched, and yet in the emotional background of the narrative it is symbolically appropriate. The conception of the whole story is dreamy.

[summarizes and quotes]

Soldiers' Pay is recommended without reservation as a novel of unusual emotional power.

5. Thomas Boyd, review, *Saturday Review of Literature*

24 April 1926, 736

Boyd (1898–1935), a journalist whose response was somewhat less favorable, wrote one novel, *Through the Wheat* (1923), based on his own experiences in the war as a marine, and another, *In Time of Peace* (1928), about a returned soldier. Barretto, mentioned favorably below, reviewed *Soldiers' Pay* similarly in the *New York Herald Tribune*.

William Faulkner's novel, *Soldiers' Pay*, is not for people of prosaic minds. From the outset this story of strange humans in the spring of 1919, following the signing of the armistice, is pitched unnaturally high; and as the tale continues it seems as if the author were struggling to break all contacts with the normal world and to vault upward into a sort of esoteric sphere of his own making.

[summarizes story]

The story begins with three drunken soldiers riding westward in a parlor car after demobilization. One of the former doughboys nonchalantly tries to push another through the window. There is such talk as this: 'You wrong me as ever man wronged. Accuse me of hiding mortgage on house? Take this soul and body; take all. Ravish me, big boy.' The answer to that is given: 'Hark, the sound of battle and the laughing horses draw near. But shall they dull this poor unworthy head? No! But I would like to of seen one of them laughing horses. Must of been lady horses all together. Your extreme highness . . . will you be kind enough to kindly condescend to honor these kind but unworthy strangers in a foreign land?'

At best such *non sequiturs* are amusing, suspiciously reminiscent of the mad dream of Leopold Bloom. They pave the way out of reality and place the action of the story on a shadowy horizon where vivid characterization is unnecessary and background not pertinent.

Thus *Soldiers' Pay* offers the reader a group of vague, abnormally behaving characters who waver uncertainly and fantastically through the story. Donald Mahon, the wounded hero, is described only by his scar. Mrs. Powers, the war widow, comes into the reader's consciousness as 'the black woman.' Januarius Jones seems like an offshoot of the personality of 'stately plump Buck Mulligan' of *Ulysses.*

[summarizes]

Mr. Faulkner submits to very little government in writing. His impressionistic manner is honest but slap-dash; often he sets down an extraordinarily vivid scene. The book has fervor and strength, but it would be more effective if it were better controlled. So far as the returned soldier is concerned, Larry Barretto made a much better job of him in *A Conqueror Passes.*

6. Richard Hughes, preface to British edition

June 1930

Like Faulkner, Hughes (b. 1900) after some early poetry published his first book of fiction, *A Moment of Time*, in 1926 and his first major novel, *A High Wind in Jamaica*, in 1929.

The novel in America, at the moment, seems to have passed into a sort of interregnum. Generations change quickly there; and names only recently become really familiar in England—Lewis, Dreiser, Cabell, Wilder—seem there already to be looming with the vague bigness of the past, rather than an actual, growing stature of the present.

Nor has any whole new generation taken their place; only a few separate writers, first among them one immediately thinks of Hemingway. Indeed, for seriousness and purity, one has to think of him quite alone. But even Hemingway is more a short story writer than a novelist; and even Hemingway, perhaps, has done now the work by which he is most likely to be remembered.

So that if I were asked who seems to me at the moment the most interesting novelist in America, I should not hesitate in naming one who is not only unknown in England but practically unknown in America also—William Faulkner. He is a Southerner, from Mississippi; and young, prolific, and unsuccessful.

'Physically, he is short in stature; but he is hardily constructed. His hair and eyes are very black. His nose, broken once, is aquiline, and his expression sharp and keen. He has a ready wit, and is a brilliant and sure conversationalist, with the talent for inventing spontaneously extraordinary and imaginative stories.' In his photographs his most expressive feature is his mouth.

Faulkner is a man who keeps outside the swirl of literary fashions and avoids literary people: he remains in his native State and (coming of an aristocratic family) follows the solid calling of a house-painter: producing at the same time, out of the natural fecundity of his spirit, novel after novel to be dropped by hesitant publishers into an ungrateful world. It goes without saying that some are better than others: but he has written at present at least three books in the first class of contemporary work: yet none of them, until now, have been published in England.

Soldiers' Pay, the first to appear here, and also the first he ever wrote, comes as a fitting complement and wind-up to the literature of the War; for it deals with an aspect of the War previously practically untouched—namely, the Peace.

Its theme is the return of the soldier, like an unwanted ghost, to the country he has 'saved'. The scene—the State of Georgia—is an unfamiliar one to most English readers, but not so unfamiliar as that they will expect; and even if it were more so, the theme would be the same in any setting. There is nothing in it that will seem foreign to anyone who is old enough to remember the years nineteen-nineteen and nineteen-twenty in England (or anywhere else, for that matter). The climactic episode of the dance, with the ex-service men huddled forgotten and disapproving in a corner, is tragic and vividly conceived: but it is, moreover, familiar enough.

After reading it, the somewhat similar last act of *The Silver Tassie* pales.

But *Soldiers' Pay* is more than just another (in the popular sense) 'War Book'. It is a tragic, fascinating, and beautiful story; told by a man who is a novelist to his finger-tips, not an amateur with a single unusual experience to relate; a man who writes because he *can*—and this point cannot be too strongly emphasized. It is not only an achievement, it is promising as well: and the promise is borne out by at least two other novels which Messrs. Chatto and Windus propose to issue shortly: by *Mosquitoes*, which is pure satirical comedy, and by *The Sound and the Fury*, a more ambitious and to my mind more impressive work than even *Soldiers' Pay*.

Reading them, one finds in Faulkner a man with an apparently inexhaustible invention of incident and quickening sense of form, and containing in him the germs of an apparently inexhaustible number of characters peculiar without ever descending quite into the grotesque or the heroic: and one sees these characters, once they are alive, handled and moulded and propelled by a mind both highly and widely educated, combining humanity, emotion, and wit.

7. Arnold Bennett, review, *Evening Standard*

26 June 1930, 7

The previous December, Bennett (1867–1931) had commented briefly on *The Sound and the Fury* as 'exasperatingly, unimaginably difficult to read. He seems to take malicious pleasure in mystifying the reader.' But he also found in Faulkner 'great and original talent.'

Last year I made some fuss in this column concerning the young American novelist, William Faulkner, who had been mentioned to me in conversation by Richard Hughes, author of *High Wind in Jamaica*. No American, and even no American publisher, whom I asked about Faulkner had ever heard of him. I sent to New York for his books, but could get only one, *The Sound and the Fury*, and that not without difficulty. Strange that Americans have frequently to be told by Englishmen of their new authors!

The first printed fuss made about Theodore Dreiser's first book was made by an Englishman. *Sister Carrie* fell flat in the United States until a review of it by myself was republished there. Then Americans said: 'Who is this man Dreiser?' and *Sister Carrie* began to sell in America. That was thirty years ago. Yet American critics say that English critics sniff at American novels.

Now Faulkner is getting a show in England. His first book, *Soldiers' Pay*, has just been published here, with a preface by Richard Hughes. His second and third will follow. *Soldiers' Pay* is labelled 'Not a war-book'. I call it a war-book. Its chief male characters are returned soldiers, and the whole story hinges on a terribly scarred aviator, who dies of war. Also war-scenes are directly described in the book, and very well described. Unless Faulkner runs off the rails, as some young men do, but as he probably will not, *Soldiers' Pay* will be an extremely valuable collectors' item in twenty years' time. Faulkner is the coming man. He has inexhaustible invention, powerful imagination, a wondrous gift of characterization, a finished skill in dialogue; and he writes, generally, like an angel. None of the arrived American stars can surpass him in style when he is at his best.

But praise of *Soldiers' Pay* must not be unreserved. It is a first book, and has the usual defects of a first book. It is clumsily constructed, being lop-sided; the opening chapters, though admirable, are far too long. Faulkner is like Schubert was: he doesn't know when to stop. Further, the book is over-emphasized throughout. Also, some of the locutions are irritating: 'His hands cupped her shoulder', 'Jones released the fragile writhing of her fingers'. Etc. Faults of youth, minor and excusable.

A more serious fault, however, is that the book is difficult to read. Not as difficult as his second book, *The Sound and the Fury*, but still difficult. To read it demands an effort. (The effort is adequately rewarded.) There is no excuse for this. The great masters are not difficult to read. You know what they mean, and in their passages of dialogue you know who is saying what. In too many novels of young authors a mathematical calculation, a counting of speeches, is needed to find out who is talking. A novel ought to be easy to read; it ought to please immediately. But too many young novelists seem to be actuated by a determination not to please. They seem to say: 'Whether you like it or not, there will be some rough going in our books. Kant's *Critique of Pure Reason* is difficult, and our books will be difficult. We will not smooth your path. Indeed we intend to make your path as hard as we know how.'

In this matter Faulkner is not guiltless. To get his full value involves some heavy work for the reader. But he is the most promising American novelist known to me; more promising than, for instance, Ernest Hemingway, author of the splendid *A Farewell to Arms*. He has in him the elements of real greatness, and *Soldiers' Pay* contains many quite marvellous pages.

MOSQUITOES

New York, May 1927
London, October 1964

8. Conrad Aiken, review, *New York Evening Post*

11 June 1927, iii, 7

By this time Aiken (1889–1973) was already an established poet—two years later *Selected Poems* won the Pulitzer Prize. *Blue Voyage*, his novel using the stream-of-consciousness method Faulkner so successfully employed later, came out the same year as *Mosquitoes*. Aiken had also written in 1919 *Scepticisms*, one of the first contributions to psychological criticism in America, and was influential in making the poetry of Emily Dickinson better known.

Mr. Faulkner has a sense of character; he has a sense of humor; he has a sense of style; and for his new novel, *Mosquitoes*, he has found an amusing and more or less original setting. He places his odd miscellaneous group of people—second-rate artists and second-rate hosts and a couple of Tough Guys (one male, and one female) on a yacht; and the greater part of the action (such action as there is) takes place in the week of a cruise.

To say that there is not a great deal of action is in the present instance no disparagement; for the charm of Mr. Faulkner's highly entertaining novel resides almost entirely in the astonishing lifelikeness and immediacy of his 'scene'; the comings and goings, the absurd actions, the drunken conversations, of his people, recorded hour by hour, almost minute by minute.

The dialogue is as good, in its way, as Mr. Hemingway's; it is 'tough talk' straight off the street and out of the dance halls; it has the unmistakable rhythm of living speech; and when Mr. Faulkner also wishes to give us 'highbrow' talk—the aesthetic discussions of his novelist (for whom one guesses a living prototype)—he does so with wit and color and an intelligence that is occasionally sharp to the point of brilliance. There is a great deal of talk in the book—so much, that one finds oneself thinking that the thing might almost better have been a play; a farce-comedy. And the talk falls naturally and easily into scenes. One suspects that it would take very little pruning and shaping to turn the thing into an actable affair, with the characters just enough broadened into caricature to make them easily actable.

To mark all this, and to mark the fact that Mr. Faulkner writes well (in the main) and that he has the gift, rare enough in writers of fiction, of making scenes and people come vividly alive before us, with something of Katherine Mansfield's sense of light and texture, and a good deal of Mr. Huxley's erudition, is to define one's appreciation of *Mosquitoes* as a distinctly unusual and amusing book. It is good enough to make one wish that it were better, and to make one hope that Mr. Faulkner will outgrow certain mannerisms which now tend rather seriously to come between him and his reader. He has, distinctly, the fault of many young writers of today (and of certain others not so young); a desire to shock, a desire to see how naughty he can be, and how very, very sophisticated he can appear. This results in a good many blemishes in the book, one or two of which are both unpardonable and useless.

If these minor episodes and anecdotes and innuendoes served any valid purpose, if they threw, for example, any sort of light on a particular character, or in any way forwarded the course of the action, then one might conceivably forgive them. But there is no such justification; they appear to be a wanton self-indulgence. This is a great pity, draws the attention of the reader away from the book's true excellence, and does, further, a good deal to invalidate it. Moreover, Mr. Faulkner has an unfortunate addiction to preciosity. He has an ungoverned appetite for purple passages; and when he is purple, his purple is of the purplest. It screams. One gets heartily sick of his blanched moons, spreading their boneless hands, or their ceaseless hands, or their boneless ceaseless hands, on the boneless and ceaseless water. One positively faints when he indulges himself (as all too frequently) in romantic fantasy, usually couched in italics, as part of the interior monologue of a character who is undergoing stress of emotion. On these occasions he gets off into a mawkish and morbid world that reeks of patchouli and Beardsley and anemic Bakst and a kind of *morbidezza* that has a sickly flavor as of Baudelaire and rose water.

One resents these pseudo-poetic intrusions—they would be somewhat out of place even if well done. For the rest of the story is excellent realistic satire; pungent to the nostril, brilliant to the eye, palpable, if somewhat coarse, to the touch. Here and there, one feels that Mr. Faulkner's hand has shaken a little. One gets the impression, for example, that when he began the book he intended to make his sculptor, Gordon, the chief character, or, at any rate, *one* of the chief characters; but Mr. Faulkner's attention was distracted, and Gordon slipped into the background, only to be rather hastily resurrected at the end. In the same way, his novelist, Fairchild, undergoes a kind of queer metamorphosis in midstream; he suddenly becomes a rather different Fairchild (and it must be admitted a more plausible one) from the Fairchild whom we encounter at the outset.

From such accidents one gathers the impression the Mr. Faulkner, having been seized by the excellent suggestion of scene and 'crowd' that his setting supplied for him, gave himself up to reckless improvisation, and allowed the story to run away from him. The story has the brilliance of improvisation, but also its shapelessness.

These defects being admitted, the critic must also admit, and without a shadow of reluctance, that the book is a delightful one. And one adds Mr. Faulkner's name to the small list of those from whom one might reasonably expect, in the course of a few years, a really first-rate piece of fiction.

9. Lillian Hellman, review, *New York Herald Tribune Books*

19 June 1927, 9

A Southern writer who in the 1930s wrote several successful plays, Lillian Hellman (b. 1905) provides reflections on this period in *An Unfinished Woman.*

Last year Mr. Faulkner wrote a novel called *Soldiers' Pay*. Many judicious readers thought it one of the few good books that came out of the war. Its tone was serious if its intent was ironic and its treatment imaginative. This year Mr. Faulkner has taken a quick turn, focusing his attention on an entirely different world. If his first novel showed more than the usual promise then this one, *Mosquitoes*, comes in time to fulfill it. But it must stand alone; a proof of the man's versatility.

It is perhaps unfair to any book, or at least unfair to an author's originality, should he have any, to compare his offering with another that has gone before. However, it remains one way to show excellence or demonstrate worthlessness. In 1923 Aldous Huxley wrote *Antic Hay*, which I think must still stand as the most brilliant book of the last few years. Since then there have been a host of people who have followed, or attempted to follow, in his footsteps. In most cases their literary worth has been as ephemeral as it was temporarily interesting. If any of these books have approached *Antic Hay* any more closely than *Mosquitoes* it must by now be forgotten. Not that the plot or the people in *Mosquitoes* are similar to those in the Huxley book. As a matter of fact the novel more closely resembles *Those Barren Leaves* in structure, but in the brilliant result it stands closer to the better book.

Mosquitoes takes place on a yacht. Mrs. Maurier, a collector of famous people in her own home town of New Orleans, has arranged a boating party for the more artistic of her friends. They come, some of them, because they have nothing better to do, some of them because they are assured of food, some because they cannot help themselves. She has gathered Gordon, a sculptor; Mr. Taliafero, a gentleman who knows much about ladies' lingerie; a young niece and the niece's mechanically inclined brother; a Jew and his sister; Mark Frost, a poet. The niece has found somewhere in New Orleans a young man and a young lady who on that particular day have nothing much to do with themselves. The niece invites them along. They are as cheap, as human, as vulgar as any two she could have found, and yet they furnish the wine for the party. It is a mad trip, this boat ride; the niece running off with the steward, an intellectual young lady pursuing the vulgar young man and most of the other gentlemen of the party keeping to their rooms for fear of the grapefruit that is served for every meal. Together these people are a fine combination of wit and sophistication and naïvete, but whatever their singularity, their problems, their frustration, are as important to you as if they were people who were more common. They are as tragic as other breeds are tragic, as authentic as your next door neighbor.

It is impossible to capture in a review the humor, the delight of Mr. Faulkner's writing. It approaches in the first half a brilliance that you can rightfully expect only in the writings of a few men. It is full of the fine kind of swift and lusty writing that comes from a healthy, fresh pen.

Undoubtedly certain portions of it are overwritten, certain Joycean passages that have no direct place or bearing, parts that are heavy and dull with overloaded description. But it is not spoilt. If it contained only the fine last scene it would still be able to stand up.

If you have waited with some feeling akin to longing to read about a modern heroine who is plausible and sympathetic in her somersaults, or to watch a foolish and pathetic woman who has wealth and wants art, or perchance a decaying man who desires his youth; if you want a treat of really amusing conversation that depends upon its wit and not upon its flourishes; if you have waited to see these important matters done really well, then this is your book.

10. Donald Davidson, review, Nashville *Tennessean*

3 July 1927, magazine, 7

These comments are part of an essay-review on the 'grotesque' in modern literature, especially in the work of Sherwood Anderson and Maxwell Bodenheim.

William Faulkner's new novel, *Mosquitoes*, is like his first, *Soldiers' Pay*, clearly an example of the principle of the grotesque in full operation. Faulkner sits in the seat of the scornful with a manner somewhat reminiscent of James Joyce, but with an easy languorousness befitting a Mississippian. And as he sits, he does dispatch mayhem, assault and battery upon the bodies of numerous persons with such gracious ease that you almost overlook his savagery. His device is simple in conception, but complicated in practice. The widow Maurier, a shallow lady who yearns after culture and patronizes genius, invites certain diverse people on a yachting party out of New Orleans; among the lot are a sculptor, a fool Englishman, a too-utterly-utter lingerie clerk with Don Juan ambitions, a flapperish niece and Penrodish nephew, a novelist, and, by the casual invitation of the quite casual niece, a tough young bootlegger and his girlish sweetheart get mixed with the crowd and supply sufficient vulgar contrast.

When the scientific-minded young nephew removes a part of the yacht's machinery, this medley of persons is stranded in mid-lake for some days. The ensuing period of boredom is punctuated, quite naturally, with some slapping and scratching as mosquitoes advance to the feast. There is also some of what the papers call 'mixed bathing,' a tragical-romantic escapade when the niece runs off to the mainland swamps with the steward, and an assortment of queer couplings and mixups. But we are chiefly aware that Mr. Faulkner is making all these people the butt of his irony. Most of them are, alas, a peckish, blood-sucking lot, like the mosquitoes. Only those who are physically and mentally spontaneous and natural escape the bite of Mr. Faulkner's wit, and even these nobler individuals are reduced somewhat to attitudes partaking of the grotesque. The novel runs on to its inconsequential end, and in spite of a really wonderful dexterity in the technical management of words to convey certain 'slices of life,' Mr. Faulkner makes us most aware, not of the people whom he is busy slaying, but of his own remorseless mind, most painfully ill at ease in Zion, wrenching his mortal world into a beautifully distorted cast, leaving us full of admiration for the skill of the performance, but conscious of some discomfort before the performer. Yet what he does, he does with buoyant zest.

11. Ruth Suckow, review, *New York World*

12 July 1927, 7—M

Ruth Suckow (1892–1960) was a Midwest novelist whose own work often deals with German-American immigrants and their descendants.

The manner of the 'South Wind' school simply does not sit easily upon our young American novelists.[1] This is being proved month by month in the writing business, but William Faulkner's *Mosquitoes* makes it fatally certain. Mr. Faulkner works so diligently at being brilliant, casual and profound that it is impossible not to give him the faint little spatter of kindly applause that always follows the perspiring efforts of the comedian who has labored too hard to raise a laugh. Some of the writing is good when it isn't Joyce. Some of the characterization is clever, although obvious bits of the conversation here and there are amusing.

But the all too recognizable mixture of suavity, brilliance, cynicism, tragedy, philosophy, obscenity, pure nature and thoughts on art into

[1] Norman Douglas's *South Wind* came out in 1916. It is a discussion novel, satiric and critical towards contemporary mores.

which the English attitude seems to either ascend or degenerate, as the case may be, when south winds blow upon it does not manage to acclimate itself to the climate of New Orleans.

The worst result of too resolute a determination to be sophisticated is the rawness of the amateurishness that shows through the fissures when the gloss cracks. That is terribly true in this book. The gloss is pretty good where it lasts, but the cracks come so often that reading the book gives the same discomfort that goes along with watching the high school graduating class put on an English comedy of manners. The device in itself is amateurish.

One has a feeling that it seemed too good to the author when he thought it up. He wanted to take off a lot of characters, and so why not pile them all together on a yacht? There is a real artist, arrogant and poor; two hard, sexless youngsters of the current fiction breed without knowledge of good and evil; a fool, a blonde, a—well, lots of others. The scintillating conversation is supplied by the novelist, 'the Semitic man' and the Semitic man's sister (the sophisticates of the party), giving the Semitic man always the last word.

SARTORIS

New York, January 1929
London, February 1932

12. Henry Nash Smith, review, Dallas *Morning News*

17 February 1929, amusements, 3

Smith (b. 1906) taught at Southern Methodist University and was on the editorial staff of the *Southwest Review* at this time. *Virgin Land: The American West as Symbol and Myth* came out in 1950.

Most people have noticed casually that the hard-boiled school of younger novelists has been getting distinguished recruits from the South. But possibly the full importance of several recent Southern novels is even yet not recognized. As a matter of fact, if Sherwood Anderson's pronounced southern associations are remembered and *The Time of Man* and *Mosquitoes*, it is possible to believe that the best novels of the last two or three years have borne a Southern imprint. This is especially true of William Faulkner's work. *Soldiers' Pay* and *Mosquitoes* undoubtedly represent one of the most promising talents for fiction in contemporary America.

Of course, there is a temptation to cry a local prophet's merits beyond their worth. But the chance of such an error is discounted in this instance by the wholly unexpected turn of Mr. Faulkner's talent. His books are simply not the thing that could have been expected from postwar Mississippi. He is, to be sure, one of the disillusioned young men who like to play with obscenity just to distress the censors, but there is disillusion and disillusion. When you get to the heart of almost any of the men called great in literature you find something a little chill and disturbing; they leave you with a sobering suspicion that perhaps life is like that. Mr. Faulkner's disillusion is of this sort. I do not mean that he is a Southern Shakespeare or a Mississippi Cervantes; for he is not. What he may become lies inscrutably with the future. He learns his trade and broadens his thought almost visibly from chapter to chapter; and he is young. But he is able to confront and assimilate postwar pessimism without falling into the sophomoric pose of his New York compeers, or the epicene dreaming indolence of Sherwood Anderson. In other words, like the hero of his newest novel, he carries his liquor steadily. From such a man one might well expect the definitive utterance of the generation who went to war and came back when it was over.

But if he is to this extent representative of his time, he is in at least two ways unrepresentative of present styles in fiction. In the first place, he has revived and refreshed a literary manner which had almost wholly disappeared; he is, for better or worse, eloquent. He likes processions of carefully accurate epithets; he likes jeweled, sensuous words shedding color and sound, words marshaled in swelling rhythms suggestive of blank verse. This is naturally heresy to the age of Dreiser; but the peculiar thing is he gets away with it. With the exception of a sentence here and there which grows too long for modern ears, his eloquence is moving, passionate, darkly remorseful. He speaks of the 'baffled and mellow expostulations' of hounds; or he says, 'About the doorstep the geese surged erratically with discordant cries, their necks undulant and suave as formal gestures in a pantomime'—but there is no use quoting snatches. I can merely suggest the full-chorded modulation of Mr. Faulkner's descriptions. The very fact that he makes words suggest music is quite unmodern. But sometimes he even expands into a sort of counterpoint, playing contrasting themes against one another; or again he flings upward in a crescendo to nothingness, only to return abruptly to a measured thin melody, light and graceful.

The other unrepresentative trait of Mr. Faulkner's writing is its poetry. His perceptions are Keats-like in their delicacy and richness; and his narrative moves among a constant series of pictures vivid beyond expectation. He is not ashamed to notice the moon; many of his figures thrown carelessly into a paragraph of conversation put the best efforts of the imagists to insipid shame, and his range includes smells and sounds even more keenly sensed and recorded than his pictures. His is a Southern countryside with the smell of boiling cane juice, of salt pork fried over a fireplace, of the reek of a negro cabin, of the banker's cigar smoke floating over a bed of salvia in the dusk.

[quotes from part four]

I have not said enough about *Sartoris*, Mr. Faulkner's newest book. Sartoris is the name of an old Southern family which has for generations sent its men into reckless, lunging careers through aristocratic lives destined to violence and death at the end. In the hero, Bayard Sartoris, Mr. Faulkner takes up again the theme of *Soldiers' Pay*—the dazed inability of men recently come from France to fit into the peace they had left so short a time before. Again he remembers the war from the cockpit of a fighting airplane, this time as a searing image of John Sartoris thumbing his nose affectionately at his brother close behind him and then jumping without a parachute from his burning plane.

But here more than usually the plot is unimportant. In *Mosquitoes* perhaps the intellectual attitude was most arresting. In *Sartoris* it is something else. Perhaps I can explain it by saying that Mr. Faulkner has got to be more of an artist and a little less of a social philosopher. He turns from scrutiny of the ideas of a certain New Orleans clique to the eternal task of the novelist—people themselves. *Sartoris* is not better than *Mosquitoes*; perhaps it is not quite so good. But with its publication Mr. Faulkner demonstrates that he is setting about novel-writing in earnest. *Mosquitoes* made the appearance of his next novel an event to be awaited with impatience and a little concern. *Sartoris* resolves a natural doubt about Mr. Faulkner's future and in no way decreases the impatience of waiting for his next.

13. Unsigned review, *New York Times Book Review*

3 March 1929, 8

We have had so many novels recently with the decaying South as background, and so many with the destinies of a single family as subject, that Mr. Faulkner's book risks all sorts of comparisons. But this author's self-confidence is considerable and best expressed in his dedicatory note to Sherwood Anderson, in which he thanks that totally dissimilar writer for his kindness 'with the belief that this book will give him no reason to regret that fact.' Unfortunately, the assurance with which Mr. Faulkner apparently undertook his labor of gratitude to a fellow-writer was not enough to prevent it from being a work of uneven texture, confused sentiment and loose articulation.

This story of a Southern family whose members one and all belong to a dying order of society has little persuasiveness and less unity. In his solicitude to present the Sartoris family as it exists today, its chronicler finds it necessary to supply a genealogical scheme of its progress from earlier times, and to do this makes frequent use of 'flashbacks' into the past, in the form of long and often unprofitable anecdotes which seriously interrupt the direct realization of the present. Also, he has obfuscated his canvas by peopling it with more characters than the dimensions of the book can sustain. By the time the several representatives of the Sartoris clan proper have begun to take on a few recognizable lineaments they are crowded from the scene by the constant ingress of wives, neighbors, and other citizens of the community. Nor are the features of the three or four main figures sharply enough established to make them stand out with due proportion. Old Bayard Sartoris never becomes much more than a Southern version of the cranky old Tory that we have encountered so often in the plays and novels of John Galsworthy. Around young Bayard, who comes nearest to affording the center of the drama, the author has built up a legend of reckless gallantry and romantic disillusion which is never quite realized. Perhaps the most clearly defined is Aunt Jenny, the garrulous and indefatigable spokesman of the female Sartorises, who is nevertheless thoroughly monotonous and one-sided.

By such superficial treatment of his major characters, Mr. Faulkner has of course weakened and obscured his theme. It is only by implication that one deduces the theme is the struggle of the old masculine hierarchy of the South to survive in a modern industrial society. But one cannot be too certain, for Mr. Faulkner appears as little interested in working out his theme as in the consistent creation of character. His principal interest, it would seem, lies in quantitative variety, in assembling within a single book the widest possible range of characters, situations, moods, effects and styles. Perhaps this indicates a spirit of enterprise not unhealthy in a new writer, and that in some future work Mr. Faulkner will be able to exercise more rigorous selection and concentration.

THE SOUND AND THE FURY

New York, October 1929
London, April 1931

14. Evelyn Scott, 'On William Faulkner's *The Sound and the Fury*'

October 1929

Evelyn Scott (1893–1963) was a poet and novelist from Tennessee, whose long, expressionistic, Civil War novel, *The Wave*, was also published in 1929.

Having had access to *The Sound and the Fury* in manuscript, Evelyn Scott volunteered these comments to Cape & Smith in a letter (R. L. Welker, *Reality and Myth*, Nashville, 1964, p. 179). They then issued the comments in a pamphlet, published in conjunction with the novel and prefaced by the following: 'This essay by Evelyn Scott, whose recent novel *The Wave* placed her among the outstanding literary figures of our time, has been printed in this form and is being distributed to those who are interested in Miss Scott's work and the writing of William Faulkner. *The Sound and the Fury* should place William Faulkner in company with Evelyn Scott. The publishers believe, in the issuance of this little book, that a valuable and brilliant reflection of the philosophies of two important American authors is presented to those who care for such things. The edition is limited to 1,000 copies.'

In this age of superlatives, one craves, despite one's disbelief in the supposed justification for censorships, a prohibition of some sort against the insincere employment of adjectives that, in an era of selection, carry rare meaning. One longs for measure in judgment. One desires above all a body of real criticism which will save the worthy artist from a careless allotment, before the public, with those whose object in writing is a purely commercial one. The sane critic, the critic who is careful of his words through his very generosity in recognizing valid talent, exists. But one doubts if the public in general has time to discriminate between the praise bestowed by such a critic, and the panegyrics of mere publicity. I want to write something about *The Sound and the Fury* before the fanfare in print can greet even the ears of the author. There will be many, I am sure, who, without this assistance, will make the discovery of the book as an important contribution to the permanent literature of fiction. I shall be pleased, however, if some others, lacking the opportunity for investigating individually the hundred claims to greatness which America makes every year in the name of art, may be led, through these comments, to a perusal of this unique and distinguished novel. The publishers, who are so much to be congratulated for presenting a little known writer with the dignity of recognition which his talent deserves, call this book 'overwhelmingly powerful and even monstrous.' Powerful it is; and it may even be described as 'monstrous' in all its implications of tragedy; but such tragedy has a noble essence.

The question has been put by a contemporary critic, a genuine philosopher reviewing the arts, as to whether there exists for this age of disillusion with religion, dedication to the objective program of scientific inventiveness and general rejection of the teleology which placed man emotionally at the center of his universe, the spirit of which great tragedy is the expression. *The Sound and the Fury* seems to me to offer a reply. Indeed I feel that however sophisticated the argument of theology, man remains, in his heart, in that important position. What he seeks now is a fresh justification for the presumption of his emotions; and his present tragedy is in a realization of the futility, up to date, of his search for another, intellectually appropriate embodiment of the god that lives on, however contradicted by 'reason.'

William Faulkner, the author of this tragedy, which has all the spacious proportions of Greek art, may not consider his book in the least expressive of the general dilemma to which I refer, but that quality in his writings which the emotionally timid will call 'morbid,' seems to me reflected from the impression, made on a sensitive and normally egoistic nature, of what is in the air. Too proud to solve the human problem evasively through any of the sleight-of-hand of puerile surface optimism, he embraces, to represent life, figures that do indeed symbolize a kind of despair; but not the despair that depresses or frustrates. His pessimism as to fact, and his acceptance of all the morally inimical possibilities of human nature, is unwavering. The result is, nonetheless, the reassertion of humanity in defeat that is, in the subjective sense, a triumph. This is no Pyrrhic victory made in debate with those powers of intelligence that may be used to destroy. It is the conquest of nature by art. Or rather, the refutation, by means of a work of art, of the belittling of the materialists; and the work itself is in that category of facts which popular scientific thinking has made an ultimate. Here is beauty sprung from the perfect *realization* of what a more limiting morality would describe as ugliness. Here is a humanity stripped of most of what was claimed for it by the Victorians, and the spectacle is moving as no sugar-coated drama ever could be. The result for the reader, if he is like myself, is an exaltation of faith in mankind. It is faith without, as yet, an argument; but it is the same faith which has always lived in the most ultimate expression of the human spirit.

The Sound and the Fury is the story of the fall of a house, the collapse of a provincial aristocracy in a final debacle of insanity, recklessness, psychological perversion. The method of presentation is, as far as I know, unique. Book I is a statement of the tragedy as seen through the eyes of a thirty-three-year-old idiot son of the house, Benjy. Benjy is beautiful, as beautiful as one of the helpless angels, and the more so for the slightly repellent earthiness that is his. He is a better idiot than Dostoyevsky's because his simplicity is more convincingly united with the basic animal simplicity of creatures untried by the standards of a conscious and calculating humanity. It is as if, indeed, Blake's Tiger had been framed before us by the same Hand that made the Lamb, and, in opposition to Blake's conception, endowed with the same soul. Innocence is terrible as well as pathetic—and Benjy is terrible, sometimes terrifying. He is a Christ symbol, yet not, even in the way of the old orthodoxies, Christly. A Jesus asks for a conviction of sin and a confession before redemption. He acknowledges this as in his own history, tempting by the Devil the prelude to his renunciation. In every subtle sense, sin is the desire to sin, the awareness of sin, an assertion in innuendo that, by the very statement of virtue, sin *is*. Benjy is no saint with a wounded ego his own gesture can console. He is not anything —nothing with a name. He is alive. He can suffer. The simplicity of his suffering, the absence, for him, of any compensating sense of drama, leave him as naked of self-flattery as was the first man. Benjy is like Adam, with all he remembers in the garden and one foot in hell on earth. This was where knowledge began, and for Benjy time is too early for any spurious profiting by knowledge. It is a little as if the story of Hans Andersen's Little Mermaid had been taken away from the nursery and sentiment and made rather diabolically to grow up. Here is the Little Mermaid on the way to find her soul in an uncouth and incontinent body—but there is no happy ending. Benjy, born male and made neuter, doesn't want a soul. It is being thrust upon him, but only like a horrid bauble which he does not recognize. He holds in his hands —in his heart, exposed to the reader—something frightening, unnamed —*pain!* Benjy lives deeply in the senses. For the remainder of what he sees as life, he lives as crudely as in allegory, vicariously, through uncritical perception of his adored sister (she smells to him like 'leaves') and, in such emotional absolutism, traces for us her broken marriage, her departure forever from an unlovely home, her return by proxy in the person of her illegitimate daughter, Quentin, who, for Benjy, takes the mother's place.

Book II of the novel deals with another—the original Quentin, for whom the baby girl of later events is named. This section, inferior, I think, to the Benjy motive, though fine in part, describes in the terms of free association with which Mr. Joyce is recreating vocabularies, the final day in this life of Quentin, First, who is contemplating suicide. Quentin is a student at Harvard at the time, the last wealth of the family—some property that has been nominally Benjy's having been sold to provide him with an education. Quentin is oversensitive, introvert, pathologically devoted to his sister, and his determination to commit suicide is his protest against her disgrace.

In Book III we see the world in terms of the petty, sadistic lunacy of Jason; Jason, the last son of the family, the stay-at-home, the failure, clerking in a country store, for whom no Harvard education was provided. William Faulkner has that general perspective in viewing particular events which lifts the specific incident to the dignity of catholic significance, while all the vividness of an unduplicable personal drama is retained. He senses the characteristic compulsions to action that make a fate. Jason is a devil. Yet, since the author has compelled you to the vision of the gods, he is a devil whom you compassionate. Younger than the other brothers, Jason, in his twenties, is tyrannically compensating for the sufferings of jealousy by persecution of his young niece, Caddie's daughter, Quentin, by petty thievery, by deception practiced against his weak mother, by meanest torment of that marvelously accurately conceived young negro, Luster, keeper, against all his idle, pleasure-loving inclinations, of the witless Benjy. Jason is going mad. He knows it—not as an intellectual conclusion, for he holds up all the emotional barriers against reflection and self-investigation. Jason knows madness as Benjy knows the world and the smell of leaves and the leap of the fire in the grate and the sounds of himself, his own howls, when Luster teases him. Madness for Jason is a blank, immediate state of soul, which he feels encroaching on his meager, objectively considered universe. He is in an agony of inexplicable anticipation of disaster for which his cruelties afford him no relief.

The last Book is told in the third person by the author. In its pages we are to see this small world of failure in its relative aspect. Especial privilege, we are allowed to meet face to face, Dilsey, the old colored woman, who provides the beauty of coherence against the background of struggling choice. Dilsey isn't searching for a soul. She *is* the soul. She is the conscious human accepting the limitations of herself, the iron boundaries of circumstance, and still, to the best of her ability, achieving a holy compromise for aspiration.

People seem very frequently to ask of a book a 'moral.' There is no moral statement in *The Sound and the Fury*, but moral conclusions can be drawn from it as surely as from 'life,' because, as fine art, it is life organized to make revelation fuller. Jason is, in fair measure, the young South, scornful of outworn tradition, scornful indeed of all tradition, as of the ideal which has betrayed previous generations to the hope of perfection. He, Jason, would tell you, as so many others do today, that he sees things 'as they are.' There is no 'foolishness' about him, no 'bunk.' A spade is a spade, as unsuggestive as things must be in an age which prizes radios and motor cars not as means, but as ends for existence. You have 'got to show him.' Where there is proof in dollars and cents, or what they can buy, there is nothing. Misconceiving even biology, Jason would probably regard individualism of a crass order as according to nature. Jason is a martyr. He is a completely rational being. There is something exquisitely stupid in this degree of commonsense which cannot grasp the fact that ratiocination cannot proceed without presumptions made on the emotional acceptance of a state antedating reason. Jason argues, as it were, from nothing to nothing. In this *reductio ad absurdum* he annihilates himself, even his vanity. And he runs amok, with his conclusion that one gesture is as good as another, that there is only drivelling self-deception to juxtapose to his tin-pot Nietzscheanism—actually the most romantic attitude of all.

But there is Dilsey, without so much as a theory to controvert theory, stoic as some immemorial carving of heroism, going on, doing the best she can, guided only by instinct and affection and the self-respect she will not relinquish—the ideal of herself to which she conforms irrationally, which makes of her life something whole, while her 'white folks' accept their fragmentary state, disintegrate. And she recovers for us the spirit of tragedy which the patter of cynicism has often made seem lost.

15. Winfield Townley Scott, review, Providence *Sunday Journal*

20 October 1929, magazine, 27

A New England poet and journalist, Scott (1910–68) at this time was an undergraduate at Brown University. By the mid-1930s he was reviewing Faulkner favorably.

The Sound and the Fury is a novel about a Southern family of descending social position. There is a father with considerable polish, a mother of far less education, a son who is a business man and another who is a Harvard student, two daughters who go wrong and a son who is a deaf and dumb idiot. There is little attempted on the part of the author beyond expression of these characters; the plot element is slight. It is the method in which the story is told that chiefly concerns us.

The narrative is divided into four sections. Three of these four are done in the manner of James Joyce, *Blue Voyage*, and Gertrude Stein. That is as near as one might approximate it. The story, in short, is told through the thoughts—jumbled, confused and wandering—of three different characters, with the exception of the last section which is written in quite conservative prose. Rambling, often capital-less or periodless or puncture-less, the prose strains on for 330 pages in no very definite manner, although the manner is what concerns the author. And when one ascertains that the first section is through the mind of the idiot, one begins to appreciate the complications.

Max Eastman recently wrote an essay on the modernistic school of writers—Joyce, Cummings, Stein, *et al.*—in which he contended that the purpose of literature, primarily, is to communicate. Of course. And the chief indictment against the modernists is their utmost complete lack of communication. Under this indictment young Mr. Faulkner must fall. His novel tells us nothing. In one or two cases only does his method justify itself by a certain dramatic vividness. On the whole, his novel, over which Evelyn Scott has waxed so enthusiastic, is downright tiresome. It is so much sound and fury—signifying nothing.

16. Abbott Martin, review, Nashville *Tennessean*

17 November 1929, 6

Martin (b. 1899) taught at the University of the South in Sewanee, Tennessee.

Several of Mr. Faulkner's admirers have at various times posed the question why he has not more quickly become generally popular with the reading public. The question is perhaps a fair one, and any well-disposed critic who holds a brief, as I do, for Mr. Faulkner's ability, may conscientiously attempt to answer it. It is perhaps a little beside the point to suggest, as De Quincey did in the case of Wordsworth, that the first line of readers is composed of young persons, who can be expected to have but little interest in Mr. Faulkner's books. For, from the point of view of style, Mr. Faulkner is distinctly a 'modern.' In the

Bookman for October, 1927, Mr. Herschel Brickell speaks of him as an 'exotic' and says further that—

> William Faulkner, of Mississippi, knows as much about how to write the prose to which we give the convenient tag 'modern' as any habitué of the corner made famous by the crossing of the Boulevards Montparnasse and Raspail in Paris.

We should therefore expect the generation under thirty to be strongly attracted by Mr. Faulkner.

It is true that more mature readers, whose taste has already been formed by feeding on authors in the canonical tradition, have some difficulty in appreciating Mr. Faulkner's style. They have perhaps ignored the injunction of Arthur Symons that we should always 'be on the watch for every stirring of new life, whether or not our reading has prepared us for it, in the form in which we find it.'

Some of Mr. Faulkner's peculiarities of style are purely mechanical, and consist in the absence of capitals and punctuation. Keen observation, however, will reveal the fact that this sort of thing is closely correlated to the characters involved. The speech of persons who jumble their words and ideas together, either from carelessness or ignorance, is here set down without capitals or punctuation. It is about as reasonable, therefore, to reproach Mr. Faulkner for this as to reproach Uncle Remus for talking like a negro.

But of course this is not the main peculiarity of Mr. Faulkner's style. He has been charged with writing like James Joyce. As a matter of fact, his style has much of the beauty and lacks some of the faults of Joyce's style. Mr. Joyce's style has been admirably analyzed by Mr. Edwin Muir, who says that the aim of writers in the great tradition of English prose has been concentration; and the method by which they achieved it was synthesis.

But the aim of Joyce and of his imitators, according to Mr. Muir, is not concentration but diffusion, the method not synthesis but analysis. Our 'floating thoughts' are capitalized for the first time out of comedy, and their organic relation to our more conscious cerebration is revealed. This diffusion makes for a certain beauty, as we see when we contrast Sophocles and Shakespeare; but in Joyce the organic relation between our random thoughts is not always apparent.

With Mr. Faulkner the case is better. His analysis of mood and emotion is very subtle, but the story does not sprawl. It possesses an organic unity, an artistic economy.

In *The Sound and the Fury* Mr. Faulkner has written of the decline and decay of an old Southern family. This is not an easy book. It cannot be read objectively; the reader, if he is to savor the best in this book, must surrender himself entirely. The story has much beauty, but it is a beauty that hath terror in it, the beauty of pathos and tragedy.

Never had I adequately known the meaning of pathos until I read the first part of this book. There, through the eyes of an idiot, we see the domestic life of an old Southern family. Only an idiot uttering with simplicity and pathos and beauty its imperfect understanding of the life that goes on about it.

This is a fitting prologue to the whole wretched history of the Compsons. Inadequate means, a weak father, a whining, nagging mother, overly ambitious, but unwilling to discipline herself or to restrain her offspring, quarrelsome children, stupid and helpless negro servants—here is the very stuff of life, and Mr. Faulkner has not averted his face.

He is a realist, but no satirist. If he cannot, like Stark Young, create beauty where no beauty was, neither is he possessed, like Ellen Glasgow, with 'the itch to deride.'

I should like to hear this story read to a group consisting of William Byrd of Virginia, Paul Elmer More, Irving Babbitt, Flaubert and Baudelaire. Old William Byrd would imagine these people to be descendants of the crackers and white trash he describes in his *Journey to the Land of Eden*; More and Babbitt would have apoplexy (I am full of contrition for this literary homicide).

Flaubert would be amazed, but would be won over, I think, by the splendidly impersonal style; Baudelaire alone might be frankly envious. For in *The Sound and the Fury* Mr. Faulkner excels Baudelaire in his treatment of sin and insanity; the book is ever beautiful and never unhealthy. It is, therefore, more truly artistic. The adverse judgment of the pseudo-humanists Mr. Faulkner can afford to ignore; but if these men ever find out about him they may cease reviling Rousseau and turn their tirades against William Faulkner.

Mr. Faulkner has been called an exotic. Surely no man is an exotic who loves the South and writes beautifully and well of a tragic phase of Southern life, even if the manner of his writing has suffered a sea-change. To call him exotic is to restrict the growing tradition of Southern letters. Byron, it is said, made English poetry for the first time European, and it is not too much to say that Mr. Faulkner has made Southern literature more worthy of European interest. It is true that

Hugh Walpole has already said of *Jurgen* 'here at last is a book that America can show Europe.' But Mr. Cabell employs an elaborate symbolism richly evocative of Europe whereas Mr. Faulkner writes of a wretched family in the Mississippi hills. Still one cannot imagine a cultivated Frenchman or Russian indifferent to this beautiful story.

Men we are, and must grieve
when even the Shade
Of that which once was great,
is passed away.

17. Henry Nash Smith, review, *Southwest Review*

Autumn 1929, iii–iv

William Faulkner's novel calls for a re-examination of our premises. It raises at least two perplexing questions: first, does an unmistakably provincial locale make a book a provincial piece of writing? and secondly, what evidences of provincialism might one expect in the style of a novel written by a man who has, in the trite phrase, sunk his roots into the soil?

The first question suggests some consideration of a new Southwestern book, *Dobe Walls*. Stanley Vestal's novel, for all its wealth of frontier incident and description, is perfectly conventional in its plot, its technique, and its heroine; only in some of the men (Bob Thatcher for instance) does the influence of the Frontier on character become evident. *Dobe Walls* escapes from the here and now of life; it is a historical tale with unusually authentic information about the period and the region it treats. In this respect it is vastly different from *The Sound and the Fury*, which is concerned with a regional tradition only as it appears in the present, and from Mr. Faulkner's earlier novels, which often lean toward satire. Yet both novels have a regional setting, and both authors are residents of the provinces. Are both books to be related to the 'new provincialism'?

The question of a provincial style is even more involved. One may always be suspicious when talk grows as theoretical as discussions of the 'rhythm of a landscape' or 'the spacious gesture of the frontier' tend to become. It seems entirely possible that some of us have been misled by an analogy, and have wandered a little into realms of speculation. Upholders of the idea of universal standards not dependent upon a genius of the age or a genius of the place have always been uneasy in the presence of such theories; and perhaps they are nearer right than we. Or maybe we are both right, but have not yet found the reconciling 'nevertheless.'

Let me, therefore, deliver myself from both points of view on the subject of *The Sound and the Fury*. No matter how universal the standard, there are certain pages in this novel which are very near great literature. I refer, for instance, to the character of Jason Compson, Senior, in which the typical cynicism of a decadent aristocracy is merged with—perhaps grows out of—an intensely individual delineation. They praise Chaucer for taking a stock character like Criseyda and, without losing typical traits, making her a person; for writing that half-allegory, half-comedy, the *Nonne Preestes Tale*, in which a remarkable verisimilitude alternates with the complete fantasy of the beast fable as colors play back and forth with the shifting light on changeable silk. In both of these respects *The Sound and the Fury* will easily bear comparison with the verses of the fat customs officer himself.

From another 'universal' standpoint—the traditional definition of tragedy—Faulkner's achievement is also remarkable. Pity and fear are not often more poignantly aroused than they are in the scene where Candace Compson stands cursing her brother for the devil he is. The subject, too, is of an imposing magnitude; for as the story spreads its fragments before the reader there emerges the spectacle of a civilization uprooted and left to die. Scope such as this is not usual in American novels.

Faulkner's handling of the tradition of the Old South, nevertheless, is distinctly related to provincialism. He has realized minutely and understandingly a given milieu and a given tradition—to all intents and purposes, the milieu of Oxford, Mississippi, where the author has lived most of his life, and the tradition of the ante-bellum aristocracy. He has avoided the mere sophistication which sometimes is evident in his earlier novels, and is certainly at the farthest remove from a metropolitan smartness. That he has borrowed the stream-of-consciousness technique from Europe seems to me of minor importance: to say the least, he has modified it to his own use and has refused to be tyrannized by conventions, even the conventions of revolt.

In short, by the only definition that means very much, Mr. Faulkner is a provincial writer. He belongs to the South, if not to the Southwest. Though he is not a folklorist, though he is more concerned with life than with regionalism, his book has shown unguessed possibilities in the treatment of provincial life without loss of universality.

18. Dudley Fitts, 'Two Aspects of Telemachus,' *Hound and Horn*

April–June 1930, iii, 445–7

Fitts (1903–68) was a translator of ancient Greek and modern Latin American poetry, a classicist, and master at Choate School in New England. This review also covers Thomas Wolfe's *Look Homeward, Angel.*

Both of these novels deal with the South, the theme of both is the decadence of a family, and both are unusually rhetorical. *The Sound and the Fury* treats imbecility, incest, alcoholism, and insanity; it is almost unreadable. The vices celebrated in *Look Homeward, Angel* are less extravagant, though no less pernicious; the book is perhaps too readable. In each case, the striking characteristic is the style. The books are really not novels, but declamations. The effects are emotional, not cerebral. Mr. Faulkner and Mr. Wolfe are poets, and they write in the manner of poets.

The Sound and the Fury is the story of a degenerate Mississippi family, dropped piecemeal from the minds of the agonists. The book begins in the chaotic brain of Benjy, a man of thirty, a mute whose mind has never developed. For ninety delirious pages the story unfolds in the disordered consciousness of an idiot. Benjy lacks time-sense, and is incapable of relating impressions; Benjy lacks judgment, and cannot distinguish between significant and insignificant, actual, remembered, and imaginary; and, of course, Benjy's mind-words are the mind-words of a child. It is through this medium that Mr. Faulkner has chosen to introduce his characters, sketch the necessary background, and supply us with tags and motives for the ensuing narrative. He has been courageous, but I question the practicability of his device. The deliberate obscurity of the opening pages repels rather than invites; and when the reader perseveres, he struggles out at the other end of Benjy's maunderings with no clearer an idea of what has happened, or may be expected to happen, than he had when he entered.* Once this section is traversed, however, the going is easier. There is still considerable incoherence: Mr. Faulkner is fond of the psychological throwback and the technic perfected in the Gaea episode of *Ulysses*; but in spite of these interruptions the story marches on vigorously and intelligibly. By the time he has reached the last pages, the reader is somewhat astonished to discover that he is being held by the force of narrative alone; and even more astonished when he realizes that the narrative is straight from the old school of melodrama—nothing more nor less than the pursuit-on-wheels of eloping lovers. And this after so much agony in stony places! Almost what the movie-blurbs would call 'a gripping story.' Especially in the last pages, once the stylistic surface has been penetrated, the scenario atmosphere is unmistakable; and looking back, the reader recovers and reaffirms a suspicion which was always felt: that the men and women of *The Sound and the Fury* are not real men and women at all, but dramatic clichés for all their individuality of vice and action. Only the idiot Benjy is realized; Caddy and Quentin and Dilsey and Miss Caroline and Jason are melodrama types.

The style, then. It is the study of Mr. Faulkner's style, the consideration of the book as a rhetorical exercise, as a declamation, that repays

* I can speak only for myself, of course. Nevertheless, armed though I was with eagerness and the best of will, I tried four times to finish the first section, and each time either fell asleep or started gnawing at the wallpaper after ten pages. It was at dawn on S. Swithin's that I finally arrived at what I think is the solution: let the reader start the book at page 93 putting off the introduction until the end. In this way he will not only reassemble the chronology of the narrative, but, thoroughly acquainted with most of the characters, he will better appreciate the significance of Benjy's meditations. In the event of a reprinting I recommend this arrangement.—D.F.

the reader. Joyce is the ultimate source, obviously; but the joycean technic has been pretty thoroughly absorbed, integrated with the author's sensibility. Much of the time the writing is on two or more concurrent planes; and Mr. Faulkner's skill in avoiding the clash, while preserving the identity, of each tone is noteworthy. A typical passage (not, by the way, from the idiot's stream-of-consciousness) illustrates his method admirably:

[quotes passage two-thirds through Quentin's section beginning 'and Gerald's grandfather always picked his own mint']

While this is by no means an original technic, it is nevertheless beautifully employed. The diction is generally natural (although I suspect a certain stagey cleverness in the interjection of 'what book . . . rowing suit' into the progressing statement 'he always said that a hamper of wine was necessary': it is improbable that two voices would combine so happily as to result in the amusing 'Geralds rowing suit of wine'); the expression of the subjective stream is balanced, rhythmic, intense, and at the same time lacking in affectation. The prose owes a great deal to Joyce—possibly too much;* but the individual impetus of Mr. Faulkner's sensibility is unmistakable.

The Sound and the Fury is an experiment in prose atonality, and, as such, is memorable. *Look Homeward, Angel* is at once less experimental and more effective. It is, no less than Mr. Faulkner's book, a rhetorical *tour de force*; only here (and not wholly because the rhetoric is recognizably of the established tradition), the impact upon the reader is stronger. This is partly due to the fact that Mr. Wolfe has been far more successful than Mr. Faulkner in the realization of his characters. Eugene and his brother, Ben, are first of all real persons; after that they may be types, symbols, or what you will. The narrative, too, is less lurid, less melodramatic, than that of *The Sound and the Fury*. The subject is the inevitable first-novel subject: Myself When Young; and undeniably the autobiographical impetus is at times so unassimilated that the emotional tone is wrenched out of all proportion; but the author has written with such élan, and at the same time with such sincerity, that he seldom falls into the artificial manner which marks the other book. *Look Homeward, Angel* is an extended oxymoron: a natural declamation.

* *Cf. Ulysses*, p. 732 (1st ed., 1922): '. . . and then I asked him with my eyes to ask again yes and then he asked me would I yes to say yes my mountain flower and first I put my arms around him yes and drew him down to me so he could feel my breasts all perfume yes and his heart was going like mad and yes I said yes I will Yes.'

19. Edward Crickmay, review, *Sunday Referee*

26 April 1931, 9

Those who read Mr. William Faulkner's *Soldiers' Pay* will in some measure be prepared for the poignant and bewildering experiences offered by *The Sound and the Fury*. It is not a book for every novel reader; indeed, I think Mr. Faulkner should consider himself lucky if he finds a hundred discerning readers in this country. But he may console himself with the thought that *Ulysses* had considerably fewer genuine appreciators on its first appearance. I am not going to insist too strongly on a parallel between *The Sound and the Fury* and *Ulysses*; but the influence of Mr. James Joyce is so strongly marked on the first hundred pages of Mr. Faulkner's new novel that one cannot let it pass without special notice. In my opinion *The Sound and the Fury* is an even tougher proposition for the general novel reader than *Ulysses*. To begin with, its outline is less strongly drawn and the emotions in which it deals are not so universal. Nevertheless, Mr. Faulkner's book, however strange and obscure it may appear, is one of the most important experiments in creative form and approach I have read for ten years; I hesitate in saying one of the most important achievements only because —although I have read the book twice—I have not yet completely grasped its inner significance. Laying the book aside for a second time, I feel that I have passed through one of the strangest experiences of my life—an experience which can only be paralleled in actual life by walking through a darkness which is lit fitfully by an electric storm and from which isolated figures emerge for a moment and disappear. That is precisely the effect the first part of the book left upon me. The early introduction to the narrative is made by Benjy, a congenital imbecile of thirty-three who has no time sense and who reacts naïvely to the surging of memory from a timeless flood of experiences. It is, I think, quite impossible, to disentangle any clear lines of movement or any consistent action from Benjy's wanderings; but characters now and then stand out with an almost supra-natural power, as, for instance, the sister, Candy, a superb sketch in idiot chiaroscuro. From Benjy we are taken back eighteen years and plunged into the last day of a young

Harvard man's life. He commits suicide under the spell of reaction to sexual crime; and then the story is in some measure rounded off and completed by a third part. But long before the end is reached the reader has made the fullest contact with the characters. Benjy's confused and distorted images of fog have gained in outline and substance, but they have gained immeasurably in creative significance by being first passed through the corridors of an imbecile mind. It will be interesting to know how the English public receives this strange and disturbing novel. I imagine that the popular public—and its fuglemen, the popular critics—will be indifferent or contemptuous or openly hostile; yet it is my conviction that *The Sound and the Fury* will exert a powerful influence on those handful of readers who can see deeper than the mirror of fashionable and commercial art forms permits. For myself, I hold that *The Sound and the Fury* will outlive most of the works that at present loom so large, for its influence will be educative and thus create a wider circle of appreciators for its own authentic creative viewpoint.

20. Frank Swinnerton, review, *Evening News*

15 May 1931, 8

Swinnerton (b. 1884) in his own novels often deals with the lower middle class of London.

[Swinnerton opens with a discussion of the general superiority of young American writers to their English contemporaries.]

Of all these newer American talents, the most powerful and the most enigmatic seems to me to be that of Mr. William Faulkner, whose *Soldiers' Pay* made something of a sensation when it was published here last year. Now a later, more ambitious, intricate, and often unintelligible work, *The Sound and the Fury*, is offered for attention. If I were to pretend that I understood this book, I should be lying. If I were to say that its obscurity seems to be justifiable, I should still exaggerate.

But at this point it may be urged that if we withhold judgment of difficult music until we have heard it again and again we may consent to do the same with original literature; and the general assumption that a book should be plain at sight is not necessarily valid. And if it is so urged I have no answer to make, beyond a reference to the brevity of life.

[summarizes book, expressing his frustration in comprehending it]

Can it be done? Mr. Hughes says it can. He speaks of the 'consummate contrapuntal skill' with which 'these drivellings have been composed.' But Mr. Hughes has read the book three times; and as yet I have read it but once. I will not, therefore, attempt to say what it is about. One reads as one would read a work in a foreign language of which one had a slight knowledge.

Every now and then the meaning is brilliantly clear. One is conscious of immense power, a terrific drive of creative invention. Then darkness follows. One can tell that everybody is agitated, that there are mysterious happenings, sudden piercing memories, hatreds, jealousies, agonies. They are all genuine. One believes in them. But these things take place behind an impenetrable curtain of words. The reader is shut off from them. He is excited, but he does not know why.

The dialogue in this book is racy and overwhelmingly convincing. All sounds, sights and memories are so wonderfully indicated that they electrify the reader into attentive belief. The fantastic adventure of the young suicide and the little girl with the loaf is glorious. Clearly the difficult technique is not a smoke-cloud to hide poverty of any kind. But the book is a teaser, and I fear that, in spite of all its qualities, it may delay general appreciation of a talent which I believe to be outstanding in our time.

AS I LAY DYING

New York, October 1930
London, September 1935

21. Unsigned review, *New York Times Book Review*

19 October 1930, 6

One comes away from *As I Lay Dying* with a commingled sense of respect for the author and an intense annoyance—emotional rather than intellectual—with him for spending his rich inventive faculty on such a witch's brew of a family as Anse, Vardaman, Jewel, Cash, Darl, and the dying mother, Addie Bundren, constitute. One also feels that one must immediately sit down to write an essay on the province and limitations of fiction. The quality of Mr. Faulkner's own mind, even when it is latent, is of a high order; the quality of the minds of the people he chooses to set before you, in fluid Joycean terms, is, on the contrary, of a very low sort. The effect of the conjunction of the two qualities is to force the reader to call into question our prevalent assumption that the artist may never be quarreled with for his selection of material. We should be the last to deny the novelist the right to poke his nose into any human territory, but faced with *As I Lay Dying*, the critic can hardly be blamed if some categorical imperative which persists in the human being (even at this late date) compels him to put this book in a high place in an inferior category.

Mr. Faulkner has chosen subtle and extended means to develop the interrelated mental and emotional life of a family more amenable to the method Ring Lardner has used on his ballplayers. The story is told through the minds of the members of the family and their acquaintances, casual or otherwise. Between the madness of Darl, the sanity of Cash and the childishness of Vardaman there is often disconcertingly little difference on first reading. Perhaps that is in line with the author's intentions. Perhaps the difference between madness and sanity is one of overt expression and action; perhaps the only fair test of Mr. Faulkner's people would be to write another and quite objective book about them from a point above the battle.

The family of Anse and Addie Bundren suggests inbreeding of the sort that undoubtedly weakens the stock in certain of our backward country districts. These Southerners of Mr. Faulkner's are close to trash; some of them have possibilities, notably Jewel, but their general fuzziness of mind serves to make them seem more hopeless than they might seem were they set before us in more externalized terms. The chief trouble with the method of the interior monologue in dealing with these people is that it makes them, as has been suggested above, seem very much alike. And the different characters are not always coherent when taken by themselves. Vardaman, for instance; what does he look like and how does he behave in any crisis that the reader wishes to propose? One would hardly venture to predict. But with Joyce's Molly Bloom, how different? Give us Molly and any situation and we would be able to tell Joyce himself the tenor of her thoughts and the meaning of her activity. We might do as much with Mr. Faulkner's Jewel, but not with the rest—unless we except MacGowan, the boor who tries to cure Dewey Dell's 'female trouble' with a 'hair of the dog that bit her.' Ironically enough, Jewel and MacGowan are put before us by no more objective means than, say, Cash or Vardaman, or mother Addie, whom the members of the family are taking in a coffin made by Cash for burial in the distant town of Jefferson, said burial being in accordance with Addie's wish.

Mr. Faulkner is in the predicament of the specialist. As he dips into the recesses of the consciousness of these various people, he finds himself discovering more and more about less and less. He makes us yearn for Dostoevski to rescue the stream of consciousness and to put it into literary channels whereby it can be handled by the human intellect. Mr. Faulkner seeks to get at the essence of his characters' thought. He is carrying on an experiment that has widened the boundaries of modern fiction. But essences, unfortunately, must be contained in outlines, or they end up by floating away in a dispersal that is so widespread that the pedestrian human mind cannot follow it without going to pieces itself.

22. Julia K. Wetherill Baker, review, New Orleans *Times-Picayune*

26 October 1930, 33

The 'Literature and Less' column of the *Times-Picayune*, first John McClure and then Mrs Baker, gave Faulkner substantial coverage during these years. Mrs Baker, according to a more recent writer of the column, Mabel C. Simmons, was 'a real southern literary lady of the old school.'

Most of the men and women of promise who have contributed to the brilliance of recent American literature have shown an unfortunate tendency, after a splendid beginning, to go backwards or to stand still. Their promissory notes have not matured. Ernest Hemingway has not advanced from the powerful sketches of *In Our Time*, though *A Farewell to Arms* was an admirable novel. What is true of Mr. Hemingway is true of most of his contemporaries and of their immediate elders in American literature. Few of them have shown any true development. William Faulkner is a noteworthy exception. He has developed steadily and impressively, and has become in a very few years an important figure in contemporary fiction. On the face of the papers, he may become the most important.

William Faulkner, a native of Mississippi who has done not a little of his writing in New Orleans, began as a poet. His first book, *The Marble Faun*, was a long poem. From that he turned to fiction, writing his first novel, *Soldiers' Pay*, in New Orleans. In that book was apparent a remarkably keen and fine sense of tragedy, a very intense zest for life. It was in every sense a promising first novel. The promise was not fulfilled in his two succeeding books, *Mosquitoes* and *Sartoris*. It was amply fulfilled, however, in *The Sound and the Fury*, reviewed on this page a few months ago. That novel, too difficult in technique to become popular, is one of the finest pieces of tragic writing yet done in

America. It has its faults, but they are minor. Its merit is major, for it is a novel of terrific intensity.

Mr. Faulkner's new novel, *As I Lay Dying*, is a worthy companion piece to *The Sound and the Fury*. It lacks the intensity and driving power that make the latter one of the most remarkable of American novels, but it has an integrity of conception and firmness of handling that make it a distinctive and noteworthy work. It fulfills the promise of *Soldiers' Pay*. It represents, in construction and technique, an advance beyond *The Sound and the Fury*. Mr. Faulkner continues to develop toward simplicity and power.

The Sound and the Fury dealt with the tragedy of the disintegration of an aristocratic family. *As I Lay Dying* deals with the tragedy of death among white trash. The tragedy of character is deeper than the tragedy of death, for death is a commonplace, whether among white trash or cavaliers. It stands to reason that *The Sound and the Fury* with its strange reverberations of madness should be a more striking novel than *As I Lay Dying* in which the action is sordidly matter-of-fact.

As I Lay Dying is a horrible book. It will scandalize the squeamish. But it is an admirable book, one to delight those who respect life well interpreted in fine fiction without attempting to dictate what subjects an author shall choose.

[summarizes story]

The style, save in the passages of conversation, which are excellent, is not strictly in dialect. Mr. Faulkner repeatedly uses rhetorical devices of his own, and a vocabulary such as a Bundren never dreamed of, to render the thought in the mind. He does this particularly when the thought is so vague that a Bundren would be inarticulate, merely sensible of his feelings.

[quotes representative passages to illustrate style]

Mr. Faulkner has in a few instances exaggerated to attain the horror he desired, but the story as a whole is convincing. *As I Lay Dying* is a distinguished novel. With *The Sound and the Fury* it entitles William Faulkner to rank with any living writer of fiction in America. All but a scant half dozen—Dreiser, Anderson, Hemingway among them—he far surpasses.

23. Gerald Gould, review, *Observer*

29 September 1935, 6

Ironically, in an article he wrote in the mid-1920s Faulkner pointed to Gould as a rare example of the sensitive and responsible critic. Gould (1885–1936) reviewed seven of Faulkner's books, none favorably.

If Mr. Faulkner were asked to tell a straight tale and tell it straight, I presume he would be physically unable to. Even in the novel-reading world, there is a mug born every minute, and certain novelists have availed themselves of this pleasing fact. But I do not suggest that Mr. Faulkner is one of these. I imagine him to be a perfectly sincere artist—which is what makes him so odd. Odder, I mean, than he would obviously be in any case! His importance is that he has created a school of worshippers. I am merely stating a fact, and making no sort of reference to his artistic powers, when I say that, by some method which I can admire but cannot understand, he has succeeded in producing what seems to me a purely reflex action in a section of his readers. Some writers are, as it were, literary Pavlovs, and, however innocently and honestly, try it on the dogs. Many whom everybody would admit to be far greater writers have never produced this automatic response. Shakespeare himself never produced it. Readers have always discriminated among the plays and passages of Shakespeare—like this more, that less, the other not at all. If a new Shakespeare manuscript were discovered tomorrow, critics would immediately begin arguing about its merits. But say certain modern names, and the victim, stiffened into an attitude of adoration, generally does not recover for some hours. Mr. Faulkner, more, I suppose, by luck than demerit, has attained this enviable position. To talk dispassionately about him is (if I may vary my metaphor) to have the fangs at your throat. Fortunately, the fangs in my experience are either amiable or negligible.

In *As I Lay Dying* we are meant—or, at least, I vaguely think we are meant, for it would be a bold man who dogmatised about Mr. Faulkner's meaning—to see a woman dying and her decomposing corpse then transmitted by her menfolk, over great physical difficulties, to a town for burial. The death affects various people in various ways, though, as they all talk the same tough poor-white idiom when they remember (and the most execrable Bloomsbury when they forget), it is difficult to tell what their relations or reactions are. It emerges that there is a child who was set to cut up a large fish just about the time of his mother's death. So we get a complete chapter headed with the child's name and running: 'My mother is a fish.' Now of course any psychologist would admit that the two events might get tangled in the child's mind and produce fantastic results: one result they could not possibly produce would be to make a boy of reasoning age think his dead mother was a fish. 'But,' the fan will reply, 'Mr. Faulkner obviously doesn't mean that: he means that one death reminded the child of another, that a body is *like* a fish' . . . and so forth. Only—if Mr. Faulkner meant that, why did he not say it? The sole conceivable answer is that that is not pretty Fanny's way. He does not seem even to have made up his mind whether his method of labelling chapters under characters is meant to represent the subconscious (or semi-conscious) flow of their minds, or what they actually say to themselves in words or thoughts. If the former, then of course he is justified in using fine language, as a poet is justified in using blank verse to express the exalted emotions of his persons—though nothing could excuse such an effort as that which describes the taming of a horse by a man: 'They stand in rigid terrific hiatus'! But then why all the colloquialisms and bad grammar? And why does the little boy, who can get his tenses right when he wants to, suddenly say: 'I did not said to God to made me in the country'? The best comment would probably be a rigid terrific hiatus; but Mr. Faulkner has in one place put so admirably the advice he ought to take for himself that I am moved to transcribe it: 'A fellow . . . his brain is like a piece of machinery; it won't stand a whole lot of racking. It's best when it all runs along the same. . . .' It is only fair to add that there are dimly discernible in this book the makings of something worth writing: if it were not so, if one did not believe that underneath all the nonsense there is possibly a genuine gift, one would not waste time in criticising Mr. Faulkner.

24. Edwin Muir, review, *Listener*

16 October 1935, 681

Muir (1885–1959) was a prolific man of letters—a poet, novelist, translator notably of Kafka, biographer, critic, and co-editor of the *European Quarterly*.

The note on the dust-cover of *As I Lay Dying* says that it 'has been long recognised in America as one of Mr. Faulkner's most powerful and remarkable works.' We may probably assume, therefore, that it is one of his earliest novels; and indeed it shows many signs of immaturity, as well as a simplicity, not achieved but unconscious, which tells us a great deal more about the fundamental elements of his work than his later novels do, with their smothering complication. The real subject of this story, simple to the point of desperation, is the corpse of a woman in late middle age. A truer title would have been 'As I Lay Dead,' but even that would give the story credit for more complexity than it has, for it is concerned not with death, but merely with the chemical changes which happen in a body after life has forsaken it. The 'dying' is very quickly and perfunctorily got over, for what Mr. Faulkner—like the detective story-writer—is really after is the body, and the history he relates is the history of this body before it is finally shovelled underground and got out of the way. To have chosen such a curious theme, to have lingered over it with such professional solicitude, conscientiously and lovingly, must show the presence of a very deep-seated obsession. It may be objected that 'Webster was much possessed by death' and that Donne was such another; but death is a normal and indeed unavoidable subject of human thought, and, as Webster and Donne conceived it, was inseparable from life. To Mr. Faulkner, on the other hand, it is a sort of death absolute, or rather a sort of post-mortem life, that has no connection with a human life at all. We are told far more about Addie Bundren's corpse, for instance, than about herself. A vision of the horror of death such as Webster's depends for its power on his sense of life. But it may be said of this story of Mr. Faulkner that the most interesting character, or at least the character in which he shows most interest, is the corpse, not in its former incarnation as a human being with feelings, affections and a soul, but simply in its dead, or rather gruesomely alive, state. What we are to deduce from such an obsession it is hard to say; for it is not a comprehensible obsession, like Webster's, but a blind one. The effect that this story produces is, in any case, one of self-indulgence, self-indulgence pushed to the point of keeping a corpse for nine days above ground on its journey to a distant town, saving it from a flood and then from a fire, and reducing the family it left behind it to such a state that they end by confusing it with fishes and horses. Yet the effect is not horror but merely disgust, a much more cold and impotent emotion.

The story is interesting, nevertheless, as showing one of the probable reasons why Mr. Faulkner complicates his method of presentation so elaborately, and why his short stories are so much better than his novels. His technique is so complicated because there is something blind, something unaccounted for by his intellect, in his vision of the world, so that it can only take the form of a series of circular wanderings making towards a circumference which it can never reach. This probably accounts also for the sulphurous and overcharged atmosphere in his novels, and the brilliance of the occasional flashes, for they always appear against this background of impenetrable darkness. There are such flashes in this book, for instance in the scene describing the fire:

[quotes from Darl's chapter, 'The stall door has swung shut. . . .']

The flash is produced in the most wasteful and amateurish way possible, amid a terrific hubbub of adjectives and adverbs; but in descriptions such as this of physical events Mr. Faulkner has shown himself to be a remarkable writer. Little can be said for this story, however, except for a few isolated accounts of violent action.

25. James Burnham on the theme of inarticulateness

January 1931

'Trying to Say,' *Symposium*, 51–9.

Burnham (b. 1905) was Professor of Philosophy at New York University from 1929 to 1953. With his colleague Philip Wheelwright he edited *Symposium*, a journal of intellectual and critical discussion, from 1930 to 1933. More recently he has been writing on politics and international relations, frequently for *National Review*.

The heaviest charge against novels is dullness. Think of to say in our own century Galsworthy, Green, Lewis, Dreiser, Bennett, Zweig, Wilder, Dos Passos, the desert Scandinavians, the wastes (to be honest) in Joyce, Mann, Proust, and how many more.

If every American novelist were to bring out a book tomorrow and I could have only one I should take William Faulkner's. I am not saying that I think his would be the 'best' novel—a meaningless judgment always, since in literature we are interested in specific and unique kinds of excellence. But I should feel at least that it would have the best chance of being not dull. It is often supposed that dullness can be most effectively avoided by thrilling plots. Using plot in its narrower sense this would leave Faulkner in the slough; his scaffolding is for the most part commonplace or melodramatic. The excitement of his books depends on gradual dramatic disclosures of relations between persons, the imaginative complexity with which so many of his characters are developed, the strained handling of emotional situations, the sometimes passionate intensity of his style.

The reviewers tell us that Faulkner writes about decadent Southern families.* With this, for all I know, Faulkner might himself agree; and

* In this paper I am concerned only with: *Soldiers' Pay* (Boni & Liveright, 1926), *The Sound and the Fury* (Cape & Smith, 1929), *As I Lay Dying* (Cape & Smith, 1930).

if it were thoroughly true his novels would take their place in the over-crowded line of genre studies so apparently indigenous to American writing. Any careful observer can describe his home district and its people (Faulkner has always lived in Mississippi). You can then judge by how life-like and 'real' things and people are. From this point of view Faulkner's success is not remarkable. His distorted, neurotic characters are too fantastic to be credible. But actually, in his last two books (*The Sound and the Fury* and *As I Lay Dying*) Faulkner is using the data of observation only as material in the construction of his own world. It is to be judged not as imitation but as creation, by the emotional integrity with which it is formed.

What in another sense Faulkner is writing about emerges from a study of what most he responds to emotionally. There is first a very special attitude toward sex, resembling the attitude of several late Elizabethans. His preoccupation with sex does not crowd nearly so much space as is usual in many contemporary writers, but its importance is evident even in his conventional first novel, *Soldiers' Pay*. Donald, before going to war, spent a moonlit night in the woods with Emmy, and the reverberation of that night is almost the sole emotional force in Emmy. Januarius Jones, with his yellow goat's eyes, has as his only strong interest the seduction of any woman he happens to meet. George and Cecily use the lawn of her house for their first encounter. The women are always shaping their thighs to tables and chairs, and the post-war young people dance just like harlots in the old days. Caddy in *The Sound and the Fury* and Dewey Dell in *As I Lay Dying* are impregnated by itinerant lovers. The idiot Benjy has been castrated after his attack on some passing schoolgirls. But the precise nature of the attitude toward sex is brought out more directly in Jason, with his genuinely Elizabethan notice of the rouge and paint Quentin uses ('She hadn't got around to painting herself yet and her face looked like she had polished it with a gun rag.' 'She had painted her face again. Her nose looked like a porcelain insulator.' Time after time.), and such remarks as, 'I'm afraid all the time I'll run into them right in the middle of the street or under a wagon on the square, like a couple of dogs.' Even Benjy begins moaning when Caddy uses perfume, and sees dirty drawers.

There is that is to say none of the romantic glory, no positive value in sexual relations. Even the occasional temporary ecstasy (George Farr's 'Moonlight on her like sweetly dividing water,' or Addie Bundren's one abandonment) is soon negatived. And this is one aspect of the general moral nihilism, pointed more directly by for instance the complete triviality of everything that happens to Quentin the day of his suicide, of Faulkner's novels. They all end flat: which might be accounted for by failure in technique, but which is at least partly quite deliberate.

The most central intuition in Faulkner, that from which arise all the most deeply emotional situations, is a feeling toward inarticulateness. Other writers of course have emphasized the inability of words to communicate, the inadequacy of all verbal expression of emotional complexities. But I know no other writer whose work may in a very real sense be said to grow from the passionate awareness of inarticulateness. The most obvious example is the idiot Benjy through whose consciousness the first part of *The Sound and the Fury* is told. Benjy cannot talk. His clearest vocal abilities range from moaning to bellowing. Indirectly throughout and in several places explicitly it is shown that this is felt as the most dreadful aspect of his idiocy:

I could hear them talking. I went out of the door and I couldn't hear them, and I went down to the gate, where the girls passed with their booksatchels. They looked at me, walking fast, with their heads turned. I tried to say, but they went on, and I went along the fence, trying to say, and they went faster. Then they were running and I came to the corner of the fence and I couldn't go any further, and I held to the fence, looking after them and trying to say.

But the feeling emerges even in *Soldiers' Pay*. What is strongly felt about Donald Mahon is not his scar or his blindness or his helplessness but his verbal isolation: he can no longer say much more than an occasional, 'Carry on, Joe.' The garrulous characters in the book, Jones and the rector, are empty. In the two most recent novels, the feeling dominates; situation after situation depend on it for their force. No words are ever possible:

We were in the hall. Caddy was still looking at me. Her hand was against her mouth and I saw her eyes and I cried. We went up the stairs. She stopped again, against the wall, looking at me and I cried and she went on and I came on, crying, and she shrank back against the wall, looking at me. . . . (Benjy's account.)

Quentin sat perfectly still, chewing. . . . Quentin had quit eating. Every once in a while she'd take a drink of water, then she'd sit there crumbling a biscuit up, her face bent over her plate . . . (Jason's section of *The Sound and the Fury*).

The effect of Quentin's ironically amusing encounter with the little Italian girl is very largely dependent on the fact that she says nothing during the whole time they are together. The conversational vocabulary of the principal characters in *As I Lay Dying* consists of a few monosyllables and worn blasphemy.

This feeling for inarticulateness is I think closely related to the method of Faulkner's two last books, and explains in part the obscurity which has been charged against particularly *The Sound and the Fury*. Faulkner does not develop his plot and situations and characters *ab ovo*; in fact there is no development in these two novels. There is an initial obscurity which gradually becomes clarified, as if the whole book were implicit in the first page. We are not presented with a sequence of events, but with the sharper perception of a pre-established pattern. This is carried out through the consciousness of the characters—of the four sections of *The Sound and the Fury*, three are in the first person (Benjy, Quentin, Jason); the fifty-nine sections of *As I Lay Dying*, all (with the exception noted below) in the first person, are distributed among fifteen characters. It would be definitely mistaken however to suppose that Faulkner is simply 'reproducing' as nearly as possible the thoughts and feelings of the 'I' through whom any given section is written, even to the extent that Joyce tries in the last part of *Ulysses*. The prose gives what might be called a poetic equivalent of the 'stream of consciousness'. It is no more a direct rendering than a painting is a sum of the canvas and paint. This is definitely clear in *As I Lay Dying*, which further justifies 'poetic': inarticulate emotions, half formed thoughts, obscure feelings are *expressed*, are thrown out objectively—which shows incidentally how different is Faulkner's feeling for inarticulateness from the attitude seen through the under-writing of the Hemingway school. Understanding this will explain many of the obscurities, particularly the curious symbolism occurring now and then in *As I Lay Dying*.

For instance, the young son Vardaman has caught a fish and has cleaned it and cut it up shortly before his mother dies and is nailed in her coffin.

> It was not her because it was laying right yonder in the dirt. And now it's all chopped up. I chopped it up. It's laying in the kitchen in the bleeding pan, waiting to be cooked and et. Then it wasn't and she was, and now it is and she wasn't. And tomorrow it will be cooked and et and she will be him and pa and Cash and Dewey Dell and there wont be anything in the box and so she can breathe. It was laying right yonder on the ground. I can get Vernon. He was there and he seen it, and with both of us it will be and then it will not be.

This ends Vardaman's first section. The next is a single sentence: 'My mother is a fish.' The following passage comes after the coffin has been upset in the river, and recovered:

> . . . My mother is a fish. Darl says that when we come to the water again I might see her and Dewey Dell said, She's in the box; how could she have got out? She got out through the holes I bored, into the water I said, and when we come to the water again I am going to see her. My mother is not in the box. My mother does not smell like that. My mother is a fish.

It is undoubtedly true that Faulkner's technique is still experimental, that he has not yet assimilated the methods he is working out. Yet I cannot believe, as has been charged against him, that he is interested in technique for its own sake or that he is obscure that he may appear profound. There is no reason why literature shouldn't be difficult; but the truth is many of the difficulties in Faulkner come from a refusal to read carefully what is there. Take one of the most talked of parts, the first section of *The Sound and the Fury*. This is written in a first person representing Benjy the idiot. About a sixth of its ninety-two pages are devoted to a perfectly coherent account of the afternoon and early evening of Benjy's thirty-third birthday, April 7, 1928, principally concerned with a hunt for a lost quarter by Luster, the negro who has charge of Benjy. Benjy has no sense of the interlocking of past time nor of any but elementary causal connections (he 'hears the roof,' not the rain on the roof). Various events or sights of the day swing his consciousness back without effort to automatically associated events of the past—though for Benjy there is little distinction between the past and the present. Now Faulkner has simplified the process of marking each transition by italics. Several situations (the initial one, the day of the grandmother's death, Caddy's wedding, etc.) and a few isolated happenings are developed parallel to and interrupting each other. The technique itself is not at all haphazard or chaotic: it is ordered and (perhaps too) self conscious.

This use of a typographical device (the italics) is a seemingly natural though uncommon exploitation of written language. Faulkner employs italics for various purposes other than marking transitions. In *As I Lay Dying* they are used for example when he wishes to throw emphasis on a particular person. Thus in one of Darl's sections every phase having anything to do with Jewel is italicized (pp. 172–174; in Vardaman's section pp. 243–246, the same toward Darl); this is done most skilfully: the section as a whole reads in a perfectly straightforward manner; and the italicized parts (which are some of them only phrases of sentences) themselves make continuous sense and have a continuous rhythm.

The italics, again, enable us to understand more easily one of the most doubtful problems of *As I Lay Dying*: the role of Darl. Of the fifty-nine sections of *As I Lay Dying*, nineteen are Darl's—more than twice the number allotted to any other character. Yet Darl emerges less strikingly than any of the others. The reason for this is suggested by the section beginning on page 43; Darl and Jewel are at this point some miles from the house where their mother lies dying, yet the part of the section printed in roman describes events at the house—in the third person, the only pages of the book written in the third person. The first and third italicized parts of this same section give Darl's consciousness in the usual manner, at the place where he and Jewel, presumably, are. Taking this together with the number and style of the Darl sections we may I think conclude that Darl is identified in a special sense as the author of the book (not at all however identified with Faulkner himself), that the whole book is Darl's. Thus, from a Tull section:

He [Darl] is looking at me. He don't say nothing; just looks at me with them queer eyes of hisn that makes folks talk. I always say it aint never been what he done so much or said or anything so much as how he looks at you. It's like he had got into the inside of you, someway. Like somehow you was looking at yourself and your doings outen his eyes.

The last Darl section shows the author-Darl observing the character-Darl being taken to the state insane asylum at Jackson; *As I Lay Dying*, like *The Sound and the Fury*, declares itself told by an idiot, signifying nothing—

When the shadow of the sash appeared on the curtains it was between seven and eight oclock and then I was in time again, hearing the watch. It was Grandfather's and when Father gave it to me he said, Quentin, I give you the mausoleum of all hope and desire; it's rather excrutiating-ly apt that you will use it to gain the reducto absurdum of all human experience which can fit your individual needs no better than it fitted his or his father's. I give it to you not that you may remember time, but that you might forget it now and then for a moment and not spend all your breath trying to conquer it. Because no battle is ever won he said. They are not even fought. The field only reveals to man his own folly and despair, and victory is an illusion of philosophers and fools. (The beginning of Quentin's section, *The Sound and the Fury*.)

SANCTUARY

New York, February 1931
London, September 1931

26. Henry Seidel Canby, 'The School of Cruelty,' *Saturday Review of Literature*

21 March 1931, 673–4

Canby (1878–1961) had taught at Yale, but more recently had helped establish both this journal and the Book-of-the-Month Club. Though a disciple of the New Humanism, he was not doctrinairely so, in fact was generally open to the new literature and worked to eliminate all forms of censorship. The following year he reviewed *Light in August* quite favorably. His favorite subject of study was nineteenth-century American literature; he wrote on Thoreau, Whitman, Hawthorne, and Twain.

In the powerful and distressing *Sanctuary* of William Faulkner, anti-romance reaches its limit. The plodding naturalism of Dreiser was merely evidence that the world was dingy, which the imaginative could disregard, the harsh staccato of Hemingway had sentiment as an undertone, Lewis's satire was at least based upon idealism. But this Mississippi writer (land of white columns draped in roses!) gives no quarter and leaves no field of the emotions unblighted. Others have written of the underworld and made it sinister, but in this story the underworld is less despicable than the frivolous creatures who descend into it. Others have done, and overdone, the trivial gin-drinking generation and the thin, hysterical debauchery of college youth, but with scorn, pity, or a secret admiration. Mr. Faulkner has come out at the further end of both Puritanism and anti-Puritanism, and in the dry light of complete objectivity weighs his subjects for their pound or ounce of life with no predilection for 'ought,' no interest in 'why,' and no concern for significance. He is cruel with a cool and interested cruelty, he hates his Mississippi and his Memphis and all their works, with a hatred that is neither passionate nor the result of thwarting, but calm, reasoned, and complete.

Unlike his fellow workers in the sadistic school, Mr. Faulkner can make character. His Popeye, the gunman, an impotent defective, without emotions and unaware of morality, is the most convincing of all his lengthening line in fiction. And better than any of them, better, I should say than Hemingway, Mr. Faulkner can write a still and deadly narrative that carries with it an unrolling series of events as vivid as modern caricature and as accurate as Dutch painting. I say *can*, for in the attempt to tell a story by its points of emphasis, omitting explanation and connectives, he is frequently elliptical and sometimes so incoherent that the reader loses his way and must go back after later enlightenment to see who was who in an earlier scene. Mr. Faulkner seems then to be trying to write a 'talky,' where the dialogue gives the situation while the continuity is left to the pictures, which, verbally presented, are not enough to clarify the reader's imagination. Yet narrative skill of a high order he undoubtedly possesses.

But the story!—It lies in two planes, an upper and lower, like a Russian ikon.

[summarizes story—the underworld is the 'lower plane,' Horace and Temple the 'upper plane']

Mr. Faulkner's Mississippi is, we trust, a partial portrait, but his vivid narrative style makes it convincing; nor can anyone doubt the force and truth of his characterizations—Popeye, the filthy politician, the bootlegger's woman, the nit-wit. Nor can any sane reader doubt that somewhere along the path he is following lies the end of all sanity in fiction. Here in this sadistic story is decadence in every sense that criticism has ever given the word, except dilettanteism—there is none of that. The emotions are sharpened to a febrile obsession with cruelty, lust, and pain which exaggerates a potentiality of human nature at the expense of human truth. These debased flappers and hideous mobs in a community which seems incapable of virtue in either the Christian or the Roman sense, are bad dreams of reality which no matter how truly set down are false to everything but accident and the exacerbated sensibilities of the author. To this disease Americans seem peculiarly liable, and there is a direct relationship between the drugged terrors, the unreal sadisms, and the morbid complexes of Poe's stories, and this new realistic decadence of which *Sanctuary* is an outstanding example.

Art is curious. Although it does not have to be representational of human life, when it does become more than design and gives form to human happenings it cannot and never has been able to go far into the abnormal, the unbalanced, the excessive without danger. Poe's more lurid stories are read now as drug fantasies, more interesting to the psychologist than to the man of letters, and so will it be with this new sadism, the novel cruelty by which the American scene with all its infinite shadings is made into something gross, sordid, or, as here, depraved with an ironic depravity in which the trivial by a kind of perversion becomes more horrible than professional evil, while what virtue exists in individuals only throws gasoline upon the lyncher's fire.

I have chosen Mr. Faulkner as a prime example of American sadism because he is so clearly a writer of power, and no mere experimenter with nervous emotion. He is distinguished above others in the cruel school by a firm grasp upon personality and his ability to enrich the flow of time with pertinent incident. No one who reads his description of the harlot's sob party and the drunken little boy will doubt his skill in prosaic horror. In *Sanctuary* I believe that sadism, if not anti-romance, has reached its American peak.

I say 'has reached,' for this is not Mr. Faulkner's last book. It was written before his imaginative and poetic *As I Lay Dying*, a book in which the intolerable strain of cruelty breaks down into one of those poetic escapes into beauty by which the real artist has always saved himself from too much logic. In *As I Lay Dying* there is again a cruel mob, but it is withdrawn, watching the spectacle of a half-mad family who tell their stories by monologue in which one finds how far less intolerable is misery and violence if one sees into the hearts of the characters. It is almost as if Mr. Faulkner had said: I am not God. I am not responsible for these people. If I look at the outward aspects of life in the Mississippi I know, they are so terrible that I respond by impulses of cruelty which lead me to describe coldly events which when read can only arouse wrath or disgust. Let me start again with simpler people, naïfs and crazy folk, uncorrupted if also unmoralized, and tell my story as they must have seen it, thus forgetting my own scorns and cruelties, and so get closer to ultimate truth.

Perhaps *As I Lay Dying* is only a reaction from *Sanctuary* into a different morbidity. I do not think so. The creative artist is usually the first to turn from excess just when the weak and the imitative are racing ahead to their own destruction. He feels a call to a more important job.

The hard-boiled era is headed toward the dust heap where the soft-boiled era of the early 1900s has long preceded it. The post-war bitterness of wounded psyches has already subsided in England. Here it seems to be like an induced electricity where the pressure is higher but the substance less. The war-hurt generation is already too old for poetry, but just ripening for fiction. The candor behind their cruelties when they escape from the hard-boiled convention and grow wiser in life will give their work a substance and an edge which American fiction has too often lacked. They are not drugged, like Poe, nor have they his abnormal sensitivity which only the rightest of all possible worlds could have kept in bounds and only the most ethereal beauty could lift into the escape of real literature. They are—and I speak particularly of Faulkner and Hemingway—men of unusual ability who are working at their craft with a conscientiousness almost unknown to the easy going journalists who constitute so many of their contemporaries, and they have developed styles and methods, not better than, but different from, the practice of their established elders, such as Willa Cather or Sinclair Lewis, and perhaps better adapted to the new decades as they and theirs will see them. Yet, hurt themselves, they have so far vented their irritation upon, and transferred, as the psychologists say, their inferiorities to, a country and a personnel which can be hated, as they hate it, only when the imagination is still fevered. That fever, as it subsides, leaves the problem of rediscovering America, for America has to be rediscovered by every generation, the problem of discovering not just the drunkards, gunmen, politicians, near virgins, and futile, will-less youths which have so deeply engaged them, but the American scene in all its complexity. They will never do it while one ounce of sadism, one trace of hysteria remains.

27. Philip E. Wheelwright, review, *Symposium*

April 1931, ii, 276–81

Wheelwright (1901–70) was one of the most original myth critics of his generation. Some of his best work is in *The Language of Poetry* (1942) and *The Burning Fountain: A Study in the Language of Symbolism* (1954). In 1931 he was teaching philosophy at New York University and editing *Symposium* with James Burnham.

It may be that the novel, or something like what we now call the novel, is the white hope of American literature. At least, there is little positive evidence to confute the suggestion, what with drama selling out to the talkies and poetry borrowing more and more of its rhythms from prose. But if the American novel is to become something of literary as opposed to merely sociological or zeitgeistian importance, it must be something more than a collection of realistic snapshots and Freudian case-book gossip. It must create form. I say 'create' rather than 'have' because it is not enough that Americans should ape the forms invented by Hudson or Gide or Joyce. For the establishment of what can seriously be called an American novel it is required: (1) that there should be writers capable of giving form to American material—meaning American with respect principally to the tone and order of the emotions involved; (2) that the form should be moulded out of the material itself rather than imposed by European plaster-casts; (3) that the form should be principally justified by its ability to convey aspects of the material that could not be conveyed without it. I am not sure that the second and third requirements are quite distinct, though the third is intended to at once qualify and interpret the perhaps nationalistic connotations of (2). For naturally I do not mean that a serious novelist in this country can ignore, for example, Joyce. I mean that what of Joyce or any other writer comes through the prism of our own culture should be treated simply as one part of the, to a contemporary American, available material; and should if necessary be plagiarized, broken up, and adapted ruthlessly—as ruthlessly as Shakespeare dealt with Montaigne and the chronicles of Holinshed. Applying the general principle there seem to be very few writers who are properly speaking both novelists and Americans. There can be however, I think, little doubt that William Faulkner is one of them. With *Sanctuary*, his sixth novel, he has at length become established; and in considering it I wish also to consider David Burnham's *This Our Exile*, which possessing the faults and ambiguous promises of a first novel and having a different tone from anything in Faulkner, does nevertheless share the one cardinal trait of striving towards a form that objectifies.

In *Sanctuary* Faulkner has used a variation of the technique that made *The Sound and the Fury* and *As I Lay Dying* such brilliant monstrosities. The principal devices are those already established in the earlier novels: a gradual clarification, chiefly through symbols, of the main events of the narrative; a type of conversation suggesting frustrated attempts at communication; a repetition of trivial statements for heightened emotional effect; a feeling for the automaton-character of bodily processes; an objectification of persons through the assignment of symbols special to each one; and an absorption of the person-symbols into the symbol arrangements that clarify the narrative and into those other symbol arrangements that sustain and intensify the emotional tone. At times these devices are used for effects almost melodramatic, as in the case of the means invoked towards the central revelation, which is accomplished by a group of partial disclosures ('I didn't know it was going to be just the other way,' 'You're not even a man!' 'There wasn't no signs,' etc.) and associations built around the roaring of the shucks, the plopping sound, Popeye's whinneying, and the seeping blood.

The characters in *Sanctuary* have fullness, but a fullness as if in some other and rarely encountered dimension. This comes about from the unusual atmosphere which the symbol arrangements sustain and into which the characters are fixed. The in this respect most consciously and thoroughly developed character is Popeye, a deformed creature who seems to cast a hypnotic evil spell all about him. His primary symbol is the eye. 'From beyond the screen of bushes . . . Popeye watched . . .' the novel begins; and out of that beginning there arise not less than thirty separate similes describing human eyes, concentrated in sections of the novel where Popeye's presence is dominant. There are Popeye's eyes 'like yellow knobs,' a blind man's eyes 'like dirty yellowish clay marbles' and 'like two clots of phlegm,' there is Temple Drake, Popeye's victim, with 'eyes like holes burned with a cigar' and who saw something 'with the tail of her eye.' Imbued with another kind of quality is Miss Reba the brothel keeper, all breasts and lushness and hot glints and thick wheezy sounds. She 'drank beer, breathing thickly into the tankard, the other hand, ringed with yellow diamonds as large as gravel, lost among the lush billows of her breast.' Her dogs and even the inanimate trappings of her brothel partake something of her quality. The dogs, 'woolly, white, worm-like . . . moved about with an air of sluggish and obscene paradox . . . or, rushing thickly in when the negro maid opened the door, climbing and sprawling onto the bed and into Miss Reba's lap with wheezy, flatulent sounds, billowing into the rich pneumasis of her breast and tonguing along the metal tankard which she waved in one ringed hand as she talked.' In her brothel 'the china figures which supported the clock gleamed in hushed smooth flexions: knee, elbow, flank, arm and breast in additudes [sic] of voluptuous lassitude.' And then from a more dissonant arrangement of images comes malignant travesty:

. . . Her open mouth, studded with gold-fillings gaped upon the harsh labor of her breathing.

'Oh God oh God,' she said. . . . She drew her breath whistling, clutching her breast. . . . 'We was happy as two doves,' she wailed, choking, her rings smoldering in hot glints within her billowing breast, 'Then he had to go and die on me.' She drew her breath whistling, her mouth gaped, shaping the hidden agony of her thwarted lungs, her eyes pale and round with stricken bafflement, protuberant. 'As two doves,' she roared in a harsh, choking voice.

Of particular interest is the quality of Faulkner's irony. The short sentence used as understatement is familiar from Hemingway and Lardner, but in Faulkner its use is specialized as a foil for an already constructed and violent complex of emotions. 'Durn them fellers,' repeated and repeated, and 'Them fellers ought to quit pesterin her' are the only ways the half-wit Tommy can express his uneasy sympathy. And 'But that girl, she was all right. . . . You know she was all right,' repeated five times against the wall of the hill woman's silence produces a vague vast sense of something unnameably wrong. His most characteristic irony, however, is displayed in the frustration of attempts to communicate. There is the imaginative but incoherent discourse of Horace Benbow drunk, given a verbal form of heightened obscurity and mock-poetry to suggest the effect of its filtration into the consciousness of Ruby and Temple, where each led by her peculiar emotion builds her half of the conversation into a structure of its own, punctuating but not responding to the conversation of the other. The result is a kind of ironical epistemic, which is supplemented by irony of situation:

Benbow's attempt to save Goodwin's neck bringing on a still more horrible death; the manner of Popeye's arrest and accidental retribution; above all, the final description of Temple—no reference to the moral enormities for which her weakness has been largely responsible—in the gray gloom of Luxembourg Gardens.

28. L. A. G. Strong, review, *Spectator*

19 September 1931, 362

Strong (1896–1958), a prolific novelist and poet whose own work is frequently marked by the macabre and the violent, reviewed four of Faulkner's novels favorably in the early 1930s.

Mr. Faulkner's third novel enormously strengthens the evidence that he is a writer of the first importance. *Sanctuary* is a book which does not allow one to beat about the bush; and, unfortunately, the first thing I am obliged to say about it is that, owing to the outspokenness with which its ugly theme is handled, it cannot be generally recommended in the columns of the *Spectator*. Yet readers who are not afraid of frankness, and who are interested in the novelist's art, can hardly afford to miss it. Mr. Faulkner is making a real addition to the scope of the novel. The addition I can best explain by a picture. In the average novel the reader travels in a car along a road. There are brakings and accelerations; he halts now and then to look at the scenery; he may even change cars, and travel for a while by a parallel road; but he makes a definite journey upon a line which is long rather than broad, and along which the events in the story lie. *Sanctuary*, however, is more like a field, in which events stand here and there like posts, with long shadows. Mr. Faulkner leads us a course among these posts. We visit some of them twice or three times. Occasionally we cross a shadow before we are allowed to see the post by which it is thrown. In other words, Mr.

Faulkner's events are fixed in space but not in time. Time is fluid in the consciousness of his characters. For all this, *Sanctuary* is not a difficult book, as is *The Sound and the Fury*. It tells how Temple Drake slipped out from High School for a joy-ride with an undergraduate. The undergraduate got drunk; they had an accident, and Temple fell into the hands of a gang of bootleggers, proceeding in swift stages of degradation to the witness-box in a sordid murder trial. Mr. Faulkner is sometimes wilful, and petulantly outrages probability in small details; but his observation, his skill in recording the impressions of the deranged mind, and above all the extraordinary authority with which he compels the reader to follow a pioneer course, fill me with admiration and envy. As a technical achievement *Sanctuary* would be astonishing enough; but it is much more than a technical achievement.

29. Rebecca West, review, *Daily Telegraph*

2 October 1931, 18

Rebecca West (b. 1892), novelist, biographer, and outspoken social and literary critic, also reviewed *Sartoris* unfavorably the following year. She charged that Faulkner was covering a poverty of imagination with literary tricks.

There are books which make a claim that their analysis of experience is of such a degree of subtlety that they should be read with deliberation, and with tolerance for the author's attempts to make an old language express new meanings. A book which makes that claim exposes itself *ipso facto* to the ridicule of persons who dislike subtlety, and do not believe that any fresh interpretations of life can be achieved. But it would seem that such a book may receive approval as automatic and indiscriminating as that disapproval, when it comes the way of those who admit that a book has the right to make those claims. Proof of this is afforded by the reputation of Mr. William Faulkner on both sides of the Atlantic, which can be tested by his most recent novel *Sanctuary*.

This tells the story of what happened to a girl who was taken to a bootlegger's den in the woods by a stupid and drunken boy who runs away and leaves her when things get difficult. It tells this story badly. The first 100 pages show a degree of narrative incompetence which will prevent all but the most obstinate readers from finding out what exactly happened in the bootlegger's den. They are also full of inherent improbabilities.

Of the events that emerge from this confusion, all show signs of borrowing. It was Pop-eye, a sadistic degenerate, borrowed from M. André Gide, who committed the murder. It was, however, a comparatively virtuous bootlegger who was accused of the crime. He had a mistress, who is borrowed from Bret Harte, one of those hard-bitten women with hearts of gold, who tell us out of the corner of their mouths of their persistence in devotion; and she had impressed with her moral worth a lawyer who had been kidnapped and released, a gentleman with a vague incestuous passion for his step-daughter, borrowed from Mr. Sherwood Anderson. He defends the comparatively virtuous bootlegger.

But nothing much can be done without the testimony of Temple, the abducted girl, who saw Pop-eye commit the crime. She, however, is detained in a Memphis brothel, itself described in passages against which the charge of borrowing cannot be made. Their filth and hideousness do, indeed, represent a new contribution to literature. The lawyer does retrieve her, but it is of no avail, as she also is borrowed, and from, in this connection, a dangerous model. She is a vulgarised version of Emily in *High Wind in Jamaica*, and like her original she gives false evidence at the murder trial and thus sends the innocent man to be lynched.

The whole book is, indeed, a rewriting in the coarsest terms of *High Wind in Jamaica*, with the bootleggers taking the place of the virtuous pirates, and Temple, the girl of 17, and Pop-eye, the man who has never reached maturity, taking the place of the cold and wicked children.

That book some of us considered one of the most terrible ever written by a man of genius, in its abandonment to a fantasy which was so murderous, so akin to that which led Herod to put the Innocents to the sword; but at least it was a work of genius.

There the fantasy was fetched from the back of the mind, it was made recognisable, criticisable. This imitation of that work of genius is nothing of the sort. One must suspect any criticism that accepts this book as being tolerant of second-rate work if only it is obscure.

Yet *Sanctuary* has a use, if only to illuminate Mr. Russell's call for values, and suggest that when he talks as if science had to look outside itself for them he is, perhaps, not accurate.[1] *Sanctuary* would seem a clear case of art that had lost its sense of values, if it were not the case that it was the case of an imperfect process of art. The book is not an analysis of experience; it is an imitation of one; the author seeks to gain prestige as a collector of information without collecting any such information. The scientists Russell denounces, Rockefeller and Edison, commit a like fault. They have collected some information, but they act as if they had collected all information. If this violation of the proper scientific process had not been committed, they might have seen authentic values of life emerging from their work.

1 Bertrand Russell's *The Scientific Outlook*, also reviewed here.

30. Granville Hicks, 'The Past and Future of William Faulkner'

September 1931

Bookman, lxxiv, 17–24. During the 1920s a lively forum for cultural debate, *Bookman* went out of business in 1933, not long after Seward Collins had taken it over as an organ of New Humanism.

Hicks (b. 1901) appreciated Faulkner's work more at the time of this article, one of the very first general appraisals of that work, than he would for several years. As he became more involved with the Communist Party and *New Masses*, he reviewed Faulkner's fiction less favorably. He resigned from the Party in 1939. In the 1950s and 1960s he wrote several favorable articles on Faulkner.

I

With *Sanctuary*, his seventh book and his sixth novel, William Faulkner moves toward the reputation that a few critics predicted for him five years ago when *Soldiers' Pay* was published. That reputation, based though it is on this his most recent novel, points correctly to the two qualities that are most conspicuous in and most characteristic of all his fiction: his preoccupation with unpleasant subjects and his experimental approach to the novel as a form. Admirers of *Sanctuary*, now turning back to Mr. Faulkner's earlier writings, are unlikely to be either surprised or disappointed; some of the subjects, they will find, are more horrible and some less, just as the methods are sometimes less ingenious and sometimes more so; but the fundamentals both in content and in form are consistently the same.

Even in their superficial aspects, his six novels give evidence of homogeneity; all of them are located in the South, and four are placed in and about a single small town, which he calls Jefferson, in northern Mississippi. This Jefferson he has populated in his own fashion, introducing several of its citizens in more than one book—Horace Benbow, for example, or fat Dr. Peabody, or the ubiquitous Snopes family. But thematic homogeneity is even more notable. Except for *Mosquitoes*, which is, as will be shown, no real exception, his novels are, at least in the looser sense of the word, tragic. In all the other five death is central, and in all these five some form of sexual irregularity furnishes either the major or a minor theme. Four have leading characters suffering from some form of mental disease, and in three the sexual irregularities are associated with pathological symptoms. Suicide or murder figures in three. The world of William Faulkner echoes with the hideous trampling march of lust and disease, brutality and death.

How persistently a single mood dominates his work becomes clear if we examine that apparent exception to the rule, *Mosquitoes*. Here Faulkner essayed a venture under the guidance of the comic spirit; a study, after the manner of Aldous Huxley, of futility. His intention is quite apparent; so apparent that his failure upon the level of that intention cannot be palliated. In telling this story of a group of New Orleans intellectuals unhappily engaged, thanks to the enterprise of a Mrs. Maurier, local patron of the arts, on a yachting trip, he was obviously trying to write a witty and cynical exposure of the pettiness of the human mind, the banality of the intelligentsia, and the general meaninglessness of life. Unfortunately such a study of stupidity itself escapes dulness only if its author has some capacity for the sophisticated manipulation of ideas. Faulkner has none. And yet the book is not a complete fiasco. When he abandons his plans, when he leaves the level of what is meant to be sophistication for the level of brutality, *Mosquitoes* becomes interesting. Whatever gifts he lacks, he has, as his handling of the eloped Patricia and David shows, when they are lost in the swamp, suffering from thirst and lacerated by insects, a very pretty talent for the depiction of the ills to which human flesh is liable. Such talents repeatedly reveal themselves and in the end dominate the book. What had started out to be a comedy of futility became instead a wry and bitter record of human suffering.

Thus, despite its author's intentions, Faulkner's second novel allied itself with the tradition established in its predecessor. This first novel, *Soldiers' Pay*, takes as its theme the return from the World War of an aviator, shell-shocked and badly wounded, lapsing through oblivion into death. Only incidentally is this a war book; any meaningless catastrophe would have served Faulkner's purposes as well. What he suggests in his account of Lieutenant Mahon's decay, Margaret Powers's passion-emptied mind, Cecily Saunders's stupid greed, and Januarius Jones's goatish strategies is a realm of wanton suffering in which protest and submission are equally comfortless.

Sartoris, coming after the comparative failure of *Mosquitoes*, made no attempt to deviate from the purposes and methods of *Soldiers' Pay*; indeed, it also portrays the return of a soldier, though it is concerned with him rather as a representative of a doomed family than as a returning warrior. *The Sound and the Fury* introduces another family of the damned: of the four children one is an idiot, one commits suicide, one becomes a prostitute, and one is harshly dishonest and insensitively cruel. A third blighted family figures in *As I Lay Dying*—the shiftless father and the mad, unhappy children who attend the body of the mother on its tortuous pilgrimage to the grave. And in *Sanctuary* the principal events are a peculiarly brutal rape, two wanton murders, a lynching, and an execution.

Once started upon his path, Faulkner has not turned back. It is amazing, when one stops to think of it, the pathological range that he has traversed: the shell-shocked Mahon, insane Darl, the feeble-minded Popeye, the idiot Benjy, to say nothing of obsession-ridden Jewel and Vardaman Bundren, Bayard Sartoris, Quentin Compson, and Januarius Jones. Beside these diseased personalities he places his weak and purposeless men—Horace Benbow, Talliaferro, Mahon's father, Bundren—and his lascivious, heartless, unprincipled women—Temple Drake, Cecily Saunders, Patricia of *Mosquitoes*, and Benjy's niece Quentin. With few exceptions, Faulkner's men and women are twisted shapes in the chaotic wreckage of a mad world.

II

Quite as conspicuous as this preoccupation with disease and violence is Faulkner's technical ingenuity. Though his methods were not fully elaborated in any of his first three novels, none is without its structural innovations. The introduction to *Soldiers' Pay*, for example, is uncommonly adroit: instead of beginning with the story of Lieutenant Mahon, Faulkner begins with the meeting between Private Gilligan and Cadet Lowe, both recently discharged from the army; they meet Mahon, and then Mrs. Powers adds herself to the party. Thus Faulkner contrives to suggest, even as he introduces his situation and his characters, the casualness, the lack of design, that gives the novel its dominant tone. As the story goes on, he unfolds brief episodes one after the other, repeatedly changing his point of view so that we see now through the eyes of one character and now through the eyes of another. Gradually the whole situation becomes clear, and yet we are never given any suggestion of a rational, of a more than accidental, organization of events. Faulkner's method deliberately keeps the story remote from him and from us; he never tries to deceive us into thinking that we know these characters well, for that we cannot know anyone is part of his philosophy.

For the purposes of *Mosquitoes* the episodic method and the rapidly changing point of view were obviously well suited, and it is not to any technical weakness that the failure of the book should be attributed. *Sartoris* made greater demands upon the technique, for five generations are involved in the story, and too rapid a manipulation of the point of view could only have resulted in confusion. Faulkner avoids the danger by focusing attention on basic Sartoris characteristics found in every generation. As in *Soldiers' Pay*, where the adventures of Januarius Jones are only slightly related to the rest of the story, he introduces a minor theme—the affair between Horace Benbow and Belle Mitchell.

Though not uniformly successful in his first three novels, Faulkner had shown uncommon ingenuity and a remarkable sureness of touch in arranging his materials; but he had done nothing that could prepare the reader for the technical finesse of *The Sound and the Fury*. Adapting the fundamental elements in his earlier method, and both elaborating and adding to them, he achieved as original, as complex, and, on the whole, as well-conducted an experiment in novel-writing as this experimental age has, at least in America, produced.

[summarizes method of the four sections]

As was natural, Faulkner did not try to repeat the particular experiment he had made in *The Sound and the Fury*. Instead, in *As I Lay Dying*, he attempted to amplify and formalize the method of brief episodes and shifting point of view that he had made the basis of his earlier work. In sixty different episodes he reflects through the minds of fifteen characters the death of Addie Bundren and the prolonged efforts of her family, cut off by a flooded river, to take the body to Jefferson. Each section mingles the observations, associations, reflections, and emotional reactions of the person whose mind is being exposed, and the reader pieces together the story as best he can. As all five of the children, who are vehicles for the greater part of the narrative, are psychologically abnormal, we see events as if on a series of distorted canvases painted by modern artists of a variety of bizarre schools. Yet the burden of the narrative is unfailingly sustained, there is a progressive revelation of character, and the incidents of the journey are clearly defined.

Sanctuary, finally, develops still another phase of the earlier method. Here the episodes are longer, the point of view shifts less frequently, and there is almost no attempt to reproduce the stream of consciousness. But the events narrated are so selected and arranged that the reader has nearly finished the book before he understands how the rape of Temple, the central action of the book, took place, and only the last chapter permits him to understand the psychological antecedents of that crime. *Sanctuary*, then, like the earlier books, forces the reader to reconstruct from piecemeal evidence the actual nature and sequence of events; but Faulkner has made the task enough easier to permit his reader to grasp, without too much effort, the main outlines of the story. He is not, as is likely to be the case in *The Sound and the Fury* and *As I Lay Dying*, distracted by his efforts to disentangle himself, and hence he does not lose the force of the ultimate revelation. Less ingenious than its two predecessors, *Sanctuary* deserves its greater popularity, as a successful adaptation of a difficult method to the actual powers of response that the reader brings. To that extent it is Faulkner's best work.

III

Thus far I have tried to describe Faulkner's novels, not to evaluate them; but his work, as much as that of any living American, cries out for evaluation, and the task is not to be neglected. Can we not, at the very outset, disregard the contention that his subjects count against him? Can we not take it for granted that there is no subject that is inherently and inevitably unsuited for fiction? That should be easy to do if we recall the subjects of Greek tragedy: Clytemnestra's bloody murder of her husband, Electra's fierce revenge, Oedipus's double crime, Laius's infanticide, and Haimon's self-slaughter. Even the mentally diseased have had their place in literature: who can forget, to go no farther in Elizabethan drama, the magnificent scene in which Lear, Edgar, and the Fool seek shelter together from the storm? The question is never what subjects an author chooses but how he treats them.

How should the artist treat insanity and murder and lust? He may, it is clear, treat them, if he has a norm of human conduct, as aberrations from that norm. If he believes in hell, he can, like Dante, make room for the most hideous sinners; that is what hell is for. Such has been, surely, the most common way of finding a place in literature for the crimes to be observed in life; and we may be moderately certain that if Faulkner had chosen this method, if he had shown the evil punished and the good rewarded, we should never have heard any objections to his subject-matter.

But presumably he is unable to take so simple and satisfying a view of the universe, and if so his scepticism is not without precedent. The moralist's view of evil is not the only one that has been dignified in philosophy and poetry. Even the most pious mind must have moments when it feels that we are to the gods as flies to wanton boys, and out of such moods men have constructed a view of the universe. When Oedipus asks

> If one should say, this is the handiwork
> Of some inhuman power, who could blame
> His judgement?

he offers an interpretation of the events of the play that seems more reasonable to many modern minds than the commentary of the chorus. How many have felt, like Isabel in Melville's *Pierre*, that 'all good, harmless men and women were human things, placed at cross-purposes, in a world of snakes and lightnings, in a world of horrible and inscrutable inhumanities!' Such an attitude may not be consoling, but it cannot be said to be ignoble, and it has inspired literature that is not to be ignored. The wild poetry of Webster's *The Duchess of Malfi* and *The White Devil*, the sustained terror of *Wuthering Heights*, the majesty of *The Dynasts*—these bear witness to the distances they can soar who find life a mist of error.

Is Faulkner of this company? One would like to think so; there is something so overwhelmingly persistent in his preoccupation with evil, so starkly resolute in his portrayal of deeds of violence. Surely, one feels, this man purges his own soul and must purge ours; nothing less than a fiery vision of cosmic baseness could inspire so intense and ruthless a summoning forth of all the demons in hell. And then—one hesitates. Is the expected catharsis achieved? Or does the reader stand, terrified and fascinated, but in the deepest reaches of his emotional organization unmoved, watching the horrible panorama unfold itself? 'Perhaps', says Horace Benbow in *Sanctuary*, 'it is upon the instant that we realize, admit, that there is a logical pattern to evil, that we die.' But suppose one never does, in any imaginative way, realize this pattern; suppose it is merely an idea, a notion, perhaps a second-hand notion. Suppose one merely uses the idea, mechanically. One describes the most brutal crimes, arranges them in sequences, heaps them one upon the other. What is the result? Is it tragedy, a tragic vision such as illuminates *The Duchess of Malfi* and *Les Fleurs du mal*? Or is it the succession of *frissons nouveaux* of *Le Grand Guignol*?

So delicate is the question, so personal any attempt to answer it, that we may shrink from too hasty or too positive a conclusion. But how, we may ask ourselves, does Faulkner fare if we compare him with the contemporary whom in choice of subject he most resembles, with Robinson Jeffers, in whose poems is paralleled every offence against human law that Faulkner's novels chronicle? The situations, obviously, are much the same; they affect the reader very differently. The madness of Darl, the suicide of Quentin, the lynching of Lee—these are ends; there is nothing more to be said about them; one reads, shudders, and forgets. But California's encounter with the roan stallion, Tamar's death in the burning house, Barclay's incest, the loving shepherdess's march to destruction—these are beginnings; they lift us above and beyond them. Jeffers has a vision, which expresses itself in symbols of lustful deeds and bloody crimes; Faulkner has strangely focused powers of observation. Jeffers writes the poetry of annihilation, Faulkner the record of thwarted lives and savage deaths. That calm detachment of Faulkner's, superficially so much a virtue, betrays a secret, for if he is not a man possessed, as Jeffers unquestionably is, what is he?

And when the suspicion enters one's mind, how much there is to confirm it! What about Faulkner's experimentalism? Have we here some new, some sharply individual view of life creating for itself new forms, or a keen but mechanical intelligence posing for itself problems that it loves to solve? The forms of Dos Passos's novels, for example, are unmistakably their own justification; one knows the themes could not have been presented in any other way. Faulkner's experiments less clearly authenticate themselves. It is not certain that Benjy was the inevitable narrator of the history of the Compson family, or that the story could only have been told in four episodes, or that in the arrangement of these episodes chronological sequence had to be violated.

There is a better case for the form of *As I Lay Dying*, for we should be the losers if we could not grasp the mental processes of the Bundren family; but even here there seems to be a wilful playing with the normal processes of narration. In *Sanctuary* there is, in the same way, no inherent reason for withholding the details of Popeye's rape of Temple, especially in view of the regularity with which events have previously been chronicled. What is gained by the throttling of the narrative at this point is a heightening of suspense, a leap in the reader's eagerness to push on with the novel. It is, in short, a mechanical device, making possible the extremely clever arrangement of spaced clues that constitutes the remainder of the story. And precisely the same mechanical aim seems to have dictated the other deviations from normal narrative form that have been mentioned. It would almost appear that Faulkner is playing a game with his readers, a game in which he displays tremendous ingenuity and gives pleasure to the reader by stimulating a like ingenuity on his part.

One wonders, however, in what sense this ingenuity is a literary virtue. One can almost imagine Mr. Faulkner inventing his stories in the regular chronological order and then recasting them in some distorted form. This is a different thing from the kind of arrangement Ford Madox Ford has given to the material in *The Good Soldier*; Ford chose a point of view that would permit a progressive revelation in the course of which certain important facts could be withheld in order to lend the climax a force based on surprise. But, given the point of view, the revelation is natural and inevitable. Faulkner, on the other hand, almost literally writes his stories backward, and what he achieves is not a form rising organically out of the material but an arbitrary pattern. The fascination of a gallery of horrors, multiplied, let us say, by some intricate arrangement of mirrors—is that too unfair an analogy to the effect of William Faulkner's novels upon their readers?

IV

But if Faulkner does not belong in the line of Webster and Baudelaire and Jeffers, there is a tradition with which he is affiliated. It is the tradition, at least so far as America is concerned, of Edgar Allan Poe and Ambrose Bierce. He is like them not merely in his preference for the macabre but also in his preoccupation with formal problems. The resemblance, if we allow for the differences between the short story and the novel and for the influence on Faulkner of contemporary psychologies and the work of such men as Joyce, strikes down into fundamental attitudes. We know that Poe constructed his tales of terror with the mechanical precision of a chess player and cryptogramist, and we suspect that Bierce, with his cheap cynicism and petty sophistries, wrought in a not dissimilar fashion his anecdotes of dying soldiers and ghost-haunted civilians. Both made pretence to a profound and dark philosophy, but neither actually had the range of intellect or the power of imagination out of which philosophies are made. The minds of both were disordered and in a way not unsuggestive of the minds of shrewdly plotting madmen.

Surely this is not the most healthy, the most fruitful tradition for a young writer to ally himself with. The reputation of Ambrose Bierce has not survived the critical examination of his work, and even for Poe admiration must always be sharply qualified. There is no depth, no substance, in the work of either man—merely glittering surface. And both men wore out their minds in the manufacture of these lurid devices, these bizarre assaults upon juvenile sensibilities. Whether there were greater resources there we cannot know, but we can see that the kind of work they engaged in would have made no demands upon such resources, which must, supposing them to have existed, inevitably have atrophied.

With Faulkner there is some reason to think that he has resources other than those on which he has thus far depended for his principal and most characteristic effects. There is another side of Faulkner, perhaps an important side. His first published work was a book of poems called *The Marble Faun*. The poetry is not, I fear, very good. It is quiet pastoral poetry of which the most that can be said is that its tone is fresh and pleasant. The mood is a mildly pagan, somewhat pantheistic appreciation of natural beauty. The descriptions are nowhere near so original or so striking as many of the descriptive passages in the novels, but they appear to grow from an honest sensitivity. When Faulkner speaks of the blackbirds like 'burned scraps of paper cast/On a lake quiet, deep and vast', or of the 'slow exploding oak and beech', or of the moon's 'fondling a wayward star', one feels no great power, perhaps, but at least there is an actual and personal emotion to which the reader responds. Mr. Phil Stone, who writes the introduction to the little volume, says justly, 'These are primarily the poems of youth and a simple heart.' A simple heart—it is not a quality one would have thought of attributing to William Faulkner, but perhaps it is there.

Reading *The Marble Faun* recalls the fact that Faulkner has not always neglected his less macabre talents in his prose. There is the description of the parsonage in *Soldiers' Pay*, of the life of the MacCallums in *Sartoris*, of the children's games in *The Sound and the Fury*. And there are other passages, not so obviously the product of a simple heart, that have a vitality and a kind of veracity that one does not find in the more lurid episodes or the more startling characterizations; the section devoted to Jason in *The Sound and the Fury* is harsh but convincing; shiftless Anse Bundren breathes life into *As I Lay Dying* whenever he appears; the visions of Gordon in *Mosquitoes*, though curiously unrelated to the rest of the story, seem to correspond to some experience of the author's. And it sometimes happens that what one remembers after reading these books is not the bravura passages—Red's funeral, the burning of the barn in which Addie Bundren's body lies, the death of Bayard Sartoris—but the slight, sometimes insignificant passages that bear the stamp of personal experience and imaginative recreation.

To say this is not altogether to belittle the peculiar gifts that have brought Faulkner his reputation. The cold, sharp vividness with which he can describe an assault or a murder argues a talent that is neither common nor insignificant; the vigour with which he can sustain throughout a novel some highly intricate device indicates technical capacities that are not to be scorned. The worst that can definitely be said is that these talents are not subordinated to finer imaginative qualities that would employ them on a level above the merely mechanical. But it is possible to suggest, beyond that, that the continued cultivation of these talents, without the development of the powers that could control them and give them meaning, is likely to end in sterility.

It may be that Mr. Faulkner's facility is his greatest danger; it is too easy for him to produce shudders for him to try to create tragedy. But if, as has been indicated, he actually has skill, though not in such great measure, in the portrayal of persons and scenes such as one imagines to be familiar to him in the daily passages of his life, that may be his salvation. One would like to see what would happen if he attempted something quite unlike what he has been writing in the last few years, something more conventional if you will, certainly something closer to his own experience and easier for his imagination to assimilate. If he had the dark genius of a Robinson Jeffers, one could condone, even admire, his abandoning himself to the guidance of his more sensational talents. But no signs of that genius have appeared. What seems to be called for is a fresh start. If he were to ignore for a time his ability to provide thrills, if he were to try to build solidly on so much of life as he understands, permitting the organic needs of his material to guide his ingenuity in the creation of new forms, he might in the end fuse all his talents into some fresh and inclusive and firmly founded attitude toward life. There is, of course, no reason for believing he will do this; but to define our hopes does at least clarify our grounds for dissatisfaction with his past and fear for his future.

31. Kenneth Roberts and Booth Tarkington on Faulkner

April 1932

This is the entry for 7 April 1932, in *I Wanted To Write* (Garden City, New York, 1949), 236–7, memoirs of the historical novelist Kenneth Roberts (1885–1957). He thought very highly of the older novelist Tarkington (1869–1946).

Woke at six and wrote 1,000 words before rising. Two gems of American literature arrived from one of those esoteric Paris publishing houses: one called *Bubu of Montparnasse*, the other *Sanctuary* by William Faulkner. They are all about sex and syphilis: all grimness and starkness: not a ray of humor or insight: two unclothed authors committing nuisances in a public park. When I expressed myself to Mr. Tarkington about the Faulkner masterpiece, and made inquiry as to who he was and how he got that way, Mr. Tarkington replied:

From your queries about Mr. Falconer, you must be an ignorant not to say loutish person literarily. I heard of him 'way last December during which by some odd mischance I stumbled upon a copy, of all things in the world! of *Scribner's* magazine for that month, and was quite startled to find that this periodical still runs—in its own way. It has an editor, evidently, and he did a kind of trumpeting for his contents, this Mr. Falconer being what was most trumpeted. According to the noise, Mr. F. is almost officially our Leader and Hero. Subsequent to the trumpeting, Mr. F. himself appeared exuding a short story, which, as I recall it, began something like this:

> *Over in the muddy field on the edge of our town a tall man in a patched overcoat glanced up toward the sky and saw (he had walked out from the town which consisted of frame houses, drug stores, etc., and was founded about 1832 by a Baptist group of pioneers and now contained every sort of people and considered itself thoroughly prosperous, having a Mayor and Council elected the preceding November) an airplane from which a peculiar dot seemed to be hanging.*

So you can see he has some pretty original ways and would like to get lots of notice from terribly literary people, and would. Outside of being different with parentheses and things now and then, and some traces of Stephen Crane, our Leader is often satisfactorily confusing in ways that demonstrate greatness.

32. Henry Nash Smith on Faulkner as lyric novelist

June 1932

This is a preface Smith wrote for *Miss Zilphia Gant*, published in a limited edition by the Book Club of Texas.

Though William Faulkner's books have already become collector's items, his work is by no means a closed issue; however much the writer of a preface might like to gesture easily towards accepted opinions and then retire, he can not attain this self-effacement in introducing Faulkner because there is no accepted opinion to invoke. Unfortunately, one has to make up his own mind.

The best way is perhaps to compare Faulkner with some traditional novelist: for instance, with Henry James.

The characters of Henry James, like those of Meredith and other novelists of the last generation, are almost all intelligence: they live in a region of the mind where mere biology does not count. If the lower levels of their existences occasionally irrupt into the subtle processes of their conscious lives, such intrusions are unexpected, even monstrous.

The characters of Faulkner, on the other hand, live for the most part below the levels of conscious thought. They are largely subconscious. They are never startled or angered by the intrusion of irrational subconscious drives into their scheme of things, because they are seldom ruled by any other forces. At most they regard the impulses which dominate them with a sort of dull hostility, like that of a man who at dawn awakes to pain from a familiar and incurable disease. Nothing could be more unlike the delicately poised minds of Henry James's characters than the terribly simple mechanisms which move most of the people in William Faulkner's books.

Faulkner, in short, has come a long way from the conception of fiction entertained by Henry James or Meredith. In *Mosquitoes*, for instance, Faulkner had a situation which seemed ideal for the Meredithian treatment: a group of characters temporarily isolated by an accident to the yacht on which they were spending the week-end. Mrs. Maurier's yacht might easily have become a counterpart of Sir Willoughby Patterne's drawing room. Faulkner does indeed set down many pages of dialogue; but instead of advancing from one idea to another, as Meredith's stories do, Faulkner's plot works itself out as a pattern of desires and frustrations which never become articulate. The conversation merely underlines the despair of characters whose intelligence can only make them half-aware of their fundamental irrationality. And in his subsequent books, Faulkner has practically abandoned conversation in favor of attempts to suggest with words mental processes which really have to be imagined as wordless.

It is evident that this simplifying of character to the basic tropisms leads Faulkner away from the world we call actual. Yet to say that his characters frequently resemble people who have been psychoanalyzed but not cured, is only to say that his characters do not resemble our conceptions of real people: it is not to deny their validity in their own universe, which has an organic unity like that of Donne's or Shelley's. The best way to understand Faulkner, in fact, is to regard him as a lyric poet whose characters have the value of symbolic projections of fragments of his mood. This lyricism is enhanced by the opulence of his descriptions. His settings are done with careful attention to visual values and to all the minutiae of sound and odor. The result is an almost stereopticon vividness: Faulkner's universe is integral and self-consistent, though it does not resemble very closely the universe which we, in our partiality, assume is real.

Yet what one remembers from his books is not so much pictures, as a mood. He seems often to be battling publicly with something deep and hostile within himself which he can not see or define. It is this struggle which causes readers to turn again to books which repel and attract them almost indistinguishably. Perhaps it is this struggle, too, which underlies Faulkner's selection of characters. He habitually chooses people who are undisciplined by any civilized pattern, and makes their savage, bewildered struggles the expression of his own inner conflict. The people of Faulkner's later novels, reduced to bundles of reflexes, seem to live in a world for which Saint Augustine and Thomas Aquinas and Shakespeare can have no significance. Their world has developed no traditions and has acquired no subtleties. Earlier, to be sure, Faulkner created characters like Jason Compson,

Senior, who remembered or preserved in themselves the feudal South . . . people who had a code and could quote Horace. But Faulkner felt the remnants of Europe in America as unreal; and he portrayed in such characters a cynical awareness that their world was moribund. It dies, and is succeeded by the jungle. The death of this world, and the savage simplicity of the new, are Faulkner's chief preoccupations. He is obsessed by decay and insanity, and by the futility of man's struggle to become godlike in his wilderness of flesh. For his characters . . . one almost says, for him . . . the only tradition surviving in America is nature, cruel, beautiful, and unambiguous.

The publication of *Miss Zilphia Gant* by The Book Club of Texas is appropriate.[1] Faulkner's work is so closely identified with the South that it seems almost out of place on an Eastern publisher's list. And he found an early recognition and critical appraisal in the *Dallas News* book page, the editor of which, John H. McGinnis, has some claim to be the reviewer who first appreciated the significance of Faulkner as a new force in American fiction. A glance at some of the reviews of Faulkner's work will reveal that he has not always been so fortunate in his critics.

[1] Smith and McGinnis accepted the article for publication in *Southwest Review*; then, deciding it might offend some of the journal's readers, arranged for the book club to print it (J. B. Meriwether, *The Literary Career of William Faulkner*, 1961, 174). Smith almost lost his job at Southern Methodist University for writing the preface (Lon Tinkle, 'William Faulkner and the Dallas News,' Dallas *Morning News*, 14 July 1957, vii, 5).

33. A. C. Ward on pathology in Faulkner

1932

American Literature, 1880–1930 (London, Methuen, 1932), 153–6.

Alfred Charles Ward (1891–1973) was a British scholar. He was the first of a series of literary historians in the 1930s to see Faulkner as representing an unhealthy trend in modern literature.

It is more difficult to speak with assurance of William Faulkner's novels, though these had been singled out for high praise by eminent critics in England and America. His excessive interest in abnormality makes it impossible to think of *Soldiers' Pay*, *The Sound and the Fury*, and *Sanctuary* in terms of literature or aesthetics, however much the author's passages of beautiful writing and his psychological penetration are admired. What is material for the pathologist is not necessarily ruled out as material for the novelist: one does not question Dostoevsky's genius on any such ground. But pathology in literature has to be justified according to aesthetic standards, not medical ones; and the pathological factor in William Faulkner's books is not transmuted. In *Soldiers' Pay*, the horror of Donald's mutilation (he was wounded while with the Air Service in France) and the horrific effect of it upon Cecily, never moves the reader from horror to pity; and other characters—Januarius Jones particularly—increase this horror. The technical devices are also only dubiously justified, except in so far as the spasmodic narrative method and the few excursions into more or less symbolic dialogue aid the stabbing sensations of slow pain left by the book. To the robust-nerved this protracted sensation may be acceptable evidence of Faulkner's genius, though he seems to fumble over things Hemingway would bring off with swiftness and certainty. At moments the clouds of misery are reft by Faulkner's flashes of beauty and light, or by such astonishing feats of descriptive and evocative power as the two pages recalling Donald's last flight above Ypres. But what Faulkner indicates in this and other books is a 'mooned land inevitable with to-morrow and sweat, with sex and death and damnation'—almost the final words of *Soldiers' Pay*. Without some preliminary explanation of what the novelist is attempting to do, *The Sound and the Fury* would be almost insoluble; and, as it is, Richard Hughes's interpretation differs from that provided by the publishers. The former notes that 'the first seventy pages are told by a congenital imbecile'; the latter that the book displays 'completely the psychology of a madman.' It is useless to quarrel with the experiment, since a prior objection must be made that the experiment is not successfully conducted. Often the conversations reported by the imbecile (or madman) are almost as lucid as if set down by a sane person. For example:

> Father said, 'I admire Maury. He is invaluable to my own sense of racial superiority. I wouldn't swap Maury for a matched team. And do you know why, Quentin?'
>
> 'No Sir,' Quentin said.
>
> 'Et ego in arcadia I have forgotten the latin for hay,' Father said.*

Since the narrator at this stage of the tale is the congenital imbecile, his reporting style seems to be far enough outside the author's convention to wreck the experiment. And however much we wish for reasonable freedom for the novelist in choice of subject and method, there must be limits of sanity beyond which literary experimentation can hope to produce only pathological documents with no significance as works of art. Art must always have some at least implicit standard of reference, but imbeciles and madmen could conceivably use completely incoherent language which, if embodied in a novel, might be held up as a masterpiece of absolute realism. Similar objections are raised, in a more acute degree, by William Faulkner's *Sanctuary*. An 'ironic study of a crime,' this novel might be described alternatively as a prolonged essay in sadism. It could also be objected that the author procures the reader's interest under false pretences, since the brief life of Popeye, held back until near the close of the book, reveals that he has been demented since childhood; and, therefore, whatever psychological interest the character would have as the study of a brutal nature disappears when he is unveiled as a sexual maniac. The irony of Popeye's execution for a crime of which he was innocent, while he had escaped the consequences of murders he did commit, is relatively unimportant as compared with the horror and agony of Temple Drake's violation and subsequent mental break-up. An inside view of a maniac's mind and sensations

* p. 41, English edn., 1931.

would be a valuable addition to human knowledge, but Willia Faulkner's studies in mania are, at best, only imagined, and, at worst, are external statements of matters dreadful and beyond understanding. There can be no justification in art for a novel concerning a boy who cuts up living birds and animals and who, later in life, turns to the torture of human beings. Faulkner has remarkable abilities; perhaps, also, something of the exceptional genius claimed for him—and his nearer approach to normality in *Sartoris* may indicate that he has passed through the stage of young devotion to vivid ghastliness.

LIGHT IN AUGUST

New York, October 1932
London, January 1933

34. James T. Farrell, review, *New York Sun*

7 October 1932, 29

In 1932 Farrell (b. 1904) published the first volume of his Studs Lonigan trilogy, an important manifestation of urban naturalism.

William Faulkner's most impressive literary virtues are an impressive stylistic competence and a considerable virtuosity in construction and organization. It is his sheer ability to write powerfully that carries many readers through the consistently melodramatic and sensational parts that occur regularly in his writings.

For instance, when one strives to reconstruct or to tell a Faulkner plot in retrospect one sees this melodrama clearly, but when one is reading, one is swept along by the man's driving pen. Technically, he is the master of almost all American writers who fit under such a loose and general category as 'realists.' He has probably forgotten more about literary tricks than such writers as Ernest Hemingway or Sherwood Anderson will ever learn.

I have recently suggested, in these pages, a comparison between Faulkner and Julian Green. Another comparison, and perhaps a more apt one, is with the Irish novelist Liam O'Flaherty. In both cases, one finds an efflorescence of literary talents that is primarily employed in themes of violence. Of the two, Faulkner is more inclined toward out and out pathological cases, and also, his conceptions of character are the more unflinching. Both use melodrama liberally. O'Flaherty is the more verbally excessive, and very often the melodrama consists in mere metaphorical exaggerations. Thus, one of his hunted characters will skulk about night-time Dublin, looking into store windows to see his face as the reflection of a ghoulish blob of flesh. With Faulkner, melodrama runs more to incident, to his sensational rapes, lynchings, and descriptions of the human being in sadistic and brutal moments. Faulkner, likewise, seems to have the more consistent viewpoint, and to grasp the social implications of his tales with greater clarity. Again and again, he has stated the problem of the intelligent individual, with some standards of justice, when he is forced to face mob fury; and with this statement, has gone a delineation of the impotency of the intelligent individual in the surge of that mob fury. A quotation, garnered from this new Faulkner novel, which might almost apply to the characters of an O'Flaherty book like *The House of Gold*, if one makes a few slight alterations regarding religion, offers an explanation why Faulkner indulges in so many insanities and violences.

[quotes, from chapter 16 when Hightower listens to the distant church music, a passage beginning, 'Yet even then the music . . .']

Faulkner and O'Flaherty both afford the reader relief from a situation in these terms, by lyrical passages, or by strong and steady writing. In the Irish writer, the confessional strain runs strong, and the personal element is more direct and immediate. O'Flaherty seems to be more involved in his stories. Withal, the comparison is not nullified. They are both miniature editions of say, Robinson Jeffers.

In *Light in August*, Faulkner adopts many of the tricks and mannerisms that have been termed 'modernistic,' and this without any great profit. Particularly in some of the early pages, he is very free with metaphors, and they grow monotonous. He adopts the habit of using two verbs where one would often do. Thus, 'The door opened, *inyawned*.' (Italics mine.) He runs words together, the same as Dos Passos does, although these words might just as easily have been separated. How 'aweinspiring,' or 'womansmell,' or 'manvoice' or many other words are more effective by being combined is something I do not understand. Also he draws out distinctions between the sexes by such neologisms which, for this reviewer at least, grow boresome. Finally, he even indulges in a bit of Gertrude Stein, again, to my incomprehension.

[quotes opening of chapter 6]

t in August, Faulkner cuts out his own chronological scheme, o complicated to be summarized here. Hence, I shall confine a mention of the leading characters.

ɔpsis]

This novel has all the Faulkner ingredients. Also, despite the comments on adopted mannerisms, there is powerful writing, particularly some of the passages that describe the life of Joe Christmas, a life heaped with injustices. As a writer, I believe that Faulkner has been overpraised. Also, I believe that his preoccupations with violence and insanity will, with the accumulation of more Faulkner novels, wear out. In other words, he is limiting himself. Because of these facts, there is no necessity of gravitating to the other pole and underpraising him. He writes with force and drive. He is worth reading, although consigning his work to posterity wholesale is another matter.

35. George Marion O'Donnell, review, Memphis *Commercial Appeal*

9 October 1932, 4—B

Before his important article on 'Faulkner's Mythology,' O'Donnell (1914–62) reviewed at least three of his novels. By 1935 he was less favorably disposed toward *Light in August*.

The scene of William Faulkner's latest novel is Jefferson, Mississippi, the locale of four of the six novels that have made him a major writer. And the story is as characteristically Faulknerian as its setting. It will be probably well to warn those to whom *Sanctuary* was distasteful that Faulkner steadfastly holds the view that an artist must not be limited as to subject-matter, must not be restrained by outside pressure from exploring any fields of life toward which he is drawn and which seem to need exploration. For though *Light in August* is more human and less mordant than *Sanctuary*, it is decidedly unconventional and decidedly tragic in tone.

Mr. Faulkner utilizes almost 500 pages in the telling of his story. The plot is luxuriant, teeming with a thousand suggestions and implications and complications, but clear-cut and lucid at last. As in his other books Faulkner sheds light gradually upon the events that make up his narrative. There are long flash-backs in which one learns the life history of each of his major characters in turn; and these flashbacks, with their abrupt transitions from the present to the past, from one set of characters to another, give to the narrative a slight looseness that stands in the way of perfection, though it does not impair the cumulative effect of the whole.

The method which Mr. Faulkner has utilized in *Light in August* is interesting. It is simpler than any other he has used in his writing, yet it is a synthesis of all these methods. The author has employed third person, past tense, and present tense narration, the stream of consciousness, first person narration and conversation, blending the various methods that he has used separately in previous books into a whole that is admirably effective if not always smooth. This synchronization gives the impression that Faulkner is striving for a novel-form in which all modes will be blended into a perfect narrative. This perfection is not attained in *Light in August*, but it is approached.

In every respect *Light in August* is quieter than the author's earlier works. It is more restrained, less brutal, more leisurely and dignified in its movement. The author still possesses his power for dramatic, gripping writing about tragic events, and his descriptive epithets are usually so apt as to be startling; but the prose is less staccato than that of *Sanctuary*, being more like the prose of *Sartoris* and of portions of *The Sound and the Fury*. Even the characters are more human and less pathological than one expects Faulkner's characters to be.

On the whole *Light in August* is a greater work than any other book William Faulkner has written. It is more mature, broader in outlook, nearer to the final, truthful revelation of human potentialities for which the author is striving. It is a novel that no one who is interested in the growth of American literature can afford to neglect. And that William Faulkner is one of the major writers of our generation is proved here anew.

36. Richard Aldington, review, *Evening Standard*

2 February 1933, 11

Poet, critic, and novelist, Aldington (1892–1962) had been involved in the Imagist group. He published his third novel, *All Men Are Enemies*, in 1932. In an early article Faulkner indicated familiarity with Aldington's verse.

Plenty of people are trying to write novels which they hope will please the public and make them some money; a few are trying to use the novel as an art form, and a very few are succeeding.

Mr. Faulkner belongs to the smallest and most distinguished category. He is gradually building up a reputation in his native America, and his English public, though small, is enthusiastic. His subject matter is usually (as in this new novel, *Light in August*) the crude violent stuff of the ordinary crook or crime story. The originality of Mr. Faulkner lies in the treatment of his material and his attitude towards it.

Most crime stories rely on ingenuity of plot and exciting incident, where the reader plays a game of hunt-the-slipper with the clues; the characters are vague, and little attempt is made at any profound analysis of motive. Though Faulkner's crime stories are very nearly faultless in their curious and unusual construction, their greatest merit is the profound analysis of character and impulse.

These bleak squalid narratives reach tragical quality through this grim relentless exposition. By the time you have read a Faulkner novel a character has been completely revealed and a doom explained. Those who dislike Mr. Faulkner's vivid studies of criminal psychology should ask themselves whether it is the psychology or the criminality they dislike. Exactly the same stories told in the false sensational way are always welcomed.

The central character of *Light in August* is a man named Joe Christmas, who has a streak of negro blood in him; and he is the murderer. His name comes from the fact that he was a foundling discovered on a doorstep on Christmas Eve—an ironic touch in the true Faulkner manner. The story does not begin in the conventional way with a mysterious murder, but gradually works up to the ghastly business, the criminal's demented fight and lynching.

The narrative is constructed in chapters which all converge on the central figure like avenues on a round point. The reader keeps wondering why new characters are introduced, only to find that they have a bearing on the murderer's fate. After a careful reading—and the book demands some attention—you will see why this horrible thing was almost certain to happen, given the man's heredity, upbringing, environment, and the crude ugly conceptions of life which exist in these remote Southern States. Incidental to the main thread of the story, this book gives a remarkable sketch of social history in certain parts of America.

In spite of the hard-boiled style in which Mr. Faulkner writes, there cannot be the slightest doubt of his meaning and sympathies. He is engaged in the not very popular task of criticising the fundamental assumptions of his own people, and it is to the credit of American tolerance that these cruel, cold expositions of their stupidities and crimes have been so widely read. But the quality of the book is so fine that it rises far above any merely topical problem novel. It is an amazingly complete statement of what human life is in that part of the country, and provides us in England with a far more plausible explanation of Southern farmer mentality (with all its narrowness and hostility to Europe) than could be accomplished by legions of self-appointed ambassadors of good will.

If Mr. Faulkner's account is accurate, then it is quite obvious why these crude harsh people, with their fanatical Calvinism and hatred of the negro, their stupefying prejudices and ignorances, their repressions, their violence, their hideous attitude to sex, are unable to understand the necessity for action in world affairs demanding a good will and intelligence they merely don't possess. *Light in August* cannot be recommended as light fantastic reading, but those who are prepared to make an effort should find an acrid enjoyment in this passionately honest dissection of the dark places in the human soul.

…pton Mackenzie, review, *Daily Mail*

9 February 1933, 4

Elsewhere in this review, entitled 'Prose Gone Bad,' Mackenzie (1883–1972) called Sinclair Lewis 'the most significant novelist of this period.'

To the 'intellectuals' on both sides of the Atlantic the work of Mr. William Faulkner has appeared much more profound than that of Mr. Sinclair Lewis. With *Light in August* Mr. Faulkner will be proclaimed by them a more significant novelist than his senior.

Unquestionably *Light in August* is a good book; possibly it is a great book. Yet with all its qualities, with its strength and brutality, with its astonishing power of evoking atmosphere, with its perfect control over dialogue and its subtlety of analysis, the book is rank with the odour of decay, and it is noteworthy how much this deliquescence of imagination is affecting even the very texture of Mr. Faulkner's prose.

[quotes opening of chapter 6]

Writing like that is the result of weakness masquerading as strength. Mr. William Faulkner has only to develop such a style a little further to collapse as utterly as so many other modern writers have collapsed, and let me add as so many Latin writers collapsed long ago, under the burden of words.

What on earth is the point of writing 'adjacenting'? What is gained by adding an English present participle to an already existing Latin present participle? While he was about it Mr. Faulkner might as well have added a French present participle, and written 'adjacentingent.'

Nevertheless, I must not suggest that the whole book is written with such a barbarous disregard of verbal decency. Mr. Faulkner is, in very fact, still too good a writer to believe that he can only attract the world's attention with the kind of funny noises that a third-rate trumpeter makes in a jazz band.

Arnold Bennett proclaimed that Mr. Faulkner 'writes ger an angel.' For this book he has plucked a quill from one c wings, and it would not be a bad experiment if he wrote his with a thin steel nib.

38. F. R. Leavis, review, *Scrutiny*

June 1933, ii, 91–3

Mr Leavis has requested that a postscript follow this review, originally entitled 'Dostoevsky or Dickens?'

Frank Raymond Leavis (b. 1895) helped found this important critical quarterly in 1932, the same year he published *New Bearings in English Poetry*, a study of Hopkins, Eliot, and Pound. For many years he was a fellow of Downing College, Cambridge. As his postscript indicates his attitude toward Dickens changed vastly after he wrote *The Great Tradition* (1948), a study of the English novel which more or less excludes Dickens from the first rank of writers.

Dostoevsky was influenced by Dickens, but they are very different. *Light in August*, which is more readable than William Faulkner's earlier books, should make it plain that he is much more like Dickens than Dostoevsky. It is more readable because in it Faulkner has been much less concerned to be modern in technique. But he has still been concerned too much.

It is his 'technique,' of course, that, together with his dealings in abnormal or subnormal mentality and his disregard of the polite taboos, has gained for him, in France as well as in America and England, his reputation as one of the most significant and peculiarly modern of writers. The technique that matters is the means of expressing a firmly realized purpose, growing out of a personal sensibility. Early in *Light in August* it should have been plain to the reader that Faulkner's 'technique' is an expression of—or disguise for—an uncertainty about what he is trying to do.

There is, for instance, that Gertrude-Steinian trick: 'Memory believes before knowing remembers. Believes longer than recollects, longer than knowing even wonders. Knowing remembers believes' etc. Here it is incidental to a rendering (for the most part in a quite unrelated manner, and one of the best things in the book) of childhood experience. But it is sporadic, applied to various kinds of characters in various circumstances, and it is never supported by that minute intimacy in the registering of consciousness which it implies. Indeed, Faulkner is seldom for long sure of the point of view he is writing from, and will alter his focus and his notation casually, it would seem, and almost without knowing it.

This pervasive uncertainty of method goes down to a central and radical uncertainty. If what is apparently meant to be the central theme of the book, the conflict in Christmas of the white and the negro blood, had been realized and active, we should necessarily have had somewhere and by some means an intimate and subtle rendering of his consciousness. But in spite of the technique and in spite of the digression—for it strikes us as that—back into childhood, he remains the monotonously 'baleful' melodramatic villain whose mysteriousness is of so familiar a kind, depending on our having only a surface to contemplate. Faulkner, in fact, in his vision of Good and Evil is like Dickens—at his best simple, at his worst sentimental and melodramatic. The brutal submorality of Christmas might have been significant in a Dostoevsky context and so, interesting; but when Faulkner rightly not trusting the job made of it by his 'technique,' pumps in the Significance straightforwardly at the death of Christmas, its quality appears in the prose of this.

[quotes from last paragraph of chapter 19]

There are, as has been implied, good parts. The account of Christmas's childhood and boyhood is one of them. But it remains, like so much else in the book, separate, unrelated organically, and the subject of it is only nominally related to the villain-hero who dies in the passage quoted above. The long history of the family of Miss Burden, the murdered paramour, is also good in its way, and the tacking on is done with an innocent directness contrasting oddly with the pervasive 'technique': 'She told Christmas this while they sat on the cot in the darkening cabin.'

The Reverend Gail Hightower, another main character, again illustrates the uncertainty of grasp and purpose. He hovers between the planes of Mr. Dick and Miss Havisham, soaring up to the latter (in cheap prose and cheap sentiment) when Significance gives the cue. The odd couple, Hines, belong irremediably to the plane of Dickensian grotesque, but they are solemnly pushed on the stage as tragic actors.

What Faulkner renders with most conviction is the simple-shrewd vegetative mentality of his rustics and small-town citizens (indeed, he finds it so congenial that he again and again uses it, quite improbably and with great technical naïveté, as the medium of presentation). His heart is with his simple heroine and hero, Lena and Byron Bunch, and where they are concerned his sentimentality is not offensive as it is in his flights of high-tragic Significance. The Old South is the strength of his book: one gets intimations of a mellow cultural tradition, still, it appears, in some degree surviving, that recall that great book, *Huckleberry Finn.* But it is too late for another Mark Twain.

In 1974 Mr Leavis wrote:
I wrote the review of *Light in August* many years ago, and I am horrified to take, from the journalistic heading of the review, the implication that Dickens, regarding whom I am now certain that he is among the very greatest, is less profound than Dostoevsky, who doesn't matter much to me. Nevertheless, the suggestion isn't fair to Dostoevsky either; he certainly exists.

39. Jean Stewart, 'The Novels of William Faulkner'

March 1933

Cambridge Review, 10 March 1933, 310–12.

Jean Stewart Pace (b. 1903) studied at Cambridge and has translated and written on French poetry. She wrote this article not in England but while on a fellowship at the University of California. It was, however, the first general appraisal of Faulkner's achievement to appear in England.

The appearance of *Sanctuary* in a popular edition, last year, made the American public suddenly aware of the savage and eccentric power of William Faulkner; but his earlier work, in some ways more significant, remains comparatively little known. It is on the assumption that English readers are even less familiar with Faulkner's writing that I venture to present my own appreciation of it.

He is so versatile and so experimental as to elude facile definition. The problems which beset the preceding generation of American writers do not concern him; he has not to rebel against Puritanism or materialism—the Menckens, Dreisers and Andersons have done that pioneer work of destructive criticism, leaving the way open for younger writers to express their vision unhampered, and Faulkner profits fully by this freedom. He is obviously aware of the latest movements of thought and expression—of Freud, Joyce, the modern poets; he adapts as much of their methods as will serve his own purpose, but is no further bound to them.

Two influences, it seems to me, must have proved vital factors in the formation of his mind and art. First, the peculiar character of that South to which he belongs and of which he writes. Faulkner is by no means one of the 'new regionalists,' bent on reproducing local colour and on consecrating their particular small corner of the earth. But the Southern landscape serves as a background, its climate provides the atmosphere for all his dramas—from the lovely luxuriant April that contrasts so poignantly with the human tragedy in *Soldiers' Pay* to the sultry summer that enhances the horror of *Light in August.* And in the remote, backward civilisation of the South he finds his store of psychological problems—among the uncultured 'poor whites,' the decaying gentry, the vivid Negro folk: he knows their mind and can convey their idiom with startling power. Whether his interpretation of the South be the accepted one, I am not competent to say; it is, at all events, an impressive personal vision, like Lawrence's Mexico or Van Gogh's Provence.

The second influence is clearly the war, which seems to have left a profound impress on his mind; this is shown not only in his grave and penetrating studies of war psychology, but in the general blackness of his view of humanity, his choice of macabre and brutal themes. To the same searing war-experience one may doubtless attribute his cult of an intricate art-form—a reaction against the horror of life akin to that of Baudelaire.

Soldiers' Pay (1926) is a study of the aftermath of war; the shadow of the storm hangs over it. This is an imperfect, but oddly moving, book, more accessible and written with more display of feeling than any of his later work; yet it is complex, rich in implications and overtones. It is compact of contrasts; the essential opposition is between those whom the tragic experience has touched, draining them of hope and desire, leaving them only pity and joyless wisdom and the power of self-sacrifice, and on the other hand those who stayed at home; the young with their egotism and shallowness, the old with their pathetic immaturity. The central figure of the book is the maimed and mindless aviator Mahon, a symbolic victim, and there is tragic irony in the contrast between his death-in-life and the passions at strife around him and on account of him, and of which he is oblivious.

The whole book, indeed, may be described in terms of contrast. The characters seem to exist on different planes; Margaret and Joe, who have suffered, are drawn with sympathy, are deeply and fully human; the others are deliberately unreal—Cecily, the flapper, is an exquisite and savage satirical etching, Mahon's father a quaint fantastic, while the preposterous Jones is a grotesque and sinister satyr. Meanwhile the ironic objectivity of the narrative is frequently interrupted by outbursts of pity and indignation; the vivid realism of the dialogue gives place, in description, to an elaborate metaphorical style, flashing into poetry, straining after conceits; and the essentially tragic theme is relieved, in

Elizabethan tradition, by satire and crude farce. Contrasts as violent as these deprive the novel of any unity of tone, but give it its peculiar savour. As for the preciosity and grotesquerie, they are a defense-mechanism against overt emotion, but one which does not always prevail.

In his next two books (there is a third, *Sartoris*, which I have not been able to procure) he pushed experimental expression still further, as though deliberately to perplex and disconcert the reader. His situations become more mysterious, his characters more irrational, their motives more obscure; abandoning traditional methods of narrative, he seeks ever more oblique ways of presentation.

In *The Sound and the Fury* (1929) he shows the disintegration of a family in which madness runs. The plot, which is woven on the themes of terror, hatred and incest, discloses itself indirectly, reflected in the minds of the characters; first, in that of the imbecile Benjy, to whom time and causality mean nothing; his dim perceptions of present happenings are intermingled with recollections of past experience, brought back by some sense-impression; only with close reading can one disentangle the chronology and get some glimpse of the situation, and even then, many of the suggestions remain unfulfilled until the story is completely told. Part II deals with an earlier act of the drama, one obscurely descried already through the confused vision of Benjy; it takes the form of an interior monologue in the mind of Benjy's brother, Quentin, a neurotic on the verge of suicide, maddened by jealousy at his sister's marriage, obsessed by phrases and images recalling the past incidents that have tortured him. In Part III we return to the later period; Quentin is long since dead, the sister has been cast off by her family; and the horrible younger brother, Jason, relates his own callous and revengeful persecution of his sister's child. Part IV, in straightforward objective narrative, pulls the threads together and sets forth the crisis.

The book conveys a sense of accumulating horror; at first, all is befogged and bewildering, but gradually loose threads connect, dark hints are developed, the impression is built up. The effect is akin to that of a cubist picture where objects are dissected and shown from different angles simultaneously, an art of pattern and of intellectual structure rather than of direct representation. And Faulkner's pattern is a cunning one; witness his use of leit-motivs, the obsessions with time, with water, with virginity, with death, that recur in Quentin's tortured mind.

His handling of the stream of consciousness, of the network of association and the obscure conflicts of the subconscious, betrays the inevitable influence of Joyce; but he shows a sensitiveness in selection, a poetic intensity in expression, that are quite individual. Perhaps the most remarkable thing in the book is the sympathetic insight with which the crazed mind of Benjy is interpreted; but I cannot forbear to mention one apparently extraneous episode, at the close of the book —the picture of the negro church-meeting—which shows yet another aspect of his power, his sympathetic grasp of primitive folk-psychology, his sense of the picturesque and his keen humour.

These novels having met with small success, he conceived a deep contempt for the public and composed *Sanctuary*, first version, to flout it, as 'the most horrific tale' he could imagine; and was forced, inevitably, to discard this for the time being. Meanwhile, working on a power plant, he wrote *As I Lay Dying* between shifts, in six weeks. It is akin to *The Sound and the Fury* in technique, but even more obscure. Here we have another crazy and ill-fated family; we witness the death of Addie Bundren, a poor farmer's wife, and the transporting of her corpse, in its home-made coffin, to her family graveyard some fifty miles away; a grotesque and gruesome journey. The story is once more told indirectly, through brief cross-sections of the consciousness of the various characters; the psychology of each, the sense of their limited mentality, of their individual obsessions, desires and hatreds, is powerfully conveyed. One is reminded of the early Sherwood Anderson by Faulkner's insight into the problems of inarticulate, frustrated and bewildered souls (though Faulkner has a sharp humour, a gift for caricature, that are lacking in the older writer), and of Joyce, by the desperate dadaism to which he resorts to express their obscure emotions. The effect here is rather of a Surrealist than of a Cubist painting, got from the juxtaposition of incongruous objects and the evocation of haunting forms from the subconscious.

Sanctuary, second version, remains a 'horrific tale' enough, but (as planned) just enough to tickle the public taste and prove a best-seller at 95 cents. It has indeed a horrible fascination; on a transcontinental train journey it held one reader spellbound and oblivious of the interminably unrolling middle-western plains. It is straight sailing compared to the two previous novels, being hardly more embroiled than an ordinary thriller; the bewilderment it causes is due to the unaccountable behaviour of the characters, judged by ordinary standards of motivation; it is perhaps a flaw that the physiological cause of the villains' sadism is only revealed in an epilogue. Otherwise it is a masterpiece of construction and narrative; Faulkner maintains strict detachment throughout, relentlessly unfolding his sinister story, relieving its tension only with such superb studies in grim humour as the picture of Miss Reba, the brothel keeper, and her friends. And if his characters are irrational, they are given nevertheless an astonishing concreteness; the girl Temple, victim of the monstrous Popeye, is a creature of impulse without mind or soul, but we can feel her physically, we share her terrors as of a hunted animal, her frenzies and her stupors.

With his latest novel, *Light in August*, Faulkner abandons the swift concentrated narrative form of *Sanctuary*. This book is diffuse, intricate, slow-moving. We are confronted with a disparate crowd of characters, whose lives have become inter-connected at the crisis of his story; we pass from one to the other, watching the repercussion on them of the central incidents, and tracing back the complex antecedents of each individual. We have thus an involved sequence of episodic stories; the time sense is abolished as we grope in the past, discovering the influences that have moulded each of his strange protagonists; if the characters are still mysterious, abnormal, yet there is an attempt to make them convincing by a searching analysis of their origins. The method is not wholly successful, since these peculiar beings hardly excite enough interest at the start to make their numerous and complicated histories worth the unravelling. The book, however, has magnificent things in it; Joe Christmas lingers horribly in the memory—a sinister figure haunted by knowledge of his negro blood, bearing a bitter grudge against humanity; for sheer tension and terror, few things in modern writing can equal the story of his desperate flight from justice. While only a poet could have made the fierce heat of a Southern August throb in his pages with such intolerable sensuous realism.

Besides these five novels Faulkner has written a number of short stories of unequal merit; a collection entitled *These Thirteen* illustrates the variety and scope of his talent. There are austere war-stories, studies of abnormal psychology, vivid pictures of Southern life—'Dry September', which describes the lynching of a negro, is particularly powerful. In this form he is perhaps at his best; the discipline it imposes corrects the tendency to diffuseness which mars *Light in August*, and the over-complication which is always a snare to him.

What direction Faulkner will take next, whether success will spoil him by leading him to repeat himself or by encouraging affectation and artifice, or whether he will gather up his very real strength for the creation of something permanent, remains to be seen. It is easy to po out his faults, his violence, his obscurity, to say his themes are too horrible, too remote from ordinary humanity, his structure over-elaborate, his characters unconvincing, his style extravagant. But he has qualities which, to my mind, outweigh these defects; he has that most precious of gifts, a vigorous creative imagination. The queer creatures that throng his pages live with an intense vitality of their own; the power of his conception compels us to suspend our disbelief, even if unwillingly. If his world seems strange and repellent to us, it is not through any lack of variety, beauty or humour in it, but because the forces of evil and terror, which we are always endeavouring to forget, are here unleased and dominant. He has the insight which pierces below the surface of life, which can apprehend and concretise the mysterious workings of the subconscious. He has that imaginative humour which bodies forth grotesques, as well as the realist's humour which is founded on an intimate knowledge of human nature. Above all, his imagination is revealed in his style, which has the force and intensity of poetry; in the strained metaphors, the impressionism of *Soldiers' Pay*, the crazy babblings of Benjy, the hallucinations of Quentin, in the tense narrative of *Sanctuary*, in the fierce attempts of *As I Lay Dying* and *Light in August* to express the inexpressible, the burden of the mystery as felt by a bewildered being.

It may be that, as Ludwig Lewisohn declares, 'this type of art can help us no more; we shall find a new idealism or our literature will perish.' Faulkner's work may be destined to dismissal as the tortured vision of a neurotic in an age of decadence and despair, and have nevertheless a vital meaning for us, his contemporaries. I only know that his art provides so potent a stimulus to my own mind as to make all soberer and saner literature pale into banality, by contrast, while the mood lasts.

. Edgar, from *The Art of the Novel*

1933

These passages come from chapter 28, 'Four American Writers: Anderson, Hemingway, Dos Passos, Faulkner,' 338–51.

Edgar (1871–1948) taught at Victoria College, University of Toronto. He wrote studies of Shelley and James, and the English novel. This is one of few sympathetic comments on Faulkner by academics.

Three of these writers have given us their measure—a satisfying measure we admit it to be. The fourth and youngest, Faulkner, has already revealed more creative energy than any of his contemporaries, but the time has not yet arrived to cast his horoscope. He is still intelligently but violently experimenting. There is much crashing in the underbrush, but he is hewing out a recognizable path. Where it will lead him is the debatable question. His full strength he has put out only in one book, *The Sound and the Fury*, and its almost incredible difficulty is not an initial recommendation. The ordinary intelligent reader does not relish such apparent contemptuous treatment from an author. But with the difficulties overcome we are inclined to admit that they may have been necessary to the plan, and that a simple approach would have deprived the book of the impressiveness it gains from its very complexity. While we admit the virtue of clarity we are not prepared to insist that a profound treatment of life shall reveal itself at a glance. The others do not strike so deep to the root of things. In Anderson and Hemingway difficulties do not exist, and in Dos Passos they are unnecessary and irritating.

[discusses subject matter of each]

In the craft of words they are all competent and interesting. When Arnold Bennett announced Faulkner as 'The coming man' he said that he wrote 'generally like an angel.' We are glad of the 'generally,' for his forcefulness betrays him often into over-emphasis. There is a too perpetual straining for similitudes, since everything is not of necessity like something else. Fertility in image-creating power is a virtue too rare in modern writing to merit condemnation, and an ultimate pruning of excess will some day permit us to expunge Arnold Bennett's 'generally.' We suspect that he does not always know the meaning of the long words he uses, and there are mannerisms in his constructions that irritate us by their frequency: 'and pretty soon there were gulls looking *like* they had pink and yellow feathers, slanting and wheeling around—and it was *like* there was a street in a city.' A mannerism confined to *As I Lay Dying* may be noted without comment. It is so constantly and confidently employed that it must rest on some obscure artistic reason which is not readily apparent. The ordinary habit in dialogue is to represent the speakers with variations in the phrase announcing them. To every speech in this book is attached the bald statement, 'he said,' or 'he says,' 'I says.'

Like most good writers of our day Mr. Faulkner conceals himself within his book. The compositional law of that strange novel, *As I Lay Dying*, is that each chapter reveals the consciousness of one particular character. Vardaman is the child of the family: 'It is dark. I can hear woods, silence: I know them. But not living sounds, not even him.' Up to this point it is a child thinking. But in a moment we are miles away from the child's consciousness: 'It is as though the dark were resolving him out of his integrity, into an unrelated scattering of components—snuffings and stampings; smells of cooling flesh and ammoniac hair; an illusion of a co-ordinated whole of splotched hide and strong bones which, detached and secret and familiar, an *is* different from my *is*'—etc. This is rather a compositional, than a stylistic flaw. When the ordinary analyst reads a mind we are often conscious of the author's presence. The psycho-analyst more rarely intrudes. An excuse for the old-time author's intervention was that it gave him an opportunity to express himself apart from the story. It was a dangerous expedient which only good writing could condone. Such deviations are extremely rare in Faulkner, but there is a passage in Part IV of *Sartoris* where the author stops his story to write a long paragraph on the mule. It is a fine specimen of undramatic writing, and he would be a captious critic who would wish it away.

[discusses Anderson's style]

William Faulkner has more to tell us about life, but he demands also much more of our attention. It requires not only a strong stomach, but a strong head to read him. He has been so short a time upon the stage that a few words upon his literary career will be justified, and an examination of his most difficult book *The Sound and the Fury* not superfluous.

There is a mathematical formula known as 'Trial by Error.' Faulkner is applying this process to fiction, and if he is fortunate enough to benefit by his mistakes he bids fair to be America's greatest novelist. He is best known by *Sanctuary*, which is not a satisfactory, hardly even a representative, example of his work. If a novelist encounters horror by the way we shall not ask him to step aside, but the calculated manufacture of superfluous horrors is another matter. In other books Faulkner is sufficiently grim, but there the tragic material is not imported but inheres in the theme. My recommendation to a reader who might wish to measure Faulkner with other writers of traditional fiction would be to read his first spirited novel *Soldiers' Pay*, or the more massively constructed *Sartoris* where he consents to use the customary devices for securing local color and achieving character. But more essential to an understanding of the man are the two experimental books *As I Lay Dying* and *The Sound and the Fury*. The last is barred from adequate recognition by its almost insuperable difficulty; the beauty of the first is concealed by the premeditated monotony of the treatment, and jeopardized by the crude horror of its theme. A simple-witted family loads the dead body of the wife and mother on a rickety wagon and for nine days trundles the putrefying corpse to its distant burial. What happens on the journey is presented by the members of this queer cortège in turn.

Some travelers enjoy a voyage throughout, however rough the weather. Some are sea-sick all the way, while others recover from their qualms sufficiently to find tonic restoration in the journey. Let this lame apologue suffice in lieu of an exposition of this strange and original book.

Can a poem, a drama, or a novel be deep without being difficult? A mathematical or philosophical treatise is shallow if too readily understood. Is a work of art to be governed by another law, and must hard thinking here and penetrating vision always issue in complete clarity of expression? If that is true one of the most significant novels of our time is an artistic failure. It is because I feel that *The Sound and the Fury* is on the contrary an artistic triumph, a book not only of profound human value but of deft and intricate architecture, that I contest the general soundness of the theory.

A first reading of this book is a baffling experience, and because the novelist is careless of his explanations the commentator must supply them. . . .

[quotes from and summarizes the novel]

. . . The last book as I have said is author's narrative, and is superb in quality throughout. It is largely Dilsey's book, but all the characters we know drift into it whether actually or by reference. The date is April Eighth, 1928.

Our confidence is established at the outset, and how well the author has availed himself of his narrative privilege is clear even from the opening paragraphs where he is describing Dilsey, the negro cook, emerging from her cabin to take up her duties of the day. Indeed, so masterly throughout is his command of traditional methods that we are permitted to wonder why he so fiercely assailed them in the earlier books of the story. The results are significant enough to reconcile us, and he has achieved an accumulative effect which straightforward narrative could not have secured. Our perspective of vision is enlarged and sharpened, the characters are inwardly and outwardly revealed, and the tragic reach of his conception is presented to us with an impressiveness that no other book of recent years has attained.

41. Granville Hicks, from *The Great Tradition*

(New York, Macmillan, 1933), 265–8

William Faulkner also seeks for symbols of despair. His characters are meaner than Jeffers'; not even suffering can endow them with nobility. But they can be more easily recognized than Jeffers' characters, though one may have met them before only on the pages of textbooks of pathology. His themes are suffering and violence. Death is central in all but one of his seven novels: death and betrayal in *Soldiers' Pay* and *Sartoris*; madness and decay and death in *As I Lay Dying*; suicide, idiocy, and prostitution in *The Sound and the Fury*; madness and murder in *Light in August*. Even the attempt at satire in *Mosquitoes* ends in a description of useless suffering and meaningless disaster. Faulkner's men and women are, with few exceptions, twisted shapes in the chaotic wreckage of a world.

Faulkner himself could not tell why he is so concerned with death and abnormality; certainly we cannot. The decline of the Faulkner family has something to do with it; so has the war; so, perhaps, have many other things. But if Faulkner's mind must remain a mystery to us, we are not wholly ignorant of the forces that have made the world he writes about what it is. He himself gives us hints. He shows us families that have lost money and social position—the Sartorises, the Compsons, and the Hightowers. He shows us families that have no hopes of rising from squalor—the Bundrens, the Groves, the Hineses. He shows us all the meannesses of a Snopes on the make. It is easy for us to recognize such phenomena, for we know how and why the South has been transformed.

But Faulkner is not primarily interested in showing us how people live in the South, and why they live as they do. Passages in *As I Lay Dying* and *Light in August* reveal a fine talent for realistic description of contemporary life. Faulkner has not only watched the people of the South carefully; he is one of them and he knows them from the inside. But he will not write simply and realistically of southern life. He is not primarily interested in representative men and women; certainly he is not interested in the forces that have shaped them. In *As I Lay Dying* he picks a period of unusual tension in the lives of the Bundrens, and he chooses to tell his story in a way that brings out all their eccentricities. *Light in August* soon forsakes the rather amusing and wholly credible story of Lena Grove to portray murder and flight through the abnormal consciousness of Joe Christmas. The ordinary affairs of this life are not enough for Faulkner; even the misery and disease born of generations of poverty and ignorance are not adequate themes for the expression of his horror and disgust. Nothing but crime and insanity will satisfy him. If he tried to see why life is horrible, he might be willing to give a more representative description of life, might be willing to occupy himself with the kind of suffering that he can see on every hand, the kind of crime that is committed every day, and the kind of corruption that gnaws at every human being in this rotten society. As it is, he can only pile violence upon violence in order to convey a mood that he will not or cannot analyze.

There can be little doubt of the intensity of Faulkner's bitterness. Despite the silliness of his talk about writing his guts out, one has to recognize in his work the most vehement effort to express a burning hatred. But what it is he hates he scarcely knows, and because he fears that he is somehow missing the mark, he has to apply every possible device for heightening the effect upon the reader. Faulkner's novels are complex because he recognizes the necessity for this heightening of effect. He tries to hammer out, as if with brute force, fit symbols for his mood. There is nothing in the story of the Compsons that requires Faulkner to use the fleeting memories of the idiotic Benjy; but disgust is made almost palpable by that device. The wild meditations of Darl and the childish hallucinations of Vardaman do very little to help us understand the Bundren family, but they intensify, even more effectively than the introduction of loathsome physical details, the horror that Faulkner wishes to arouse in the reader of *As I Lay Dying*. An enormous ingenuity has gone into the construction of Faulkner's novels, but it has not been devoted, as James's ingenuity was devoted, to discovering 'the way that most presents the subject and presents most of it'; but rather to discovering the way that creates in the reader the most violent loathing.

It is apparent that Faulkner's methods are not altogether illegitimate: if what he chiefly wants to express is his disgust, he must use whatever means are available. But it is also apparent that, if he understood more completely the reasons for his disgust, he would not have to resort to arbitrary devices. And there is the danger of his becoming a mere showman, mechanically manufacturing thrills in the Grand Guignol manner. How real this danger is *Sanctuary* shows. The method of presentation has no inherent relation to the theme: information is withheld from the reader merely to create as violent a climax as possible. There is nothing but cleverness to distinguish the book from any cheap shocker. And what is true of *Sanctuary* as a whole is true of parts of other novels. Faulkner's unwillingness to try to understand the world about him not only robs his novels of true importance but brings them dangerously close to triviality.

It is significant that *Sanctuary* has been much the most popular of Faulkner's books. Though it is the poorest of his later books, it is the one that comes closest to providing the kind of thrill beloved by readers of detective stories. The situation is a little ironic: Faulkner, who obviously wants to force his readers to recognize what he calls 'the logical pattern to evil,' helps them to forget, for a few hours, their s the price he has to pay for his particular kind of blind- a novelist who gave a comprehensive account of life based not only on a disgust with misery and vileness but erstanding of why misery and vileness exist and how they ated, would be in no danger of becoming a Sax Rohmer sticated.

42. Milton Waldman, 'Tendencies of the Modern Novel'

December 1933

Fortnightly Review, cxl, 722–4.

In this section of a multi-part article on trends in fiction Waldman (b. 1895), an English critic and historian, focused on America. He emphasized the new realism of Sinclair Lewis and his contemporaries, their social criticism, and their untraditional prose styles.

The effects of this influence [Proust] were not only marked in writers who had been directly exposed to it—writers so diverse as Mr. Ernest Hemingway and the usually orthodox Mr. Louis Bromfield, who had long lived in Paris—but spread to others who, like Mr. William Faulkner and Mr. James Cozzens (*vide* his recent novel, *A Cure of Flesh*), have, so far as I know, passed nearly the whole of their lives in the United States. What that effect is will be recognized only by those familiar with the Proust substance *cum* Joyce or Stein method—that sensation of looking at characters a great way off, whose voices and gestures seem remote, yet who are brought physically close to us by a powerful glass which serves simultaneously as a screen between their and our reality. This method is not conducive to popularity, particularly where the personages and the scene retailed are otherwise unfamiliar; and I am inclined to think that one of the most important of contemporary American novelists, Mr. Faulkner, has failed of wide appreciation in this country because so much of his work produces that particular sensation.

Mr. Faulkner has published five novels, all of which are laid in the Southern states, a setting much less well known to English readers than the Eastern or Middle Western. The first impression that these books convey (apart from their eccentricities of language, to which I shall revert later) is of an intense violence and a close sectionalism. Drunkenness, the most brutish lusts, lunacy and every conceivable crime of blood make up the action of these novels; and one is never permitted to forget that all this passes in one small and restricted locality in the lower basin of the Mississippi River.

Yet, out of violence that is at first sight incredible in its horror and variety, and with characters as grotesque as those of Dostoevsky, Mr. Faulkner has contrived to fashion novels that are as genuinely works of literature as they are unmistakably American. Somehow one believes that all the bizarre sequence of idiocy, incest, suicide and greed of *The Sound and the Fury* are natural to a decadent white family like the Compsons, nurtured on the hatreds and the ruin of the Civil War. All the nightmare of rape and murder in *Sanctuary* is conceivable in a community whose rulers descended from the carpet-baggers. The same is true of *Light in August*, the latest and, I think, the best of Mr. Faulkner's books, for in it many of the crudities of style and of factitious melodrama are ironed out, leaving a novel which is notable for the clarity and subtlety of its narrative and for the unsentimental brooding pity that lights it from within. And in *Sartoris* he shows that he is capable of other moods, a feeling for heroic family memories (such as the reminiscences of the gallant cavalry General Stuart and of the glamour of pre-Rebellion days), which Miss Cather herself could not have surpassed, and of the ability to draw a woman of wit, nobility and breeding in Miss Jenny, one of those characters whose presence in it justifies any work of fiction.

In sum Mr. Faulkner, with less social consciousness and perhaps less absolute genius than Mr. Lewis, has advanced further toward the pure art of the novel which is to be grown in the soil of America. His sectionalism is a virtue rather than a vice—Dickens and Hardy were none the less English for being so narrowly occupied with their respective small corners of England.

[illegible] exhibits a queer mixture of influences. Much of the [illegible] negro, and that part seems to be excellent, including the [illegible]gro dialect on the speech of whites, both cultured and [illegible] But apart from dialogue he frequently adulterates his own [illegible] style with solecisms derived from negro speech. Over and over he uses 'like' for 'as if' in a way to make one shudder: 'He continued that thick movement, like he could neither stop it nor complete it.' He invents compounds like a German—'frictionsmooth', 'womenvoices'. And every now and again he writes a passage which distinctly echoes Miss Stein.

43. Robert Penn Warren on drama in Faulkner

February 1934

These are the last three pages of 'T. S. Stribling,' *American Review*, February 1934, ii, 483–6. Implicit in it are the assumptions of the New Criticism. Warren (b. 1905) the following year published his first collection of poems and helped found the *Southern Review*. Except a brief review of *These Thirteen* this was his first commentary on Faulkner.

[Warren has argued that Stribling's fiction interests us as propaganda or social polemic but not as art]

The point, I think, may come clear if Stribling's work is compared with that of certain other novelists who have treated the same material; for instance, William Faulkner. Take the 'poor whites' of Faulkner's *As I Lay Dying* as compared with those of *Teeftallow* or *The Store*. As a citizen, in his practical and public rôle, Faulkner may want to see a broadened way of life possible for the back-country people of Mississippi; but he is too much of an artist to commit himself to the easy satire of the reformer or aesthete. And it is doubtful that Faulkner, the citizen, approves of Pop Eye, the gangster, or of Temple Drake; but his distaste as a citizen is not the theme of *Sanctuary*. And when the mother in *The Sound and the Fury* rebukes her child for using a nickname, saying nicknames are common, the effect is not a piece of satire on her pretensions, but something more immediate, human, and profound; it is perhaps a pathos at this clinging to a symbol of gentility and self-respect in the midst of decay, and if the scene is complicated with irony it is an irony that the symbol should, after all, be so futile and stupid.

Light in August employs all the material familiar in Stribling's work, race prejudice, class prejudice, sectional prejudice, and violence, but with a far different effect. Christmas, the white Negro of *Light in August*, unlike Toussaint of *The Store*, is caught in an insoluble problem that can only end in tragedy; it is a problem so fundamental that he cannot evade it, no matter what he does or where he goes. The implication in *The Store* is that if Toussaint could go North, and get an education, and pass as white, and, as Gracie wishes, have a white wife, his problem would be solved. But Christmas does pass as white, even in the South, and does go North, and does have, not one, but many white women; but these things are ultimately irrelevant to the circumstance of his life. Even if he were rich and successful, his character being given, they would remain irrelevant. The death of Christmas has some tragic dignity; the lynching of Toussaint is a mere butchery, or on another view, a competent piece of legerdemain to point a moral if not adorn a tale.

The primary difference, a difference perhaps more of intention than of achievement, between the work of Stribling and that of Faulkner seems to be this: the drama that engrosses Stribling is a drama of external circumstance, a conflict involving, to some degree at least, the spiritual integrity of a character. It is this quality of Faulkner's work that has provoked such a remark as the following from a review by Morris Schappes:[1]

> But despite his [Faulkner's] apparent unconsciousness of the complex background that would permit us to understand fully the merely personal situation he explores—a background that would reveal the multiple social relations among the old landed 'aristocracy', the newer industrialists, the small peasant

[1] 'Faulkner as Poet,' *Poetry*, October 1933, xliii, 49.

farmers, the share cropper, the proletariat of textile and steel mill, the Negro farmer and worker—we still find some meaning in the very surface tension of his world.

It is a question as to which drama, that of Stribling or that of Faulkner, is a 'surface tension.' The answer may be as simple as this: social constructions and social propositions can only be endowed with value in terms of the individual experience. If that is an answer, obvious as it is, then it is the drama of Stribling, not that of Faulkner, which is concerned with surface tension. And it may well be, in the end, that the work of Faulkner, rather than that of Stribling, is of the order that can give social conscience a meaning.

But the difference may be stated as it relates to method. With Stribling, as I have said, a novel is a device for communication, that is, a device for illustration. The author 'intellectualizes' his perceptions so that their vitality is forfeited. The work approaches allegory. But Faulkner, and a considerable group of the younger Southern novelists, are more conservative; they conceive of the novel as *itself* the communication. They are interested in putting, so far as their powers permit, the question about the destiny of certain obscure individuals, their characters, so that the question will remain alive. Perhaps the questions, or some of them, are unanswerable. But that sort of passionate, yet disinterested and patient, contemplation is, presumably, the business of an art, even the art of the novelist. It is a contemplation rooted in the poetic attitude.

But to the critical realist poetry, like religion, would be, I take it, somewhat 'greasy'.

44. Philip Blair Rice, 'The Art of W[illiam] Faulkner,' *Nation*

25 April 1934, 479

Rice (1904–56) taught philosophy at Kenyon College and was on the staff of the *Kenyon Review*. This is the first half of a review of *Doctor Martino and Other Stories*.

Although Mr. Faulkner is on a number of counts the most interesting contemporary American writer of fiction there is good ground for doubting that he is on his way to becoming quite first-rate as a novelist. All his readers agree that he can tell a story and that his use of language is dazzling; the general public buy his novels also because he gives them shivers and satiates their prurience; while the aestheticians are fascinated by his experiments in form. He is perhaps the only American whose achievement in this latter respect is at all comparable with that of Joyce, Mann, or Mrs. Woolf. After their several fashions, these writers have brought the novel closer to poetry, which in turn has aspired to the condition of the even more formal arts of music and painting. It is likely that the novel can no longer be the amorphous and pedestrian affair that it has been too often in the past, but there is also reason to believe that its matter will continue to be no less important than the manner. Mann and Joyce are bulky at least partly because they have something of consequence to say, while Mrs. Woolf's work appears slighter and Faulkner's tangential because their virtues reside almost wholly in the saying.

If Faulkner as a novelist is something of an eccentric, he is nevertheless quite in the main tradition of the short story. One hesitates to mention a novel of his in the same breath with *Tom Jones*, *War and Peace*, *The Brothers Karamazov*, or *The Magic Mountain*, but he seems the legitimate heir of Poe, Maupassant, Bierce, and Gorki. It is not only that the short story is largely a feat of craftsmanship: Faulkner's violent and morbid subject matter is better suited to the briefer type of fiction.

.n the short story a kick is obligatory; a few cocktails in the hour before dinner are in order, though one soon becomes groggy in the attempt to make an evening of them.

Faulkner's principal structural device, likewise, is more adequate to the short story than to the novel. It has been remarked that for all the abundance of action in his writings most of Faulkner's characters are static. The interest lies in the gradual revelation of character and of situation rather than in their development. When, toward the end of *Sanctuary*, the reader at last finds out what happened in the barn and what is the matter with Popeye, he may very easily conclude that it was not worth all the mystification and the pother. This method, however, with the jolt of realization on the last page, is an admirable device of economy in the short story, and it supplies the structure of many of the best tales in the present volume. . . .

45. Laurence Bell, 'Faulkner in Moronia,' *Literary America*

May 1934, 15–18

Though short-lived, *Literary America* was one of the most eclectic journals of the mid-1930s. The March 1935 issue included a satirical portrait of Faulkner by W. J. V. Hofmann.

Bell, who grew up in the South, at this time was a free-lance writer in New York City, and later in the 1930s contributed regularly to *American Mercury*.

Ever since the publication of *The Sound and The Fury* in this country in 1929, its author, William Faulkner, has been an easy target for that company of critical gentlemen which includes unsuccessful novelists, more successful but envious contemporaries, the Agrarians (an esoteric group of Southern pseudo-aristocrats whom Gerald Johnson defines as people who want to sit on the verandah of a plantation house, sipping a mint julep while a nigger mows the lawn), and aging LL.D.'s hanging over from the Humanist regime. I say 'easy target' because Faulkner is probably the one man in the world who doesn't give a damn what the rest of its inhabitants might think, so long as he has a place to sleep, eat and write, with an occasional jug of corn thrown in for recreational hours.

It was *The Sound and the Fury*, if I reminisce ably, which provoked Dr. Henry Seidel Canby, arch-deacon of the Humanists since the departure of Prof. Dr. Stuart P. Sherman, piously to deplore the rise of the Faulknerian 'school of cruelty.' This indictment has been echoed by practically every lady bookreviewer in the hinterland at one time or another. However, the practice of putting Faulkner on the spot, which is now a favourite pastime among dilettante conservationalists, really originated in New Orleans about seven years ago when a certain group of arty poseurs awoke one morning to find themselves cruelly but accurately satirised in the novel called *Mosquitoes*. The gleeful roars of those New Orleanians fortunate enough not to be included in the *dramatis personae* became so irksome to the victims that they began to retaliate by inventing tales about Faulkner's mental and moral delinquencies. Thus, the origin of those now threadbare stories that he lives on gin and tea biscuits; that he was fired from the postmastership at the University of Mississippi for embezzling*; that he habitually goes barefoot; that he is uncommonly rude to visitors, and so on.[1]

The Agrarians, who occasionally break into print in such weighty periodicals as *The Hound & Horn*, *The American Review* and even the allegedly liberal *New Republic*, look upon Faulkner as the Dixie Anti-Christ. Their high priest, Dr. Donald Davidson of Vanderbilt University, the Sorbonne of the Jake Leg Belt, has been known to admit that Faulkner is somewhat of a writer, but whatever forthright praise he has received from these aesthetes is hardly comparable to their panegyrics to John Crowe Ransom and others of their cabal.

It is not strange that other American writers have adopted a sneering attitude toward Faulkner's work, since literary men are notoriously jealous fellows, but it is surprising that Ernest Hemingway, whose following approximates that of Faulkner, should exhibit such pettiness. This exhibition, in the form of a patronising reference to Faulkner in *Death in the Afternoon* as a glorifier of bawdy houses, immediately created a schism in the ranks of the army of aspiring critics and novelists. The Faulknerites usually ignore Hemingway altogether, but the devotees of *the aficionado* become positively enraged at the hearing of Faulkner's name, and emit such frenzied tirades that one would imagine the Mississippian to be a menace to civilisation.

Although I have heard dozens of these Hemingway addicts hold forth vocally, it is not until recently that I have run across any of them in print except for the newspaper reviewers referred to in preceding paragraphs. It remained for *The American Spectator*, that gadfly whose editors imagine it to be a hooded cobra, to print in its columns essays

* Faulkner resigned from the job after complaints had been made that he spent his working hours writing poetry instead of waiting on customers. He once told an interviewer that he got fired for paying too close attention to the contents of people's mail. I have it on authority of George Healy, city editor of the New Orleans *Times-Picayune* and a classmate of Faulkner's at Ole Miss, that after Faulkner had turned his books over to the postal inspector he turned to a friend and remarked: 'I suppose I'll always be more or less dominated by the wealthy classes, but I'm damned if I'll ever again be at the beck and call of any freshman who has two cents to buy a stamp.'

[1] For a copy of the letter charging Faulkner with neglect of his duties as postmaster, see *New Yorker*, 21 November 1970, 50.

by two aspiring critics who fairly froth at the mouth in discussing Faulkner. The *Spectator*'s editors carry on in the somewhat anachronistic fashion of belabouring whatever persons or institutions are held in esteem by less discriminating citizens, the idea being to capitalise on the theory that every knock is a boost. The fact that some thirty thousand people buy the folder every month, the learned hecklers observed editorially at the close of its first year on the stands, is ample reason for them to continue. Horace Gregory was probably right when he wrote of the *Spectator* that its editors are 'leaning backward into an immediate past that always seems more conservative, more out of step with present problems than any other period in history.' This supposition fits four of the editors at any rate. Outside of the drama George Jean Nathan reminds one of a little lost boy with no Mencken to guide him; Ernest Boyd is so fanatically Anglo-Irish as to be contemptuous of all American literary wares. Eugene O'Neill and James Branch Cabell take no apparent hand in the destinies of the *Spectator*, and since the Neo-Catholic life-line has failed to hoist O'Neill out of the slough of his own subconscious and Cabell still pines for the mythical field of Poictesme, it may be assumed that they know and care nothing about either Faulkner or his critics. But with Sherwood Anderson it is another matter. Assuming that Anderson, as one of the editors, sanctioned the printing of these attacks, he has performed an about-face that is amazing when one remembers that it was he who persuaded Faulkner to write his first novel, and that three years ago he wrote a piece for *The American Mercury* in which he stated that Faulkner was one of the two most gifted writers in America. Can it be that the master is envious of his pupil?

It is upon the opening sentences in Chapter VI of *Light in August* that the two essayists, the Messrs. Robert Linn and Stanley K. Wilson, base their positive assertions that William Faulkner can't write for apples. I quote the 'chaotic' passage: *Memory believes before knowing remembers. Believes longer than knowing recollects.*

'Fustian! Wind! Showing-off! Attitudinising!' cries Mr. Wilson in bewildered fury, and Mr. Linn chants in antiphony: 'Yellow journalist! Unforgivable literary snob!' Mr. Wilson's brain must certainly be highly sensitised to be so irritated by these puzzling but innocuous sentences, and if obscuring of meaning constitutes literary snobbery then the editors of the *Spectator* must doubtless realise that at least three of their clique, Cabell, Anderson and O'Neill, are doomed to hell for the same heinous offence.

I would like to mention here that I have asked at least twenty people who read *Light in August* for their interpretation of the passage, and every one of the lot agreed that Faulkner merely used this method to differentiate between the retentive subconscious of Joe Christmas and his earliest actual memory. It is a psychological fact that the subconscious harbours childhood incidents that are transmuted to the tangible reminiscences of the conscious only in occasional fleeting moments.

Mr. Wilson's name is not well enough known to be a household word, and never having seen him in print before the appearance of his tirade against Faulkner, I have not even a hint from which to divine his favourite author (perhaps he hates all writers), but when he prefaces his hymn of hate with babble about 'clarity, economy, force and colour' he is quoting from the handbook of the Hemingway addicts. Indeed, if I may be permitted to fall into the gentleman's own low comedy style of writing I will say that he has to all appearances gone the Hemingway of all flesh. Nobody but a devotee of the First Reader I-see-the-dog-isms of Hemingway would raise such a disturbance over a sentence that stymies his intellectual capacity, even if it brought about canonisation by *The American Spectator*.

Lest it be said that I drag Hemingway into the controversy as a red herring, let me state that I have learned from close observation that only in rare instances do the same people like both writers (Faulkner and Hemingway, if you don't follow). I know innumerable dilettantes who wade through one of Mr. Hemingway's allegedly forceful commentaries on the lives of *cocottes*, eunuchs, fairies, punch-drunk boxers, dipsomaniacs, and other pleasant creatures, and then rush madly about looking for an opportunity surreptitiously to boost their champion of the abattoir, of belittling the talent and style of Mr. Faulkner. I can but agree with the publishers of successful tabloid newspapers that submorons still like their realism served up raw and unadorned with polysyllabic subtleties. Personally, I prefer the artifice of sterility due to fire and pre-natal *spirochoetae* to sterility through the device of shrapnel wounds below the fouling line.

If I have not advanced a sufficiently clear case for Faulkner, let me add that I, as an unbiased Southerner reasonably familiar with the rural classes in Mississippi, his state, can vouch for his integrity in portraying vicious decadents who fit in not at all with the Swords and Roses traditions. His Snopes family, his Sartorises, his Lee Goodwin, and his Januarius Jones are there, in the flesh. There are even prototypes of

Popeye, less volatile perhaps, but none the less he remains a symbol ot the combination bootlegger-pimp type common to every Southern tenderloin.

In parting, I suggest that the gadfly critics read *As I Lay Dying*, *The Sound and The Fury*, and the short stories 'A Rose for Emily,' 'Victory,' 'Lizards in Jamshyd's Courtyard' and 'That Evening Sun Go Down'; read the first novel, *Soldiers' Pay*, which was a best seller in more enlightened England long after it had been shunted to the remainder counters in the United States. There is beautiful writing even in the horrific *Sanctuary* if you are not too biased to look for it. I quote from page 205: *At the top of the hill three paths diverged through a broad grove, beyond which, in green vistas, buildings in red brick and grey stone gleamed, and where a clear soprano bell began to ring.*

Turn over a page and begin at: *Bright, trembling with heat* and read on. Open the book at any page and read through a chapter. Forget the melodramatic interludes and read Faulkner for some other purpose than snooping for dirt. And remember that when the late Arnold Bennett said that William Faulkner wrote like an angel, he wasn't thinking of the harp-twanging Elsie Dinsmore types pictured in the Methodist Sunday School tracts.

ey Starke, 'An American Comedy'

December 1934

'An American Comedy: An Introduction to a Bibliography of William Faulkner,' *Colophon* (1934), part 19. This was not only the first scholarly checklist of Faulkner materials but also the first attempt to relate the short stories to the novels.

Colophon: A Quarterly for Collectors and Lovers of Books, founded in 1928, was printed by Pynson Printers in New York. Each article was supplied by a different press, Starke's by Walpole Printing Office, New Rochelle, New York.

Those who know William Faulkner only as a novelist know him less well than those who know him chiefly from the magazines, and as a writer of short stories. Though it is with his novels that Faulkner has won his fame, and for them that he has been accorded critical consideration—because of them indeed, that many of his stories, previously rejected, have been published—it is in the stories that we discern most clearly Mr. Faulkner's purpose to produce a comedy, following the precedent set by such novelists as Balzac (his favorite author), Cabell, Galsworthy and Van Vechten. The novels are the major chronicles of the world of his comedy, but the short stories form a chain by which the novels are bound. And as story has succeeded story, it has become increasingly evident that Mr. Faulkner's world was one carefully conceived from the beginning and is both varied and conceivably real.

For the collector, then, Faulkner's work holds a three-fold interest. There is the interest in gathering—and not without difficulty—some fifteen principal titles, in various states, at least nine other volumes containing contributions by Faulkner, and numerous uncollected short stories (aside from other magazine and newspaper work),—an impressively long list for an author whose first book appeared only ten years ago. There is the interest in reading the work of a young novelist who, in spite of the horror and brutality of his most famous novel, has made even conservative critics his enthusiastic admirers and his staunch defenders, and who gives more promise of becoming a great humorist than any other American writer since Mark Twain. And there is the problem—which at times proves as exciting as a Van Dine mystery novel—of determining the relation each novel and story has to the comedy, of identifying recurring localities and reappearing characters, of tracing through richly varied work the essential steps in the building of a carefully integrated whole. A bibliography in the case of Faulkner is essential not merely as a collector's check-list but as a reader's guide, and as the best substitute for an analytical chart.

[summarizes the novels and stories through August 1934, also referring to the 'eagerly awaited "Snopes Saga",—chief title on Mr. Faulkner's list of unpublished work']

There are other reappearing characters besides those already named: for instance, Surratt, the sewing machine agent, who tells the story of 'A Bear Hunt,' Hawkshaw, the barber, and Judge Stevens. There are other recalled incidents, such as the incident of the German captive, of 'Ad Astra,' recalled in 'Honor.' And as we have seen a paragraph in *Sanctuary* grow into a story, 'Lizards in Jamshyd's Courtyard,' a sentence from *As I Lay Dying* become a story, 'Spotted Horses,' we may be quite sure that other incidents mentioned only casually in one or another novel or story of the comedy will yet become itself a novel or story; and until the future proves us wrong, we may insist that such stories as 'Fox Hunt,' 'Dr. Martino,' *Idyll in the Desert*, and 'Artist at Home'—even 'Black Music'—belong in the comedy, in spite of no at present apparent connection; that 'Once Aboard the Lugger' and 'Divorce in Naples,' for instance, are connected with the comedy artistically and in intention as well as through common origin in Mr. Faulkner's experience, and by accident. Compsons and Sartorises we may yet find were long ago mating, if not marrying; and we should not be surprised to find characters from *Soldiers' Pay* and *Mosquitoes* meeting citizens of Jefferson and Mottstown. And even if *The Snopes Saga* were not already promised we could safely predict that Mr. Faulkner would continue for some time to come the story of the Snopeses, for the rise of the class to which the Snopeses belong and the decay and disintegration of the class to which Sartorises and Compsons belong is surely the central, symbolic theme of Mr. Faulkner's comedy, as it—more than the traditional color problem—is the central problem of that part of the world in which Mr. Faulkner lives.

There is not space to speak here of the variety in characterization of the people of Mr. Faulkner's novels and stories, and of the wide range of emotions—of tenderness and pity, as well as brutality and horror—of which Mr. Faulkner (in spite of the denial of certain critics) is master. The point to be made here is that Mr. Faulkner has created so great a number of characters and carried some of them at least successfully through several novels and numerous stories, each complete in itself, so that no one story seems merely a sequel to another and the characters reappear not in the forced and requested manner of most sequels but with the naturalness of life.

When we realize how carefully Mr. Faulkner has constructed his comedy, we must absolve him of the charge made against him (and largely as a result of a statement he himself made in the introduction to the Modern Library reprint of *Sanctuary*, and of another statement concerning *Idyll in the Desert*) that he writes merely to make money. His artistic intentions as revealed by an analysis of his comedy, if not by the force and beauty of the work itself, are sincere and serious—and the more creditable in the light of Mr. Faulkner's youth. He is only thirty-seven; the first chronicle of Jefferson appeared when he was thirty-two; and some of the short stories of Jefferson may well have been written at an even earlier age (for it is quite certain that the order of publication does not even approximate order of composition of the short stories. Even of the novels, *Sanctuary* is an earlier work though published later than *As I Lay Dying*.)

[a primary and secondary bibliography follows]

47. W. J. V. Hofmann on Faulkner's notoriety

March 1935

'Contemporary Portraits: IV. William Faulkner,' *Literary America*, March 1935, ii, 193–5. Facing the first page of this satirical sketch is a caricature depicting Faulkner against a background that includes a gallows, an open-jawed skull, a mannequin, a cracked wall, and a table with lamp and book. It is signed 'Fouts.'

In ten years, William Faulkner has emerged from the comparative obscurity of the smaller literary magazines into the floodlight of the five-cent weeklies. He has accumulated the fame, notoriety, money, and Hollywood attention that any beginning writer lusts after, and through it all he has preserved his status of one of the leading American literary white hopes. In his career there are implicit several important lessons for you industrious boys and girls who, at this moment, are selecting just the proper word for that great story you're finishing off.

First—we'll take for granted you were born in the Southland. If, by a topographical error, your parents selected some other region, pause to check back carefully among your ancestors for some Southern stock—and if you fail, lose all hope. There is only one road to take if you can't write glibly about the Southern poor white or the appealing negro—and that road leads to perdition, Stalin, and proletarian literature. For you will have noticed that the *important writing* of to-day is Southern writing. Aside from Mr. Faulkner who is several laps ahead of the field, the Pulitzer Prize just has to be awarded every second year to some inspired unknown from way down yonder.

So you have now achieved a Southern ancestry. The second step is to move far, far away from New York—since, in your innocence, you have probably haunted this metropolis, imbued with a Horatio Alger slant of wild eyed editors clutching your precious manuscript from your hands, pushing a colossal wad of money into your fist (they all pay on acceptance, you know—hah! hah!) and being able immediately to dash into the charmed circle of the urban literati. Give up this feverish hope, my lads and lassies. Take a tip from Massa Faulkner. Never, never pal around with the Broadway wits or the Madison Avenue publishers. Hie yourself to some little town that has to be exhumed from the U.S. Postal Guide when an editor wants you, and sit down there, shooting your manuscripts hither and yon.

If all this very sincere advice seems to run counter to the copybook maxims, remember it can be proven by stern facts. For exhibit A (Mr. Faulkner) came of a very distinguished Southern ancestry. His birthplace was Ripley, Mississippi and his chosen home is Oxford, Mississippi. Now there's something insidious and wily in the choice of Mississippi as a habitat. The state is notorious for its lack of reading matter, averaging thirty-eight printed pages to a county, and one and one-eighth literatures to a township. It has done its best to earn Mr. Mencken's title of the Sahara of the Bozarts. So if you can find yourself a place like that, your literary fortune is practically assured.

That assurance comes from two important sources. First, if you're the only writing man in town, nobody is going to drop in evenings and upset your prose style with discourses on the declining use of adverbs or Stypm's theory of the editor's place is in the wastebasket. No, sir! You can just sit and turn out your quota of words a day, and in the evening go down and watch a lynching—if it's a holiday—or insult the local girls as they pass by the pool-parlor. Such a lack of literary stimulus is vital to the present day successful artist.

The second reason for sojourning in such a bookless desert is the acclamatory reception your work will receive in editorial offices. One Faulkner in Mississippi is worth ten Shakespeares in New York. The literary editor is capsized by the thought that someone can put words together in such a place. The circulation manager insists your story be bought, on the chance he'll get ten or so subscriptions from the state. Of course, once the editors form the habit of buying your material, you're made. So we'll drop this angle right here. (Incidentally, if you're both a denizen of a little crossroads store in Mississippi—and a Syrian or an Armenian, the editors of *Story* will buy your first 110 stories sight unseen.)

Equipped with all these essentials, you are now on your way to fame. You must be for you're patterning on a famous career. This, with one exception, completes your basic requirements. Any other little quirks you may have will undoubtedly help. You must remember that while your start will be slow, your ultimate success is assured.

Mr. Faulkner is gifted, however, with an intuitive knowledge which most lack—the ability to understand and unearth the strange aberrations humanity is prey to. This gift is invaluable for portraiture of the submerged four-fifths of the South. It was undoubtedly part of the allure he had for the first editors who published him. This knowledge you will have to garner from obscure and enormous tomes—a disheartening but needful task. For the discovery of a new perversion is coincidental with being tapped for O'Brien.

So hop a train and disappear for a little while—to emerge in 1937 as the Faulkner of that year. You need have no fear that you will be pushing a literary idol from his pedestal. By that time, Mr. Faulkner will have been submerged by the popular magazines and his unspeaking prose will be twisting and snarling through the back pages next to the advertisements.

The progress of the artist is akin to that of the politician. The French claim to tell an officeholder's politics by his age—at nineteen, a communist; at fifty, a conservative fascist. So too the usual fate of the American writer. At nineteen, striving for form, for expression of true realities; at forty, lulled by his agent's cheques, sliding into the National Academy.

Mr. Faulkner has merely speeded up this process. Retaining his sense of language, his ability of intense story-weaving, he has thrown his gallery of thwarted creations into the laps of the psychiatrists, his knowledge of the life that lives beneath the surface into a convenient niche of forgetfulness. He is plunging ahead to a success, which, if he moves with the speed of former years, will soon place him beside Irvin S. Cobb and Octavus Roy Cohen as an interpreter of the dreams, the frailties, in the wandering, pathetic lives of a Southerner.

PYLON

New York, March 1935
London, March 1935

48. Laurence Stallings, 'Gentleman from Mississippi,' *American Mercury*

April 1935, xxxiv, 499–501

Stallings (1894–1968) was an American playwright and motion-picture scenarist, who knew Faulkner well in Hollywood.

It is possible that one of the three writers struggling for possession of Faulkner's heart may be a genius. That writer is hard to distinguish because so much nonsense has been written about him, as every man of high talent provokes critical nonsense. For example, the short story 'A Rose for Emily' is an immensely comic piece; but its significance can be left to those critics who wish to draw some sociological inference from every piece of fiction—even from the fact that once upon a time in Mississippi an old maid fed rat poison to her faithless lover. One hopes Faulkner lends no ear to the jitney sociologists who patronize him; for this truly comic side of his work is his best side, and the conversation of the bedraggled lily who ran the Memphis house—in *Sanctuary*—is downright genius. Faulkner has a whole gallery of tragi-comic figures from the back-waters of Huey Long's kingdom; but I think he would have peopled this gallery with similar studies had he been born in Swampscott. So much for the number one Faulkner.

There is a second Faulkner; and this second one has a yearning for the halcyon. Witness his recent story of the old pioneer woman who remembered the fine things brought on from the Old North State.

That story had the gift of lending enchantment and grace to past things lovingly remembered. However, the natural animosities athwart our unseen frontiers have hailed his delineation of the more sullen streams of human conduct in Dixie as being the whole South itself. It is true that Faulkner has never done as well with his Gascons as with his Freudian clowns: witness his failure to make a fine novel out of *Sartoris*. Yet in a summary of all his work, it will be discovered that at least a third of Faulkner's writing is teeming with an affectionate regard for the ante-bellum gallantries of Thomas Nelson Page.

It is still another Faulkner who has written the new novel *Pylon*. This is the Faulkner who writes with a rush of prose engendering enormous technical friction which inexorably overheats the oil of narration. There is always a great difficulty—at least for Faulkner—in this method of narration. I can only think, for a simile, of a jockey rating the pace when he is in at top weight and the distance is a mile-and-a-half. When Faulkner goes the full distance and writes a novel, he breaks with a great deal of smartness and the reader is instantly plunged into the shifting field of his rushing characters.

In *Pylon* these characters are typically Faulknerian in their curiously compelling sympathies which transcend a natural impulse of disgust. These are a barn-storming pilot, a parachute-jumper, and a woman shared by the two; there are also a little boy whose parentage was settled by a throw of the dice, a stupid mechanic, and a dipsomaniacal newspaperman. Faulkner is all eyes for the woman. She is the dark horse of the race, the unknown entry.

The barn-storming group is competing with a worthless old crate for a speed trophy at a New Orleans aviation meet (incidentally, Faulkner stubbornly persists in referring to the city as New Valois). Of necessity in the dash of the opening chapters, Faulkner cannot stop for a breather. And inevitably, he must pull up to do so later on; he must place and unmask his characters in their proper positions. Were it not for his superb technical facility as a writer, he would be out of the running at the first sudden check. *Pylon* is written in this manner of sprints and breathers. It is a strange, incalculable story which he has to tell, and he tells it for all he is worth, whipping heavily in the home-stretch to bring the woman in under the wire. I put down the novel with the feeling that the thing has not come off, and yet with the curious satisfaction of a reader who has been incited to pity, to terror, and to laughter throughout.

Pylon has a wonderful feel of the aero about it. The speed-race around the closed course must be a First in the comparatively meager literature of the air, but it is all secondary to 'a woman not tall and not thin, looking almost like a man in the greasy coverall, with the pale strong rough ragged hair actually darker where it was sunburned, a tanned heavy-jawed face in which the eyes look like pieces of china.' It is this woman upon whom Faulkner lavishes his innate love of modernism which is never better exemplified than when he writes of airplanes. He has in other stories, such as 'All the Dead Pilots,' revealed this feeling before. One could almost say that so committed is Faulkner, a war pilot himself, to a zest for the empyrean, that he is only within those characters who, like Faulkner, have learned to spurn the earth. The sheer description of the air-race is superbly brilliant. The birdman's scorn of the earthbound is profoundly voiced, so profoundly that I believe the man will only rise above the limitations of the comic novelist by heeding this voice and giving himself over to it.

Faulkner's pilot and his parachute-jumper, who between them share the bovine woman dumbstruck by her two tramps of the bright blue sky, are themselves a group-hero of the age which the Wright brothers ushered in at Kitty Hawk. For those who love to discern symbolism in modern work attention is drawn to the studious passion of Jiggs the mechanic for his boots. These boots are made for men of a pedestrian psyche, men earthbound and unwinged. Much of *Pylon* is told among the sodden morass which is the mind of Jiggs. The unconscious heroism of two boys throwing their lives away in provincial aviation meets is the quality the novelist is intent upon divining; it is rendered striking by the lack of divination which Jiggs brings to his task of overhauling valves and adjusting superchargers.

The desire of the hen-brained woman to fly, and to love carnally all men who fly, is not as brilliantly wrought. Faulkner is hesitant in revealing in her the things which he has brought to her; had he let go at full rev he would have given his novel wings. She is of a piece with Faulkner's women characters—endowed with a grotesque motivation. She eludes recognition as a palpable character, shifting as Temple Drake changed in *Sanctuary*. Her last despairing curse as her lover breaks his ship in mid-air against the final pylon is hardly human, hardly understood. The little boy whose parentage must remain in question forever is an eaglet, and it suffices that he was sired by an eagle, and was born on a parachute pack. Yet these things are not shown clearly in the continuity of the novel, but are revealed in cut-backs which appear awkwardly and in spell-breaking pauses. Those who follow Faulkner, and like myself maintain an unflagging interest in the work of an artist, can dismiss such disappointing turns, and once more find it pleasant to adventure into the imagination of the curious gentleman from Mississippi,

49. William Troy, review, *Nation*

3 April 1935, 393

Troy (1903–61) was one of the first critics to explore analytically patterns of myth and ritual in literature.

For his central observer or 'reverberator' in this new novel Mr. Faulkner has chosen a character that is like a grotesque caricature of the typical hero of the post-war generation of poets and novelists. From one of the chapter-headings, Lovesong of J. A. Prufrock, it is apparent that Mr. Faulkner himself would have us make some such ironic connection. The unnamed reporter in the story is the bedraggled heir of the pallid Laforguian celibate of the early Eliot, the masochistic intellectuals of Aldous Huxley, and the sterile *aficionados* of Ernest Hemingway. The outward and visible sign of his impotence is his almost ghostly physical fragility: 'a scarecrow in a winter field,' 'a paper sack of empty beer bottles in the street,' 'a dandelion burr moving where there is no wind.' From such comparisons it should also be plain that he is being made to serve as the whipping boy for Mr. Faulkner's whole generation. He is, or has been, the image which that generation has found staring back at itself every morning in the mirror. And the mirror must somehow and in some way be broken.

Although the image is not once and for all shattered in Mr. Faulkner's novel, it is at least temporarily dissolved in the blinding light of a rather new and certainly stirring expression of human indifference to the discomforts of living and the menace of death.

[summarizes story]

Of course it is a familiar romanticism which causes Mr. Faulkner to turn to what is for our time the most spectacular expression of that perennial instinct of flight. These reckless nomads of the air are not essentially different from the graceful toreadors that court death so beautifully in the pages of Hemingway. (And it may be remarked that they are presented with the same remoteness and opaqueness: none of them is quite so real as the sensibility for which they exist with such charm and fascination.) Admiration of their careless intrepidity does not drown the burden: 'Tomorrow and tomorrow and tomorrow; not only not to hope, not even to wait: just to endure.' If the novel manages to be much the best that Faulkner has yet written, therefore, it is not because this writer has at last discovered a permanent balm for his generation. It is not because one can point to any growth in a philosophical sense, any modification or enlargement of his theme. It is rather that in this book he has found an almost ideal subject for the presentation of his theme. By writing about fliers and flying machines he has indeed made his subject indistinguishable from the theme of flight into the life of action, which has been one of the three or four dominating themes in contemporary fiction. And he has given to the treatment of that theme an interest and power which one had believed that it was no longer capable of sustaining.

50. Cyril Connolly, review, *New Statesman and Nation*

13 April 1935, 525

Connolly (1903–74) was a journalist and essayist whose novel, *The Rock Pool*, appeared the same year as *Pylon*. From 1939 to 1950 he edited *Horizon*.

When a writer is sufficiently established nowadays he is no longer appreciated by the quality of his work. He enters the realm of higher criticism. Mirsky (I was a Prince!) discusses his attitude to the social revolution. Wyndham Lewis ties an offensive label round his neck—Fascist, dumb ox, childmind, simpleton—and tries to drown him in a sack. Gertrude Stein accuses him of dark crimes against the spirit and of smelling badly. Only his personal behaviour and the political implication of his books are mentioned, and nobody alludes to the one fact of supreme importance about him: how well he writes. For this reason writers, like music-hall turns, are often mentioned in couples, Hemingway and Faulkner, Firbank and Huxley, Eliot and Pound, Joyce and Stein. If people realised they were saying Paul and Barnabas it would be all right, but they don't. They confuse a certain specious similarity in treatment with a resemblance in degree. In my opinion America possesses one great writer, Hemingway; another who, if he could resolve some mysterious equation inside him, would be great, Scott Fitzgerald; several others of enormous competence and talent, headed by William Faulkner and Dashiel Hammett, and a tail that produces the most entertaining and readable trick stuff—the postman with his double knock, Bessie Cotter in her shift, the trapeze virtuoso, etc.

But Hemingway is a great writer: I can think of no other novelist living who unites to such purity of emotional content such mastery of form.

And this is where Faulkner fails. In his most ambitious moments the chisel skids and slithers, and the emotion, the intensity he puts into his writing, is often suspect. There's gold in that thar cob! Nevertheless he is among the half-dozen American authors from whom a new book is an event. The morbidity of his imagination is beyond suspicion, he excels above all in combining a passionate hatred of the city, every sputum of which is familiar to him, with an appreciation of everything that is relaxed, corrupt, and phosphorescent in the southern countryside. It was this mingling of the vice of the town with the decay of the country, Pop-eye's city's clothes reflected in the tropical bogwater, that gave *Sanctuary* its extraordinary quality.

[summarizes story]

The characters of the flying family are admirably portrayed, their attraction for the reporter is quite understandable, but the reporter himself does not come to life so well. It is a source of major irritation, for instance, that one is never told his name.

The scenes at the aerodrome, however, are highly dramatic. The treatment of the spoken word is masterly, the two or three nights of carnival roll the characters through every combination of love and hate in an inspissated gloom of money, sex, and alcohol: 'Yair, I could hear all the long soft waiting sound of all womanmeat in bed behind the curtain.' This book, incidentally, brings Faulkner into much closer relation with the accepted modern masters. He has borrowed widely from the crowd scenes in *Ulysses*, one chapter is called 'The love song of J. A. Prufrock,' and the style, with its rolling turgidity, forced images, and cumbrous and uncouth eye to the main chance—the scarifying of the reader—is often pure Dreiser. I do not see any virtue in the long sentence unless it expresses a genuine nuance of observation or prolonged subtlety of thought. With Faulkner it is simply degenerating into a bad habit:

> Hagood entered stiffly, like an old man, letting himself down into the low seat, whereupon without sound or warning the golf-bag struck him across the head and shoulder with an apparently calculated and lurking viciousness, emitting a series of dry clicks as though produced by the jaws of a beast domesticated though not tamed, half in fun and half in deadly seriousness, like a pet shark.

There are several hundred other sentences which the writer seems to be gabbling through as if himself convinced that they do not come off, but resolved that anyhow it's too late to change. And he uses 'immobile' a dozen times; for him it is the sinister epithet; and why not, as in the poem, J. A. Prufrock? And why make five adjectives do the work of one? These are questions one cannot help asking as one reads this work of real power and importance, and wonders why it isn't twenty thousand words shorter. For when this modern Juvenal comes off, how good he is, as in this passage, where the conscious echoes of Eliot and his London suburra are blended with the atmosphere of the tropical creole city which Degas painted, and which was so charmingly described by Heredia's daughter.

[quotes passage beginning, 'It would be there—the eternal smell of the coffee, the sugar, the hemp. . . .']

51. Sean O'Faolain, review, *Spectator*

19 April 1935, 668

O'Faolain (b. 1900) has done his best work in the short story, but has also written novels, biography, and history. In 1957 he continued to question Faulkner's achievement, in 'William Faulkner, or More Genius Than Talent,' a chapter in *The Vanishing Hero*.

There was once a man in the West of Ireland who was the butt of his village. Baited and tormented beyond patience, he sprang up one night in a rage and cried out: 'Oh, Heavens! If I were only Almighty God for five minutes! . . .' Mr. Faulkner seems to begin his novels in much the same spirit of misanthropy. It is rather extraordinary that so many modern authors, with the power to recreate the world to their heart's desire, should have wished to do it in a like spirit of misanthropy. Not that there is any lack of joy of life in Faulkner. But it is a masochistic joy. *Pylon*, his new novel, is the story of a bizarre group of aeroplane racers—in the words of the publishers' 'talkie-ese'—'slaves of speed, reckless and indomitable people flying from pylon to pylon behind roaring motors on fragile projectors of cloth and steel.'

[summarizes story]

Mr. Faulkner is obviously very much excited by the lives of these strange circus folk—excited, indeed, beyond coherence, so that he can only present them as if they were not human beings at all; as if he felt that petrol and not blood ran in their veins, and they were the half-doped robots of a brutal half-doped world. Yet if it is not a pleasant world he has created it is exciting, disturbing, Dantesque, with all the compulsion and terror of a great talent driven to frenzy. In fact, so much so, that his language, always inclined to be rhetorical, becomes here at times so elusive that many who will begin his novel with interest will finish it more as a duty than as a pleasure. So, when Laverne enters the editor's office, he thinks of himself as looking at 'a canvas conceived in and executed out of that fine innocence of sleep and open bowels of crowning the rich, foul, unchaste earth with rosy cloud where lurk and sport oblivious and incongruous cherubim.' Or the reporter, in his drink, feels his destination and purpose 'like a stamped and forgotten letter in a coat which he had failed to bring.' His eyes, while he is still drunk, are 'like two dead electric bulbs set in his skull.' And so on. Faulkner is one of the finest American writers of today, but he has not yet learned, and may never learn, that brutality is not strength, nor facetiousness wit, and that, if America holds nothing sacred, art still does.

52. T. S. Matthews, parody of *Pylon*

January 1936

'Eagles Over Mobile, or Three Yairs for Faulkner,' *American Spectator*, January 1936, 9, 12.

Thomas Stanley Matthews (b. 1901) was with *New Republic* in the late 1920s, then was an editor of *Time* from 1929 to 1953. He now lives in England, and has written a biography of T. S. Eliot. In 1934 he reviewed *Dr Martino* unfavorably. *American Spectator* printed several unfavorable articles and reviews on Faulkner during this period.

'Baby wants a new pair of shoes.'

'Shoes?' the clerk said. 'The pair in the window?'

'Yair,' Maggie said. 'How much?' But the clerk did not move. He leaned back on the counter, looking down at the infant figure, the hard, tough, button-nosed, dish-face, wall-eyed, cauliflower-eared and in which the hot green eyes seemed to whirl and sputter like a snake's do approaching for the first time the moulting season; at the dirty swaggering diaper, held precariously in place by one huge rusty horseblanketpin, the short, thick, musclebound body streaked with dirt, oil and sweat.

'Oh yair?' he said, staring.

'Yair.'

'Twenty-two bucks.'

When the baby dug her hands into her jeans the clerk could follow it, filthy fingernails and stubby knuckle, the entire length of the diaper like watching the author in the suspensestory swallow his adamsapple. The hand emerged a fist with a wad of greenbacks which it tossed grumpily up onto the counter. The clerk made no move to touch the money, he stared fixedly at the smouldering child. 'Yair,' he thought. 'It ain't the money. It ain't that. . . . Yair.'

'A tough baby,' he said. 'Yair?'

Maggie's lips curled back from her stumpy teeth. 'You bastard,' she said quietly, 'you gonna gimme them shoes?'

It wasn't until she was actually out on the plane's wing that he could see she was nervous about something. He sat in the back cockpit with the airplane in position, holding the wing up under her weight, gesturing her on out toward the wingtip, almost angrily. As she edged slowly on, she kept dropping off pieces of clothing which the wind snatched away like they were butterfly spawn against the choraldrop of the dawn's biding white wings. He saw her looking at him with that blind and completely irrational expression of protest and wild denial on her face, her mouth open like she was about to vomit.

He cut the engine and listened. She was screaming, 'You bastard, you bastard rotten pilot'—over and over.

'You want to take your pants off?' he said.

'They are off.'

'Oh yair. I forgot.' He could see now, as the wind whipped the hem of her skirt out of the parachute harness about her loins, that she had on no undergarment, pants.

'I see you have on no undergarment, pants.'

'Yair.'

She looked like she was about to start screaming again, so he cut in the motor to drown her noise. 'Jump!' he whispered to himself through tight clenched teeth. 'Why don't you jump? Can't you see the lake?'

They had been up here a long time. He started to figure the months in his head, but he was too dizzy. Was it nine, or ten? This diet of cylinderoil, nothing but cylinderoil, was beginning to get him down. That and the air, the heavy, damp, bayou-and-swamp-suspired air. He remembered that Saturday afternoon months ago, when it had all started. When she came scrambling and sprawling into the cockpit he had tried to fight her off for a while, but she had had the author, the perennially undefeated, the victorious, on her side. Just before he lost consciousness he thought, 'Anyway, a record!'

When he came to, the plane was standing on one wing, and she was holding a can of cylinderoil to his lips. After that she never let him land except to refuel. He had begun to feel like a character in a book. And now at last she had decided she was tired of it, she wanted to get off and walk for a while. He had not noticed her condition because he was so preoccupied with his own, and besides, every time she came near him he shut his eyes.

She was still out there on the wing, and still shouting, like she was mad at something. He saw now that she had taken off all her clothes, and was covered with nothing more than the parachute harness. She was clinging to the inner bay strut and shouting at him. He cut the engine again.

'Why don't you jump?'

'Jump, you bastard? The two of us?'

That was how Maggie was born.

Yair, the reporter thought, clashing the unhermetic screendoor of the comfortstation behind him, it was about time I found my way to this place. Yair. And I suppose there'll be a corncob hanging here instead of the Sears-Roebuck catalog. He looked with naked and urgent concentration at the old countryman, goatbearded, rheumy-eyed, who was splashing away at the only water basin like he was trying to accomplish total immersion. The old farmer looked up, fumbling with the towel.

'Them eagles,' he said disgustedly, wiping his eye. 'Them durn birds.'

The reporter watched him abstractedly in the mirror, fingering gently the left side of his face, leaning to the blunt, wavering mirror the replica of his tentative grimace as he contemplated his diploma-colored flesh.

'Yair,' he said quietly. 'Yair. It's lucky cows don't fly. . . .'

53. Harlan Hatcher, 'Ultimate Extensions'

1935

Creating the Modern American Novel (New York, Farrar & Rinehart, 1935), 234–43. This is a chapter in a survey of modern American fiction.

Hatcher (b. 1898) taught at Ohio State University until 1951, when he became president of the University of Michigan. He has also written novels and histories of the American Midwest.

There is another side to the fiction of the War generation that is concerned with war only by reference or by indirection. It did not use the materials of war, but it carried over into post-War civilian life the tone, the mood, the point of view natural to young men who had gone through the violent reversal from the 'humanitarianism' of the War years to the collapse into disillusion and unrest in the aftermath. It would be diverting to contemplate what our literature would be like now had the poetic impulse released in 1912 been permitted to unfold in an atmosphere of peace. But it was thrown into the hysteria of hate and its hope was blighted. One priceless if fragile portion of human values embalmed in the words *human*, *love*, *friendship*, *mercy*, *charity*, *peace*, and *good will* was crushed and battered from much of our literature by the fury of organized destruction and the callous indifference of men in high place as they scrambled for the profits in the boom. The inevitable result was a literature unparalleled in violence. For every noteworthy tendency in the great fiction whose development we have been following was intensified and extended to its ultimate capacity by the talented young men in the twenties.

There were many of them. Quite necessarily, since they were born in the late nineties, they began to find themselves around 1925. After his unromantic report on life in the War, John Dos Passos, as we have seen, published his *Manhattan Transfer* in 1925, and Ernest Hemingway's first novel appeared in 1926. In the same year William Faulkner came forth with *Soldiers' Pay*. The novel made no great appeal at the time, and it was not until the publication of *Sanctuary* in 1931 after the reputations of Dos Passos and Hemingway were firmly established that the sensational gifts of the new author were generally recognized. He now stands among his generation, individual and aloof, the most distinguished of the many who have applied to civil life the 'torches of violence' characteristic of the War. Every reader of contemporary fiction can call up dozens of examples; therefore we may be permitted to center this brief study around their most brilliant representative.

[surveys Faulkner's novels up through *Pylon*]

These are the Faulknerian materials in the novels upon which his reputation is based, but it is unjust to summarize so baldly. For they are frequently and with a curious contradiction beautiful in their poetic perceptions, and they often handle revolting situations with delicacy without weakening their power to stab the reader with a sense of extreme horror. And it is the effect of horror made acceptable by masterly presentation that William Faulkner leaves with his readers. For beginning with sick and dying men back from the War, he has deepened and advanced the element of meaningless suffering by transferring it to common life and specializing in it to the exclusion of all tenderness and gentle living. This is a world comparable to that of the *Inferno*, burning with evil and abnormality. It is peopled with a collection of monstrous beings beside whom Cowperwood, Hurstwood, and Hugh McVey are apostolic. It comprises perverts, imbeciles gentle or vicious, gangsters, prostitutes, bootleggers, sadistic religiouses, and numerous pathological specimens engaged in horrific self-expression. It also includes judges, lawyers, university students, decayed plantation-owners, poor whites, drugstore clerks, and politicians. But there is little difference between these groups except a traditional social distinction. Their motives and their lusts are not dissimilar. Not since Swift's conclusion to *Gulliver's Travels* (with the possible exception of some of the pages of Aldous Huxley) has humanity in all walks of life been pictured as such contemptible vermin. Nor has anyone probed with greater power into the volcanic fury, the corruption, the depravity in the black hearts of men who are only incidentally dwellers in the South, or written of such matters in more brilliant prose, or with finer control of mood and suggestion and careful spacing of atrocities. One is led to wonder whether this elaborate collection of abnormalities is not more accurately accounted for as a reversal of the humanitarian and poetic mood trampled to earth by the psychology of the War than by the jargon of the psychoanalysts applied to it by Dr. Lawrence S. Kubie. For it is the natural and ultimate extension of the materials and the moods clearly to be discerned in the literature of the contemporary period.

We have seen with some completeness the rise and triumph of realism and how it explored and reported previously neglected segments of American life. Although there was nothing in the realistic theory to preclude the presentation of beautiful living, in actual practice it commonly preferred to picture the evil and the sordidness of modern life. Almost from the beginning, therefore, the realistic movement was associated with repellent materials and motivated by the desire to strip away the hypocritical masks from the faces of men, to reveal the spiritual and moral ugliness which deforms them, and to uncover the miseries which are their lot. Its exponents rightfully insisted that their purpose was not to make anyone miserable, or needlessly to harrow his feelings with terrifying incidents, but to face life as it is, even when it is filthy and without redemption.

This was quite apparently the purpose of William Faulkner in his serious work. But it is impossible to bring any large portion of this complex life into the confines of a book and hold it there in realistic dimensions. The ugly and the vicious can drive out of focus the beauty and the tenderness that are equally true. And unless the artist is wary and incorruptible, in a period such as ours he may become absorbed with the violent and the grotesque moments in the activities of men. And such moments are appallingly frequent in American news.

If we may take at its face value the preface William Faulkner wrote for the Modern Library reprint of *Sanctuary* (and why should we not?) then it would appear that the author, after attempting to state his view of the life of his period in novels that got but a limited notice, deliberately invented a tale that would give readers a more violent stimulation than the realistic stories had provoked. And starting with the worthy purpose of revealing life as it is without rearrangement, and proceeding to the cruelty and brutality of war as really experienced, we arrived at *Sanctuary* with the avowed intent of exaggerating to the limit the evil of life and the grimness of death for the ulterior purpose of creating not truth but a sense of horror in the Mississippians. It is a blot on the integrity of the artist, and it is a comment upon criticism and the reading public in America. For William Faulkner's calculations were correct. His work was acclaimed, he was given a French and an

English as well as an American reputation, and the *Saturday Review of Literature* ostensibly disapproving, has given more columns to *Sanctuary* than to any three books issued since the *Review* was founded.

The Freudian materials were developed in the same way and apparently for the same reasons. It became clear early in the realistic period that the limits to accurate reporting of life as it appears objectively to the eye are narrow and rigid, and omit the seething world in the dark recesses of the soul. We have seen how Sherwood Anderson and his compeers, following and contributing to the fashion set by D. H. Lawrence, James Joyce, August Strindberg, turned literature inward not to discover peace in the will of God, but to ferret out the unsuspected demons lurking behind innocent-appearing masks, and to expose incredible terrors and lusts normally kept under control and away from the eyes of men by severe self-discipline.

The external and often gratuitous horrors—the smell of putrefaction, the buzzards hovering above a too-long-exposed coffin, a broken leg set in raw cement, the absurd pairs of eyes flashing luminous rays through the dark where there is no light to reflect—these Gothic thrills are mild when set over against the emotional twistings and torturings of imbeciles and perverts. If the road is straight from the hesitant music of Sherwood Anderson's style to the brilliant and magic prose of William Faulkner at his best, it is also direct from Winesburg, Ohio, 1919, to Jefferson, Mississippi, 1931. And when you have extended the comparatively mild derangements of Wing Biddlebaum of Winesburg to the criminally perverted Popeye inflicting lacerating cruelties upon his victims in *Sanctuary*, you have lost sight of the original purposes and produced a monstrosity not to be improved upon. And when you project the libidinous perplexities of Curtis Hartman until they become the confused fragments in the mind of an imbecile who has been three years old thirty times as in *The Sound and the Fury*, you are again at end point. For a literature of shock and horror prepares its own defeat, since it must depend upon continuous intensification to maintain its effect, and since there is a point beyond which the jolt of incest, ravishment, and pathology cannot be sustained.

The work that William Faulkner has so far done now appears to be the end of one era rather than the beginning of a new. In an age inured to horror and indifferent through repetition to the cruelty and the crudity of decadent people, he has succeeded in extending their potency for shock. He is not a novelist of ideas but of mood and action, physical and psychic. And he is at his best in the portrayal of men of low mentality undergoing the torture of fear. His work is the flaming focal point of ultimate extension of the characteristics of the literature of his time: the realism of exposure, the sinister distortions of Freudianism, the pain and the preoccupation with violent death revealed in the War literature. And he defines the farthest limits to which the innovations and revolts that were at one time necessary to the continued well-being of our literature can be carried without final self-defeat.

ABSALOM, ABSALOM!

New York, October 1936
London, February 1937

54. George Marion O'Donnell, review, Nashville *Banner*

25 October 1936, magazine, 8

In 1935 O'Donnell reviewed *Pylon* quite unfavorably, suggested Faulkner should return to his Yoknapatawpha materials, and argued that he had been declining ever since *Sanctuary*.

[O'Donnell opens with a summary of Sutpen's story]

Returning for his setting to the Mississippi country of *Sartoris* and *As I Lay Dying* and *The Sound and the Fury*, Mr. Faulkner has built his new novel, *Absalom, Absalom!*, around this man, who stands out as a new sort of figure in Southern fiction, in all his demoniac fierceness and strength. And with him in the book live also the people who lived around him and wondered at him during his lifetime. For in this novel, Mr. Faulkner has presented at once one man's life, the way in which he existed, a whole section of the country, and a whole passing of time.

But the story and the characters are not revealed in any conventional fashion. Mr. Faulkner is still experimenting with form; and this is presumably a healthy sign, indicating that he is not yet finished as a novelist and is not likely to be finished for some time, despite the major artistic defects of his two previous books, *Light in August* (the formal structure of which does not stand the test of rereading) and *Pylon* (which is probably the worst of Mr. Faulkner's novels). For this new book, Mr. Faulkner has adopted a strange device: the story is revealed only as it takes form in the understanding of Quentin Compson. . . .

[summarizes Quentin's role, that of 'a Special Listener', and suggests Faulkner's difficult style may obscure the story to the point of being a fault]

Moreover, when Quentin's roommate tells Quentin all over again the parts of a story which Quentin himself must have told to the roommate, then the process seems a little ridiculous. It cannot fail to call to mind the device by which inexperienced dramatists make their exposition of antecedent action, those tense moments in which a husband reminds his wife that they have been married for five years and now have two children.

However, these are not major faults. Though the method of construction in this book is a dangerous one, it appears to succeed. The book seems narrowly to evade formlessness; yet it does manage the evasion, because of Mr. Faulkner's device of using Quentin as his Special Listener, even if it does not achieve perfect formal coherence.

One might question at times the realism of the narrators' speech, because they speak often in a kind of prose-poetry familiar to readers of *The Sound and the Fury*. But this is defensible in *Absalom, Absalom!* on the ground that Mr. Faulkner is dealing with characters who speak and think in the elaborate, Latinesque, sometimes oratorical style characteristic of the antebellum South. And it is defensible on the different ground that Mr. Faulkner is not writing just what can be said in narrative speech; he is writing all that cannot be said (trying thereby to project the very experience itself) along with what can be narrated. And experiences actually are projected in *Absalom, Absalom!* by means of this style. Here, too, Mr. Faulkner is daring; here, once more, he is flirting with failure. A novel can not be so complex and artistic a presentation of experience as a poem, since a novel necessarily excludes more of the minutiae of an experience, giving only the essentials where a poem may give much more of rich detail. And the ignoring of this limitation is a dangerous thing. Mr. Faulkner, however, is a conscientious and profound artist. And it is more likely that he deliberately accepts the danger than that he accidentally stumbles into it. That he does accept the danger, and still manages to defy it successfully, is one more evidence of Mr. Faulkner's artistry. For by this acceptance Mr. Faulkner manages to recreate the story of Sutpen whole, as it would be revealed in life, yet richer than life itself because of the strong, controlled power of his art.

With all of its minor stylistic and formal defects, *Absalom, Absalom!* is fiction of a high order of excellence, strong from its roots in the life of a people and in a land and in a time, rich from the experience of that people, and beautiful from its sincere telling by one of that very race who has mastered his art as have very few of his contemporaries.

55. William Troy, 'The Poetry of Doom,' *Nation*

31 October 1936, 524–5

Much confusion will be saved if one applies to Mr. Faulkner's new book not the usual standards of the realistic novel but whatever standards we are accustomed to apply to lyric poetry of the most subjective sort. All writing is personal, to be sure, and in the last analysis so-called objective fiction represents just as temperamental a view of the facts as the frankest lyric. But in fiction usually there is some line of demarcation between the facts and the writer's vision of them, some pretense of establishing a norm or mean in their presentation. Leaving aside obvious examples of the realistic or documentary, we need only turn to such a work as *Wuthering Heights*, which Mr. Faulkner's book helps us recall, to recognize how safely we are removed from the tempestuous center of feeling by the device of a narrator who is a model of sober and balanced vision. Even in James, through his 'frames' and his politely colloquial style, and in Proust, through his sustained abstract logic, we are permitted within the work itself something like a normal or social angle on the facts. Nothing so distracting is allowed us by Mr. Faulkner. From first to last we are plunged into the same world, and everything that we see and feel and think is saturated with the special atmosphere of this world. Through neither the form nor the style do we escape from the closed universe of his intensely personal vision. Despite the elaborate orchestration—the story is told through at least a half-dozen voices—the voice that we hear throughout is always the same. Whether it is Miss Rosa Coldfield, frustrated Southern belle of 1866, or Shrevlin McCannon, matter-of-fact Harvard undergraduate of 1910, rhythm and vocabulary are identical; all the characters have fallen under the influence of Mr. Faulkner's later prose style. As for the method of multiple point of view borrowed from James and Conrad, it has not here any real justification. It does not give us those contrasts of perception for which it was invented nor is it actually required for the order. At best it adds a little factitious intensity to a work already sufficiently fraught with intensity of the most genuine sort. The aggravating ventriloquism of method does not disguise the fact that everything in it is the product of the same unrelieved and unrelieving vision of existence.

Through the uniformity of his image-laden and mournfully cadenced style Mr. Faulkner gives most reason for being considered as a poet rather than as a novelist; but there is also the peculiar operation of his imagination. Given a view of living as 'one constant and perpetual instant when the arrasveil before what-is-to-be hangs docile and even glad to the lightest naked thrust,' he is more concerned with the potentials than with the actualities of experience. Life being a very bad dream in which anything might happen, his imagination posits isolated people, actions, gestures, even speeches, broods upon them until they take the full shape of his vision, and then attempts to relate them in some sort of pattern. The reader will be struck by the recurrence of phrases like 'Just imagine,' 'Conceive only,' 'Listen,' all springing from the passion to make us realize, in the most literal sense, the unique person or event. Young Tom Sutpen turned away from the front door by a Negro butler, Henry throwing the dead body of his sister's fiancé at her feet, old Tom Sutpen killed by a rusty scythe—each of these scenes is something separate, complete, and detachable. Each is a symbol of the same uniform vision. The work is put together not out of a logical sequence of such symbols, for the imagination does not recognize the pattern of logic, but according to order of ascending horror. Even to speak of pattern or order is perhaps inaccurate. It is rather the scale or gamut of all possible human misery and depravity.

Mr. Faulkner's imagination, that is to say, does not operate by filling in some design that has been constructed by the rational mind. It will be disappointing, for example, to try to discover in the career of Thomas

Sutpen—who migrated from West Virginia by way of the West Indies to Mississippi, where he acquired a hundred miles of land and built an enormous mansion, only to be defeated in his effort to found a family by the intervention of the Civil War and bad luck with his sons—a demonstration of the social and economic contradictions of the Old South. Nor is it possible to stop at the explanation that his domestic troubles are all traceable to a social attitude that regards miscegenation as a more heinous crime than incest. Undoubtedly these circumstances of history and geography affect the *form* of the Sutpen saga, but its meaning will be found in a much deeper and broader interpretation of life as a whole. According to this interpretation, everything that has happened could have happened anywhere else in the world. The little drop of Negro blood that runs through Sutpen's destiny becomes no more than the symbolical materialization of that irrational element which exists to thwart the most carefully planned designs of the human will. The ultimate cause of everything is that 'sickness somewhere at the prime foundation of this factual scheme,' that sickness inherent perhaps in the imagination itself which always sets before it more than it can ever accomplish and enjoy.

It is because of the depth and the scale and the cumulative grandeur with which Mr. Faulkner presents this intuition that his book seems not only the best that he has yet given us but one of the most formidable of our generation. His vision of existence, which is a product of temperament, will be ultimately accepted or rejected according to the temperament of the reader. But to reject the vision is not necessarily to reject the book. T. S. Eliot refers somewhere to the mark of the great poet as the ability to understand and communicate 'the essential strength and weakness of the human soul.' For most readers Mr. Faulkner will fail of this mark through giving us too much of the weakness and not nearly enough of the strength. Unquestionably, his book will suffer from the limitations of his vision. But there is also no question that it owes most of its astonishing qualities to these same limitations. It possesses the awful impressiveness that comes from exhausting any attitude or vision, however wrong and one-sided, of its last measure of intensity.

56. Bernard De Voto, 'Witchcraft in Mississippi'

31 October 1936

Saturday Review of Literature, 3–4, 14.

A cultural and social historian best known for his work on Mark Twain and on the American West, De Voto (1897–1955) was a proponent of American Realism.

Numerous reviewers in 1936 said that Faulkner resorted to narrative tricks and pathological sensationalism to obscure his incomprehension of the psychological and historical complexities of his topic.

It is now possible to say confidently that the greatest suffering of which American fiction has any record occurred in the summer of 1909 and was inflicted on Quentin Compson. You will remember, if you succeeded in distinguishing Quentin from his niece in *The Sound and the Fury*, that late in that summer he made harrowing discoveries about his sister Candace. Not only was she pregnant outside the law but also, what seared Quentin's purity much worse, she had lost her virginity. In the agony of his betrayed reverence for her, he undertook to kill both himself and her but ended by merely telling their father that he had committed incest with her. This blend of wish-fulfilment and Southern chivalry did not impress Mr. Jason Richmond Compson, who advised his son to take a vacation, adding, in one of the best lines Mr. Faulkner ever wrote, 'watching pennies has healed more scars than Jesus.' Quentin went on to Harvard, where, however, the yeasts of guilt, expiation, and revenge that are Mr. Faulkner's usual themes so worked in him that he eventually killed himself, somewhere in the vicinity of the Brighton abattoir. But at the end of *The Sound and the Fury* not all the returns were in. It now appears that only a little while after he was pressing a knife to Candace's throat—I make it about a month—Quentin had to watch the last act of doom's pitiless engulfing of the Sutpens, another family handicapped by a curse.

Mr. Faulkner's new fantasia is familiar to us in everything but style. Although the story is told in approximations which display a magnificent technical dexterity—more expert than Mr. Dos Passos, and therefore the most expert in contemporary American fiction—and although the various segments are shredded and displaced, it is not a difficult story to follow. It is not, for instance, so darkly refracted through distorting lenses as *The Sound and the Fury*. Though plenty of devices are employed to postpone the ultimate clarification, none are introduced for the sole purpose of misleading the reader, and in an access of helpfulness, Mr. Faulkner has included not only an appendix of short biographies which make clear all the relationships, but also a chronological chart which summarizes the story. If you study both of them before beginning the book, you will have no trouble.

[summarizes story]

Mr. Faulkner, in fact, has done much of this before. This off-stage hammering on a coffin—Charles Bon's coffin this time—was used to make us liquefy with pity in *As I Lay Dying* where it was Addie Bundren's coffin. And when Addie's coffin, with the corpse inside, slid off the wagon into the flooded river, the effect then gained discounted the scene in *Absalom, Absalom!* where the mules bolt and throw Thomas Sutpen's corpse and coffin into the ditch. Much of Henry Sutpen's ambiguous feeling for his sister Judith was sketched in Quentin Compson's attitude toward Candace. When Charles Bon forces Henry Sutpen to shoot him, moved by some inscrutable inertia of pride and contempt and abnegation (or moved by unmotive)—he is repeating whatever immolation was in Popeye's mind when he refused to defend himself against the murder charge of which he was innocent, near the end of *Sanctuary*. These are incidental repetitions, but many fundamental parts of *Absalom, Absalom!* seem to come straight out of *Light in August*. It is not only that Etienne Bon undergoes in childhood cruelties as unceasing as those that made Joe Christmas the most persecuted child since Dickens, not only that he is moved by the same necessity to wreak both revenge and forgiveness on both black and white that moved Joe, not only that he commits some of the same defiances in the same terms, and not only that the same gigantic injustices are bludgeoned on the same immeasurable stubbornness and stupidity in the same inexplicable succession. It is deeper than that and comes down to an identity of theme. That theme is hardly reducible to words, and certainly has not been reduced to words by Mr. Faulkner. It is beyond the boundary of explanation: some undimensional identity of fear and lust in which a man is both black and white, yet neither, loathing both, rushing to embrace both with some super-Tolstoian ecstasy of abasement, fulfillment, and expiation.

The drama of *Absalom, Absalom!* is clearly diabolism, a 'miasmal distillant' of horror, with clouds of sulphur smoke billowing from the pit and flashes of hellish lightning flickering across the steady phosphorus-glow of the graveyard and the medium's cabinet. And it is embodied in the familiar hypochondria of Mr. Faulkner's prose, a supersaturated solution of pity and despair. In book after book now he has dropped tears like the famed Arabian tree, in a rapture of sensibility amounting to continuous orgasm. The medium in which his novels exist is lachrymal, and in *Absalom, Absalom!* that disconsolate fog reaches its greatest concentration to date. And its most tortured prose. Mr. Faulkner has always had many styles at his command, has been able to write expertly in many manners, but he has always been best at the phrase, and it is as a phrase-maker only that he writes well here. Many times he says the incidental thing perfectly, as 'that quiet aptitude of a child for accepting the inexplicable.' But, beyond the phrase, he now—deliberately—mires himself in such a quicksand of invertebrate sentences as has not been seen since *Euphues*. There have been contentions between Mr. Faulkner and Mr. Hemingway before this; it may be that he is matching himself against the Gertrude-Steinish explosions of syntax that spattered *Green Hills of Africa* with bad prose. If so, he comes home under wraps: the longest Hemingway sentence ran only forty-three lines, whereas the longest Faulkner sentences run eighty lines and there are more than anyone will bother to count which exceed the thirty-three line measure of his page. They have the steady purpose of expressing the inexpressible that accounts for so much of Mr. Faulkner, but they show a style in process of disintegration. When a narrative sentence has to have as many as three parentheses identifying the reference of pronouns, it signifies mere bad writing and can be justified by no psychological or esthetic principle whatever.

It is time, however, to inquire just what Mr. Faulkner means by this novel, and by the whole physiography of the countryside which he locates on the map of Mississippi in the vicinity of a town called Jefferson. This community is said to be in the geographical and historical South, and the Sutpens, together with the Compsons and the

Benbows and the Poor Whites and the Negroes, are presented to us as human beings. Yet even the brief summary I have made above shows that if we are forced to judge them as human beings we can accept them only as farce. Just why did not Thomas Sutpen, recognizing Charles Bon as his mulatto son, order him off the plantation, or bribe or kill him, or tell Judith either half of the truth, or tell Henry all of it? In a single sentence toward the end of the book, Mr. Faulkner gives us an explanation, but it is as inadequate to explain the tornadoes that depend on it as if he had tried to explain the Civil War by the annual rainfall at New Granada. Not even that effort at explanation is made for most of the behavior in the book. Eulalia Bon's monotone of revenge is quite inconceivable, and her demonic lawyer is just one more of those figures of pure bale that began with Januarius Jones in *Soldiers' Pay* and have drifted through all the novels since exhaling evil and imitating the facial mannerisms of the basilisk. Miss Rosa (another Emily, without rose) is comprehensible neither as a woman nor as a maniac. Why do the children suffer so? Why did Rosa's father treat her that way? Why did Sutpen treat Henry and Judith that way? Why did Judith and Clytie treat Etienne that way? Just what revenge or expiation was Etienne wreaking on whites and Negroes in that Joe Christmas series of attempts at self-immolation? Just what momentary and sacrificial nobility moved Wash Jones to kill three people? Just what emotion, compulsion, obsession, or immediate clairvoyant pattern of impotence plus regeneration plus pure evil may be invoked to explain the behavior of Charles Bon, for which neither experience nor the psychology of the unconscious nor any logic of the heart or mind can supply an explanation?

Well, it might answer everything to say that they are all crazy. As mere symptomatology, their behavior does vividly suggest schizophrenia, paranoia, and dementia precox. But that is too easy a verdict, it would have to be extended to all the population of Jefferson, the countryside, New Granada, and New Orleans, and besides the whole force of Mr. Faulkner's titanic effort is expended in assuring us that this is not insanity.

A scholarly examination might get us a little farther. This fiction of families destroyed by a mysterious curse (beginning with the Sartorises, there has been one in every novel except *As I Lay Dying* and *Pylon*), of ruined castles in romantic landscapes, of Giaours and dark 'unwill,' may be only a continuation of the literature of excessive heartbreak. The Poe of 'Ligeia' and kindred tales, Charles Brockden Brown, Horace

Walpole, and Mrs. Radcliffe suggest a clue to a state of mind, which after accepting the theorem that sensation is desirable for itself alone, has moved on to the further theorem that the more violent sensation is the more admirable, noble, and appropriate to fiction. Surely this reek of hell and the passages to and fro of demons has intimate linkages with Eblis; surely Vathek saw this ceaseless agony, this intercellular doom, and this Caliph's heart transparent as crystal and enveloped in flames that can never be quenched. Surely; and yet that tells us very little.

Much more central is the thesis advanced in these columns a couple of years ago, that Mr. Faulkner is exploring the primitive violence of the unconscious mind. Nothing else can explain the continuity of rape, mutilation, castration, incest, patricide, lynching, and necrophilia in his novels, the blind drive of terror, the obsessional preoccupation with corpses and decay and generation and especially with the threat to generation. It is for the most part a deliberate exploration, Mr. Faulkner is at pains to give us Freudian clues, and he has mapped in detail the unconscious mind's domain of horrors, populated by anthropophagi, hermaphrodites, Hyppogypi, acephalites, and cynocephalites. It is the world of subliminal guilt and revenge, the land of prodigy which D. H. Lawrence thought was peopled exclusively by beautiful, testicular athletes, but which is inhabited instead by such races as Mandeville and Carpini saw. These are the dog-faced men, the men whose heads do grow beneath their shoulders, who feed on corpses, who hiss and bark instead of talking, whose custom it is to tear their own bowels. A far country, deep under the mind's frozen ocean. In Mr. Faulkner's words, a 'shadowy miasmic region,' 'amoral evil's undeviating absolute,' 'quicksand of nightmare,' 'the seething and anonymous miasmal mass which in all the years of time has taught itself no boon of death.'

Haunted by the fear of impotence and mutilation and dismemberment, hell-ridden by compulsions to destroy the mind's own self and to perpetrate a primal, revengeful murder on the old, cataleptic in the helplessness of the young, bringing the world to an end in a final fantasy of ritual murder and the burning house—the inhabitants of the prodigyland of the unconscious are also fascinated by those other primal lusts and dreads, incest and miscegenation. In Joe Christmas and Etienne Bon, neither white nor black, repudiating both races, inexplicably ecstatic with love of both, mysteriously wreaking revenge and expiation on both, we face a central preoccupation of Mr. Faulkner, a central theme of his fiction, and, I think, an obligation to go beyond the psycho-analytical study of his purposes. In spite of his enormous labor to elucidate these two mulattoes and their feelings and their symbolism in society, they are never elucidated. What is it that bubbles through those minds, what is it that drives them, what are they feeling, what are they trying to do, what do they mean? You cannot tell, for you do not know. A fair conclusion is that you do not know because Mr. Faulkner does not know. I suggest that on that fact hinges the explanation of his fiction.

It is a fact in religion. For the energy derived from primitive sources in the mind projects a structure of thought intended to be explanatory of the world, and this is religious, though religious in the familiar reversal that constitutes demonology and witchcraft. William James has told us how it comes about. The simple truth is that Mr. Faulkner is a mystic. He is trying to communicate to us an immediate experience of the ineffable. He cannot tell us because he does not know—because what he perceives cannot be known, cannot therefore be told, can never be put into words but can only be suggested in symbols, whose content and import must forever be in great part missed and in greater part misunderstood. This is a mysticism, furthermore, of what James called the lower path. There are, James said, two mystical paths, the one proceeding out of some beatitude of spiritual health which we may faintly glimpse in the visions of the saints. It is from the lower path, the decay of the vision, that witchcraft always proceeds. And witchcraft, like all magic, is a spurious substitute for fundamental knowledge.

The crux of the process by which witchcraft came to substitute for the ordinary concerns of fiction in Mr. Faulkner's work may be observed in *Sartoris*. His first book, *Soldiers' Pay*, introduced the overwhelming despair finding expression in lachrymation and the creatures of unadulterated evil that have appeared in all his later books—curiously combined with the glibness and tight technique of magazine fiction. His second book, *Mosquitoes*, was his *Crome Yellow* effort, and had in common with his other work only a pair of lovers moving on some manic errand through a nightmare world. With *Sartoris* (which was published, if not written, before *The Sound and the Fury*), he became a serious novelist in the best sense of that adjective. He undertook to deal fairly with experience, to articulate his characters with a social organism, and to interpret the web of life in terms of human personality. Wherever he was factual and objective—in Loosh, Miss Jenny (who is his best creation to date), the unmystical Negroes, the crackers, the old men, Dr. Alford—he imposed a comformable and convincing world of his own on a recognizable American experience, in symbols communicative to us all. But he failed in the principal effort of the novel. What he tried to do, with the Sartorises themselves, was to deliver up to us the heart of a mystery—to explain the damnation, the curse, of a brilliant, decayed, and vainglorious family doomed to failure and death. And he did not do it. They were a void. We did not know them and he could not tell us about them. They were without necessity, without causation. When he faced the simple but primary necessity of the novelist, to inform us about his characters, he backed away.

He has been backing away ever since. All the prestidigitation of his later technique rests on a tacit promise that this tortuous narrative method, this obsession with pathology, this parade of Grand Guignol tricks and sensations, will, if persevered with, bring us in the end to a deeper and a fuller truth about his people than we could get otherwise. And it never does. Those people remain wraiths blown at random through fog by winds of myth. The revelation remains just a series of horror stories that are essentially false—false because they happen to grotesques who have no psychology, no necessary motivation as what they have become out of what they were. They are also the targets of a fiercely rhetorical bombast diffused through the brilliant technique that promises us everything and gives us nothing, leaving them just wraiths. Meanwhile the talent for serious fiction shown in *Sartoris* and the rich comic intelligence grudgingly displayed from time to time, especially in *Sanctuary*, have been allowed to atrophy from disuse and have been covered by a tide of sensibility.

57. Malcolm Cowley, 'Poe in Mississippi,' *New Republic*

4 November 1936, 22

This was the second review of Faulkner by Cowley (b. 1898), ten years before *The Portable Faulkner* appeared with Cowley's now famous preface. One of the American expatriates in the 1920s, he published in 1934 *Exile's Return*, a study of that group. *After the Genteel Tradition* (1937) reviews the American literary renaissance after 1910. Neither says much about Faulkner; but after 1935 he regularly covered Faulkner's work as his respect for it increased.

Among all the empty and witless tags attached to living American authors, perhaps the most misleading is that of Southern Realist as applied to William Faulkner. He writes about one section of the South—that much is true—and he writes in what often seems to be a mood of utter distaste. But critics have no excuse for confusing realism with revulsion, or rather with the mixture of violent love and hatred that Faulkner bears toward his native state. No, there is only one possible justification for classing him with the novelists who try to copy the South without distortion. It lies in the fact that he can and does write realistically when his daemon consents. He can and does give us the exact tone of Mississippi voices, the feel of a Mississippi landscape, the look of an old plantation house rotting among sedge-grown fields. On occasion he even gives us Mississippi humor (like the scene between Uncle Bud and the three madams, in *Sanctuary*) that is as broad and native as anything preserved from the days of the steamboat gamblers. But Faulkner's daemon does not often permit him to be broadly humorous or to echo the mild confusions of daily life. The daemon forces him to be always intense, to write in a wild lyrical style, to omit almost every detail that does not contribute to a single effect of somber violence and horror.

And this gives us a clue to Faulkner's real kinship. He belongs with the other writers who try to produce this single and somber effect—that is, with the 'satanic' poets from Byron to Baudelaire, and with the 'black' or 'terrifying' novelists from Monk Lewis and the Hoffman of the 'Tales' to Edgar Allan Poe. The daemon that haunts him is the ghost of the haunted castle—though it is also Poe's raven and Manfred's evil spirit. And the daemon is especially prominent in his new novel. Not only is *Absalom, Absalom!* in many ways the strongest, the most unified and characteristic of his twelve books, but it is also the most romantic, in the strict historical sense of the word.

Thomas Sutpen, in 1833, comes riding into a little Mississippi town with twenty coal-black Negroes straight from the jungle. He despises his new neighbors, who in turn regard him as Satan in the flesh. He is the lonely Byronic hero with his mind coldly fixed on the achievement of one design. And the plantation house built with the help of his naked slaves—the great mansion literally hewn from the swamps—is the haunted castle that was described so often in early nineteenth-century romances. Like other haunted castles, Sutpen's Hundred is brooded over by a curse. Years ago in the West Indies, Thomas Sutpen had deserted his wife and his infant son after discovering that they had Negro blood. He now marries again; he has two children and a hundred square miles of virgin land; but in the midst of his triumph the curse begins to operate: the deserted son reappears and tries to marry his own half-sister. Here the note of incest suggests Byron, but elsewhere it is Poe whose spirit seems closest to the story—especially at the end, where Sutpen's Hundred collapses like the House of Usher. And indeed one might say that Faulkner is Poe in Mississippi—Poe modernized with technical and psychological devices imported from Joyce's Dublin and Freud's Vienna.

But this is a great deal different from saying with Granville Hicks that Faulkner is 'in danger of becoming a Sax Rohmer for the sophisticated.' It is different from saying that 'he is not primarily interested in representative men and women; certainly he is not interested in the forces that have shaped them.' Hicks's judgment seems to be based on the false theory that romantic authors are always trying to evade the life of their own times. The truth is that they know and can write about nothing else. The men and women they represent in romantic disguises are their own selves, with their friends, mistresses and enemies. The issues they deal with are derived from their own lives and are frequently social as well as personal or pathological. And the general result is that romantic novels are likely to be written on two planes, with one subject below, in the foreground, and above it another subject that is half-revealed by conscious or unconscious symbolism.

In Faulkner's new book, the second or hidden subject is the decline of the South after the Civil War. Sutpen's Hundred, the mansion that rotted and finally burned, is obviously a symbol of Southern culture. Thomas Sutpen himself seems to represent the Southern ruling caste, though here the symbolism is confused by the fact that he also represents the proud Byronic hero hated by his fellow men. But it is clear enough that Sutpen's curse is a result of his relations with Negroes, and that he is finally murdered by a poor white. Forty years later, when his mansion collapses in flames, the only survivor among his descendants is Jim Bond, a half-witted mulatto. And one of the other characters tells us, on the last page, 'I think that in time the Jim Bonds are going to conquer the western hemisphere. . . . In a few thousand years I who regard you will also have sprung from the loins of African kings.'

But Faulkner is not presenting this picture as the reasoned conclusion of an essay on the South. He is not arguing that Southern society was ruined by its own injustice toward the Negroes, nor again that a mixed race will survive after the heirs have vanished from the great plantations. He is not arguing anything whatever. He is giving us perceptions rather than ideas, and their value is not statistical but emotional. To the critic their importance lies in the fact that they explain a great deal not only about *Absalom, Absalom!* but also about Faulkner's earlier novels. His violence here and elsewhere is not a means of arousing pointless horror: it is an expression of a whole society which the author sincerely loves and hates and which he perceives to be in a state of catastrophic decay.

But Faulkner's new book falls considerably short of the powerful mood that it might have achieved. Possibly this is because he has failed to find a satisfactory relationship between the horror story in the foreground and the vaster theme that it conceals: the two subjects interfere with each other. But the partial failure of *Absalom, Absalom!* is chiefly explained by the style in which his daemon forced him to write it—a strained, involved, ecstatic style in which colloquialisms and deliberate grammatical errors are mingled with words too pretentious even for Henry James. Too often it seems that Faulkner, in the process of evoking an emotion in himself, has ignored the equally important task of evoking it in the reader.

58. Philip Rahv, review, *New Masses*

24 November 1936, 20–1

Rahv (1908–73) put much of his energy in the 1930s into political writings. He was also a founder of *Partisan Review*. In the 1940s he was a leader in the Henry James revival.

The difference between William Faulkner and most American novelists suggests the difference between a character and a type. Whether he attracts or repels us, his individuality and its vision, his world and its tonality are complete enough, and his identity firm enough, to evoke response. All the more unfortunate it is that, though his gifts and importance are unquestionable, he seems quite unable to realize himself in a truly significant work.

To my mind, Faulkner's new book demonstrates once again the gap between his talent and its realization. He is influencing our awareness of the range and variety of the modern novel without, however, affecting its direction or power in the shaping of ideas and attitudes. What he feels and knows he renders in the deep terms of an imagination of the first intensity; all the more formidable and menacing, then, become the weight and pressure of the manifold things, crucial and charged with illumination, that he knows not and perhaps cannot even grasp but that are essential to his full understanding of the world he has been impelled to create. Moreover, that understanding which his conception had refused to integrate and make his own perforce attaches itself to him, even if only as his Nemesis. Denied access in the light of day, it reappears in the dark of night, now no longer open-eyed but sightless. Herewith we touch one source, at least, of the sinister suspense and horror that pervade his pages. The very surplus of uniqueness in him is but the mask of his solitude and of his limitations. Hemmed in by his own consciousness, he beats his fists against its walls, finding a forced release only in violence and melodrama. But what needs to be clearly understood here is that Faulkner's plight does not so much reveal a private failing in aptitude or temperament as a type of creative frustration not uncommon to American literary history. Within this stream his work represents a subtle and intricate ramification, steeped in and formed by his special sectional background, of the ways in which the mind and art of the American intellectual mirrors the dissolution of an old order of values.

In his new novel Faulkner again immerses himself in the destructive element. But this time he is bending its fury into the very heart of that theme towards which he has been beating his way through all his preceding books, and which, in a sense, can now be regarded as his medium of preparation for the supreme effort to come. It is as if the life of the Old South, deep and dead, is so sacred and meaningful to him that he could not have trusted himself at it ere he had rehearsed its parts in more recent locales and on less worthy subjects. With the dear anguish of the past as his trophy, he has used the contemporary world, as it were, merely as his running start.

The rise and catastrophic end of a plantation family, the Civil War, the defeat that peopled the ravaged land with 'garrulous outraged baffled ghosts' whose fear and pride and glory you live and breathe, a thing that you, the outsider, cannot understand, for 'you would have to be born there'—all this is the classic avowal and exhortation of the peculiar trauma induced by the heritage of the Confederate South. The old ghost-tides come to life in a tide of events and emotions and in men and women as peculiar to Faulkner as the Karamazovs to Dostoevsky. Tom Sutpen, who bursts out of the wilderness to father a domain and a race, his son, Henry, the incestuous lovers Judith and Charles, the illicit drop of Negro blood in the family swirling and boiling till it rises like the very flood of fate to engulf the scene of crime and evil and single insane purpose—all placed within the pattern of an imagination as absolute and exacting as any in modern fiction.

Only, the book actually makes dull reading. What has happened is that his pattern and imagery have been impaired and dispersed by an unsuccessful method of presentation. This method, however, has not been arbitrarily chosen; and the clue, I think, lies in the language, which is formal, prolix, tortuous, running over into passages of psychological theorizing that arrest the dramatic development. In a writer who depends so much on drama to carry him forward, anything that blocks the dramatic movement is bound to disintegrate his structure. The language, in its turn, is shaped by a narrative form that, instead of recreating the story for the reader, laboriously pieces it together and interprets it for him through several narrators who all speak in the same voice, the monotonous and sorrowful voice of the author's contemplation of his world. The material is not explored objectively to provide the vision; it is manipulated to illustrate and fit the vision, which is preconceived. Thus the language becomes a function of the author's metaphysics, of spiritual relations, and of reverie: it no longer sticks to the object, but to the author's idea of the object. And as Eliot once observed, language can only be healthy when it directly presents the object, when 'it is so close to the object that the two are identified'; otherwise it becomes morbid and unreal.

The form this narrative takes suggests that Faulkner is following the itinerary of an ideological dream, rather than that of history. And since to him the historic process is a mystery of human fate doomed by a 'sickness somewhere at the prime foundation of this factual scheme,' his reproduction of this process in creative terms is always in danger of degenerating into mystification, is ever on the brink of the dilettantism of horror. It is at this point that his actual qualities as a novelist are directly penetrated by his ideology, whose matrix, it seems to me, is to be located in his tortured consciousness of the defeat of the Old South and the annihilation of its way of life. But inasmuch as on this and other grounds he implicitly rejects the industrial civilization that replaced the Old South, and at the same time his mind still runs absolutely counter to materialist ideas, the final sum of his thought is a kind of social despair distended to hold the scheme of things entire. And the best symbol I can think of to represent the bond that ties him to the South he so desperately loves and hates is the very symbol he has himself inscribed into his novel. That symbol is incest. For is not Faulkner's relation to his incestuous lovers, and to the land whose agony they bear, as sterile and desolate, though at times inspired by the grandeur of defiance and death, as their relation among themselves?

59. Wallace Stegner, review, Salt Lake *Tribune*

29 November 1936, 13—D

Stegner (b. 1909) won the Little, Brown novelette contest the following year. His many novels and stories often have a realistic rural setting. He continued to review Faulkner favorably.

It is occasionally salutary for a reviewer to read other reviews of a book before he writes his own, if only for the caution it will give him about mistaking subjective judgments for truths. Where the book in question is difficult or involved or revolutionary in its approach, he will be astonished also to find how few critics are willing to let a writer do as he wishes, how few will judge a book on the standards it sets for itself instead of on standards the critic would impose upon it.

So, after reading half a dozen reviews of *Absalom, Absalom!* one is led to preface all his utterances with 'I suspect.' I suspect, for example, that Clifton Fadiman's review in *The New Yorker* is not only imperceptient and lazy, but silly as well. I suspect that three other reviews in reputable papers are at least impercipient and probably lazy. I suspect that the only review that does Faulkner's last book anything like justice is that by Bernard DeVoto in the *Saturday Review*.

I suspect further that one cannot dismiss *Absalom, Absalom!* as 400 pages of turgid and invertebrate sentences about psychopathic ghosts. It is true that with isolated lyrical exceptions the experimental sentences do not come off; they are frequently not only invertebrate but downright bad syntax. The characters are admittedly ghostly and fleshless; the technique 'cocks its snoot' at chronology and logic. Granted one reviewer's charges that Faulkner writes his guts out trying to tell a simple story in the most complex way possible, there is still reason to believe that he probably knew what he was doing, and why he was doing it.

If Faulkner had wanted to tell simply the simple story of demonic

Thomas Sutpen's rise from poor white to opulent planter, his matrimonial experiments with whites and Negroes, his desire for a son and a perpetual name, and the final dissolution of that dream in a flaming house haunted by the whimperings of a half-wit mulatto who is the only survival of the Sutpen blood, he could have told it as simply as that. The very fact that he didn't is proof enough that he didn't want to, that the manner is more important to him than the matter.

Instead of assuming the omniscience of motive and impulse and reaction that even the most realistic novelists in the past have felt obliged to assume, Faulkner presents his story through the mouths of seven different people, in what DeVoto calls 'a series of approximations.' While there is plenty of character analysis here, it is frankly tentative, frankly the attempt of one character to understand another. The whole book, therefore, gives the impression of wavering uncertainty as Quentin Compson, Harvard freshman, tries to unravel the tangled threads of a tale which has reached him from a dozen incomplete sources, mutually contradictory in spots, filled with dark gaps where informants' knowledge gave out.

In other words, this novel, despite its shadowy, nightmarish quality, is in one respect the most realistic thing Faulkner has done. It reconstructs historical materials as any individual in reality has to reconstruct them—piecemeal, eked out with surmise and guess, the characters ghostly shades except in brief isolated passages. As in life, we are confronted by a story whose answers even the narrator does not know, whose characters he (and we with him) guesses at and speculates upon, but does not attempt to explain fully.

What Faulkner is actually saying, as explicitly if not as simply as it has ever been said, is that no man, novelist or otherwise, can know another except in the trivial superficies of his life; that the mind and emotions of another are mysteries as deep as the hereafter; that we arrive at our knowledge—or, rather, our surmises—of other people through these approximations, these dribbles of information from six or 600 sources, each driblet colored by the prejudices and emotions of the observer.

That is how we know Demon Thomas Sutpen; how we arrive at a conception of Miss Rosa and her thwarted emotional life; how we know what little we do of the motives of Henry Sutpen and of Charles Bon, who was to marry Henry's sister and whom Henry killed. We know as much as Quentin does, as much as Faulkner does; and at the end of the book Quentin and his roommate are frankly guessing, extemporizing, trying to piece out sections of the plot which are wholly dark, creating plausible but wholly imaginary characters to fill in the gaps, endowing them with motive and action to fit the few surviving facts.

Perhaps that is what the critics are howling about, that they don't know any more about these 'psychopathic ghosts' than they do about the people they associate with every day. Accustomed to having our fictional characters complete, fully rounded, we feel cheated if an author rejects the omniscient lie at the basis of most fiction. Perhaps, too, Faulkner doesn't entirely succeed; certainly the style is tortured beyond what most readers will stand. But I suspect, and strongly, that the mere technique of this novel may prove to be a significant contribution to the theory and art of fiction; that *Absalom, Absalom!* will not be the last, or the best, to approach its materials in this way.

60. Paula Snelling, 'Mr Faulkner Adds a Cubit,' *Pseudopodia*

Fall 1936, 4, 16

A liberal Southern quarterly published in northern Georgia by Lillian Smith and Paula Snelling (b. 1899), *Pseudopodia*—later *North Georgia Review*—covered Faulkner regularly; but by the late 1930s Miss Snelling was less certain of the value of his accomplishment.

A parable recommends that tares be permitted to grow along with wheat until harvest lest an attempt to weed out the former result in uprooting the latter. Mr. Faulkner has adhered literally to the admonition. During the years he has developed a quality of wheat unsurpassed in many of its attributes. The tares have been cultivated almost as assiduously. When the critic in his temerity essays the role of reaper and would harvest first the tares to be burned then the wheat to be stored, he is confronted with a problem which Matthew 13:30 takes no cognizance of. For the two have become so entangled that a separation is well-nigh impossible.

No one can read William Faulkner's books without arriving at the conclusion that the man has truly remarkable powers. Nor can one read these books without recognizing that the stigmata of the third-rate recur in them with a frequency which cannot be dismissed. The writer demonstrates again and again an intuitive awareness of the hidden maelstrom of the unconscious, a mature knowledge of the sufferings an individual must endure when impulses are in too severe conflict with the demands of his civilization, a fierce hatred for the unnecessary suffering which man puts upon man, a deep pity for the victim of uncontrollable forces. And when he is writing of these things there is in his cadenced prose a surging power which few have achieved. These are qualifications of the very first order. But seldom can the reader turn a dozen pages without being confronted with some gratuitous horror; some spectacle which might have been lifted with no extenuations from the most shameless thriller. Or he encounters an appeal to race fears and prejudices having about the connection with the essential story that dinosaurs have with the superiority of a particular kind of motor oil. Or he is led to the brink of what seems a significant revelation only to have the scene shifted to a different time and place—often for the praiseworthy purpose of revealing a new facet which will make the delayed comprehension more complete; almost as often in what seems the spirit of moron Luster jerking the spoon from imbecile Benjy's opening mouth.

Several hypotheses, none wholly tenable, present themselves by which to account for the existence of such seeming incongruities in a mature and gifted artist. Perhaps he originally had (or early acquired) a 'positive tropism' for all manifestations of the gruesome, as did Poe, and as he developed had the discrimination to bring his mature powers to bear primarily on those of deepest present significance; but has not rid himself of the vestigial inclination to display whatever hodgepodge of horror he can incidentally collect. Or, granted this fascination with the shocking, it may be that the emotional drive which carries much of his writing to so high a level, and which by its very potency testifies that it taps the writer's unconscious, short-circuits when its goal is too distant and requires frequent small stimuli to keep the circuit flowing.

Or, again, it may be that he thinks as sorrily of mankind as the preface to *Sanctuary* indicates and believes that a reading public cannot be found for his books save through the lure of more and worse monstrosities; and is willing to barter his integrity. To shift the suppositions to a more philosophic level, it is possible that man is such that he cannot look directly at Truth. That when Jehovah would dole out a minimal decalog he can present it to even the great prophet only through the veil of a thick cloud and to the ludicrous and sorry fanfare of thunder and lightning, smoke and fire. Small wonder the prophet returns with not only a graven stone and a shining face, but with reverberations of thunder and after-images of lightning by which to bemuse himself and his people.

Mr. Faulkner's newest book reaches a higher level than do even *Light in August* and *Sound and the Fury*, in which the merely sensational and titillating had yielded the center of the stage to comprehension and portrayal. Though the primary object of his attention here as always is cruelty and decadence, he recognizes and throws more light upon the existence of these qualities in others than freaks. Yet here too he negates much of the major significance of his writings (that the 'perversions' at which we shudder in the 'abnormal' have their roots and often their more dire manifestations in the drab and circumspect 'normal') by investing with a spurious and sinister halo of unusualness the very characters whom he otherwise draws so truly and understandingly. The tall tale element of which he so entertainingly showed himself the master in *Spotted Horses* and in the Indian stories of *These 13*, and which played a large part in *As I Lay Dying*, scarcely enters here. In his twelve books Yoknapatawpha county and the town of Jefferson, Mississippi, have become so thickly peopled with real and interesting characters whose lives overlap that the map and the genealogy appended to *Absalom, Absalom!* are useful as well as interesting. This last book centers around a man, Sutpen, whose silence concerning his past (and his present and future) and whose singleminded and at times ruthless pursuit of his uncommunicated ambition shroud him in unholy mystery in the eyes of Jefferson people of the early and middle nineteenth century; so that now, in 1909, when most of the victims of the drama and destruction which came to those closely associated with Sutpen have died and the survivors are not willing or not able to unravel all the threads of mystery, the attempt to reconstruct the story resolves itself frequently into the speculations of first one and then another. The section in which Rosa Coldfield relives her part (tenuous, yet the core of her life and sufficient to make of her a poet and philosopher) is perhaps the richest section of the book. It would be unfair to summarize baldly a story whose value is derived largely from the significance and overtones which accrue as the reader learns first one incomplete part, then another tantalizing fragment and gradually arrives, as he does in life, at as full a comprehension as is permitted him. But it touches on several matters which have, at intervals, troubled man's sleep: ambition, conflicts of personalities, murder, poverty, war, gossip, courage, miscegenation, hate, love, marriage without love, sympathy, slavery, incest, friendship, blood ties, family pride, torture, reputation, loyalty, inadequacy, hope, imbecility, wealth, betrayal, suspense, loneliness . . . ; and is well worth anyone's reading.

61. Cecil Day Lewis, review, *Daily Telegraph*

19 February 1937, 7

C. Day Lewis (1904–72) in the 1930s formed with Auden, Spender, and MacNeice an active and socially conscious group of poets. For a brief period a member of the Communist Party, he wrote in 1934 a manifesto for revolutionary poetry, *A Hope for Poetry*.

When Mr. Faulkner's earlier novels appeared, they were received by the critics with an orgy of enthusiasm from which they are now suffering the inevitable hang-over. I myself think that *Soldiers' Pay*, *The Sound and the Fury*, and *Sartoris* are three of the most remarkable novels written since the war; but I have to admit that some of his later work does lie very heavy on the stomach.

For one thing, his style—once crude, violent and robust—has tended to become, like the face of a *bon viveur*, purple and congested. Mr.

Faulkner seems to have been taking a course of Henry James. Sentence after sentence in *Absalom, Absalom!* meanders dreamily along, winding like a sluggish river in great loops that keep on bringing you back to where you started from. These sentences are ill-adapted to the tense, melodramatic quality of the author's vision, his faculty for giving us the spiritual 'feel' of violence and frustration.

If it does not come off in practice, theoretically at least this slow, repetitive, accumulative method is justified here by the distance of 50 years which separates the narrators from the events they are recalling. *Absalom, Absalom!* is the story of Thomas Sutpen, a settler in Mississippi about the time of the American Civil War—a story pieced together by a Harvard undergraduate out of the reminiscences of two of Sutpen's contemporaries.

[summarizes story]

This continuity and inescapableness of ancestral guilt is the theme of the book. If the book fails, it is because the orchestration is too heavy, too elaborate for the basic motifs. But, as always, Mr. Faulkner contrives to charge individual incidents with a strangeness, a tension, a colour and vitality which go a long way towards redeeming his defects of style and structure.

62. Graham Greene, 'The Furies in Mississippi,' *London Mercury*

March 1937, xxxv, 517–18

Greene (b. 1904) published his first major novel, *Brighton Rock*, the following year.

Mr. Faulkner's reputation has suffered lately from the exaggerated claims his admirers made for him on the strength of the rather obvious technical experiments in his early novels, *Soldiers' Pay* and *The Sound and the Fury*. He isn't another Joyce, any more than he is another Stein, that bogey of the Sunday reviewer. Indeed in his historical novels he is rapidly matriculating into the Book Society. Horsemen riding at night, the clank of holsters, niggers shrieking in the dark, Southern gentlewomen and the scent of wistaria, family Honour and family Doom: his historical novels are full of quite charming, traditional, bogus romance: a little of Stevenson, of Meredith, of Shiel, even a little of Amanda M'Kittrick Ros in such passages as this:

> I . . . who even at nineteen must have known that living is one constant and perpetual instant when the arras-veil before what-is-to-be hangs docile and even glad to the lightest naked thrust if we had dared, were brave enough (not wise enough: no wisdom needed here) to make the rending gash. Or perhaps it is no lack of courage either: not cowardice which will not face that sickness somewhere at the prime foundation of this factual scheme from which the prisoner soul, miasmal-distillant, wroils ever upward sunward, tugs its tenuous prison arteries and veins and prisoning in its turn that spark, that dream . . .

and so on to the sentence end ten lines later.

Let the devil's advocate have his way for awhile, explain how Mr. Faulkner's new novel belongs to the worst, the Sartoris, side of his achievement: the deep South and the picturesque Civil War costumes, the doom-ridden hero, 'this Faustus, this Beelzebub', riding in from nowhere with a couple of pistols, buying land from the Indians, hiring a French architect, working naked on the house with his niggers, marrying the most respectable girl in the town, overtaken by his Fate, his son murdering his daughter's betrothed to save her from incest and the taint of black blood, all culminating years later, in 1910, in a huge conflagration and the last survivor's death in the flames. That advocate will point out that the method of the novel, the story related by various people years later, the events falling into their order in the mind only on the last pages, has been far more skilfully managed by Mr. Ford who knows how to give intrinsic value and character to the narrators —all Mr. Faulkner's narrators speak the same bastard poetic prose. And as for this prose the advocate will remark how often it falls into blank verse rhythms, how fond the author is of resounding abstractions so that sometimes we are reminded of Mr. McDonald's cloudy oratory: '. . . turned upon his contemporary scene of folly and outrage and injustice the dead and consistent impassivity of a cold and inflexible disapproval.' (In the first paragraph of the novel—a devil's advocate is always a bit of a pedant—there are forty-one adjectives in twenty-seven lines qualifying only fifteen nouns.) And the advocate will wind up his speech with the claim that Mr. Faulkner has not created a single character of recognizable humanity and that the intellectual content of his novel is almost nil. Strip away the fake poetry, and you have the plot of a 'blood', while Mr. Faulkner disguises the complete absence of a theme with pseudo-tragic talk of doom and fate and the furies.

Alas! it is all true. Mr. Faulkner's is a talent quite easy to condemn, but there does remain over—Something: at the least a gift of vivid phrase heard too seldom through the Otranto thunder ('the ghost mused with shadowy docility as if it were the voice which he haunted where a more fortunate one would have had a house'; pigeons which 'wheeled in short courses resembling soft fluid paint-smears on the soft summer sky'); at its best—not to be found here or in *Sartoris*—an individual blend of the romantic and the realistic which makes the gangster Pop-Eye in *Sanctuary* so memorable a figure, a sense of spiritual evil which away from the contemporary scene becomes unconvincing and stagey. And finally we should consider whether, if the romantic costume subject is to be treated at all (if Southern gentlefolk, horsemen at night and wistaria blossom, which do speak in certain moods like common songs to the imagination, deserve an occasional appearance), it can be treated in any other way. It can't be treated plainly, like Pop-Eye's rape on the cornhusks of the college girl, or the crazy antique planes in *Pylon*; the artificial subject has to be carried by an artificial manner, and even at its vaguest and most resounding Mr. Faulkner's style is welcome when we consider the alternatives: *Anthony Adverse* and *Gone With the Wind.*

THE UNVANQUISHED

New York, February 1938
London, May 1938

63. Kay Boyle, review, *New Republic*

9 March 1938, 136–7

Kay Boyle (b. 1903) is a short story writer, poet, and novelist, who often works with psychological themes.

There are two Faulkners—at least to me there are two: the one who stayed down South and the one who went to war in France and mixed with foreigners and aviators; that is, the Faulkner of the Sartoris saga (and the countless other savagely and tenderly chronicled documents of the South) and the Faulkner who wrote 'Turn About', for instance, and 'All the Dead Pilots' and *Pylon* with no perceptible cooling of that hot devotion to man's courage although the speech, the history, the conflict were no longer his strict heritage. I believe these two separate Faulkners (separated more by a native shyness of the foreigner than any variance in ideology or technique) possess between them the strength and the vulnerability which belong only to the greatest artists: the incalculable emotional wealth, the racy comic sense, the fury to reproduce exactly not the recognizable picture but the unmistakable experience, the thirst for articulation as well as the curiosity and the vocabulary—that rarity—to quench it. The weaknesses there are, the errors, the occasionally strained effects, are accomplished by the same fearless, gifted hand.

It is not difficult to reconcile the two Faulkners; perhaps as simple as recognizing that man is a good host or a good guest, but rarely both.

On his own ground Faulkner is explicit, easy, sure; on someone else's he is a little awed, a little awkward, provincially aware of the chances he is taking. But I believe it is in the willingness to take these risks that Faulkner's whole future lies. That *The Unvanquished* happens to be one more chapter in the Sartoris saga is no valid description of it, nor that it is a book about the Civil War—a Civil War in which the issue of black and white is lost in the wider issue not of justice and tyranny, subjection and freedom, or even sin and virtue, but merely of life and death. For one who loves Faulkner's work and has followed it closely and impatiently, the difficulty lies in isolating this book or any book from the others and trying to say this or that of it: his genius is not this book or perhaps any given book but resides in that entire determined collection of volumes which reveal him to be the most absorbing writer of our time.

[summarizes and quotes from story]

It is, then, the sentimental and glamorous story of one old lady who set out to find and ask a Yankee Colonel to return to her a chest of family silver tied with hemp rope, two darkies, Loosh and Philadelphy, and the two confiscated mules, 'Old Hundred' and 'Tinney'; and like a single and undaunted fife still playing, it is as well the essence of that war, a thing as intrinsically and nationally and gallantly the South's as the revolution is France's and the rebellion Ireland's: become now a legend, almost a fable of tattered banners, makeshift uniforms, incredible courage and inhuman ferocity. It has those weaknesses which can be found throughout Faulkner's work: the full-length portraits which abruptly become caricatures not likenesses of the living, the 'ladies' without face or substance, the repetitions, the maudlin lapses, the shameless voice of the evangelist declaiming in solemn, flowery passages. But it has that fabulous, that wondrous, fluxing power which nothing Faulkner touches is ever without. The word for it may be glamor or may be sentiment, but both these words are mutable and I have used them here without contempt, applying them in their best sense as attributes to fact. They can confuse, they can disguise, but they can as well bring to the familiar a heightened, an isolated and a therefore truer legibility. They were elements in that electric atmosphere and mystic climate in which Poe's men and women lived and have survived and they are a vital part of Faulkner's quicker, more comprehensive world. Faulkner and Poe, set far enough apart in time, are strangely kin: unique in our history in their immunity to literary fashion, alike in their fanatical obsession with the unutterable depths of mankind's vice and even more with his divinity.

If writing remain one of the Arts—with a capital A and be damned to the current mode of splitting it two ways in a poem or a fresco on a wall—if its sensitive execution still demand the heart and the endurance which have kept artists lying prone on scaffoldings painting year in, year out, and if its success depend on its acceptance as convincing tragedy or comedy, then it can quite simply be said of Faulkner that he is the rare, the curious, the almost ludicrously authentic thing. In this book, as in his others, he writes with that 'fierce desire of perfection' which contemporaries said Michelangelo evidenced when 'flinging himself on the material of marble,' vehemently seeking expression for 'the human elements of fervor and tenderness.'

64. V. F. Calverton, 'Southerner at Large,' *Modern Monthly*

March 1938, 11–12

Calverton (1900–40), born George Goetz, was an American Marxist opposed to Stalinism. He wrote several literary and social studies of America, and in 1933 founded *Modern Quarterly*, a journal of the Left less doctrinaire than *New Masses*. It became *Modern Monthly* in 1938.

William J. Faulkner interests the English reading public for the same reason that Ernest Hemingway and Sinclair Lewis do—because he is so American and because his Americanness is not provincial but universal. The people he describes and the situations he depicts are national, or, what is even more limited, sectional, but the emotions he evokes are unconfined by geography or tradition. What makes American literature

American or French literature French is something so subtly and inextricably involved with attitude, approach, emphasis that they can be easier recognized and felt than defined but the differences are there, however elusive and indefinable they may seem. Faulkner's approach to his people is as singularly American as Thomas Hardy's approach to his rustic mayors, school teachers, and commoners is unmistakably English. Faulkner is not concerned with the agrarian he has met, known, shaken hands with, lived with, in the deep south, in his native state of Mississippi, which is the most backward state in the nation. That fact is very significant in understanding Faulkner's fiction. He is dealing with a people who are inferior to all other Americans, who are living in a state of intellectual barbarism which is infra-medieval. In *Sanctuary*, one of his revealing portraitures in Southern degeneracy, and in *Light in August*, his best novel to date, he introduces his reader to a collection of people who are totally incredible unless one lives in or has lived in Mississippi. What Caldwell and Kirkland did in *Tobacco Road* was gentle and generous compared with what Faulkner has done with the Mississippians he has described in so many of his novels.

To people who do not know the South, or Mississippi, Faulkner's characters seem fantastic, impossible creations, off-shoots of a morbific imagination, but the fact of the matter is his characters are so absolutely and completely real, so forthrightly actual, that the very dregs of the country live in them, seep through them, distort and disfigure them. It is this fact which explains Faulkner's failure to create inspiring or admirable characters; to date, for instance, he has yet to create a single character of emulative quality. In his most recent novel, *The Unvanquished*, he comes closer in his depiction of the grandmother than anywhere else to providing us with a character whose experiences we can share with some slight degree of sympathy instead of with complete revulsion. No American writer since Poe has created such wild, macabre, forbidding characters. Poe, however, a child of the post-Waterloo romanticism of Europe, which found a fertile though remote rebirth in his work, invented his characters, contrived them out of the recesses of his weird imagination; Faulkner, on the other hand, gifted though he is with something of Poe's penchant for the macabre, didn't need to resort to *such invention and excogitation*. He had the characters before him, near him, with him.

Aside from his war experience, from which he emerged a lieutenant and a hero with wounds resulting from a plane crash (his novel *Pylon* is a product of that aspect of his career), he has lived practically his entire life in the South and that, in itself, is an endurance test of a supreme variety. His work, therefore, has been inevitably soaked in Southern soil. His people are no more queer, relatively speaking, than Sherwood Anderson's characters in *Winesburg, Ohio*. Whatever difference exists results from the fact that the South is bankrupt and degenerate, living still upon forgotten frontiers of experience, whereas the Midwest, though stodgy, possesses something of promise and futurity. The Midwest characters in Sherwood Anderson, Sinclair Lewis, and Willa Cather are corrigible; the Southern characters in Faulkner's fiction, however, are incorrigible. They are nothing more than the sick, stinking backwash of a dead but still rotting civilization.

The proliterati have complained that Faulkner does not deal with the class struggle and is not interested in the more progressive forces of American civilization. The truth of the matter is that the class struggle plays a relatively minor role in the semi-feudal life of Mississippi. There are abundant classes in the state but little struggle between them. Industry has made too little headway in Mississippi to have introduced the class conflict on a vast, active, belligerent scale. The majority of the Mississippians are an impoverished, exploited lot but they accept that lot without much protest or opposition.

In *The Unvanquished* Faulkner goes back to the Civil War for his types, and it must be said at once that as types these people are far superior to those in *Sanctuary* and *Light in August*. But these characters spring from a South which was old and defeated but not yet decadent, and there is a naturalness about their developments, their actions, their devotions, their deaths, and a simplicity which Faulkner has never attained in his previous novels. This is the least involved, the least obscure, and the least affected of his works. It is free of the literary tricks which made certain of his earlier novels sound 'phoney' in places. It is free of all artifice, and it is to be fondly hoped that Mr. Faulkner's novels in the future will follow this novel as a model rather than go back to the distorted and contorted models of his earlier fiction.

65. Earle Birney, 'The Two William Faulkners,' *Canadian Forum*

June 1938, 84–5

Birney (b. 1904) is a Canadian poet who has written his best work since World War II. In the mid-1930s he was active in Trotskyist affairs in both Canada and Utah, then was literary editor of *Canadian Forum* prior to the war.

Two writers have been struggling with each other for a long time inside the skin of William Faulkner. One of them is a stylized and morbid mystic attempting a sequence of novels on the scale of an epic. The other, the less publicized but more authentic author, is a sharp and brilliant narrator of short stories. The peculiar promise of Faulkner has always been that he has never been able either to unite or to untangle his two powers within one book.

None of the nine novels which have given him a place in the immediate sun of American fiction can stand alone, nor do they make a satisfactory unit together. It is not merely that a major character in one work can be understood only by a knowledge of his sufferings in an earlier or a later book; or even one not yet written; it is not only that Faulkner eternally shies at his own plots, deliberately prancing and curvetting about a vital incident until a reader screams vainly to know what did happen and when and why. Deeper than this is his inability to do what he evidently most wants to do, that is, to make, out of the microcosm of 'Yoknapatawpha County', Mississippi, a life-cycle of the essential American South from plantation days through the Civil War down to the World War and the present.

Such a theme demands an observation wide enough to scan the new industrial South and its problems as well as the decadent pastoral Confederacy and its anachronistic psychology, and the understanding which can unify the two. Instead Faulkner has given us a broken series of novel-fragments, each in turn disintegrated by separable passages of verbal experimentation. Octopus sentences emerge in fine undulating terror and then proceed to strangle themselves in their own straining tentacles; phrases soar into music and brilliant picture, and sink into discord and cubism. Motivation is equally incoherent; crime and sex abnormalities (constants in his fiction) are treated one moment as psychopathic, the next as products of Southern idealism, and finally as inexplicable, motiveless. By long reminiscences—all his characters are incurable brooders with prodigious and masochistic memories—the reader is led down the nightmare alleys of a character's mind, and then suddenly abandoned while the author leaps to a snorting horse of narrative and, like the schoolboy's cavalry officer, gallops away in all directions.

In other words Faulkner's handling of action is that of the short story, flashing, dexterous and brief, while his characterization and theme can be enclosed only in the epic cycle which he does not write. That is why the most steadily admired of his writings are not the once-fashionable *Sanctuary*, self-confessed pot-boiler, nor even that amazing tour de force, *The Sound and the Fury*, but contes like 'That Evening Sun Go Down' or 'A Rose for Emily.'

The Unvanquished, latest of his books, is a striking epitome of the two Faulkners. Its sections first appeared as separate stories in popular magazines; they have been insufficiently revised to appear as a novel and are now neither one thing or the other. 'Ambuscade' was originally a fine simple story of two twelve-year-old boys, one black and one white, who played Civil War behind the Mississippi farmhouse while the white's father was playing it in earnest fewer miles away than they thought. Lying 'in ambush' with a real blunderbuss they shot the horse from under the advance scout of the first Yankee invaders, fled to shelter beneath their white granny's skirts and were saved by the shrewd courage of the old lady and the contemptuous chivalry of a northern officer. A Hollywood story-idea, perhaps, but made real by Faulkner's ability to step within the minds of both the adolescents and the aged, the rocket speed of his action at the moment of climax, and by that curious unsmiling humor-at-remote-control which pervades his best work. But, now that the story is fitted into a continuous book one is unable to forget that the white boy is Bayard Sartoris I who, as an old man, had already brooded over this incident in an earlier novel, *Sartoris*, and that this Bayard's father, John, is now by the killing of two carpet baggers apparently setting in motion a family curse which was already being expiated in the earlier *Light in August* and which will probably pop up again in 1940.

Yet despite its curses, curse-words, and dozen-odd murders, *The Unvanquished* represents, as De Voto has remarked, 'a new high in purity and romance' for Faulkner. Even rural Ontarians might risk a copy on the parlor settee. There is a blueblooded virgin who remains such despite a year's fighting in pants with Southern guerilla corps. There's a treasure box buried, stolen, recovered, and reburied. There's Bayard's cocky grandmother who defrauds Sherman's men of mules, sells them back to them, and washes her sins away with prayer. Her spirit is conveyed in the title; she is eventually defeated but never licked. There is a sunny clarity about all this which is positively dazzling from Faulkner.

For the real Faulkner fan there are still a number of non-stop sentences, preposterous similes about whites of eyes, mystical smells (Bayard sniffs a 'will to endure' on his pappa's uniform), a spot of corn-cob philosophizing, and the above mentioned entanglements with other Faulkneriana.

The reader looking for Faulkner's definitive treatment of the South must however continue to look. True, here is at last a book of his planted square in that Civil War which has been the great Trojan doom behind or before the melodramas of his other books; here he tackles the primum mobile; but at the best all that results are a few brilliant side-glances into the back-waters of the war. The movement of masses of men, the impact of great historic forces, of ideas and ideals, of economic motives and conflicts as reflected in the minds of representative men —all these are still over the horizon.

The one exception is a fine chapter, 'Raid,' which vivifies the mass hysteria of 'freed' and bewildered slaves trooping like lemmings down the dusty roads to the rivers, chanting that Sherman is leading them to Jordan. But even this heart-compelling theme becomes a blurred Grand-Guignol, for Faulkner can see no real motive, no suffering negro race, behind the phenomenon. He looks at the black still through the dulled and provincial eyes of a slaveholder, ignorant of the humanity he surrounds himself with, ignorant of the essential anachronism of plantation feudalism, and ignorant of the real barbarousness of the equally outdated wage-slavery under which the contemporary black groans.

The Unvanquished, like Faulkner's other books, is a timepiece with a number of tiny jewels and delicate wheels, oiled and sparkling and ingeniously fitted; but there is no mainspring and the watch doesn't tick. Nevertheless, the wheels, regarded separately, are delights in themselves and the book is no worse, if no better, than Faulkner's others; as such it contains as good 'action' fiction as any being written in the United States today.

THE WILD PALMS

New York, January 1939
London, March 1939

66. Edwin Berry Burgum, review, *New Masses*

7 February 1939, 23–4

Burgum (b. 1894), a Marxist critic who taught at New York University, was one of few reviewers to perceive the close relationship between the two stories in the book. In 1947 he wrote a less favorable overall assessment of Faulkner in *The Novel and the World's Dilemma.*

In his distinguished career Mr. Faulkner has not written a more thoroughly satisfying novel than *The Wild Palms*. He has been unusually sensitive to manner of expression and extraordinarily persistent in technical experimentation. Since he has at the same time insisted upon grappling with significant themes, his work has either presented the obvious flaws of construction of *Light in August* or achieved a form, like that of *The Sound and the Fury*, almost incomprehensible to the average reader. But in this latest novel he has come very near the successful expression he has been groping for. It not only reads easily; it grips the attention.

If such is really Faulkner's accomplishment in *The Wild Palms*, the comments the critics are making can scarcely be right. Puzzled, apparently, by the fact that two unrelated stories unroll in alternate chapters, some of the critics have failed to find any organic connection between them, while others have discovered too simple a relationship.

These latter believe the one story to be the mere opposite to the other. As the blurb puts it, the two themes are flight and refuge. On the one hand, a woman leaves the security of marriage for the hazards of life with an unstable young doctor. On the other, a prisoner, virtually given a chance to escape when he is sent to aid persons marooned by the overflowing Mississippi, prefers to return to his prison walls.

But the real relationship between the two stories must be more complex, for they both end within the 'security' of prison walls. The pursuit of freedom, the escape from the conventional, has in neither instance been satisfactory. This is the basic ironic theme which both stories hold in common: in a demoralized age the prison affords the illiterate hillbilly and the educated neurotic doctor alike the only possible framework of social compulsions within which they can exist, if not with what Malraux would call man's natural hope and dignity, at least with the approximation of tranquillity. In this fundamental orientation of the novel, one can find a development of the paradox of Dostoevski. In Faulkner peace does not come after crime and suffering simply as a result of the compulsion imposed by society. The irony is more bitter, since these men who suffer and go to jail have become better men, better integrated men, than their sadistic jailers and the average respectable citizens outside. The 'wretched of mankind' are in no mood to arise in Faulkner, but they have at all events escaped that pretense of freedom which our competitive world sets up as an ideal and translates, as these two stories hint, into the actuality of the undernourished body and the neurotic personality.

The dominant story, the story of Dr. Wilbourne, is in its general outline only the better retelling of Dreiser's *American Tragedy*. Wilbourne is the same sort of virtuous inexperienced weakling, whose suppressed sexual urges burst into control of him at the age of twenty-seven, and whose lack of that core of resolute selfishness which comes naturally to the boy on the street corner makes possible his eventual crime. But Faulkner is not content to leave Wilbourne the plaything of heredity and environment. He centers his attention on the intricate immediate conflict within the personality. He depicts the ineffectual rise of a deep masculine discontent with mere satisfaction in love, which leads Wilbourne, not to reject the 'stability' (as the critics would say) of his being supported by his mistress, but to wipe out the offense to his pride in not being able to support her himself. And so they trek to the snowbound mine in Utah, where he fails as a doctor because he has fallen victim to a shady capitalistic enterprise.

One value of the subordinate story now begins to become apparent. It throws into contrast with the neurotic instability of this educated middle-class doctor the contrasting virtues of the proletarian. At the very time when the doctor is becoming hysterical because of his mistress' pregnancy, caught between her desire for an abortion and his fear and dislike of performing it, the criminal of the second story is rescuing from the swollen Mississippi a woman who is also pregnant. Actually the event, like the rest of the second story, occurred some ten years earlier. But the fact that Faulkner inserts this particular episode into his novel at this point can only mean that he intends the reader to learn something from the contrast of the two situations. If the doctor could hardly endure the cold of Utah winters, the hillbilly illiterate rises equal to his physical emergency. These scenes in which the man —who is never given a name, who is only described as tall and lean, as though the prototype of the underprivileged, not worth individualization in the eyes of dominant respectability—these scenes in which he is shot at by officers on the bank to which he has dragged her no more weak with exhaustion than himself, may well be isolated in our textbooks as instances of Faulkner's mastery of the art of narration. But in the novel they furnish dramatic relief to the spasms of passion, the alternations of despair and futile ecstasy, the impotent hesitations, among which Wilbourne has been wallowing. They restore to the reader the pleasure and the confidence of certain elemental qualities which seem to have retreated from the higher social levels. But it has been nature and not society which has inspired this heroism in the tall lean man. And if after these weeks of heroism he returns to his prison, indifferent to the ten years which have been added to his sentence, 'for escaping,' it is because he knows he will enjoy there the friendship of his fellow prisoners and the comfort of tomorrow's hand upon the plough, which not merely his crime, his absurd, unsuccessful train robbery, but the very complexion of respectable society denies him outside.

It is not, however, on this note that Faulkner ends his novel. The heroism has been exceptional, something to be recounted with simple joy of recollection to his fellow prisoners, among whom some day, perhaps, Wilbourne, shorn by years of imprisonment of both his respectability and his neuroses, forgetful at length of love and the grief it has brought him, may be content to listen. For society has reduced these prisoners to the habitual level of Hardy's peasants who expect no more than toil and discipline. They get pleasure out of the day because they expect so little from it, and if they are deprived of love, remember with a laughter which has lost all bitterness that it does not submit to routine.

67. Paula Snelling, review, *North Georgia Review*

Spring 1939, 24–5

In *Light in August* and in *Absalom, Absalom!* Mr. Faulkner seemed well on his way towards making of his vices the virtues they potentially are. About *Pylon* there was little good to be said. *The Wild Palms* lies somewhere between the two extremes. In it, the publishers say, he has 'achieved a straightforward and smashing dramatic story in the best manner of his *Sanctuary* and *As I Lay Dying*.' Their shelving is correct, and one quarrels only with the inclusion of the word 'straightforward'; —Mr. Faulkner's most cherished trick in trade here and elsewhere being to march his readers through partially unintelligible, powerfully charged pages until they find themselves almost deciding what it is the author wishes to (or not to) tell them, then to jerk them into a new series of pages designed to the same end. For the rest of it, one looks again through the preface to the Modern Library edition of *Sanctuary*, glances through the subsequent corroborating pages, considers *The Wild Palms* and concludes that the author has not changed his spots. He even goes a step further here in that he tells two unrelated stories which have been placed in the same volume for little other discernible purpose than to afford him the pleasure, after engrossing you in one story to the point where you have forgotten what occurred in the other and have lost all interest in its characters, of transporting you to the other, there to remain until the same disinterest has arisen concerning the first set; then back again. Which bears more resemblance to the manner in which a fisherman disports himself with reel, rod and sucker than to the preoccupations of a serious and talented artist whose realm is the human soul. (The two stories, concerned with different characters, different locales, different times do of course permit the reader to make certain comparisons and contrasts, but the author does little in the choosing and the shaping of his stories to impress us with a relationship —unless it be the basic inevitability underlying the beguiling opulence of phrase in the 'take-it-off, knock-it-off, or have-the-crow-to-pick-it-off' alternatives life frequently restricts us to.)

And yet Faulkner has gifts which, were his core of the same caliber, would place him in the foreranks of twentieth century novelists. For that reason only does one not accept his performances with equanimity. Those to whom ten talents have been given cannot escape the hard requirement that they produce therewith another ten. Whereas Mr. Faulkner seems to have selected as his goal the search for a corrosive with which to overlay each of his ten rarely duplicated talents. Yet it is perhaps useless, even stupid, to rail out at Mr. Faulkner for this. His books, more than those of any other American writer, seem to draw their power and their poison from their author's unconscious. They seem to be fashioned: just as certain of our dreams are charged with an emotion far in excess of the requirements of their ostensible subject-matter, yet not too great for the deep elemental forces for which the dream symbols unrecognizedly stand, so Faulkner's novels have a surcharge of power and terror which though fully warranted by certain under-currents and conflicts of life, yet remain definitely excessive for the matters he chooses to write about. Or perhaps he no more chooses what to write about than we choose what to dream about —the subject-matter in both cases being that compromise material which simultaneously affords outlet for pent-up unconscious emotions and screen against conscious recognition of the basis of those emotions. One feels even that Faulkner's mad search for ever more and more bizarre material may be an attempt to find something spectacular enough, something awe-ful enough, to justify to his conscious mind (compelled to rationalize where it fears to reason) the emotion which he has and which he recognizes is out of proportion to what he sees in more conventional subject-matter—he not having attained that rare maturity of vision which sees that the most turbulent, the most distressing, the most exquisite emotions a human being can feel are not the outcroppings of lurid adventures, but have their roots in simple experiences which are the common lot of man; and that the booger-men, the horror tales, the envisioned and the enacted perversions with which from time to time we confound ourselves are but feeble and inaccurate projections of simple and terrifying and hidden thoughts, conflicts, experiences that basicly disturb us.

We are grateful to Mr. Faulkner for his certainty, and for his repeated powerful affirmations of this certainty, that life is not the stereotyped, mediocrity-encrusted affair which the conventional mind in and out of books contents itself that it is. That his fiction should impatiently and angrily state and overstate the inadequacy of customary assumptions concerning what is important in life is understandable and valuable. But it is not sufficient. There is great potential virtue, both artistic and psychological, in Mr. Faulkner's tendency to isolate one compelling factor, instinct, drive, perversion, character trait, in a person's life, taking a bulldog grip on it, following the person where this compulsive motive power leads him, refusing to be diverted from the scent by the false trails human beings lay to bemuse themselves and their fellow-travelers. But Mr. Faulkner does not give continuous evidence that he discards conventionalities discriminately or for the honest purpose of learning what lies beneath. More frequently he seems to be flaunting in our faces the cheapness in which he holds us—and himself; or to be following compulsions of his own which only coincidentally take him into the rich, inadequately explored bottom lands of civilization.

68. Edwin Muir, review, *Listener*

30 March 1939, 701

There are two main categories of modern prose fiction. The first deals with the outside of life; the second with the inside. The outside world is a world of counters, the inside world a world of flux, and they rarely come together in a novel. The first is described with intelligence and sensibility in *The Thibaults*, by Roger Martin du Gard, which almost succeeds in being a great novel; the second is evoked in fits and starts in Mr. William Faulkner's *The Wild Palms*. The world of *The Thibaults* is a world of families, posts, careers, civil and religious institutions, law-courts, towns, and other countries. In Mr. Faulkner's world there is a Freudian Censor but no civil authority, mother-fixations but no mothers, a racial unconscious but no race, a communal curse but no community. Or rather when such things appear they are like projections of a dream: policemen and gaolers against a vacuum, mothers seen through a mother-fixation, the community as a mirage of the glazed inward eye. Gaolers, mothers, murder, flood, guns, indifferent faces, flash past that eye; chaos is the background; the most that can be predicted of it is that if you commit murder or manslaughter a police-man will arrive for you, though where he comes from it is hard to say. Mr. Faulkner's world of imagination is really a prolonged dream or rather a nightmare, into which civil functionaries from another dream intrude now and then; but the tortured inner eye cannot account for these people, for to it the ordinary is the sharpest surprise of all. Mr. Faulkner has flashes of genius; he has probably more of that quality than M. Roger Martin du Gard; but his novel accounts for nothing, and *The Thibaults* does.

[a paragraph on *The Thibaults*]

Civilisation results in measure, an ability to judge what things in human life are and are not important. In this sense Mr. Faulkner has no measure at all; he is like a traveller from some remote country who has rushed through civilisation and viewed it with a burning eye. His glance falls like a vivid searchlight on certain things: lust, pregnancy, abortion, homicide, flood, ruin; but behind these there is darkness. The result is a half-savage, melodramatic vision made up of a few in-tensely real figures in a limbo without ordinary people and ordinary households, schools, municipal buildings, theatres and clubs, but con-taining several hospitals, gaols, brothels and cemeteries. This melodrama at its best resembles that of the Elizabethan drama, and at its worst is wild caricature. The note recurs again and again:

> the profound and distracted blaze of objectless hatred in the strange woman's eyes . . .

> a Pole, with an air fierce proud and wild and a little hysterical. . . .

Nevertheless, Mr. Faulkner is a writer with moments of genius; if he sees things one at a time, against a featureless darkness, he sees them with intensity. The intensity is ultimately destructive; it not merely outlines the characters but dissolves them, sometimes bit by bit, sometimes in a blaze; but before that happens there are always moments of strange and brilliant clarity. It is not entirely chance that the best thing in the book is a long description of the Mississippi in flood, a superb picture of ruin. This is over-written, like most of the rest of the book; but there are intervals of curious lucidity, as when the escaped convict looks round him after paddling in vain for hours:

> after a while it no longer seemed to him that he was trying to put space and distance behind him or shorten space and distance ahead, but that both he and the wave were now hanging suspended simultaneous and unprogressing in pure time.

This gives an immediate sense of the wide chaos of water, though the convict was probably not a man who was capable of thinking of pure time. But Mr. Faulkner gets very close to things before his imagination obliterates them. The novel consists of two stories: one of a man who was destroyed by his resolve to stick to love and freedom, in spite of the world; the other of a man so accustomed to imprisonment that he turns against love and freedom, and after having escaped by chance goes thankfully back to his chains again. This probably embodies Mr. Faulkner's judgment of the world, but the world, nevertheless, is left out: all that remains is this narrow and intense vision.

69. George Marion O'Donnell, 'Faulkner's Mythology'

Summer 1939

Kenyon Review, i, 285–99. This article appeared in the third issue of *Kenyon Review*, among contributions by John Berryman, Randall Jarrell, Kenneth Burke, Peter Taylor, Philip Rahv, and John Crowe Ransom.

In 1936 O'Donnell received his B.A. from Vanderbilt University. In 1939 he received his M.A. and held a fellowship in creative writing under Donald Davidson. Later he taught at Auburn and Louisiana State Universities.

William Faulkner is really a traditional moralist, in the best sense. One principle holds together his thirteen books of prose—including his new novel, *The Wild Palms*—giving his work unity and giving it, at times, the significance that belongs to great myth. That principle is the Southern social–economic–ethical tradition which Mr. Faulkner possesses naturally, as a part of his sensibility.

However, Mr. Faulkner is a traditional man in a modern South. All around him the anti-traditional forces are at work; and he lives among evidences of their past activity. He could not fail to be aware of them. It is not strange, then, that his novels are, primarily, a series of related myths (or aspects of a single myth) built around the conflict between traditionalism and the anti-traditional modern world in which it is immersed.

In a re-arrangement of the novels, say for a collected edition, *The Unvanquished* might well stand first; for the action occurs earlier, historically, than in any other of the books, and it objectifies, in the essential terms of Mr. Faulkner's mythology, the central dramatic tension of his work. On one side of the conflict there are the Sartorises, recognizable human beings who act traditionally. Against them the invading Northern armies, and their diversified allies in the reconstruction era, wage open war, aiming to make the traditional actions of the Sartorises impossible.

The invaders are unable to cope with the Sartorises; but their invasion provides another antagonist with an occasion within which his special anti-Sartoris talent makes him singularly powerful. This antagonist is the landless poor-white horse-trader, Ab Snopes; his special talent is his low cunning as an *entrepreneur*. He acts without regard for the legitimacy of his means; he has no ethical code. In the crisis brought about by the war, he is enabled to use a member of the Sartoris family for his own advantage because, for the first time, he can be useful to the Sartorises. Moreover, he is enabled to make this Sartoris (Mrs. Rosa Millard) betray herself into an act of self-interest such as his, and to cause her death while using her as his tool.

The characters and the conflict are particular and credible. But they are also mythological. In Mr. Faulkner's mythology there are two kinds of characters; they are Sartorises or Snopeses, whatever the family names may be. And in the spiritual geography of Mr. Faulkner's work there are two worlds: the Sartoris world and the Snopes world. In all of his successful books, he is exploring the two worlds in detail, dramatizing the inevitable conflict between them.

It is a universal conflict. The Sartorises act traditionally; that is to say, they act always with an ethically responsible will. They represent vital morality, humanism. Being anti-traditional, the Snopeses are immoral from the Sartoris point-of-view. But the Snopeses do not recognize this point-of-view; acting only for self-interest, they acknowledge no ethical duty. Really, then, they are a-moral; they represent naturalism or animalism. And the Sartoris–Snopes conflict is fundamentally a struggle between humanism and naturalism.

As a universal conflict, it is important only philosophically. But it is important artistically, in this instance, because Mr. Faulkner has dramatized it convincingly in the terms of particular history and of actual life in his own part of the South—in the terms of his own tradition.

[O'Donnell turns to several of Faulkner's novels, including *The Wild Palms*, to delineate 'the conflict between traditional (Sartoris) man and modern (Snopes) man, dissociated into a sequence of animal functions, lacking in unity under essential morality.' The entire article is reprinted in most general collections of Faulkner criticism.]

William Faulkner's myth finds expression in work that is definitely romantic; when he comes near to tragedy, it is the tragedy of Webster. His art, like Webster's, is tortured. In form, each of his novels resembles a late-Elizabethan blank verse line, where the meter is strained, threatens to break, sometimes breaks, but is always exciting. He is an original craftsman, making his own solutions to his problems of form, often blundering, but occasionally striking upon an effect that no amount of studious craftsmanship could achieve. Consequently, like Dostoievski, or like Miss Djuna Barnes in our own time, he is very special; and his work cannot be imitated except futilely, for he works within no general tradition of craft and hands on no tradition to his successors.

But Mr. Faulkner's difficulties of form derive, in part, from the struggle that he has to make to inform his material. The struggle is manifest, even in the prose itself. Discounting the results of plain carelessness in all of the books, the correlation between the fictions and the quality of the prose in Mr. Faulkner's books is instructive. It appears significant that *The Unvanquished* contains his least tortured, *Pylon* his most tortured prose.

He has worked to project in fiction the conflict between his inherent traditional values and the modern world; and the conflict has affected his fictional projection, so that all of his work is really a *striving toward* the condition of tragedy. He is the Quentin Compson or the Bayard Sartoris of modern fiction. He does not always fail; but when he does, his failure is like theirs—he ends in confused or meaningless violence. And for the same reasons: His heritage is theirs, and it is subject to the same opposition to which they are subject as characters. When he is partially successful, the result is tortured but major romantic art.

Now, in 1939, Mr. Faulkner's work may seem melodramatic. Melodrama differs from tragedy only in the amount of meaning that is subsistent in the pattern of events; and in our time the values of Mr. Faulkner's tradition are available to most men only historically, in the same way that, let us say, medieval values are available. The significance of the work as myth depends, then, upon the willingness of the reader to recover the meaning of the tradition—even historically.

70. Benjamin T. Spencer, 'Wherefore This Southern Fiction?'

October–December 1939

Sewanee Review, xlvii, 502–4.

Spencer (b. 1904) is the author of *The Quest for Nationality: An American Literary Campaign*. Now retired, he has taught since 1930 at Ohio Wesleyan University. In this article he analyzed the obsession with confusion, disorder, and chaos, and conversely the thirst for order, so prevalent in recent Southern fiction.

In the Southerner's deeply traditional reliance on social and political order, combined with the decay of the liberal hope which arose in the Reconstruction, one may find in appreciable measure, I believe, the compelling force and dominant mood of such renascence of literature as is now present in the South. With those who regard literature in general as an attempt to clarify some confusion, to resolve some social or personal quandary, to recover some order, one may agree that Southern literature is not unique in its archetypal situations. Yet the degree and nature of the confusion are in a measure distinctive; and Allen Tate has weighed well his metaphor in speaking of the 'fascinating nightmare called the South'.

Beneath the surface of Southern literature, then, whether it deal with sharecropper or mountain white or the old families, one may discern through plot and image and style and texture its essential Southerness—its concern for order. Melodramatic much of it is, but it is the melodrama not of the West or the sharp violence of J. M. Cain or the sentimentalized violence of Steinbeck, but rather that of the Jacobean dramatists, intense and bewildered in the insecure decades after Elizabeth's death. Faulkner, Caldwell, and Thomas Wolfe are authentic Southern writers, not so much by reason of their material as by this temper. Violence, the long search, the ironic social joke, the blundering, childlike adult, the casual blasphemy—all are integral in their Southern imagination. Even had their books extra-Southern settings, they would, like Shakespeare's plays, betray their origin.

In Faulkner the theme of violence and confusion is most dominant and is most brilliantly expressed. The wanderer and fugitive are most notable among his characters, and the restless journey among his plots. The plot of *As I Lay Dying* stands as a metaphor of modern Southern life: the inept family, blundering about the hot Mississippi countryside with the decaying body of the mother in an attempt to reach a burial place: the pathetic and incongruously carnal concerns of the burial party in search of a ford, and the unceremonious immersion of the coffin in the river; and at last the fantastic burial. *Pylon* is built around the same theme of confusion, but with an urban setting: the inescapable doom of desperate and non-human stunt flyers in a mechanized era. Or, to turn from the larger elements of plot to character, in *Light in August* there is the unforgettable Hightower, lost in a lawless age, so obsessed by those stable and heroic days of the Confederacy that he could not divorce his preaching from 'galloping cavalry and defeat and glory', preaching like 'a sort of cyclone that did not even need to touch the actual earth. . . . It was as if he couldn't get religion and that galloping cavalry and his dead grandfather shot from the galloping horse untangled from each other . . . born about thirty years after the only day he seemed to have ever lived in'. And in *The Wild Palms*, to take Faulkner's recent novel, there is Henry Wilbourne's frantic search for certainty, his dash to the West, and grief and death and imprisonment as a result of his attempt to find assurance in only himself and another's wife; and there is also the tall convict, swept hither and yon in a great Mississippi flood so that he didn't 'know even where I want to be' or 'where I wanted to go', finally rowing back to prison with a strange woman and her new-born baby and, amidst ludicrous political chicanery, receiving even gratefully the security afforded by ten years added sentence 'if that's the rule'. Significantly enough, Faulkner's *The Unvanquished*, with its Civil War setting, marches more certainly ahead in deliberate action than any of his other books. It is not to be wondered that Faulkner has vouched for the portrayal of the older Mississippi in Stark Young's *So Red the Rose*: 'Lived once? Shucks, those people in your book not only once lived, they are living now.' The stability which Young attributes to his McGehee family and the delirious search in Faulkner's characters are obverse and reverse of the same medal, struck off in the same South.

71. Conrad Aiken, 'William Faulkner: The Novel as Form'

November 1939

Atlantic Monthly, clxiv, 650–4.

Outside of scattered comments in reviews this was the first serious attempt to analyze the function of Faulkner's unusual stylistic devices. Aiken published several volumes of poetry in the 1930s and in 1939 his third novel, *Conversations*.

The famous remark made to Macaulay—'Young man, the more I consider the less can I conceive where you picked up that style'—might with advantage have been saved for Mr. William Faulkner. For if one thing is more outstanding than another about Mr. Faulkner—some readers find it so outstanding, indeed, that they never get beyond it—it is the uncompromising and almost hypnotic zeal with which he insists upon having a style, and, especially of late, the very peculiar style which he insists upon having. Perhaps to that one should add that he insists *when he remembers*—he can write straightforwardly enough when he wants to; he does so often in the best of his short stories (and they are brilliant), often enough, too, in the novels. But that *style* is what he really wants to get back to; and get back to it he invariably does.

And what a style it is, to be sure! The exuberant and tropical luxuriance of sound which Jim Europe's jazz band used to exhale, like a jungle of rank creepers and ferocious blooms taking shape before one's eyes,—magnificently and endlessly intervolved, glisteningly and ophidianly in motion, coil sliding over coil, and leaf and flower forever magically interchanging,—was scarcely more bewildering, in its sheer inexhaustible fecundity, than Mr. Faulkner's style. Small wonder if even the most passionate of Mr. Faulkner's admirers—among whom the present writer honors himself by enlisting—must find, with each new novel, that the first fifty pages are always the hardest, that each time one must learn all over again *how* to read this strangely fluid and slippery and heavily mannered prose, and that one is even, like a kind of Laocoön, sometimes tempted to give it up.

Wrestle, for example, with two very short (for Mr. Faulkner!) sentences, taken from an early page of *Absalom, Absalom!*

Meanwhile, as though in inverse ratio to the vanishing voice, the invoked ghost of the man whom she could neither forgive nor revenge herself upon began to assume a quality almost of solidity, permanence. Itself circumambient and enclosed by its effluvium of hell, its aura of unregeneration, it mused (mused, thought, seemed to possess sentience as if, though dispossessed of the peace—who was impervious anyhow to fatigue—which she declined to give it, it was still irrevocably outside the scope of her hurt or harm) with that quality peaceful and now harmless and not even very attentive—the ogre-shape which, as Miss Coldfield's voice went on, resolved out of itself before Quentin's eyes the two half-ogre children, the three of them forming a shadowy background for the fourth one.

Well, it may be reasonably questioned whether, on page thirteen of a novel, that little cordite bolus of suppressed reference isn't a thumping aesthetic mistake. Returned to, when one has finished the book, it may be as simple as daylight; but encountered for the first time, and no matter how often reread, it guards its enigma with the stony impassivity of the Sphinx.

Or take again from the very first page of *The Wild Palms*—Mr. Faulkner's latest novel, and certainly one of his finest—this little specimen of 'exposition': 'Because he had been born here, on this coast though not in this house but in the other, the residence in town, and had lived here all his life, including the four years at the State University's medical school and the two years as an intern in New Orleans where (a thick man even when young, with thick soft woman's hands, who should never have been a doctor at all, who even after the six more or less metropolitan years looked out from a provincial and insulated amazement at his classmates and fellows: the lean young men swaggering in the drill jackets on which—to him—they wore the myriad anonymous faces of the probationer nurses with a ruthless and assured braggadocio like decorations, like flower trophies) he had sickened for it.' What is one to say of that—or of a sentence only a little lower on the same page which runs for thirty-three lines? Is this, somehow perverted, the influence of the later Henry James—James the Old Pretender?

In short, Mr. Faulkner's style, though often brilliant and always interesting, is all too frequently downright bad; and it has inevitably offered an all-too-easy mark for the sharpshooting of such alert critics as Mr. Wyndham Lewis. But if it is easy enough to make fun of Mr. Faulkner's obsessions for particular words, or his indifference and violence to them, or the parrotlike mechanical mytacism (for it is really like a stammer) with which he will go on endlessly repeating such favorites as 'myriad, sourceless, impalpable, outrageous, risible, profound,' there is nevertheless something more to be said for his passion for overelaborate sentence structure.

Overelaborate they certainly are, baroque and involuted in the extreme, these sentences: trailing clauses, one after another, shadowily in apposition, or perhaps not even with so much connection as that; parenthesis after parenthesis, the parenthesis itself often containing one or more parentheses—they remind one of those brightly colored Chinese eggs of one's childhood, which when opened disclosed egg after egg, each smaller and subtler than the last. It is as if Mr. Faulkner, in a sort of hurried despair, had decided to try to tell us everything, absolutely everything, every last origin or source or quality or qualification, and every possible future or permutation as well, in one terrifically concentrated effort: each sentence to be, as it were, a microcosm. And it must be admitted that the practice is annoying and distracting.

It is annoying, at the end of a sentence, to find that one does not know in the least what was the subject of the verb that dangles *in vacuo* —it is distracting to have to go back and sort out the meaning, track down the structure from clause to clause, then only to find that after all it doesn't much matter, and that the obscurity was perhaps neither subtle nor important. And to the extent that one *is* annoyed and distracted, and *does* thus go back and work it out, it may be at once added that Mr. Faulkner has defeated his own ends. One has had, of course, to emerge from the stream, and to step away from it, in order properly to see it; and as Mr. Faulkner works precisely by a process of *immersion*, of hypnotizing his reader into *remaining immersed* in his stream, this occasional blunder produces irritation and failure.

Nevertheless, despite the blunders, and despite the bad habits and the willful bad writing (and willful it obviously is), the style as a whole is extraordinarily effective; the reader *does* remain immersed, *wants* to remain immersed, and it is interesting to look into the reasons for this. And at once, if one considers these queer sentences not simply by themselves, as monsters of grammar or awkwardness, but in their relation to the book as a whole, one sees a functional reason and necessity for their being as they are. They parallel in a curious and perhaps inevitable way, and not without aesthetic justification, the whole elaborate method of *deliberately withheld meaning*, of progressive and partial and delayed disclosure, which so often gives the characteristic shape to the novels themselves. It is a persistent offering of obstacles, a calculated system of screens and obtrusions, of confusions and ambiguous interpolations and delays, with one express purpose; and that purpose is simply to keep the form—and the idea—fluid and unfinished, still in motion, as it were, and unknown, until the dropping into place of the very last syllable.

What Mr. Faulkner is after, in a sense, is a *continuum*. He wants a medium without stops or pauses, a medium which is always *of the moment*, and of which the passage from moment to moment is as fluid and undetectable as in the life itself which he is purporting to give. It is all inside and underneath, or as seen from within and below; the reader must therefore be steadily *drawn in*; he must be powerfully and unremittingly hypnotized inward and downward to that image-stream; and this suggests, perhaps, a reason not only for the length and elaborateness of the sentence structure, but for the repetitiveness as well. The repetitiveness, and the steady iterative emphasis—like a kind of chanting or invocation—on certain relatively abstract words ('sonorous, latin, *vaguely* eloquent'), have the effect at last of producing, for Mr. Faulkner, a special language, a conglomerate of his own, which he uses with an astonishing virtuosity, and which, although in detailed analysis it may look shoddy, is actually for his purpose a life stream of almost miraculous adaptability. At the one extreme it is abstract, cerebral, time-and-space-obsessed, tortured and twisted, but nevertheless always with a living *pulse* in it; and at the other it can be as overwhelming in its simple vividness, its richness in the actual, as the flood scenes in *The Wild Palms*.

Obviously, such a style, especially when allied with such a *concern* for method, must make difficulties for the reader; and it must be admitted that Mr. Faulkner does little or nothing as a rule to make his highly complex 'situation' easily available or perceptible. The reader must simply make up his mind to go to work, and in a sense to cooperate; his reward being that there *is* a situation to be given shape, a meaning to be extracted, and that half the fun is precisely in watching the queer, difficult, and often so laborious evolution of Mr. Faulkner's idea. And not so much idea, either, as form. For, like the great predecessor whom at least in this regard he so oddly resembles, Mr. Faulkner could say with Henry James that it is practically impossible to make any real distinction between theme and form. What immoderately delights him, alike in *Sanctuary*, *The Sound and the Fury*, *As I Lay Dying*, *Light in August*, *Pylon*, *Absalom, Absalom!* and now again in *The Wild Palms*, and what sets him above—shall we say it firmly—all his American contemporaries, is his continuous preoccupation with the novel *as form*, his passionate concern with it, and a degree of success with it which would clearly have commanded the interest and respect of Henry James himself. The novel as revelation, the novel as slice-of-life, the novel as mere story, do not interest him: these he would say, like James again, 'are the circumstances of the interest,' but not the interest itself. The interest itself will be the use to which these circumstances are put, the degree to which they can be organized.

From this point of view, he is not in the least to be considered as a mere 'Southern' writer: the 'Southernness' of his scenes and characters is of little concern to him, just as little as the question whether they are pleasant or unpleasant, true or untrue. Verisimilitude—or, at any rate, *degree* of verisimilitude—he will cheerfully abandon, where necessary, if the compensating advantages of plan or tone are a sufficient inducement. The famous scene in *Sanctuary* of Miss Reba and Uncle Bud in which a 'madam' and her cronies hold a wake for a dead gangster, while the small boy gets drunk, is quite false, taken out of its context; it is not endowed with the same *kind* of actuality which permeates the greater part of the book at all. Mr. Faulkner was cunning enough to see that a two-dimensional cartoon-like statement, at this juncture, would supply him with the effect of a chorus, and without in the least being perceived as a change in the temperature of truthfulness.

That particular kind of dilution, or adulteration, of verisimilitude was both practised and praised by James: as when he blandly admitted of *In the Cage* that his central character was 'too ardent a focus of divination' to be quite credible. It was defensible simply because it made possible the coherence of the whole, and was itself absorbed back into the luminous texture. It was for him a device for organization, just as the careful cherishing of 'viewpoint' was a device, whether simply or in counterpoint. Of Mr. Faulkner's devices, of this sort, aimed at the achievement of complex 'form,' the two most constant are the manipulation of viewpoint and the use of the flashback, or sudden shift of time-scene, forward or backward.

In *Sanctuary*, where the alternation of viewpoint is a little lawless, the complexity is given, perhaps a shade disingenuously, by violent shifts in time; a deliberate disarrangement of an otherwise straightforward story. Technically, there is no doubt that the novel, despite its fame, rattles a little; and Mr. Faulkner himself takes pains to disclaim it. But, even done with the left hand, it betrays a genius for form, quite apart from its wonderful virtuosity in other respects. *Light in August*, published a year after *Sanctuary*, repeats the same technique, that of a dislocation of time, and more elaborately; the time-shifts alternate with shifts in the viewpoint; and if the book is a failure it is perhaps because Mr. Faulkner's tendency to what is almost a hypertrophy of form is not here, as well as in the other novels, matched with the characters and the theme. Neither the person nor the story of Joe Christmas is seen fiercely enough—by its creator—to carry off that immense machinery of narrative; it would have needed another Popeye, or another Jiggs and Shumann, another Temple Drake, and for once Mr. Faulkner's inexhaustible inventiveness seems to have been at fault. Consequently what we see is an extraordinary power for form functioning relatively *in vacuo*, and existing only to sustain itself.

In the best of the novels, however,—and it is difficult to choose between *The Sound and the Fury* and *The Wild Palms*, with *Absalom, Absalom!* a very close third,—this tendency to hypertrophy of form has been sufficiently curbed; and it is interesting, too, to notice that in all these three (and in that remarkable *tour de force*, *As I Lay Dying*, as well), while there is still a considerable reliance on time-shift, the effect of richness and complexity is chiefly obtained by a very skillful fugue-like alternation of viewpoint. Fugue-like in *The Wild Palms*—and fugue-like especially, of course, in *As I Lay Dying*, where the shift is kaleidoscopically rapid, and where, despite an astonishing violence to plausibility (in the reflections, and *language* of reflection, of the characters) an effect of the utmost reality and immediateness is nevertheless produced. Fugue-like, again, in *Absalom, Absalom!* where indeed one may say the form is really circular—there is no beginning and no ending properly speaking, and therefore no *logical* point of entrance: we must just submit, and follow the circling of the author's interest, which turns a light inward towards the centre, but every moment from a new angle, a new point of view. The story unfolds, therefore, now in one color of light, now in another, with references backward and forward: those that refer forward being necessarily, for the moment, blind. What is complete in Mr. Faulkner's pattern, *a priori*, must nevertheless remain incomplete for us until the very last stone is in place; what is 'real,' therefore at one stage of the unfolding, or from one point of view, turns out to be 'unreal' from another; and we find that one among other things with which we are engaged is the fascinating sport of trying to separate truth from legend, watching the growth of legend from truth, and finally reaching the conclusion that the distinction is itself false.

Something of the same sort is true also of *The Sound and the Fury*—and this, with its massive four-part symphonic structure, is perhaps the most beautifully *wrought* of the whole series, and an indubitable masterpiece of what James loved to call the 'fictive art.' The joinery is flawless in its intricacy; it is a novelist's novel—a whole textbook on the craft of fiction in itself, comparable in its way to *What Maisie Knew* or *The Golden Bowl.*

But if it is important, for the moment, to emphasize Mr. Faulkner's genius for form, and his continued exploration of its possibilities, as against the usual concern with the violence and dreadfulness of his themes—though we might pause to remind carpers on this score of the fact that the best of Henry James is precisely that group of last novels which so completely concerned themselves with moral depravity—it is also well to keep in mind his genius for invention, whether of character or episode. The inventiveness is of the richest possible sort—a headlong and tumultuous abundance, an exuberant generosity and vitality, which makes most other contemporary fiction look very pale and chaste indeed. It is an unforgettable gallery of portraits, whether character or caricature, and all of them endowed with a violent and immediate vitality.

'He is at once'—to quote once more from James—'one of the most corrupt of writers and one of the most naïf, the most mechanical and pedantic, and the fullest of *bonhomie* and natural impulse. He is one of the finest of artists and one of the coarsest. Viewed in one way, his novels are ponderous, shapeless, overloaded; his touch is graceless, violent, barbarous. Viewed in another, his tales have more color, more composition, more grasp of the reader's attention than any others. [His] style would demand a chapter apart. It is the least simple style, probably, that was ever written; it bristles, it cracks, it swells and swaggers; but it is a perfect expression of the man's genius. Like his genius, it contains a certain quantity of everything, from immaculate gold to flagrant dross. He was a very bad writer, and yet unquestionably he was a very great writer. We may say briefly, that in so far as his method was an instinct it was successful, and that in so far as it was a theory it was a failure. But both in instinct and in theory he had the aid of an immense force of conviction. His imagination warmed to its work so intensely that there was nothing his volition could not impose upon it. Hallucination settled upon him, and he believed anything that was necessary in the circumstances.'

That passage, from Henry James's essay on Balzac, is almost word for word, with scarcely a reservation, applicable to Mr. Faulkner. All that is lacking is Balzac's greater *range* of understanding and tenderness, his greater freedom from special preoccupations. For this, one would hazard the guess that Mr. Faulkner has the gifts—and time is still before him.

THE HAMLET

New York, April 1940
London, September 1940

72. F. W. Dupee, review, *New York Sun*

2 April 1940, 40

Frederick W. Dupee (b. 1904) was affiliated in the 1930s with *New Masses* and *Partisan Review*. He taught for many years at Columbia University.

It is a common device of satire to show animals in the role of men. A more unusual and perhaps subtler way of excoriating human weakness is to show men behaving like animals. And this is the kind of satire which certain Southern writers of today seem to be practicing. For the poverty-debased humanity of the South exhibits in their most naked form the cruelties and lusts that lie buried in people everywhere. So in *Tobacco Road* Erskine Caldwell gave you more than a genre picture of domestic misery among share-croppers. He showed you the jungle passions rooted in all family life, no matter how civilized.

William Faulkner, though less frankly a satirist than Caldwell, less clear as to his aims in general, exploits his Southern material in much the same fashion. It is the satirical impulse, indeed, which accounts for the celebrated violence and extravagance of these writers. They are the remote descendants of Ben Jonson.

In *The Hamlet* Faulkner's anger at humanity has put forth another bitter flower. All the usual Faulknerian passions are in it, but primarily it is a tale—or rather a string of anecdotes—about money, greed and rapacity as typified by a family named Snopes. The weasel-like Snopes lurked in the background of several of Faulkner's early novels. Here they swarm out of their holes and literally overrun the country.

[summarizes story]

Flem is the archetype of the Snopeses, the super Snopes. And Faulkner seems to have conceived him as a kind of inverted folk-hero, a Paul Bunyan of the cashbox, the sort of rogue who incarnates the desperate fantasies of poor and envious men. In any case he is at the bottom of everything that happens in the story and he gives it a certain unity. Otherwise it is simply a series of episodes, and episodes, moreover, which are quite uneven in quality. The tale of the wild horses which Flem imports from Texas and contrives to sell to his neighbors against their better judgment is as vivid as Mark Twain. Then there is the story of Eula Varner, who has to be driven to school because she is too lazy to walk. The episode is wonderfully amusing so long as it keeps to the level of an extravagant anecdote; but once Eula's passivity is made to symbolize the eternal female, the thing is ruined with lushness and cheapness. And so it is with most of the other episodes: that of Mink Snopes, who kills a man in a feud and is in turn attacked by hounds. In nearly every case Faulkner's exuberance gets the better of his taste and intelligence. You grow tired of big swaggering adjectives like 'outrageous,' 'incredible,' 'irrevocable.' You seem to hear the author licking his lips over the too too 'inscrutable' Flem Snopes, the too too 'pleasant' Ratliff. And his oblique way of telling a story is becoming a mannerism. A French critic once said that Faulkner's narrative method gave you the feeling of riding in a car backwards: you only perceive things when they already have passed. In *The Hamlet* the landscape is so thick with involved and flying events that the rider becomes a little sick and dizzy.

Certainly Faulkner is the most brilliant and fertile novelist in America today. Yet critics have always deplored his tendency toward disorder and inflation. These tendencies seem to be gaining on him in his recent work. And *The Hamlet*, which appears to have been planned as a sort of parable of the workings of monopoly capitalism, falls a little short of its intentions.

73. Burton Rascoe, 'Faulkner's New York Critics,' *American Mercury*

June 1940, i, 243–7

Rascoe (1892–1957), a journalist and editor, was for many years himself a 'New York critic.' By this time the *American Mercury* had strongly conservative politics.

William Faulkner certainly goes to the heads of New York reviewers who have never lived in the South and know nothing about it. His new novel, *The Hamlet*, causes Mr. Milton Rugoff of the New York *Herald Tribune* to commit Adonic verse (that Greek verse form consisting of a dactyl followed by a spondee), which he sets forth in the straight line of prose. Let's break it up, boys, thus:

— ◡ ◡ — — — ◡ — —
Out of the / rank hu/mus of / de cay
Formed by the mouldered traditions and the
Rotted manor mansions of the Old South
Crawls a breed of characters
Who call William Faulkner master.
Rising, like marsh phantasms, out of the
Mississippi bottomlands and the canebrakes,
They come to play out their grotesque dramas
On the stage of each of his novels.
Debased by poverty, degenerate through inbreeding,
They struggle hopelessly with the soil,
Cheat, lie, murder and commit acts
Of such depravity
As beggars description.

Isn't that a lulu? Mr. Rugoff ought to be writing those poetic prose introductions for Hollywood historical sagas—those runes which roll on and on until you begin to gag or go to sleep, just before the colossal drama begins; those scanned, sonorous runes, printed on the film with Spencer Tracy and Robert Young eating acorns and wading through rapids in the background. Mr. Rugoff has talents which are lost in book-reviewing. Maybe it's a little unfair to call attention to his misapplied talents. For, after all, he is only typical of the New York reviewers whose brains are so easily addled by a Faulkner novel.[1]

Mr. Faulkner probably gets more fun out of reading the New York reviews of his novels than he gets out of writing the novels. He is a sardonic soul; and I can easily see him as he sits at his typewriter, cooking up a tall tale—for the fun of it, to be sure, but also for the further fun of seeing how New York reviewers swallow it. Take Mr. Rugoff, but only because he is representative of the way New York reviewers, including Clifton Fadiman, write *apropos* a Faulkner novel. He has got into his mind the idea that down South—where it is inconceivable that he has ever been—there are 'rotted manor mansions,' in which 'crawl a breed of characters' who are 'debased by poverty, degenerate through inbreeding,' who 'struggle hopelessly with the soil' and who 'cheat and lie and murder and commit acts of such depravity as beggars description.' The multitudinous fallacies which go to make up the machinery of his thinking are compact in those quotations. But they are not idiosyncratic with Mr. Rugoff: they are typical of what passes for intellectual accoutrements in the quasi-intellectual circles of New York.

Has Mr. Rugoff never read Marcel Proust? Is it his conception from reading Proust that France is a country entirely populated by Barons Charlus? Does he imagine that the functionary who examines his baggage at Le Havre or Bordeaux and inquires, 'No cigar, no cigarette, no *chocolat*?' is a degenerate whose psychopathic compulsions put him in constant fear of the police? Does he conclude from Proust that his innocent *concierge* owns a hotel, secretly, in which to conduct Heliogabalian debaucheries such as Proust describes? If Mr. Rugoff doesn't think so, why does he (and so many of his naïve fellow reviewers) imagine that the South is filled with rotted old mansions, swarming with degenerates? He must have seen that picture taken by Margaret Bourke-White in Clinton, Louisiana, and reproduced in *You Have Seen Their Faces*, by Erskine Caldwell and Miss White. It shows a young

[1] Rugoff's review, which appeared 31 March, is actually quite favorable; and though he does emphasize Faulkner's preoccupation with abnormality, he also praises the humor, 'a humor that comes sometimes out of the very excess of horror, a humor like that evoked by the subhuman images that stare back at us from crazy mirrors.' Although Rascoe correctly points out the frequent failure of reviewers to recognize Faulkner's humor, New York reviewers, including May Cameron, Harold Strauss, and Ralph Thompson, generally gave *The Hamlet* favorable reviews.

woman sitting, with a child on her lap, on the steps of an ante-bellum mansion. There are five huge Doric pillars visible, so there must be eight huge Doric pillars altogether. The pillars are potmarked, weather-worn, scarred and scratched; rubble has accumulated at their bases and on the steps. The caption reads: 'I don't know what ever happened to the family that built this house before the War. A lot of families live here now. My husband and me moved in and get two rooms for five dollars a month.' That is the only picture of its kind that Miss Bourke-White seems to have found in the South. And I doubt very much that Miss Bourke-White would say that the quite personable young woman —a woman much more personable than nine out of ten of the women I have seen at the Stork Club or the Colony—is 'debased by poverty, degenerate through inbreeding,' and given to 'cheat and lie and murder and commit such acts of depravity as beggars description.' Let us not shed any tears about this 'rotted old mansion' in Clinton, Louisiana. There are fewer of these rotted old mansions *in the entire South* than you will find in a motor drive 100 miles North from Spuyten Duyvil—the first thing you see to your right, after you cross the Henrik Hudson bridge is an abandoned monstrosity of architecture built by some big-wig.

Have these reviewers read the conclusions of the Rockefeller Institute's researches on inbreeding and outbreeding? Not only are the finest cattle and the finest horses, but also the finest animals of all sorts —including men—often produced by inbreeding. The reviewers apparently get their scientific knowledge from a quack book which was supposed to be a history of an anonymous 'Jukes' family in Northern New York. That book was a sort of Bible of Eugenists Society in the 'nineties. All the members of the 'Jukes' family were alleged to have come to bad ends on account of inbreeding. The Eugenists set up a family—The Jonathan Edwardses—who were supposed to have been exemplars of what outbreeding can do in the way of making great statesmen, law-makers, generalissimos, etc. Clarence Darrow, trying to use this 'Jukes' family myth to clear a client of a murder charge, learned too much about their history for his client's good. He made such an exhaustive study of the 'Jukeses' and the Edwardses, that he discovered that the descendants of the 'Jukeses' were faring quite as well, in his generation, as the descendants of the Edwardses. Moreover, they conspicuously showed more intelligence.

Perhaps Mr. Faulkner's greatest fault is that he doesn't write *down* to the knowledge and experience of his New York reviewers. Maybe he ought to write a confidential letter to all of them, explaining in the simplest terms that what they are liable to take as profound criticism of the socio-economic situation in the South and as a document of utmost social significance, is only a joke which every Southern reader will understand. But I suppose if he did this they would conclude he hasn't the real stuff in him; that he is a jackanapes and not serious the way they imagined him to be.

Let's take an example. I have seen no New York review of *The Hamlet* which shows the slightest indication that the reviewer got the point of the longest and best tale in the novel—one of the most hilarious tall tales in all literature. They all took it seriously. The tale is Ratliff's about the horse traders. It is far better than *David Harum*. And yet it is in the strictest tradition of oral tall tales in the South. It runs for page after page—with interruptions—like all Southern horsetrading tales. The teller tries to see how long he can drag the thing out and still keep his audience, before he arrives at the masterpiece of his imagination. He tells dozens of stories of contests between two horse-traders both of whom think they are pretty slick. That is only to lead up to the tall tale the teller has thought up. Faulkner has followed this tradition. He wins the prize.

What is the climax story in Ratliff's recital? It is that, after two horse-and-mule traders have tried for a long time to out-smart each other, the really smart guy trades back to the sap the horse the sap has brought in to palm off on the smart guy. The sap, going into town to cheat the smart trader, feeds a spavined and decrepit horse gobs of salt with his fodder, so the horse will drink a lot of water at every creek on the way to town and thus swell out his belly until he *looks* pretty good. Besides that, the sap has covered the nag with shoe-polish to make the sorrel look like a roan. The slick trader spots the deception, sends the sap away from his auction tent into town under some sort of pretext, turns the hose on the horse, washing off the shoe-polish, and then gets busy. He opens up a hole in the horse's foreshoulder, according to Ratliff (who goes into such precise nonsensical details that they would fool a New York reviewer who never saw a horse except in a parade) and, with a bicycle pump, pumps in air all over the horse's body, between skin and flesh, until the nag looks like a percheron! Then he trades it back to the sap. The horse falls apart twenty minutes after the trade is made.

Mr. Faulkner never even suspects that New York reviewers can be so ignorant of physiology that they accept such a tale literally and don't know you can't pump up a horse with a bicycle pump. When he writes superb stories like that and I see how New York reviewers take them, I begin to believe that the South ought to secede again. What's the use of writing if you have to submit what you write to the critical estimate of persons who haven't the slightest idea what your words mean? It doesn't help if the reviewer goes enthusiastically gaga or writes Adonic verse in praise; for, after all, he is praising you for something you haven't written and never had any intention of writing.

Mr. Faulkner is an extremely talented man, with a fine sense of values, which is sometimes confused by his inordinate comic sense. It is his misfortune—and his fortune perhaps—to be ecstatically praised by people who haven't the vaguest notion what he is writing about.

74. Unsigned review, *Times Literary Supplement*

21 September 1940, 481

It is not a bit of good—Mr. Faulkner's talent may be prodigious and highbrow fans of his and the critically knowing in general may be right in singing his praises, but he is difficult to read. He is, at any rate, more nearly unreadable in this new novel than in any previous one. In the past one was willing, up to a point, to put up with his terrific churning of words and his laboured passion for violence because some sort of queer illumination of mind or soul showed through. Here everything is as incomprehensibly opaque as the eyes of Flem Snopes, Mr. Faulkner's lunatic marionette of a hero. Those who find this novelist 'one of the few significant writers of our age, &c., &c.,' have heard of the Snopes before. What they will make of this full-length study of the sinister Flem there is no means of telling.

[summarizes story]

It is a chaotic narrative, and the chaos is deepened by what seems to be a degree of mystification in the telling even more deliberate than that exhibited in earlier books by this author. His copiousness of language is as remarkable as ever, but here it takes on the character of mere intoxication; the spinning and winding sentences are yards long, crammed with trivial detail or flamboyant imagery, and not once in a hundred times does a clear picture emerge from them. The time-sequence seems, as usual, fantastically erratic, and is made more bewildering by long-winded anecdotal digressions. And, on the dismally characteristic subject of Eula Varner and her aura of sexual energy, fecund nature and the rest, Mr. Faulkner's gush of words, if one may say so, is rather silly. He has, it is plain, unusual aspirations and commanding gifts of a secondary importance in the writing of fiction, but there seems little sense in the use he makes of them here.

75. Robert Penn Warren, 'The Snopes World,' *Kenyon Review*

Spring 1941, iii, 253–7

Warren's first novel, *Night Rider*, came out in 1939. It deals with a tobacco war in Kentucky in approximately the same time period as *The Hamlet*. In 1938 and 1943 respectively Warren and Cleanth Brooks published their very influential textbooks, *Understanding Poetry* and *Understanding Fiction*, texts that brought the emphasis on close reading of literature typical of the New Criticism to classrooms around America.

The Hamlet is William Faulkner's fourteenth published book of prose fiction. With its opening sentence it proclaims itself a part of that world of Jefferson, Mississippi, and its back country, which has been the scene of almost all of Faulkner's fiction: 'Frenchman's Bend was a section of rich river-bottom country lying twenty miles southeast of Jefferson.' By its sub-title, 'A Novel of the Snopes Family,' it proclaims a personal, and perhaps thematic, as well as geographical and sociological continuity with the previous books, for members of the Snopes family have appeared before and have already defined for themselves a characteristic rôle. But the relation of *The Hamlet* to Faulkner's other books has, naturally, other aspects, aspects concerning which various reviewers have bitterly contradicted each other. For instance, one prominent reviewer has professed to see a new development in the Faulkner of *The Hamlet*, a new, healthy, earthy humor, a new realism, an issuing forth from the moonlit 'gothic ruins' of the earlier books into the light of day. It is difficult to understand how the reviewer could commit himself to the opinion that such elements, however they may be interpreted, are new in Faulkner, for the best examples of this 'new' humor, the 'tall-tale' episode of the Texas ponies and that of the horse-swapping, appeared some years ago as short stories and are only slightly rewritten for the present occasion; and in any case, humor, though humor of a peculiar ambivalence, has not been absent even from novels like *Sanctuary* and *Light in August*. Another reviewer, taking exactly the opposite approach to *The Hamlet*, has seen here, in the story of the idiot Snopes's fixation on the cow, the ultimate and irresponsible development of what he interprets as Faulkner's obsession with the horrible and disgusting. Each of these reviewers is, apparently, so much concerned with a certain aspect of the atmosphere of *The Hamlet* (one finds humor, one finds disgust, dominant) that he never feels it incumbent upon him to investigate the relation of the aspect which engages his attention to the totality of the novel. On the evidence of the particular aspect taken in isolation, the reviewer has leaped to an evaluation, when it would seem that evaluation is impossible until after an investigation of the total structure of the book—that is, of the relation of the horror, for example, to the other factors. It may be objected that such an investigation is necessary only to a purely aesthetic evaluation of the book, but I suggest that the purely moral evaluation is also impossible without such an investigation. The second critic implies that Faulkner's work is morally reprehensible, that he invites us to 'let our virgin fancies wallow in the sloughs of Zolaism.' But before accepting such a view, we should perhaps try to discover what such a story as that of the idiot Snopes and the cow is intended to mean in the novel—however disgusting and horrible it may be in isolation. One is entitled to know the moral intention at least, before accepting the moral judgment.

[summarizes story]

A good starting point for any discussion of the frame of ideas in Faulkner's work is provided by an essay published in this journal (Summer, 1939) by George Marion O'Donnell, 'Faulkner's Mythology,' which is probably the most enlightening and provocative commentary yet written on the subject. Mr. O'Donnell sees the basic situation in Faulkner's work as a conflict between the Sartoris world and the Snopes world, between traditionalism and modernism, between humanism and naturalism. 'It is a universal conflict. The Sartorises act traditionally; that is to say, they always act with an ethically responsible will. They represent vital morality, humanism. Being anti-traditional, the Snopeses are immoral from the Sartoris point-of-view. But the Snopeses do not recognize this point-of-view; acting only from self-interest, they acknowledge no ethical duty. Really, then, they are a-moral; they represent naturalism or animalism.' The Sartoris world is fighting a losing fight, and is either finally corrupted by a direct acceptance of the Snopes world, as in *The Sound and the Fury*, or betrayed, in combatting the Snopes world, by a traditional response so formalized and isolated that it has no reference to the immediate realities of the situation, as in the story 'There Was a Queen.' But Mr. O'Donnell has not, as the Sartoris–Snopes antithesis would seem to imply, intended an aristocrat-Snopes opposition. He attributes to the family of *As I Lay Dying* the same 'ethical will' which is possessed by the Sartoris world.

In *The Hamlet*, the Sartoris world does not, specifically, appear. There is, in the background, the gutted ruin of a mansion, but no one even remembers the name of the man who built it. Nor does the past (which is so important in so much of Faulkner's fiction) appear; or rather, it appears only in so far as it is implied by the fact that Frenchman's Bend is an old community which has developed its own stable way of life and wisdom. The contrast here, then, is between the non-aristocratic Frenchman's Bend world, unconscious of its past, and the Snopes world, which Ratliff, the characteristic Faulkner commentator, recognizes as the enemy. But even within the Snopes world differences are to be discriminated. Ab's amiable habit of barn-burning is non-Snopes in its motivation, a kind of vengeance for his defeat, an act of pride; Mink's murder of Houston, too, springs from his long defeated pride. There is some human element in them, contrasted with the pure Snopes mind, which can demand of Mink, 'Do you mean to tell me you never even looked?'—never even looked in the victim's pockets—and which can then try to exploit the murderer's crime; or contrasted with Flem, who has no pride to forbid his marriage with Varner's pregnant daughter, or contrasted with Lump, who can try to make a good thing of exhibiting his idiot cousin's perversion.

The structure of the book depends on the intricate patterning of contrasts, for instance, the contrast of the Flem-Eula story with the Houston-wife story, the Eula-seducer story, and the idiot-cow story. In this connection, I am not sure that Mr. O'Donnell's terminology can be strictly applied. Flem does not stand, it seems to me, as 'naturalism or animalism' in the terms of the contrast; he stands outside the scale which runs from the idiot to Houston, from groping animalism to a secret poetry; in his cunning, he stands beyond appetite, passion, pride, fidelity, exploiting all of those things. Nor do I see him as equated with the barn-storming aviators of *Pylon*, whom Mr. O'Donnell interprets as the dehumanized products of a world dominated by 'naturalism or animalism'; the aviators are mixed cases, I imagine, for in their complete lack of calculation and lack of concern about the future, they exhibit a sort of heroism, the stoical discipline of the Hemingway hero, who by his discipline tries to humanize at least some corner of the world. But Flem is all calculation. In Faulkner's mythology, however, Flem, as pure Snopes, may represent modernism, as Mr. O'Donnell suggests; and if this is so, the ironical point of *The Hamlet* is that, in the end, Flem gets Eula Varner, the fertility goddess, but only after she has been possessed, willingly, by her first violent, courageous lover, and only after we know that she has always referred to Flem as 'that man'—a nameless creature.

Before concluding this review I should like to comment on a certain formal difference between *The Hamlet* and Faulkner's other novels. In the previous novels, as Conrad Aiken has pointed out, Faulkner has exhibited a concern very much like James's concern with fictional organization. His movement has not been linear, but spiral, passing over the same point again and again, but at different altitudes. From this method has derived the peculiar suspense which is present in Faulkner's best work. But in *The Hamlet* there is no such central suspense; the various stories refer, finally, to Flem, the various contrasts are patterned about the theme, but in comparison with *Light in August*, for instance, the effect is loose and casual. It might be argued that for the present purpose the form is adequate, but I hope that the author will not cease to concern himself with the formal problems which have apparently engaged him in earlier work and which, sometimes, he has so brilliantly solved.

76. H. E. Bates on Faulkner's style

1941

The Modern Short Story: A Critical Survey (London, Thomas Nelson, 1941), 181–3.

Bates (1905–74) was a short story writer, novelist, and critic from the English Midlands.

Faulkner is contemporary with Hemingway. Of the same embittered generation, soured less by the futility of war than the aftermath, he is a disoriented romantic. His early stories dealt, like *A Farewell to Arms*, with the war in Europe, and were largely of flying; in these stories he was striving, like Hemingway, to use a stricter, more rigidly muscular language than literature had previously known, but for various reasons he never mastered it. Language, and the emotion behind it, always mastered him; Hemingway pruned the branches of his style until they stood clean as skeletons; Faulkner began by pruning, only to allow the tree to break and blossom more prodigiously, so that at last he could luxuriate in its shade. As he went on, turning from the stories of war in Europe to stories of the older, perhaps more cynical war in the Southern states, where white is at war with negro even down to the segregative notices in public places, Faulkner permitted himself more and more the luxury of a warmer, more emotional style. This gives his stories a certain shapelessness, almost florid beside the spare boniness of Hemingway, together with a quality of atmospheric passion and grandeur which Hemingway never aimed to achieve. Faulkner's subjects being what they are—the decaying Southern aristocracy, passionate spinsterhood, mass fury, racial injustice, murder, sexual conflict, and so on, and his backgrounds being what they are—the decaying Southern towns steeped by sunlight with a kind of ominous lethargy, this floridity, passion, and high atmospheric pressure all seem legitimate and in keeping. For Faulkner is primarily an atmospheric writer. His stories owe their life not to rigidity of structure, to clean energy of direction, to the denial of emotion, but to strength of mood. Once that mood is caught and then held by the corresponding rhythms of Faulkner's recklessly beautiful style, nothing can break it; the emotional force must play itself out. The characters too are caught up by the dark forces of these moods, and are borne relentlessly on to tragic and predestined conclusions.

[quotes from chapter 5 of *Light in August*, 'He went on, passing still between the homes of the white people. . . .']

The manner has a parallel in Conrad, whose characters also are shaped less by conscious and rational forces than by the vaguer, larger forces of atmosphere and destiny. And the characters too have a certain resemblance; for if Conrad reserves his deepest pity for the isolated, for men in lonely conflict against the forces of existence and destiny, Faulkner reserves his for the oppressed: the poor, the negroes, the beaten children, the frustrated, the decaying aristocracy, the frightened, and the framed. There is anger in his work: the social anger of a romantic gifted, or cursed, with a realistic pair of eyes. For Faulkner, like others of us, can never reconcile the opposing forces of existence, the justice and injustice, the simplicity and the cynicism, the beauty and the ugliness; he can never align life as it is with life as it seems to be. Out of this natural and discomforting conflict arises the righteous moody anger of his work.

Such a manner, shaped by so much that is emotional, is bound to have many faults difficult to eradicate. In spite of these—a certain affected poeticism and turgidity, a striving for atmospheric effect, a tendency to introduce violence for its own sake, and some attempt at verbal experiment—Faulkner's stories must and should be read. He makes many mistakes, but they are the mistakes essential to a talent that cannot stand still.

77. Warren Beck, 'Faulkner's Point of View'

May 1941

College English, ii, 736–49.

Beck, an American novelist and critic, wrote four articles on Faulkner in the early 1940s, this, one on 'Faulkner and the South,' and two on his style. In 1961 he published *Man in Motion*, a study of the Snopes trilogy. His first collection of stories, *The Blue Sash*, came out in 1941. For many years he taught at Lawrence College in Wisconsin.

Criticism of William Faulkner's novels has diverged conspicuously between two tendencies. Some of the most discerning have praised Faulkner highly; for instance, six years ago Mark Van Doren spoke of his possessing 'one of the greatest natural gifts to be found anywhere in America,' and Conrad Aiken's recent article in the *Atlantic* was on the whole constructively appreciative.[1] Even Henry Seidel Canby, after having written of *Sanctuary* that it showed 'no concern for significance,' 'no predilection for "ought,"' came around two years later to say of *Light in August*, 'It is a novel of extraordinary force and insight . . . and filled with that spirit of compassion which saves those who look at life too closely from hardness and despair. . . . I think that no one can deny it the praise of life caught in its intensities both good and bad.' Yet much journalistic criticism of Faulkner has continued to be detractory, sometimes even abusive; and such is almost always the tone toward him in those volumes on contemporary fiction which American professors write for their students and for one another.

This failure of much American criticism properly to evaluate and support the novels of William Faulkner seems based chiefly on two erroneous propositions—first, that Faulkner has no ideas, no point of view, and, second, that consequently he is melodramatic, a mere

[1] Van Doren's comment appears in a review of *Pylon* in the *New York Herald Tribune*, 24 March 1935. Canby's review of *Light in August* appeared in *Saturday Review of Literature*, 8 October 1932.

sensationalist. One academic critic has called his work the *reductio ad absurdum* of American naturalism and complains that there is 'no cosmic echo . . . behind his atrocities'; another calls Faulkner's profound masterpiece *Absalom, Absalom!* disappointing, in that it presents 'an experience of limited value'; another says Faulkner 'is not a novelist of ideas but of mood and action, physical and psychic'—as though mood and action were antithetical to ideas, instead of their legitimate artistic media in fiction. Of Faulkner's whole work a dogmatic sectarian critic (who within three pages makes four mistakes of fact about the stories) says that 'to read these books is to cross a desert of terrifying nihilism' and accuses Faulkner of almost mathematically computing a maximum of shock. Another, characterizing *Light in August* as 'murder and rape turning on the spit over the flames of arson,' says that in this book 'nothing is omitted, except virtue.'

One of the most recent insults to Faulkner's artistic integrity is Burton Rascoe's suggestion that he plays with his material and his readers, that he writes with his tongue in his cheek. Following the vogue of denying Faulkner any philosophic outlook and purpose, another academician accuses him of 'the calculated manufacture of superfluous horrors.' 'He is a belated literary descendant of Edgar Allen Poe,' writes one of the professors, in a favorite and utterly false correlation. 'He works like Poe,' says another, 'to freeze the reader's blood'; still another says, 'He stresses the grotesque and horrible to the point where they become simply ludicrous.' Taking up where the pedagogues leave off, one leading periodical reviewer hurls the epithet 'Mississippi Frankenstein'; another, in a title, sums up Faulkner's achievement as 'witchcraft.'

Perhaps the most obvious of these errors is the comparison to Poe. The association of ideas is typical of these critics' superficiality; Poe deals in horror, Faulkner presents horror—therefore Faulkner is like Poe. Horror is of different kinds, however. The essence of Poe's frightful fiction is unreality, product of a morbid taste for prearranged nightmares and self-induced hallucinations, that narcissism of the imagination which is the seamy side of romanticism. Faulkner, on the other hand, is a brilliant realist. In Poe's most typical stories there is little evidence that he studied other human beings, but it seems certain that Faulkner, like his character Gavin Stevens the attorney, might have been seen 'squatting among the overalls on the porches of country stores for a whole summer afternoon, talking to them in their own idiom about nothing at all.'

Indeed, if Faulkner in all his work does not have his eye studiously on the object, a locale and its *dramatis personae*, his has been a very foresighted piece of fabrication, for *The Hamlet*, published in 1940 but telling a story of the 1890's, is glanced back at in its details in *As I Lay Dying* (1930) and in *Sanctuary* (1931), and there are many other systematic connections back and forth between the novels, especially in reference to the tribes of Sartoris, Compson, Sutpen, and Snopes. On the map of Yoknapatawpha County appended to *Absalom, Absalom!* Faulkner writes himself down as 'sole owner and proprietor,' but this community centering in Jefferson either has more than a coincidental resemblance, however synthetic, to real Mississippians white, black, and brown, or else William Faulkner is running both God and the devil a close second as a creator and confounder of human beings. Unmistakably, whatever horror there is in Faulkner—and there is a great deal—is out of life.

It may be the very brilliance of Faulkner's realism that has confused others of the critics; details may have so startled them that they have missed the subtle implications of idea in the novels. Certainly the implications are there. While Faulkner differs radically from Poe in being a close observer and realistic reporter of the human tragedy, he departs just as radically from the naturalistic school's baldly objective, documentary method. He is constantly interpretive; he sees his subjects in the light of humane predilections, and thus his realism always intends signification. This lifts his most extreme passages above sensationalism; and striking as his scenes are, his conception of novels as meaningful wholes is still more impressive, at least for qualified attentive readers.

Faulkner's interpretive bent has also led him to transcend the modern realists' cult of a simply factual diction and colloquial construction and to employ instead a full, varied, and individual style. Perhaps, too, some of the unappreciative critics may have evaded the challenge of this style, with its overtone, ellipsis, and suspension, and so may have missed Faulkner's themes in somewhat the way of a high-school student reading *Hamlet* only as a melodramatic series of murders. However, the widely proclaimed frustrations over Faulkner's style, like the revulsions against his realism, will be dispelled once his point of view is grasped, for this style is a powerful instrument handled for the most part with great skill for the realization of his ideas.

William Faulkner's view of human life is one of the most pessimistic ever voiced in fiction, and his writing, like Mr. Compson's 'sloped whimsical ironic hand out of Mississippi attenuated,' is of a predominantly melancholy tone. 'All breath,' he says in *The Wild Palms*, has as its only immortality, 'its infinite capacity for folly and pain.' Not often, however, does Faulkner speak in his own right, out of the omniscience of third-person narrative, for he is devoted to dramatic form and to the perspective it supplies, and most of his stories are told largely through the consciousness of participant characters. And even when Faulkner himself speaks, through third-person narrative, he usually keys his utterance to the mood of the scene and makes himself the lyrical mouthpiece of his characters' experiences. Consequently, it is not possible to comprehend Faulkner's point of view from separate quotations but only from implications in his novels as wholes and from the positions of his various characters in relation to these implied themes.

His critics have sometimes failed to make the necessary distinction between the statements of his dramatic characters and his own ideas. The words of Mr. Compson, 'history is an illusion of philosophers and fools,' are shoved back into Faulkner's own mouth by one recent critic and are made basis for asserting that Faulkner never transcends the level of bare perception but sees the universe as 'bereft of authentic proprieties and the accents of logic,' when certainly his keen sense of authentic proprieties and the accents of logic is part of Faulkner's artistic inspiration—a central part of that superhuman unrest in him which has produced so prolifically and so passionately.

Undoubtedly Faulkner, like any other novelist or dramatist, stands behind some of his characters, but which are his spokesmen cannot be decided except in terms of the preponderance and system of his ideas. Therefore it should be noted, for example, that in *Mosquitoes* it is not Faulkner but the flippant Semitic who declares that man's tendency to follow illusions to his death must be 'some grand cosmic scheme for fertilizing the earth'; it is an ignorant, bitter man crazed by greed for supposed treasure—Armstid in *The Hamlet*—whom the author describes as digging himself 'back into that earth which had produced him to be its born and fated thrall forever until he died'; and it is a man heartbroken by his wife's death—Houston in *The Hamlet*—who felt himself 'victim of a useless and elaborate practical joke at the hands of the prime maniacal Risibility.'

Even Faulkner's dramatization of such negative characters need not mislead the critic if he contemplates such portraits in their entirety—Houston's disenchantment, for instance, does not include a surrender to apathy, for he not only viewed the idiot Ike Snopes at his worst with 'furious exasperation which was not rage but savage contempt and pity for all blind flesh capable of hope and grief,' but he gave the poor fellow what help he could. Thus the reporter in *Pylon* says you 'walk the earth with your arm crooked over your head to dodge until you finally get the old blackjack at last and can lay back down again,' but in spite of that despairing view he is sympathetic and aggressively philanthropic.

Pity is significantly a common emotion among Faulkner's characters. The old justice who appears incidentally but vividly in the closing pages of *The Hamlet* looks at Mrs. Armstid, the victim of her husband's stubborn folly and Flem Snopes's rapacity, 'with pity and grief.' Hightower, in *Light in August*, murmurs 'Poor man. Poor mankind,' and his words encompass not only the negro murderer but his victim and the people who now pursue him. Such humane sensitivity is epitomized when Faulkner calls the reporter in *Pylon* 'patron (even if no guardian) saint of all waifs, all the homeless the desperate and the starved,' and describes him as manifesting 'that air of worn and dreamy fury which Don Quixote must have had.'

In many of Faulkner's stories there is the compassionate troubled observer—Quentin Compson in *The Sound and the Fury* and in *Absalom, Absalom!*, a whole chorus of country folk one by one in *As I Lay Dying*, Benbow in *Sanctuary*, Hightower in *Light in August*, the reporter in *Pylon*, and Ratliff in *The Hamlet*. In *The Unvanquished*, Bayard Sartoris, while closely involved in the action, also evolves into a typical Faulknerian observer as he matures. It is no doubt significant of Faulkner's own attitude that these compassionate observers so largely provide the reflective point of view from which the story is told and thereby determine its moral atmosphere. This typical technique is in itself refutation of the charge that Faulkner is nihilistic and merely sensational. Indeed, it shows that the intention of Faulkner's temperament is idealistic, while its awareness of the preponderant realities of human behavior is pessimistic, and hence its conviction is a melancholy which recoils in protest. This protest is, of course, not didactic but rather inheres in an implicative tone, which the imaginative reader will not miss and will respect for its art as well as its idealism.

The skeptical may test this thesis fairly by re-reading *Sanctuary* (not the most skilful or organic of Faulkner's narratives) with attention fixed primarily on Horace Benbow. His unrest amid hypocrisies and viciousness and his fanatical resistance suffice to throw the events of the book into their true ethical perspective. Faulkner's exuberant and as yet undisciplined realism at times carried him into digression, as with Virgil and Fonzo at Madame Reba's house, or Red's riotous funeral, or the unassimilated and hence anticlimactic documentary chapter on Popeye's youth; however, behind the main events of the plot is the brooding corrective spirit of the perfectionist Benbow, bringing the rich imagery and profusion of fact into harmony with the dire theme. And what Faulkner achieves not without extravagances in *Sanctuary* can be found done better in *Light in August* and done to perfection in *Absalom, Absalom!*

Naturally revulsion often carries these compassionate observers into aloofness. The clergyman Hightower, perhaps the most broadly sympathetic of all, is also the most detached. Deprived of his pulpit because of his wife's scandalous behavior, he has lived alone and inactive for years; and when he hears that the posse is about to catch Joe Christmas, he refuses to be involved, saying to himself, 'I won't! I won't! I have bought immunity. I have paid.' Later when Byron Bunch comes to him with Lena's troubles and those of Mrs. Hines and Joe, the tears run down his cheeks like sweat as he says, 'But it is not right to bother me, to worry me, when I have—when I have taught myself to stay—have been taught by them to stay—That this should come to me, taking me after I am old.' Quentin Compson's revulsion is still more acute, for he is more severely involved through his sister's disgrace, and he retreats all the way into self-annihilation. Even the quizzical self-possessed Ratliff, in *The Hamlet*, pauses somewhere between despair and defiance to thank God 'men have done learned how to forget quick what they ain't brave enough to try to cure.' Benbow makes a more direct and moodier self-accusation—'I lack courage: that was left out of me. The machinery is all here, but it won't run.' And Ratliff, after stepping in several times on the side of the angels, cries out to a companion, 'I could do more, but I won't. I won't, I tell you!'

These retreats are not repudiations of principle; they are simply a natural human weakness and weariness, which Faulkner represents dramatically for purposes of characterization, and which serve also the artistic method of vicissitude. It is significant that the pendulum of mood usually swings back to positive assertion; Hightower and Benbow and the reporter, for instance, return again and again to the struggle. Even the crazed Quentin Compson realizes that beyond despair is something still more intolerable—indifference; he says, 'It's not when you realize that nothing can help you—religion, pride, anything—it's when you realize that you don't need any aid.' Benbow, oppressed by 'the evil, the injustice, the tears,' lets himself think it might be better if Goodwin, the woman and her child, Popeye, and he himself too were all dead, 'cauterized out of the old and tragic flank of the world,' and goes on to imagine 'perhaps it is upon the instant that we realize, admit that there is a logical pattern to evil, that we die'; but he does not cease to postulate and appeal to a logical pattern of good in his efforts to save a falsely accused man and to befriend that man's family. Quentin Compson is obsessed by his father's teaching that 'all men are just accumulations dolls stuffed with sawdust swept up from the trash heaps where all previous dolls had been thrown away the sawdust flowing from what wound in what side that not for me died not,' but nevertheless he cannot accept his father's argument that virginity is just words.

These characters' refusal to surrender principle even when they seem overmatched by circumstance not only intensifies their melancholy, and Faulkner's, but enhances it with human dignity. Indeed, in the darkest pages of these novels Faulkner and his compassionate spectators often exemplify Carlyle's dictum that a man's sorrow is the inverted image of his nobility. The reporter in *Pylon* tells his editor that he tried to let the fliers alone but couldn't—couldn't refrain, that is, from the impulse to help them, in spite of their desperate state beyond his help, and his own acknowledged awkwardness. Benbow says he 'cannot stand idly by and see injustice,' and when Miss Jenny suggests Pilate's cynical query, Benbow declares himself still moved to oppose what he identifies as 'that irony which lurks in events.' When Goodwin's woman assumes that she must give herself to Benbow in lieu of cash payment for his legal services, he says, 'Can't you see that perhaps a man might do something just because he knew it was right, necessary to the harmony of things that it be done?' Ratliff similarly asserts that in opposing the Snopes clan he was 'protecting something that don't want nothing but to walk and feel the sun and wouldn't know how to hurt no man even if it would and wouldn't want to even if it could, just like I wouldn't stand by and see you steal a meat-bone from a dog.'

Even the skeptical Mr. Compson often shows awareness that the moral issue is not figmentary. He sees human virtue manifested sometimes in acts of apparent evil—'Have you noticed,' he asks Quentin, 'how so often when we try to reconstruct the causes which lead up to the actions of men and women, how with a sort of astonishment we find ourselves now and then reduced to the belief, the only possible belief, that they stemmed from some of the old virtues? the thief who steals not for greed but for love, the murderer who kills not out of lust but pity?' Thus the man whose motives the Compsons try to reconstruct

—Thomas Sutpen—is driven on in his acquisitiveness, they find, by a boyhood complex of honor; and even in his materialistic pride he holds himself to a code which will not let him traduce the wife who deceived him. The persistence of such moral resolution in Faulkner's beset and melancholy characters is typified in Judith Sutpen's feeling that 'it can't matter . . . and yet it must matter because you keep on trying.'

Closely related to this attitude, and furnishing another fixed point in the ethics of Faulkner's characters, is an idealization of honesty. The aristocratic Rosa Millard, in *The Unvanquished*, never whipped her grandson for anything but lying and prayed for pardon for herself after she had lied to a Yankee officer to protect her family; later, having obtained mules by forged requisitions upon Union troops and having sold them back to other Union troops for gold, she confesses before the congregation, asks their prayers, and then distributes the money among them as she had intended. When at last she is murdered by carpet-baggers, the negro boy Ringo says discerningly of her, 'It wasn't him or Ab Snopes either that kilt her. It was them mules. That first batch of mules we got for nothing.' Nor is this integrity represented as limited to the aristocrats of the Old South. Addie Bundren, the country woman, believed 'deceit was such that, in a world where it was, nothing else could be very bad or very important.' Her carpenter son Cash holds to what he calls 'the olden right teaching that says to drive the nails down and trim the edges well always like it was for your own use and comfort you were making it,' and so great is his passion for rightness that when asked how far he fell when he broke his leg, he answers, 'Twenty-eight foot, four and a half inches, about.' Relevantly, honest Cash is the Bundren who judges most fairly the erratic brother Darl, crediting his motives even while condemning his acts. Byron Bunch is another honest workman; he keeps his own time strictly when he works alone at the mill, and he says, 'It beats all how some folks think that making or getting money is a kind of game where there are not any rules at all.' No wonder that, when Hightower hears Byron's class disdainfully called 'hillbillies,' he says, 'They are fine people, though. Fine men and women.' Another example is in *The Wild Palms*; the lost convict has the woman wash his prison suit, while he goes barebacked in the blistering sun; then he wraps up the clean suit, saving it for his return; and Faulkner himself remarks that the woman said nothing, 'since she too doubtless knew what his reason was, . . . she too had stemmed at some point from the same dim hill-bred Abraham.'

Often the unassuming virtue of simple people provides the foil to evil and furnishes the atmospheric tension in Faulkner's scenes, as, for instance, an incidental character in *The Hamlet*, a farmer whose gentility is symbolized by the spray of peach blossoms he holds in his teeth, who plows the Armstid field so that Mrs. Armstid won't be forced to do it but who will not answer when Ratliff asks how many hours he has put in for his neighbor, this detail pointing up Henry Armstid's brutality to his wife and Flem Snopes's ruthless seizure of the five dollars she had earned weaving. In the same way the professional integrity and chivalry of the flier Roger Shumann, in *Pylon*, contrasts with the commercial trickery and inhumanity of the airport promoters. Thus Faulkner furnishes frames of moral reference, not only by suggesting ideals through his repellent pictures of their opposites but by showing protagonists of them among all sorts of men and women.

And thus Faulkner's deep pessimism does not proceed from a denial of values but from a melancholy recognition of the great weight of evil opposition to very real values. Not much can be done for the Mrs. Armstids in a community overrun by rapacious Snopeses, nor can Benbow effectually help Goodwin and his woman against Popeye's viciousness, Temple's treachery, and the mob's intolerance and brutality. Thus when Faulkner's compassionate observers actually intervene, they are quite often defeated. Byron Bunch is the most successful of them all, and that perhaps because he largely shifts to Hightower the paralyzing contemplative function and himself seeks simply to protect and cherish the abandoned Lena and her child. Lena is a still simpler character, representing the will to life in an elementary human form, and she passes through Jefferson at the time of Miss Burden's murder and the mobbing of Joe Christmas as untouched and unperturbed as Eck Snopes's little boy among the wild horses that injured grown men. Most of Faulkner's characters are more complex and less stable than Lena; they are far gone in all sorts of involvements, either with others or with their own fantasies. Hence conflict and impasse in lives where suffering prevails and succor is difficult.

Under the resultant emotional strain Faulkner's characters sometimes attribute malevolence to the cosmos, but they more often see men themselves as the direct agents of evil. The whole theme of Faulkner's early work, *Mosquitoes*, seems to be that humans pester one another insufferably by passionate encroachments of one egotism upon another. Seeing these aggressive tendencies accumulated in social pressures, Wilbourne, the lover in *The Wild Palms*, who attempts with

Charlotte to escape out of the world, thinks 'you are born submerged in anonymous lockstep with the teeming anonymous myriads of your time and generation; you get out of step once, falter once, and you are trampled to death.' And the ironic repercussions of consequence are inevitable. In *Sanctuary* young Gowan Stevens says he has injured no one but himself by his folly, whereas his drunken blundering had actually set into motion the whole chain of events that brought, besides Temple's debauchment, the deaths of Tommy, Red, and Goodwin. Hightower thinks 'it is any man's privilege to destroy himself, so long as he does not injure any one else,' but then almost at once he realizes that his ego had been the instrument of his wife's despair and shame.

When the parachute jumper in *Pylon* tells the reporter goodbye, he thanks him for 'trying to help,' but he advises, 'Stick to the kind of people you are used to after this.' That, however, is difficult counsel, not only for the reporter, but for most of Faulkner's characters. They are not used to one another, never become used to one another; they are as Addie Bundren sees human beings, 'each with his and her secret and selfish thought, and blood strange to each other blood.' A key to the enigma of this separation may be found in a bit of omniscient narrative where Faulkner says, 'Man knows so little about his fellows. In his eyes all men or women act upon what he believes would motivate him if he were mad enough to do what that other man or woman is doing.' *If he were mad enough.* To the spectator, mankind seems predominantly irrational. This does not mean that Faulkner himself repudiates rationality; he seems rather to hold with the judge, in the short story 'Beyond,' who says he cannot divorce himself from reason enough to accept the pleasant and labor-saving theory of nihilism.

Faulkner's own inclination is shown by his endowing his most positive characters, his observers, with two primary elements of rationality—inquiry and disinterestedness—and with the reasonable man's idealization of justice. Yet in the whole body of Faulkner's work the results thus far of man's struggles toward rational self-control and social adjustment are not shown to be encouraging. The rector in *Soldiers' Pay* is convinced that man learns scarcely anything as he goes through this world and nothing whatever of help or benefit. The open conflict between human passions and rationality, and, alternatively, the unsatisfactory compromises of that conflict in woodenly conventional restraints, create the paradoxes so poignantly dramatized in Faulkner's most abstractly symbolic story, *The Wild Palms*. Wilbourne repudiates man's self-imposed systems and tries to live all for love; the convict, swept away on the flooded river, laboriously returns himself, the woman he had been told to rescue, and even the boat he was sent in; both men get prison sentences. The ironic dissonances of this somber novel, its dilemmas of escape and surrender, love and suffering, freedom and fate, and basically of reason and passion, give an incomparable suggestion of the confused and turbulent life of man in his present stage of imperfect mental and moral development.

Tull, in *As I Lay Dying*, suggests a severe functional limitation of the human brain: 'It's like a piece of machinery: it won't stand a whole lot of racking.' Perhaps Faulkner's frequent inclusion of feeble-minded characters is the result not only of their horrid fascination for his own acutely sensitive and subtle consciousness, but also to emphasize the precariousness and difficulty of rationality, the resemblance of the supposedly sane and the insane, and the short distance thus far traveled in the evolution of mind. The idiot, in the cow-stealing episode in *The Hamlet*, is described as one who 'is learning fast now, who has learned success and then precaution and secrecy and how to steal and even providence; who has only lust and greed and bloodthirst and a moral conscience to keep him awake at night, yet to acquire.' Thus far human rationality is not strong enough to rule out lust, greed, and bloodthirst; it can only recoil at them, usually after indulging them. And Cash suggests that there is little distinction between the various stages of supposed rationality in man: 'I ain't so sho that ere a man has the right to say what is crazy and what aint. It's like there was a fellow in every man that's done a-past the sanity or the insanity, that watches the sane and the insane doings of that man with the same horror and the same astonishment.'

There may be no such detached and perceptive fellow in every man, or even in most men; but there is such a fellow in William Faulkner, and all his works show his horror and astonishment, proceeding from an exacting and outraged idealism. Faulkner's integrity is all the more obvious in that his is an advanced outpost's stand against odds, the odds of the predominance of base passions over supposed rationality and their resultant confusions in the average man. The desperateness of the issue, as he pictures it, is what gives his books their startling intensity, unequaled in our contemporary fiction. Faulkner's own extreme mood, growing out of his absolute demands, has been so powerfully communicated that reading him is like an actual experience of catastrophe —not only the 'lightning and tempest, battle, murder, and sudden death' from which all men would be delivered, but, what is still more terrifying, 'all inordinate and sinful affections.'

His is, indeed, an apocalyptic vision of sin and of its complex consequences. He is unsurpassed in recording those spasms of greed and lustfulness and animosity that eclipse human qualities and saddle men with fixations which are not so much ideas as appetites. He has epitomized such crises in his record of Jiggs, the mechanic in *Pylon*, as he goes on drinking: 'He could have heard sounds, even voices, from the alley beneath the window if he had been listening. But he was not. All he heard now was that thunderous silence and solitude in which man's spirit crosses the eternal repetitive rubicon of his vice in the instant after the terror and before the triumph becomes dismay—the moral and spiritual waif shrieking his feeble I-am-I into the desert of chance and disaster.' Faulkner can picture as well the despair of the rational and well-intentioned when they contemplate uncontrollable suffusions of passion in others and oppose their results. Such, on a broad narrative scale, is Ratliff confronting Snopes, Benbow maneuvering against Popeye and the townspeople, Bayard Sartoris resisting his father and Drusilla, and Quentin Compson viewing his family in *The Sound and the Fury* and the South's evil genius in *Absalom, Absalom!*

Those who lack Faulkner's knowledge of good and evil, or lack his courage in facing knowledge, may shut their eyes and put their hands over their ears while they gibber about Frankenstein or nihilism. Such ostrich tactics become increasingly ridiculous in a world where a recrudescence of irrationality and brutal passions have pointed up for even the most impercipient those melancholy facts about human nature and progress which Faulkner has confronted all along and has unequivocally attacked. A virile critical approach will first recognize the coherent rationality and humanity of Faulkner's point of view, and might then profitably go on to its particular sources, in Faulkner's own experience and in his contemplation of his native South, past and present, and so might finally come to a reappraisal of his narrative techniques, so brilliantly adapted to his profound artistic visions.

78. Delmore Schwartz, 'The Fiction of William Faulkner'

Summer 1941

Southern Review, vii, 145–60.

Schwartz (1913–66), poet and short story writer from New York, had published by 1941 *In Dreams Begin Responsibilities* and *Shenandoah*, the latter a verse drama. He won the Bollingen Prize in 1960.

Sanctuary was the novel which established William Faulkner as an author from the point of view of publishers. It even awakened the Hollywood version of consciousness. In an introduction to the Modern Library edition of *Sanctuary*, Faulkner speaks of his work in the tough lingo many American authors appear to find necessary to any discussion of their work and their profession:

> I began to think of books in terms of possible money. I decided that I might just as well make some of it myself. I took a little time out, and speculated what a person in Mississippi would believe to be current trends, chose what I thought to be current trends, and invented the most horrific tale I could imagine and wrote it in about three weeks.

The effort was successful from several points of view. Now Faulkner has written eight books since the appearance of *Sanctuary*. These books have not only helped to dissipate the corncob immortality *Sanctuary* won for him; but for some time a quickly recognized quality has been defined and made various by the successive thunder-and-lightning of each book. It was an astonishing and just experience five years ago to attend a film named 'Slave Ship,' be struck by the Faulkneresque quality of the way in which the story was presented, and find later that Faulkner had written the scenario.

The consecutive sum of fourteen books read over a period of ten years and then brushed through again for the advantages of retrospect brings one the conviction that the Faulkneresque idiom is something of permanent interest. In reading these books and in bringing them freshly or fadedly to mind each time a new one appears, one naturally cannot help but mark the recurrence and repetition of elements newly and differently. No more can one help interpreting these elements in their togetherness and seeing them as a kind of constellation. A constellation is an artificial order which helps one to see and to recognize the stars. If one keeps in mind the possibly artificial character, it is perfectly safe to look at the elements as such a constellation.

A Mississippi Constellation

There are many stars in the blackness of the sky. The star of the World War as a theme appears in *Soldiers' Pay*, *Sartoris*, and several of the stories in *These Thirteen*. Two sub-themes are the return of the soldier and the soldier as an American in France or England during the World War.

Far more important, yet connected underground with the World War theme, is that of the Civil War. Often the soldier back from France behaves as if he had just lost the Civil War: this is the case with Bayard Sartoris, whose behavior is far in excess of the motive given for it, the death of his twin brother as an airman.

Obviously the Civil War theme cannot be separated from the White–Black theme which runs through almost all the books, but is especially prominent in *Light in August* and *Absalom, Absalom!*. In both these books the leading characters are trying to escape from having the stigma of negro blood in themselves or in their families. Or this theme might better be named that of the Old South and its ruin.

Then there is the theme of the poor white and the peasant, seen most strikingly in the two books just mentioned: in both of them the poor white rises to a tragic dignity by simple tenacity and faithfulness. Wash Jones kills Colonel Sutpen, who has made his daughter pregnant, when Sutpen speaks with contempt of her; and in *Light in August*, Lena Grove follows her fugitive lover for hundreds of miles and hundreds of pages without a word of criticism or dismay; she is at least one reader's favorite character in the *dramatis personae* of all the books.

Then there is the theme, richest of all, of the primitive, the abnormal, and the virtually insane.

The primitives are the delightful Indians in *These Thirteen*, and the Negroes when they are left to themselves, or when, as in one fine story, the Indians and the Negroes are together, and the white man's absence is a positive thing, like a sudden silence.

The abnormal has no better example than the celebrated Popeye, impotent like the hero of *The Sun Also Rises*, who rapes a co-ed with a corn cob and gains sexual satisfaction by regarding the sexual act and neighing by the bed like the horse who injured him. A number of other characters compete with Popeye, but without comparable success.

The insane figures occur many times also, in such an idiot as Benjy (in *The Sound and Fury*), obsessed with a day in his childhood fifteen years back, or as Ike Snopes in *The Hamlet* who engages in sexual congress with a cow after a rapturous love affair: there are more novels which contain idiots than novels without them. But it is the peculiar use of them by Faulkner and the emphatic value placed upon their perceptions which make them most important elements.

The star of the obsessed lovers shines many times too, as in *The Wild Palms*, where the passionate pair are in flight from every aspect of society which weakens or intervenes or intermits their obsession with each other; or as in *The Hamlet* where a football player tackles the impassive schoolgirl he has been lusting after for months. In passing, it might be said that nowhere is Faulkner less successful than with this theme.

The star of the intellectual shines weakly. He is such a lawyer as Horace Benbow, who appears in several books, chiefly in *Sartoris* and *Sanctuary*, or he is such a minister as the Rev. Gail Hightower in *Light in August*. Both are ruined men and cuckolds. In dealing with the intellectual in himself, in attempting to present his states of mind, Faulkner does very poorly, almost as poorly as with his obsessed lovers, because of a failure of style, which then becomes literary in the worst sense.

But the intellectual is impressive and moving when, no longer alone and soliloquizing, he is caught into the story's movement. Then he expresses the failure of rationality, the failure of law and order and justice in an irrational world. This is what happens to Horace Benbow in *Sanctuary* when he tries to defend an innocent poor white accused of murder and in the course of his passion for justice in the abstract violates Southern mores by revealing publicly the shame of Temple Drake, a young lady of good family.

The brightest reddest star of all is that of violence and horror, the violent act and the violent man, and the emotion of horror conjured up by the forms of violence. This is what we see almost always, whether in the killing of Temple Drake's lover, the violence for generations of Thomas Sutpen, the murder and lynching in *Light in August*, the suicide in *The Sound and Fury*, the desperate driving of a car in *Sartoris* and the equally desperate driving of a plane in *Pylon*, the cutting of a navel-cord with an empty jagged-edged tomato can during birth in *The Wild Palms*. The stage has not been so loaded with corpses since late Elizabethan tragedy.

Other themes, related and mixed with the mixture of those already mentioned, need only be marked: the city slicker theme and the village slicker theme: the latter is a trader and business man of one kind or another, best embodied in the many appearances of the Snopeses. And most successfully the comic theme, the immense and overwhelming comedy in which Faulkner too seldom engages his characters, as in the great Miss Reba of *Sanctuary*, the Indians already mentioned, and the tall tales of horse-trading in *The Hamlet*. Lastly there is the South as a region and landscape, described with strength and vividness by Faulkner, who rises to the truly poetic in his descriptions, as in his versions of the minds of intellectuals, he echoes the worst kind of poetry.

The constellation which gives these elements unity for at least one reader is that of obsession with the endless horror and irrationality of life. Again and again, violence ensues, horror triumphs, injustice is the victor, irrationality overcomes all, all human purpose and effort is vain, mistaken, and defeated. No author has more right than Faulkner to the much-used lines in *Macbeth* about the tale told by an idiot full of sound and fury, signifying nothing. In Shakespeare, however, this view of Life is uttered by a murderer virtually at the end of his rope; not by the author. In Faulkner, signifying nothing signifies all, it is the ultimate revelation. Thus the critical question often becomes, does Faulkner's story bring itself to the point which Macbeth occupies when he makes his speech.

The conclusion of meaningless defeat can hardly be exaggerated. For in the end, Temple Drake is left hopeless and empty in the sanctuary of Paris, Joe Christmas is lynched, Popeye is hanged for a crime he did not commit, the righteous minister who would protect Joe Christmas is killed, the family mansion is burned down in *Absalom, Absalom!* and Thomas Sutpen's passion to found a landed white family ends in a half-breed idiot son, Quentin Compson kills himself, and the aviators in *Pylon* are killed purposelessly.

The obsession with violence and evil is such that it is difficult to think of a crime not committed in the corpus of Faulkner's work. Simple murder is almost the least among such acts as incest, cannibalism, rape, various forms of sodomy, patricide, fratricide, and filicide, adultery, and castration.

The Style and Method of Horror

This vision of Life is delivered to the page by a variety of devices appropriate in their sum, but not always under the author's control, and often directed as much *against* the reader as upon the story to be told.

Most prominent is the deliberate *mystification* of style and method. The reader is deliberately kept from knowing the full significance of the action he is reading about and some of the characters are often kept in like ignorance. The mystification is achieved by the use of interior monologue, especially that of idiots; or it is achieved by a description of the action in the most detailed physical terms, terms so overwhelmingly physical that the motive of the action is not discernible and is purposely kept unknown. Frequently a related device is used, the narration of the action is separated from the narration of the motive by hundreds of pages. One reason for this is that the character responsible for the action conceals his motive, or his motive has its roots in the distant past, as in Popeye's rape of Temple Drake, or Sutpen's desire to found a landed white family because of the families he has seen in Virginia during his boyhood. Sometimes, however, the character himself does not know or is unsure of the motive for his action, and sometimes it appears that Faulkner himself does not know or does not care: thus the plot of *Absalom, Absalom!* is almost annihilated by the conflict between Thomas Sutpen and his white son over the marriage of his daughter to the son who has colored blood: but this conflict directly contradicts Thomas Sutpen's initial and most important motive, to have a family free of colored blood: for his white son is the most important element in the fulfillment of this desire, and next to him, the marriage of a daughter to one with colored blood, though regrettable, is hardly sufficient cause for the conflict between father and son. This is an amazing example of forgetfulness on an author's part.

Frequently, too, a number of characters play a choric role. They stand by to be astonished, shocked, and enthralled by the action, as for example, the newspaper reporter in *Pylon*, Ratliff the sewing machine agent in *The Hamlet*, the friend of the obsessed lovers in *The Wild Palms*, the two students who ponder the story of *Absalom, Absalom!*, and various idiots here and there.

Sometimes these bystanders are normal human beings whose normality serves to define the shock of the abnormal action. Sometimes they are abnormal themselves and serve to heighten the fury. And sometimes they are so fascinated by the spectacle they regard that they are drawn into it: this is particularly the case with the reporter in *Pylon*.

These choric characters are present perhaps to instruct the reader, perhaps to help him discount his initial disbelief by admitting the cogency of his normal response.

But over and above all is the effort of the author to mystify his reader and to compel his characters to feel his vision of the horror and irrationality of life.

It is plain enough that there is a connection between a mystification of style—a deliberate effort to make the story difficult to apprehend—and a vision of Life's irrationality. That such a literary method is justified by such a vision is not plain.

Again, it is easy to see why the author attempts to compel his reader into the emotion of horror. But there is a serious distinction between compelling him by the story in itself, and compelling him by mystifying him or forcing a furious style upon him.

The same thing happens to the characters. The reader can quickly distinguish between occasions when the character's emotions are compelled by his situation, and occasions when they are compelled by the author's style. One sometimes sees Faulkner shaking his characters to make them hysterical, jogging them up and down like a hysterical ventriloquist to gain the fury he wants.

This repeated distinction between what the subject makes available because of its nature and what the author attempts to compel in his subject, out of all reason, serves to define the primary cause for Faulkner's successes and failures.

When Faulkner has a subject extreme enough in its horror and abnormality, his style is measured, under control, and directed at the specific description of specific things. His writing is genuinely poetic and exact, his delaying obscuring method of presentation is matched and required by the nature of the story, and he has no need of the hysterical passion and the rapturous denunciation of Life in his style because the subject is sufficient unto the evil. The reader is left to respond to the subject without the author's obsessive coaching.

When the subject does not justify the author's horror, the devices of style become clumsiness and tricks, the writing is a stale version of the Swinburnian high poetic, and worst of all the style becomes purple, empty of specific objects, and sometimes insufferably periodic.

The distinction comes to the difference between boxing and shadowboxing. Faulkner is able to get a subject to fight with about half the time. This would be good enough, were it not true that the boxing and shadow-boxing alternate in the same book: certainly this is the case in what seems to me to be Faulkner's best book, *Absalom, Absalom!*

Yet this is too pat and neat to explain everything. No doubt an irreducible factor is Faulkner's literary admirations. Another factor is an inveterate carelessness, as Mr. George Marion O'Donnell observed in his essay on Faulkner, a carelessness which results in contradictory motivation, repetitiousness, and undue prolongation of the story. The lush love of such words as *proud, gallant, subtle, myriad, richly*, especially in pairs, coupled with rare or polysyllabic words of Latin derivation —'a sound meaningless and profound, out of a suspirant and peaceful following silence'—is a more complex vice of style.

The forced intensity in the texture of the writing is often close to the excellence which results when Faulkner is content to seize definite objects; here is an example where virtue and defect are an inseparable mixture:

> The sunny air was filled with competitive radios and phonographs in the doors of drug- and musicstores. Before these doors a throng stood all day, listening. The pieces which moved them were ballads simple in melody and theme, of bereavement and retribution and repentance metallically sung, blurred, emphasized by static or needle—disembodied voices blaring from imitation wood cabinets or pebble-grain horn mouths above the rapt faces, the gnarled slow hands long shaped to the earth.

It is plain that 'ballads simple in melody and theme . . . ' is a characterization too general, too far from the concreteness of the other phrases. The 'bereavement, repentance, and retribution' note is wrong in the same way and flows, though not as strikingly as many other passages in Faulkner, from the false sense of the highly poetic, just as 'disembodied voices blaring from imitation wooden cabinets' is right because the word is seeking to define an object before compelling an emotion.

The carelessness suggests itself as that of an author who is in an immense hurry (impatience is a form of laziness, said Kafka) and who writes his books quickly, driving ahead without looking back at the previous pages. Malcolm Cowley has remarked that Faulkner, like few American writers, has a daemon: this seems to be true, but it is hardly the daemon of Socrates, who always said No. Faulkner's daemon is utterly positive.

Faulkner himself provides an image which seems most appropriate in his introduction to *Sanctuary*. He describes how he wrote *As I Lay Dying* in the boiler room of a power plant all night long in the intermissions of loading a wheelbarrow with coal for the fireman to put into the boiler while nearby 'a dynamo ran. It made a deep constant humming noise.' The book was written in three weeks. Better books have been written in a shorter time and worse books have taken years. It is a question of one's attitude to one's art, rather than a question of time.

A further point is that Faulkner is one of the many American writers for whom writing and reading have no necessary relationship. He has profited by the example of such an author as Joyce, but beyond this there is little to show that he makes such a use of the reading of criticism and of other men's novels as a French author would make almost instinctively. One would never guess that America has had such writers as Hawthorne, Melville, and James, all of whom might have been of an immense usefulness to an author of Faulkner's character and uncontrollable gifts of sensibility.

The danger of imitation would not have been serious. The formal example of James might have kept Faulkner from such arbitrary, forced, superposed, and essentially pointless devices as the alternation of two stories in *The Wild Palms*.

But more than that, any serious reading might have kept Faulkner from being the victim of his own great gifts as well as the victim of the self-indulgence of his style. One comes finally to the guess that perhaps Faulkner does not even read his own books. This is one way to explain some of the superfluities and misorganizations which mar so fine a novel as *Light in August*.

In like manner, one has the sense that Faulkner has been the victim of his youthful reading in writers like Wilde, Symons, Pater, Dowson, and other writers of prose in the grand manner who may be responsible for the sudden occurrence, amid much good writing, of such a phrase as 'her voice was proud and still as banners in the dust.'

A final note on Faulkner's method rests on another guess. Faulkner's best writing almost invariably has to do with the locale he names Yoknapatawpha County, Mississippi, and the town of Jefferson. Many of the characters return through the successive novels. Sometimes they rise from the dead backward in time, like the redintegration of an explosion in a newsreel; for Quentin Compson kills himself in *The Sound and Fury*, but returns in *Absalom, Absalom!* at a point six months earlier to tell a story four hundred pages in length, no doubt as much to the creator's surprise as to that of the reader of *The Sound and Fury*.

The Sartorises, the Compsons, the Sutpens, the Snopeses, and the Benbows suggest the guess that Faulkner has models of actuality to draw from. As soon as he goes from this region, as soon as he seems to invent *ex nihilo*, the forced quality becomes least tolerable and the characters become plainly incredible: this seems especially true of *The Wild Palms* and *Pylon*.

The suggestion is that for Faulkner, as for most authors, actuality is an inexhaustible well or mine; imagination and invention are bogus unless they are bound to actuality and inspired by it. This is one of the most important senses in which art is an imitation of life, beyond any assent to the doctrines of naturalism and realism. There are inconceivably more possibilities in Life for the author with gifts than anything his imagination can construct. As there is nothing in the mind not first in the senses, so there is no richness in the imagination which is not surpassed by the richness of Life when it works upon the imagination.

Genesis and Audience

On certain occasions, a literary critic feels that he ought to have call letters, like radio stations: followed by an announcement of the city from which the bodiless voice proceeds. It is obviously necessary to assume a common denominator between reader and writer. But in discussing so extraordinary an author as Faulkner, perhaps something ought to be said about the immense distance between the region of the critic and that of the author. Few readers of Faulkner or of this essay are likely to have heard of Washington Heights unless they have lived in New York City and even then they may be ignorant. But it should be said that a Washington Heights view of our time and our country may weaken or make wholly incorrect the following discussion of Faulkner as the product of a *milieu*, the agent of a body of fiction, and an author aware of his audience. The soul may be composed of the external world, Wallace Stevens has suggested: 'I am what is around me.'

If this seems to make too much of the bare region of it all, some prominent instances from the decade of the 'thirties are available. Is it conceivable that Steinbeck would have written *The Grapes of Wrath*, if his audience had not been yearning to hear about the dispossessed? if a certain section of the populace had not been dispossessed? Would James T. Farrell's Studs Lonigan trilogy or William Saroyan's endless happiness jag about how wonderful it is to be alive and on the WPA

('Aspirin is a member of the NRA' is the title of one of his early stories) have been possible in the 'twenties?

The issue is not in the least that of mechanical causation: the age strikes the author in the sensibility and the author strikes back with a book. If this meant anything, it would mean that authors of the same period would have to be very much alike. But the assumption here is merely that the age and the author's *living* are necessary conditions, among other necessary conditions, of the specific character of his work.

What, then, can be found in Faulkner's social background to satisfy the literary historian; also to make possible a nice discrimination between the *causes* of a work and the work itself and the audience at which it may be aimed and the mind of the audience which accepts or rejects the work?

Faulkner was an aviator during the World War. This probably explains the aviators in some of his stories and the World War theme of his earlier novels. The World War may also suggest a factor in the leading obsession with violence. It is matched by other authors of Faulkner's generation, though not of his region: Jeffers, O'Neill, and Hemingway. The Prohibition Era too (Popeye, for example, is a bootlegger) must have provided its violence for Faulkner's imagination.

It is evident enough, too, that the White–Black theme, the memory of the Civil War, and other like subjects begin in Faulkner's being a Southerner, making the critic with naturalist or realist assumptions look at Faulkner as the spokesman or literary representative of 'decadent Southern families.'

But the specific and dominant quality of his work is not explained by these general factors, which must have operated upon many other authors. What is it,—can we say what it is?—which compels Faulkner to be obsessed with the horror and irrationality of life, in his writing? Every period has such writers. But what has helped to make Faulkner such an author in our time and in our country?

The question will have to be answered with conviction by one who knows a great deal more about a number of things than the present critic.

But I would like to suggest a hypothesis (merely a hypothesis): the conflict between the idea of the Old South and the progressive actuality of the New South has brought Faulkner to the extreme where he can only seize his values, which are those of the idea of the Old South, by imagining them being violated by the most hideous crimes. Thus Temple Drake must be violated by a corn cob: mere rape is not enough.

What are the values of the *idea* of the Old South (I should say here that I know of these phrases only at second- and third-hand and may use them too inaccurately)? The emphasis on pride and gallantry, the attitude toward the Negro, the behavior of the decadent Southern families always remarked by reviewers, illustrate these values broadly. One of the best examples is in *Sartoris*.

Here one is greatly impressed by the story, told by one of the characters in the present, about a member of the Sartoris family in the Civil War who is an officer with Stuart. Stuart has captured a Northern officer during a raid made for the sole purpose of getting coffee. The captured officer is without a horse, much to Stuart's distress. Out of courtesy, Stuart determines to get his captive a horse by making another unnecessary raid. The Northern officer protests that this is foolish and rash behavior, especially for a mere prisoner. Stuart replies that it is not for a prisoner, but 'for an officer suffering the fortunes of war. No gentleman would do less.' The Northern officer answers that 'no gentleman has any business in war. There is no place for him here. He is an anachronism, like anchovies. At least General Stuart did not capture our anchovies. Perhaps he will send Lee for them in person.'

Bayard Sartoris, astride his mount nearby, hears the interchange, charges forward on his horse, though Stuart shouts a protest at him, attacks the commissary tent of the Northern company to get the anchovies, and is killed by a scared cook, as the captured Northern officer begs Stuart to go to his rescue, saying: 'What is one man to a renewed belief in humanity?'

This story is told to illustrate the character of the Sartoris family. It is told in half-humor and not without a strong critical attitude. Yet despite the overtone of amusement and irony, there can be no doubt that this is where Faulkner's allegiances abide: his values are enacted and fulfilled in such an episode.

But enacted and fulfilled only in the Civil War, which has been over for a long time: the later Sartorises must exist in a society in which such behavior often seems meaningless: when the later Bayard Sartoris comes home from the World War, he has no way to express such values; consequently he expresses his frustration and despair by driving his car at hair-raising speeds.

So too with all the noble and heroic human beings who exist in the present: they have no medium in which to operate. They have carried forward inherited values to a period of time in which the dominant powers of the community do not so much oppose these values (opposition is obviously recognition, of a sort) as refuse to be aware of their existence.

Given those values, how can one experience them in modern life? How, except through the violence and abnormality which betrays them so brutally that, by a recognizable dialectic, their existence is recognized. The criminal helps one to remember the judge.

Moreover, from the point of view of those values, the irrationality of Life is seen in two ways: the alien environment is irrational because those values are foreign to it; and Life is irrational because those values fail to be embodied, are always frustrated and destroyed.

To repeat once more, this is merely a hypothesis: but many other examples might be cited to add to its persuasiveness.

The important point is that, though this state of being is responsible for Faulkner's defects as well as his virtues, the result is much more than a body of fiction representative of a *milieu*. For plainly, Faulkner's dominant situation, though extreme, is a permanent point on the compass of human fate, and Faulkner's effort for the most part is to see it in its generality, not as a piece of local color.

The local color appears, however, especially in the regional obsession with the White–Black theme. At the end of *Absalom, Absalom!* Quentin Compson, who has been telling a story of the Old South and a family as ridden by the Furies as the House of Atreus, is asked by his auditor, a Canadian student at Harvard, 'Why do you hate the South?'

' "I don't hate it," Quentin said, quickly, at once, immediately; "I don't hate it," he said. *I don't hate it* he thought, panting in the cold air, the iron New England dark; I don't. *I don't! I don't hate it! I don't hate it!*' This concludes the book.

A moment before, the Canadian boy has just made a prophecy about the interbreeding of whites and Negroes:

'I think that in time the Jim Bonds are going to conquer the Western hemisphere. Of course it won't quite be in our time and of course as they spread out towards the poles they will bleach out again like the rabbits and the birds do, so they won't show up so sharp against the snow. But it will still be Jim Bond; and so in a few thousand years, I who regard you will also have sprung from the loins of African kings.'

This is the regional interest at its best. One must distinguish with the greatest care between what an author writes because of the life he has lived and known, and the objectives he sometimes give his writing because of a sense of his audience. A Grosset & Dunlap reprint of *Sartoris* speaks on the jacket, in pure publishers' prose, of how 'Every reader of *Sanctuary* and *Light in August* will want to read this other novel of life in the raw in the New South.' This is rather raw, even for a publisher. But the worst thing is that Faulkner shows signs now and then of writing horror stories of the South for an urban audience. Certainly this is what his audience reads to look for. In *The Hamlet*, the sexual act of an idiot with a cow, regarded by the village people, makes one think that perhaps Faulkner has heard of the success of *Tobacco Road*.

But in the main, the body of his writing, both in its successes and its failures, seems to be engendered by an obsession with values which cannot be realized with sufficient intensity except through violation and perversion.

Judgment as Comparison

Is it not true that literary judgment in the end is literary comparison? One work is better than another work. If one did not think of better works, one might be satisfied with what is not good at all.

When we consider a body of work in itself, does not our past reading stand behind us and tug the hair on our heads, like the goddess Athena? Are not countless intuitive comparisons made when we recognize false notes or enjoy the rendering of actuality in language?

Considered in itself, the whole body of Faulkner's writing contains no work which seems completely successful. *Absalom, Absalom!*, *Light in August*, and several of the short stories in *These Thirteen* come close to complete success. The first of these falls short because of a self-indulgence of style and a carelessness in the plot; *Light in August* suffers from an obscurity in Joe Christmas' motivation and poor organization at the end of the book; two of the novels are made difficult from the start by the fact that Faulkner has tried to work them up out of successful short stories, though unlike Hemingway, who does the same thing, Faulkner rewrites the short story which he is planting in his novel. But on the other hand, no volume of Faulkner's lacks pages and passages which are as remarkable as any American fiction of our time and worth all the expense of spirit which a reading of Faulkner requires.

There is a mixture of success and failure throughout and there need not have been such a mixture so often, with a little more active respect for literature as an art. But on the other hand, the mixture is a great deal better than nothing: it is a body of work which bears the marks of permanent interest.

When we look for comparisons outside the work, a considerable choice presents itself: one thinks of *Wuthering Heights*. One hardly thinks of Dostoievsky, as some critics have suggested; though Dostoievsky's Slavophilism is comparable to Faulkner's feeling about the South, the religious and intellectual motivations of Dostoievsky's novels are lacking in Faulkner.

But Faulkner's work is of sufficient ambition to suggest Shakespeare and of sufficient horror to bring to mind *King Lear*. Lear on the heath during the storm, calling on Nature to wipe out the works and the ungrateful heart of man is perhaps a suitable touchstone. What other better example of the horror and brutality of Life can we find? A fool the equal of Faulkner's idiots is present too.

Yet two important differences become plain. Shakespeare does not have to break down the framework of dramatic form in order to express his horror; he does not have to engage in the formal mystifications Faulkner uses; and most important of all, the genuine fool is matched by a rational man who makes believe he is a fool: rationality presides and triumphs over the scene, despite the irrationality of life.

Nevertheless, if the comparison shows how Faulkner falls short, it shows too that his work has the power and the seriousness to suggest the comparison. And with all its failures it is especially edifying in the winter after the year 1940, for as the true Fool so wisely remarks:

'This cold night will turn us all to fools and madmen'!

79. Maxwell Geismar, 'William Faulkner: The Negro and the Female'

1942

Writers in Crisis (Boston, Houghton Mifflin, 1942), 143–83. The selections reprinted are from 144–5, 178–83.

Writers in Crisis: The American Novel, 1925–1940 was the first of four books Geismar (b. 1909) wrote surveying American fiction since 1890. His general theme in that book is the movement from detached aestheticism in the 1920s to social concern and affirmation in the 1930s.

For in William Faulkner there is no such conversion as Hemingway and Dos Passos acquaint us with, no effort however imperfect at the integration of artist and society, or indeed of artist and modern life itself. With Faulkner the descending spiral of isolation, rebellion, and denial, the heritage of American negation, reaches its final emphasis. With him, we make our last study of the influence of the nineteen-twenties, forming, lasting over, and wholly conditioning the artist of the 'thirties. If the writing on the wall has already changed, each generation reading anew the chronicle of its origins and midwife to its own destiny, this one novelist stands and defies the vanishing script, like the Hightower of *Light in August*, hearing still the thunder of martial hooves upon a cloud of phantom dust. The causes of this in Faulkner's work form an interesting sequence. Here is in some respects the history of a dissipated talent, but the history of the dissipation becomes as remarkable as the talent. So let us make our little pilgrimage to Jefferson, Mississippi (as certain respectable scholars are wont to visit Hardy's Wessex or the Lake district of the English romantics), though here we shall hardly glimpse a rugged yeomanry, thatched cottages, musing shepherds, pastoral games. The Faulknerian countryside has its own customs nevertheless—deep southern region of Baptists and brothels, of attic secrets, land of shadows and swamps alike in its interior and outward scene, presided over by its twin Furies, the odd conjunction in the Faulknerian epic of the Negro and the Female. Coming to Jefferson, Mississippi, we touch the capital of this world, which reaches backward in time to the origins of southern culture, forward to the horrid prophecies of its extinction; and ranges down in social strata from the Sartoris nobility to the new commercial aristocracy of the Snopeses; down to the last extremes of the modern dispossessed: the poor-white Bundrens of *As I Lay Dying*, the criminal Popeye of *Sanctuary*, the negro Christmas turned brute again by the society which had raised him from the animal. And even in these extremes and others—its overdone idiocy, its agglomeration of perverts and fanatics, all the excesses of disease, its labored anguish and fabricated horrors—the Faulknerian geography is often quite compelling, memorable, if hardly to the Wessex tourist, quite respectable. It is certain that William Faulkner not merely represents, but is the deep South as no other American novelist may quite claim to be. And whatever the sequence we shall trace here, it is certain that Faulkner remains in a double sense the unreconstructed rebel; living as he does in two pasts—that of his own youth, and in the other youth, tropical, cultivated, evanescent, of the South itself.

[Geismar surveys Faulkner's novels up through *The Hamlet*, which 'ends with the rise to power of Flem Snopes who cheats the inhabitants of Jefferson into believing there is buried treasure on Flem's acres. Worthless land, and worthless people. Thus Faulkner fills the pages of his latest novel with the folklore of imbeciles.']

What is curious, however, is the tone in which this last account is rendered. The sense of tragedy in *The Sound and the Fury*, or that of disgust which lies behind the morbid action of *Sanctuary* and the inversions of *Light in August*, these have been succeeded by a sense of comedy, even gaiety, in *The Hamlet*. Faulkner seems now to accept the antics of his provincial morons, to enjoy the chronicle of their low-grade behavior; he submerges himself in their clownish degradation. And in one sense why should he not? If the Snopeses are all the writer can discover in the modern world, the descendants of the gangling and giggling Wash Jones, if they now tread omnipotently the southern acres where Sutpen had his vision of dynasty, they are after all the victims and not the victors, they are the blind vessels of the final wrath. For in the Faulknerian mythology, the Wash Jones of *Absalom*,

Absalom! will himself be superseded by another sort of Sutpen, the illegitimate Sutpen from the colored branch, the Jim Bond of the novel, the final type of brutish negro idiot:

I think that in time the Jim Bonds are going to conquer the western hemisphere. Of course it won't quite be in our time and of course as they spread toward the poles they will bleach out again like the rabbits and the birds do, so they won't show up so sharp against the snow. But it will still be Jim Bond; and so in a few thousand years, I who regard you will also have sprung from the loins of African kings.

And tell me one thing more, says Shreve to the Quentin Compson who we know is about to commit suicide,

'Why do you hate the South?'
'I dont hate it,' Quentin said, quickly, at once, immediately; 'I dont hate it,' he said. *I dont hate it* he thought, panting in the cold air, the iron New England dark; *I dont. I dont! I dont hate it! I dont hate it!*

So we see, just as Faulkner was punishing the northern woman in *Light in August*, now he threatens the entire western hemisphere with the rape of the Negro. And what better images, after all, could the artist have found to express his discontent—this great hatred of the entire complex of modern northern industrial society—than the Negro and the Female? The emancipated negro who to the southern writer is the cause of the destruction of all he held dear. And now showing this negro as Joe Christmas, as Jim Bond, as the inhuman criminal, the degenerate who will dominate the civilization which freed him, Faulkner proclaims at once his anger and his revenge upon those who have destroyed his home. What more appropriate symbol than the woman, who to the southern writer is the particular treasured image of the bygone, cavalier society he is lamenting and lost in: the southern Lady, elevated and sacrosanct, the central figure of the southern age of chivalry, of those gallant agrarian knights who, very much like Quixote, went forth in 1861 to perish in combat with the dynamo. How shall the artist better show the universal debasement of modern times than to turn the pure Lady into the contemporary Female, now wanton, graceless, and degraded? The woman is both the homemaker (this new home in which the southern artist feels himself the exile) and the original source of life itself (this new life against which all of Faulkner's work is the incessant protest). How shall the artist more aptly convey his total protest than to portray the Female source of life as itself inherently vicious? And as the last step in his sequence of discontent, Faulkner mates the Female with the Negro, the savage as Faulkner feels for whom the southern Lady was sacrificed, and spawns out of his modern union the colored degenerate who is to reign supreme, the moronic emperor of the future.

As against his discontent, we have now reached the complex of that double childhood in which apparently the positive emotions of Faulkner are caught: by contrast, all his affection, hope, and sense of human grandeur. There is first the pattern of the writer's personal involvement in childhood, in early family relationships. We have noticed in Faulkner's work the continual warmth of his childhood ties, the passion of siblings, the affection of brother for brother and brother for sister—Bayard and John Sartoris, Horace and Narcissa Benbow, Caddy and Benjy and Quentin Compson, Henry and Judith Sutpen and Charles Bon the half-brother in *Absalom* where the nature of Faulkner's love becomes quite explicit:

Perhaps in his fatalism he (Bon) loved Henry the better of the two, seeing perhaps in the sister merely the shadow, the woman vessel with which to consummate the love whose actual object was the youth. . . .

Yet, however distorted or infantile in its forms, this *is* love as against the always unsatisfactory nature of Faulkner's mature relationships, and at its best Faulkner's achievement is that we may ignore the form of his emotion and are moved by its content. And beneath his personal emphasis on childhood values, and reinforcing it, there is Faulkner's involvement with a cultural past, with the birth and early growth of all those southern aristocratic values which the Civil War and the modern industrial age were to shatter—his involvement, as it were, with the youth of his southern society itself which never came to its destined maturity, which was cut off in its own early blossoming. But in this curious complex of a double childhood in which our writer seems caught, we must admit our own belief that it is the sociological rather than the personal patterns which dominate. For the meaning of Faulkner's work comes directly out of that whole web of historical southern emotionalism which colors the thought even of so fine a traditionalist as Allen Tate and so extreme a rebel as Thomas Wolfe. Disentangling themselves from this web, treating similar themes, but their ideas often in direct opposition to Faulkner's, we may nevertheless find out Faulknerian connections also in the plays of Paul Green or the stories of Erskine Caldwell. The symbolism in Faulkner comes, as it were, out of a cultural psychosis of which his work manifests the extreme hallucinations, but which still colors the dreams of those who seem most free of it. In his total rejection of the modern South, portraying it only in terms of bestiality, Faulkner is held by the historical southern myth as surely as that great-grandfather of his, whose *White Rose of Memphis* would now find itself blooming from such strange soil. The great-grandson is perhaps the greater romanticist. For while his ancestor delineated the graces of an age which never quite existed, Faulkner is caught by one which now can never possibly exist. And we may now say that Faulkner's characters never grow up because there is no world for them to grow up into.

Held in such reversionary superstition, moreover, to what distortions can the psyche not bring itself? What a strange inversion it is to take the Female and the Negro, who are if anything the tragic consequence, and to exhibit them, indeed to believe them as the evil cause! This turning of the logical coin is psychological prestidigitation which ends with the head becoming the tail, and all respectable sense lost! The using of the one object that is certainly not responsible for our woes as being the single creator of them (so the Fascists use the Jew)—this is an inversion all too familiar to us today in other areas, another symptom of the confused emotions of our time. What genuine ills can be ignored by this again infantile preoccupation with scapegoats (so the child blames its mother), the infatuation with chimeras, what terrible ills can be created by it. Here is a dangerous quirk of the psyche, a trick once learned never wholly forgotten, a temptation once indulged in perhaps never to be wholly denied, a trick which may end by deceiving the trickster. I have used the title of Maurice Samuel's penetrating study of the Fascist superstitions, *The Great Hatred*, to best describe Faulkner's work as a whole. For it is in the larger tradition of reversionary, neo-pagan, and neurotic discontent (from which Fascism stems) that much of Faulkner's writing must be placed—the anti-civilizational revolt which has caught so many modern mystics, the revolt rising out of modern social evils, nourished by ignorance of their true nature, and which succumbs to malice as their solution. It is not accidental that in Faulkner's novels we have watched the retrogression from the affecting era of infancy to that of infantile corruption; and that returning in *Absalom, Absalom!* to the only society he can believe in, Faulkner's affection is nevertheless thinner, and the pretension of his novel greater. Hatred, as we know, feeds upon itself, while living in the past is apt to be an attenuating process.

Yet these are dangers dormant in parts of the Faulknerian reversion rather than immediate. It would be a tragedy if the major talent of Faulkner were to yield to any such gross chicanery, or to any other smaller trickeries. But it would be unjust to claim that on the whole, really, it has. (And it is a vital fact that no major American writer has as yet succumbed, in the manner of Knut Hamsun, to the Fascist ethics, even though some of our popular entertainers have shown the signs.) If we notice the dangerous possibilities of Faulkner's position, moreover, we must remember it is still the southern world of the nineteen-twenties that the novelist rejects. It is the earlier impact of the American industrial ethics he denies, the ethics embodied so brilliantly in the Jason of *The Sound and the Fury*, whose final citadel is perhaps Mississippi, and whose last deity is Snopes. In the repudiation of our society from 1860 to 1929, Faulkner thus presents another aspect of the total cultural rejection of the American artist over this epoch. Alone among the major writers of the 'twenties Faulkner has remained without change, our unreconstructed rebel, like the Hightower of *Light in August* still bemused in the vision of a nobler southern past where his life began and ended. Yet to Faulkner as to Lardner, viewing the modern scene, what may have seemed like perpetuity was after all only an American adolescence. The new age, as it reached the Michigan woods of Hemingway and the metropolis of Dos Passos, may yet rout the phantoms and ghouls of Faulkner's Jefferson. The crisis and indeed the new world war may bring another glimpse of that high and impossible American destiny which for Faulkner was ended by the Civil War. A developing American maturity, this maturity that Faulkner despairs of, must at last penetrate even to Jefferson, even to the Snopeses; and may awaken in our artist that magnificent compassion which he has vouchsafed only to the children of a disintegrating aristocracy. Like his Hightower, waiting, our author may once again hear 'the wild bugles, and the clashing sabres' and the thunder of martial hooves, but not dying now nor forever lost in the phantom dust. And, like Hightower, will he also find then 'something to pant with, to be reaffirmed in triumph and desire with'?

GO DOWN, MOSES AND OTHER STORIES

New York, May 1942
London, October 1942

---

80. Lionel Trilling, 'The McCaslins of Mississippi,' *Nation*

30 May 1942, 632

Trilling (b. 1905) joined the faculty of Columbia University in 1931. Beginning with his early study of Matthew Arnold, he has always combined a liberal humanism with the insights provided by several branches of modern criticism. His only earlier articles on Faulkner were an unfavorable review of *The Sound and the Fury* and a mixed review of *These Thirteen.*

William Faulkner's latest volume is brought out as a collection of stories, but six of the seven stories deal with a single theme, the relation of the Mississippi McCaslins to the Negroes about them, and they have a coherence strong enough to constitute, if not exactly a novel, then at least a narrative which begins, develops, and concludes. The seventh and alien story, 'Pantaloon in Black', is inferior both in conception and in execution; why it was placed in the midst of the others is hard to understand, for it diminishes their coherence. But conceivably Mr. Faulkner intended it to do just that, wishing to exempt the collection from being taken for a novel and judged as such. Yet it is only as an integrated work that the group of McCaslin stories can be read.

Mr. Faulkner's literary mannerisms are somewhat less obtrusive than they have been, but they are still dominant in his writing, and to me they are faults. For one thing, I find tiresome Mr. Faulkner's reliance on the method of memory to tell his stories. No doubt we can accept what so many Southern novelists imply, that in the South a continuous acute awareness of regional, local, and family history is one of the conditions of thought. But the prose in which Mr. Faulkner renders this element of his stories is, to me, most irritating; it drones so lyrically on its way, so intentionally losing its syntax in its long sentences, so full of self-pity expressed through somniloquism or ventriloquism. Then, too, while I am sure that prose fiction may make great demands on our attention, it ought not to make these demands arbitrarily, and there is no reason why Mr. Faulkner cannot settle to whom the pronoun 'he' refers. Mr. Faulkner's new book is worth effort but not, I think, the kind of effort which I found necessary: I had to read it twice to get clear not only the finer shades of meaning but the simple primary intentions, and I had to construct an elaborate genealogical table to understand the family connections.

These considerations aside, Mr. Faulkner's book is in many ways admirable. The six McCaslin stories are temperate and passionate, and they suggest more convincingly than anything I have read the complex tragedy of the South's racial dilemma. The first of the stories is set in 1856; it is the humorous tale of the chase after the runaway Tomey's Turl—it takes a certain effort to make sure that this is a slave, not a dog—of how old Buck McCaslin is trapped into marriage by Miss Sophonsiba Beauchamp and her brother Hubert (rightfully the Earl of Warwick), and of the poker game that is played for Tomey's Turl; the humor is abated when we learn that Turl is half-brother to one of the poker players. The last story is set in 1940; its central figure is the Negro murderer Samuel Worsham Beauchamp, descendant of Tomey's Turl and related to the McCaslins through more lines than one.

The best of the book does not deal directly with the Negro fate but with the spiritual condition of the white men who have that fate at their disposal. The Edmonds branch of the McCaslin family—there are three generations of Edmonds, but Mr. Faulkner likes to telescope the generations and all the Edmondses are really the same person: this does not exactly make for clarity—represents the traditional South; Isaac McCaslin, who is by way of being the hero of the narrative, represents the way of regeneration. The Edmondses are shown as being far from bad; in their relation to their Negroes they are often generous, never brutal, scarcely even irresponsible; but they accept their tradition and act upon their superiority and their rights, and the result is tragedy and degeneration both for the Negroes and for themselves. The effects are not always immediate and obvious; one of the best passages in the book, and one of the most crucial, is that in which, as a boy, Carothers Edmonds asserts his superiority over his Negro foster-brother and then, seeking later to repent, finds the tie irrevocably broken and his foster-family, though wonderfully cordial, stonily implacable; and the failure of love which Edmonds's tradition imposed upon him seems to affect his whole life.

As against the tradition which arrests the dignity of possession and the family, Isaac McCaslin sets the dignity of freedom and the unpossessable wilderness. The experience by which his moral sensibility is developed is a kind of compendium of the best American romantic and transcendental feeling. Cooper, Thoreau, and Melville are all comprised in what he learns from Sam Fathers, the Chickasaw Indian (but he was enough of a Negro to be glad to die), from the humility and discipline of hunting, from the quest after the great bear, a kind of forest cousin to Moby Dick, from the mysterious wilderness itself. So taught, he can no longer continue in the tradition to which he is born; at great and lasting cost to himself he surrenders his ancestral farm to the Edmonds branch.

It will of course be obvious that so personal and romantic a resolution as Ike McCaslin's is not being offered by Mr. Faulkner as a 'solution' to the racial problem of the South; nor, in representing that problem through the sexual and blood relations of Negro and white, is he offering a comprehensive description of the problem in all its literalness. (Though here I should like to suggest that Mr. Faulkner may be hinting that the Southern problem, in so far as it is cultural, is to be found crystallized in its sexual attitudes: it is certainly worth remarking of this book that white women are singularly absent from it and are scarcely mentioned, that all the significant relations are between men, and that Isaac McCaslin is the only man who loves a woman.) But the romantic and transcendental resolution and the blood and sexual ties are useful fictional symbols to represent the urgency and the iniquity of the literal fact. They suggest that its depth and its complication go beyond what committees and commissions can conceive, beyond even the most liberal 'understanding' and the most humanitarian 'sympathy'. Mr. Faulkner not only states this in the course of his book; he himself provides the proof: the story 'Pantaloon in Black' is conceived in 'understanding' and 'sympathy', like every other lynching story we have ever read, and when it is set beside the McCaslin stories with their complicated insights it appears not only inadequate but merely formal, almost insincere.

81. Unsigned review, *Times Literary Supplement*

10 October 1942, 497

It needs to be said every time a new book of his appears: Mr. William Faulkner is an exasperating writer. Sometimes, as on the present occasion, it needs to be said quite firmly. His peculiar talent is not in question. He has a sombre force of imagination, a smouldering and smoky pictorial power, a harsh striving intensity of nervous passion. Nothing that he writes, whatever the effort of reading him, can be lightly turned down as sound and fury. Yet the effort, it must be confessed, grows more grudging rather than less, the impression of sound and fury grows more insistent. It becomes increasingly difficult, in fact, even while conceding Mr. Faulkner's individual virtues, to avoid being preoccupied with his glaring and rather enervating faults. To those who have still to discover Mr. Faulkner, then, this new volume of his may be recommended for a degree of seriousness, an integrity of sentiment and a power of visual concentration that between them project what is obviously a high creative purpose. For others the principal interest of the volume may lie in the doubtful pleasures of critical analysis.

Mr. Faulkner gives us seven stories of varying length, all of them concerned with the social history of the American South at different periods during the past hundred years or so. Once more he seems to draw upon a private universe of surcharged experience, where names and genealogies and remote echoes from the past have all sorts of emotional associations for himself but not necessarily for anyone else. He is, indeed, a little like the poet content to speak the private tongue of a clique of his fellows. In each of the seven stories the scene is laid in the neighbourhood of the McCaslin plantation, in the country around

Jefferson, Tennessee;[1] the same characters, or their descendants, white and negro, move in and out of the stories; and the collection thus acquires a premeditated unity of theme and temper. Mr. Faulkner's object, at least in part, is clearly to exhibit the transition from the patriarchal verities of slavery in the South to the grosser verities of an unstable system of Southern democracy to-day. This is something he seems to have had in mind in several earlier books, which may explain why he pursues the changing pattern of social relationships with an air of repressed conviction even more vehement than usual. Although in his nostalgia for the past he hymns the glories of blood and soil in a way that is faintly alarming, it seems obvious that this is a poetic rendering of his slightly Rousseau-ish primitivism where the deep South is concerned. For the Mississippi negro as he was and is, at any rate, he has a fraternal sentiment that almost transcends speech.

Almost, but not quite. Mr. Faulkner's creative purpose is one thing, his verbal performance is another. His three characteristic failings are strongly in evidence in these stories, all three at the same time in most of them. There is, first, his passion for bizarre or uncouth violences of situation. It is less pronounced here than in other books of his, but even where there is neither murder nor sudden death, neither torment nor terror, the air is thick with nameless frenzies and obsessions. Then there is his tortuous, tangential, elliptical style of narrative construction. In the past the trick of breaking off abruptly at a point of climax and resuming at another and seemingly arbitrary point has sometimes justified itself as a device for increasing tension, but now it is too often a mechanical trick and merely evasive at that. And then there is Mr. Faulkner's prodigious, mountainous, dizzily soaring wordiness. This is his most intimidating vice. Where he is trying, as so often, to express some more or less difficult idea or an exceptionally complex state of mind he may be allowed his head, however trying the result. For instance, of the negro Lucas Beauchamp, who had a white grandfather:—'Instead of being at once the battle-ground and victim of the two strains, he was a vessel, durable, ancestryless, non-conductive, in which the toxin and its anti stalemated one another, seetheless, unrumoured in the outside air.' But in page after page Mr. Faulkner pours forth a torrent of words to communicate an undistinguished trifle of observation. The act of opening or shutting a door is made portentous by a flood of random accretions of insignificant fancy or cogitation. It is too, too much.

[1] English reviewers occasionally identified his state as Georgia or Tennessee or Alabama.

The stories, nevertheless, have their Faulkneresque point; even the accumulation of desperately groping and fretted words catches fire for a lurid moment in the most protracted of them, 'The Fire and the Hearth' and 'The Bear'. Perhaps the most impressive tale is 'Pantaloon in Black', in which a powerful young negro goes crazy at the death of his wife, cuts the throat of a white man and dies a hideous and uncomprehending death.

82. Malcolm Cowley, 'William Faulkner's Legend of the South'

Summer 1945

Sewanee Review, liii, 343–61.

This is the longest of three articles on Faulkner that Cowley published in 1944 and 1945. They were all incorporated into the Introduction to *The Portable Faulkner*, published only in America (Viking, 1946). The central thesis, of a legend being incrementally developed in each novel, Cowley had hinted at in earlier reviews of *The Hamlet* and *Go Down, Moses*.

I

William Faulkner is one of the writers who reward and even in a sense demand a second reading. When you return to one of his books years after its publication, the passages that had puzzled you are easier to understand and each of them takes its proper place in the picture. Moreover, you lose very little by knowing the plot in advance. Faulkner's stories are not the sort that unwind in celluloid ribbons until the last inch of them has been reflected on a flat screen, with nothing to imagine and nothing more to see except the newsreel, the animated cartoon and the Coming Repulsions; instead his books are sculptural, as if you could walk round them for different views of the same solid object. But it is not merely a statue that he presents: rather it is a whole monument or, let us say, a city buried in the jungle, to which the author wishes to guide us, but not at once or by following a single path. We start out along one road, winding between walls of jungle growth in the humid afternoon, and it is not long until we catch a glimpse of our destination. Just beyond us, however, is a swamp filled with snakes, and the guide makes us turn back. We take another road; we gain a clearer picture of the city; but this time there are other dangers in front of us, quicksands or precipices, and again the guide makes us return. By whatever road we travel, we always catch sight of our goal, always learn more about it and are always forced back; till at last we find the proper path and reach the heart of the city just as it is about to be overwhelmed by fire or earthquake. . . . Reading the same book a second time is like soaring over the jungle in a plane, with every section of the landscape falling into its proper perspective.

And there is another respect in which our judgment of the author changes when we return to not one but several of his novels in succession. On a first reading what had chiefly impressed us may have been their violence, which sometimes seemed to have no justification in art or nature. We had remembered incidents and figures like the violating of Temple Drake, in *Sanctuary*; like the pursuit and castration of Joe Christmas, in *Light in August*; like the idiot boy who fell in love and eloped with a cow, in *The Hamlet*; and like the nameless woman, in *The Wild Palms*, who bore her child unaided in the midst of a Mississippi River flood, on an Indian mound where all the snakes in the Delta had taken refuge. After a second reading, most of these nightmares retain their power to shock, but at the same time they merge a little into the background, as if they were the almost natural product of the long unbearable Mississippi summers; as if they were thunder showers brewed in the windless heat. We pay less attention to the horrors as such, and more to the old situation out of which they developed and the new disasters it seems to foreshadow.

The situation itself, and not the violence to which it leads, is Faulkner's real subject. It is, moreover, the same situation in all his books—or, let us say, in all the novels and stories belonging to his Yoknapatawpha County series. Briefly it is the destruction of the old Southern order, by war and military occupation and still more by finance capitalism that tempts and destroys it from within. 'Tell about the

South,' says Quentin Compson's roommate at Harvard, who comes from Edmonton, Alberta, and is curious about the unknown region beyond the Ohio. 'What's it like there?' Shreve McCannon goes on to ask 'What do they do there? Why do they live there? Why do they live at all?' And Quentin, whose background is a little like that of the author and who often seems to speak for him—Quentin answers, 'You can't understand it. You would have to be born there.' Nevertheless, he tells a long and violent story that he regards as the essence of the Deep South, which is not so much a region as it is, in Quentin's mind, an incomplete and frustrated nation trying to recover its own identity, trying to relive its legendary past.

There was a boy, Quentin says—I am giving the plot of *Absalom, Absalom!*—a mountain boy named Thomas Sutpen whose family drifted into the Virginia Tidewater. . . .

[summarizes Sutpen's story and Quentin's retelling of it, concluding, 'I don't hate it! I don't hate it.']

The reader cannot help wondering why this sombre and, at moments, plainly incredible story had so seized upon Quentin's mind that he trembled with excitement when telling it and felt that it revealed the essence of the Deep South. It seems to belong in the realm of Gothic romances, with Sutpen's Hundred taking the place of the haunted castle on the Rhine, with Colonel Sutpen as Faust and Charles Bon as Manfred. Then slowly it dawns on you that most of the characters and incidents have a double meaning; that besides their place in the story, they also serve as symbols or metaphors with a general application. Sutpen's great design, the land he stole from the Indians, the French architect who built his house with the help of wild Negroes from the jungle, the woman of mixed blood whom he married and disowned, the unacknowledged son who ruined him, the poor white whom he wronged and who killed him in anger, the final destruction of the mansion like the downfall of a social order: all these might belong to a tragic fable of Southern history. With a little cleverness, the whole novel might be explained as a connected and logical allegory, but this, I think, would be going beyond the author's intention. First of all he was writing a story, and one that affected him deeply, but he was also brooding over a social situation. More or less unconsciously, the incidents in the story came to represent the forces and elements in the social situation, since the mind naturally works in terms of symbols and parallels. In Faulkner's case, this form of parallelism is not confined to *Absalom, Absalom!* It can be found in the whole fictional framework that he has been elaborating in novel after novel, until his work has become a myth or legend of the South.

I call it a legend because it is obviously no more intended as a historical account of the country south of the Ohio than *The Scarlet Letter* is intended as a history of Massachusetts or *Paradise Lost* as a factual description of the Fall. Briefly stated, the legend might run something like this: The Deep South was settled partly by aristocrats like the Sartoris clan and partly by new men like Colonel Sutpen. Both types of planters were determined to establish a lasting social order on the land they had seized from the Indians (that is, to leave sons behind them). They had the virtue of living single-mindedly by a fixed code; but there was also an inherent guilt in their 'design,' their way of life, that put a curse on the land and brought about the Civil War. After the War was lost, partly as a result of their own mad heroism (for who else but men as brave as Jackson and Stuart could have frightened the Yankees into standing together and fighting back?) they tried to restore 'the design' by other methods. But they no longer had the strength to achieve more than a partial success, even after they had freed their land from the carpetbaggers who followed the Northern armies. As time passed, moreover, the men of the old order found that they had Southern enemies too: they had to fight against a new exploiting class descended from the landless whites of slavery days. In this struggle between the clan of Sartoris and the unscrupulous tribe of Snopes, the Sartorises were defeated in advance by a traditional code that prevented them from using the weapons of the enemy. But the Snopeses as price of their victory had to serve the mechanized civilization of the North, which was morally impotent in itself, but which, with the aid of its Southern retainers, ended by corrupting the Southern nation. In our own day, the problems of the South are still unsolved, the racial conflict is becoming more acute; and Faulkner's characters in their despairing moments foresee or forebode some catastrophe of which Jim Bond and his like will be the only survivors.

II

This legend of Faulkner's, if I have stated it correctly, is clearly not a scientific interpretation of Southern history (if such a thing exists); but neither is it the familiar plantation legend that has been embodied in hundreds of romantic novels. Faulkner presents the virtues of the old order as being moral rather than material. There is no baronial pomp in his novels; no profusion of silk and silver, mahogany and moonlight and champagne. The big house on Mr. Hubert Beauchamp's plantation (in *Go Down, Moses*) had a rotted floorboard in the back gallery that Mr. Hubert never got round to having fixed. Visitors used to find him sitting in the spring-house with his boots off and his feet in the water while he drank a morning toddy, which he invited them to share. Visitors to Sutpen's Hundred were offered champagne: it was the best, doubtless, and yet it was 'crudely dispensed out of the burlesqued pantomime elegance of Negro butlers who (and likewise the drinkers who gulped it down like neat whiskey between flowery and unsubtle toasts) would have treated lemonade the same way.' All the planters lived comfortably, with plenty of servants, but Faulkner never lets us forget that they were living on what had recently been the frontier. What he admires about them is not their wealth or their manners or their fine houses, but rather their unquestioning acceptance of a moral code that taught them 'courage and honor and pride, and pity and love of justice and of liberty.' Living with single hearts, they were, says Quentin Compson's father:

> . . . people too as we are, and victims too as we are, but victims of a different circumstance, simpler and therefore, integer for integer, larger, more heroic and the figures therefore more heroic too, not dwarfed and involved but distinct, uncomplex, who had the gift of living once or dying once instead of being diffused and scattered creatures drawn blindly limb from limb from a grab bag and assembled, author and victim too of a thousand homicides and a thousand copulations and divorcements.

The old order was a moral order: briefly that was its strength and the secret lost by its heirs. I don't wish to give the impression that Faulkner is the only Southern writer to advance this principle. During the last few years, it has been stated or suggested in a considerable body of Southern fiction and poetry, including the work of Allen Tate, Robert Penn Warren, Caroline Gordon and several others. The fact is that most of the ideas embodied in Faulkner's legend are held in common by many Southern writers of the new generation; what Faulkner has done is to express them in a whole series of novels written with his own emotional intensity and technical resourcefulness. But his version of the legend also has features that set it apart: most notably its emphasis on the idea that the Southern nation (like most of his own fictional heroes) was defeated from within.

In Faulkner's reading, the old order not only had its virtues of dignity and courage and love of justice; it also bore the moral burden of a guilt so great that the War and even Reconstruction were in some sense a merited punishment. There is madness, but there is a metaphorical meaning too, in Miss Rosa Coldfield's belief that Sutpen was a demon and that his sins were the real reason '. . . why God let us lose the War: that only through the blood of our men and the tears of our women could He stay this demon and efface his name and lineage from the earth.' Quentin's father is quite sane, in his sober moments, and yet he expresses almost the same idea about Sutpen's guilt and its consequences. He is telling the story of the Sutpens when he remarks that the Civil War was '. . . a stupid and bloody aberration in the high (and impossible) destiny of the United States, maybe instigated by that family fatality which possessed, along with all circumstance, that curious lack of economy between cause and effect which is always a characteristic of fate when reduced to using human materials.'

Colonel Sutpen himself has a feeling, not exactly of guilt, since he has never questioned the rightness of his design, but rather of amazement that so many misfortunes have fallen on him. Sitting in General Compson's office, he goes back over his career, trying to see where he had made his 'mistake,' for that is what he calls it. Sometimes the author seems to be implying that the sin for which Sutpen and his class are being punished is simply the act of cohabiting with Negroes. But before the end of *Absalom, Absalom!* we learn that miscegenation is only part of it. When Charles Bon's curious actions are explained, we find that he was taking revenge on his father for having refused to recognize him by so much as a single glance. Thus, heartlessness was the 'mistake' that had ruined Sutpen, not the taking of a partly Negro wife and Negro concubines. And the point becomes clearer in a long story called 'The Bear' (in *Go Down, Moses*), probably the best single piece that Faulkner has written. When Isaac McCaslin is twenty-one, he insists on relinquishing the big plantation that is his by inheritance; he thinks that the land is cursed. It is cursed in his eyes by the deeds of his grandfather: 'that evil and unregenerate old man who could summon, because she was his property, a human being because she was old enough and female, to his widower's house and get a child on her and then dismiss her because she was of an inferior race, and then bequeath a thousand dollars to the infant because he would be dead then and wouldn't have to pay it.' It follows that the land was cursed—and the War was part of the curse—because its owners had treated human beings as instruments; in a word, it was cursed by slavery.

All through his boyhood, Faulkner must have dreamed of fighting in the Civil War. It was a Sartoris war and not a Snopes war, like the one in which he afterwards risked his life in a foreign army. And yet his sympathies did not wholly lie with the slaveholding clan of Sartoris, even though it was his own clan. The men he most admired and must have pictured himself as resembling were the Southern soldiers—after all, they were the vast majority—who owned no slaves themselves and suffered from the institution of slavery. The men he would praise in his novels were those 'who had fought for four years and lost . . . not because they were opposed to freedom as freedom, but for the old reasons for which man (not the generals and politicians but man) has always fought and died in wars: to preserve a status quo or to establish a better future one to endure for his children.' You might define his position as that of an anti-slavery Southern nationalist.

His attitude toward Negroes will seem surprising only to Northerners. It seems to have developed from the attitude of the slaveholders, which was often inhuman but never impersonal—that is, the slave might be treated as a domestic animal, but not as a machine or the servant of a machine. Apparently the slaveholding class had little or no feeling of racial animosity. Frederick Law Olmsted, a sharp and by no means a friendly observer, was struck by what he called 'the close cohabitation and association of black and white.' In his *Journey in the Seaboard Slave States*, the record of his travels in 1853–54, he said: 'Negro women are carrying black and white babies together in their arms; black and white children are playing together (not going to school together); black and white faces are constantly thrust together out of the doors, to see the train go by.' He described the relation between masters and servants as having 'a familiarity and closeness of intimacy that would have been noticed with astonishment, if not with manifest displeasure, in almost any chance company at the North.' In Faulkner's historical novels, we find this closeness of intimacy compounded with closeness of blood, for the servants are very often the illegitimate half-brothers or sisters of their white companions—not only more often than in life, a mild way of putting it, but also more often than in any Abolitionist tract. He describes the old South as inhabited by two races that lived essentially the same life on their different levels. Thus, he says in *Absalom, Absalom!* that the young planters were

. . . only in the surface matter of food and clothing and daily occupation any different from the Negro slaves who supported them—the same sweat, the only difference being that on the one hand it went for labor in fields where on the other it went as the price of the spartan and meagre pleasures which were available to them because they did not have to sweat in the fields: the hard violent hunting and riding; the same pleasures: the one, gambling for worn knives and brass jewelry and twists of tobacco and buttons and garments because they happened to be easiest and quickest to hand; on the other for the money and horses, the guns and watches, and for the same reason; the same parties: the identical music from identical instruments, crude fiddles and guitars, now in the big house with candles and silk dresses and champagne, now in dirt-floored cabins with smoking pine knots and calico and water sweetened with molasses.

'They will endure. They are better than we are,' Ike McCaslin says of the Negroes, although he finds it more painful to utter this heresy than it is to surrender his plantation. 'Stronger than we are,' he continues. 'Their vices are vices aped from white men or that white men and bondage have taught them: improvidence and intemperance and evasion—not laziness . . . and their virtues are their own: endurance and pity and tolerance and forbearance and fidelity and love of children, whether their own or not or black or not.' In Faulkner's novels, the Negroes are an element of stability and endurance, just as the octoroons (like Charles Bon and Joe Christmas) are an element of tragic instability. His favorite characters are the Negro cooks and matriarchs who hold a white family together: Elnora and Dilsey and Clytie and Aunt Mollie Beauchamp. After the Compson family has gone to pieces (in *The Sound and the Fury*), it is Dilsey the cook who endures and is left behind to mourn. Looking up at the square, unpainted house with its rotting portico, she thinks, 'Ise seed de first and de last'; and later in the kitchen, looking at the cold stove, 'I seed de first en de last.'

The increasing hatred between two races is explained in Faulkner's novels partly by the heritage of slavery and Reconstruction; partly by the coming into power of a new class which, so far as it consists of families with landless and slaveless ancestors, has a tradition of hostility to the Negroes. But Faulkner also likes to think that the lynch mobs were often led by the descendants of his old enemies, the carpetbaggers—

> . . . that race threefold in one and alien even among themselves save for a single fierce will for rapine and pillage, composed of the sons of middle-aged Quartermaster lieutenants and Army sutlers and contractors in military blankets and shoes and transport mules, who followed the battles they themselves had not fought and inherited the conquest they themselves had not helped to gain . . . and left their bones and in another generation would be engaged in a fierce

economic competition of small sloven farms with the black men they were supposed to have freed and the white descendants of fathers who had owned no slaves anyway whom they were supposed to have disinherited, and in the third generation would be back once more in the little lost county seats as barbers and garage mechanics and deputy sheriffs and mill and gin hands and power-plant firemen, leading, first in mufti then later in an actual formalized regalia of hooded sheets and passwords and fiery Christian symbols, lynching mobs against the race their ancestors had come to save.

III

Faulkner's novels of contemporary Southern life continue the legend into a period that he regards as one of moral confusion and social decay. He is continually seeking in them for violent images to convey his sense of despair. *Sanctuary* is the most violent of all his novels; it is also the most popular and by no means the least important (in spite of Faulkner's comment that it was 'a cheap idea . . . deliberately conceived to make money'). The story of Popeye and Temple Drake has more meaning than appears on a first hasty reading—the only reading that most of the critics have been willing to grant it. George Marion O'Donnell went over the novel more carefully and decided that it formed a coherent allegory. Writing in the *Kenyon Review* (Autumn, 1939), he said that the pattern of the allegory was something like this:

> Southern Womanhood Corrupted but Undefiled (Temple Drake), in the company of the Corrupted Tradition (Gowan Stevens, a professional Virginian), falls into the clutches of amoral Modernism (Popeye), which is itself impotent, but which with the aid of its strong ally Natural Lust ('Red') rapes Southern Womanhood unnaturally and then seduces her so satisfactorily that her corruption is total, and she becomes the tacit ally of Modernism. Meanwhile Pore White Trash (Goodwin) has been accused of the crime which he, with the aid of the Naif Faithful (Tawmmy), actually tried to prevent. The Formalized Tradition (Horace Benbow), perceiving the true state of affairs, tries vainly to defend Pore White Trash. However, Southern Womanhood is so hopelessly corrupted that she willfully sees Pore White Trash convicted and lynched; she is then carried off by Wealth (Judge Drake) to meaningless escape in European luxury. Modernism, carrying in it from birth its own impotence and doom, submits with masochistic pleasure to its own destruction for the one crime that it has not yet committed—Revolutionary Destruction of Order (the Murder of the Alabama policeman, for which the innocent Popeye is executed).

Mr. O'Donnell deserves very great credit as the first critic to discuss Faulkner as a moralist, the first to compare him in passing with

Hawthorne, and almost the first to see that he is engaged in creating Southern myths. In his comments on *Sanctuary*, however, he has been entirely too ingenious. There is no doubt that his allegorical scheme can be read into the novel, but it hardly seems possible that the author intended to put it there. Faulkner tells us that *Sanctuary* was written 'in about three weeks.' It was completely rewritten two years later, in the effort 'to make out of it something which would not shame *The Sound and the Fury* and *As I Lay Dying* too much'; but I doubt that Faulkner had or took the time to give every character a double meaning. Lee Goodwin, for example, is not Pore White Trash, capitalized, but a tough, frightened moonshiner dishonorably discharged from the Army. Tawmmy is not the Naif Faithful, capitalized; he is simply faithful and stupid. If Temple Drake has any symbolic value, she represents the South as a whole, or the younger generation in the South, rather than Southern Womanhood (a phrase that makes Faulkner wince) but it is also quite possible that she represents nothing but a rather silly co-ed. Popeye, however, is another question; and at this point Mr. O'Donnell's reading is not only ingenious but comes very close to Faulkner's conscious or unconscious intention.

Popeye is one of several characters in Faulkner's novels who stand for something that might be called 'amoral Modernism,' considering that they are creatures of the time and have no social morality whatever; but it might also be called—more accurately, I think—the mechanical civilization that has invaded and partly conquered the South. Popeye is always described in mechanical terms: his eyes 'looked like rubber knobs'; his face 'just went awry, like the face of a wax doll set too near a hot fire and forgotten'; his tight suit and stiff hat were 'all angles, like a modernistic lampshade'; and in general he had 'that vicious depthless quality of stamped tin.' He was the son of a professional strikebreaker, from whom he inherited syphilis, and the grandson of a pyromaniac. Like two other villains in Faulkner's novels, Joe Christmas and Januarius Jones, he had spent most of his childhood in an institution. He was the man 'who made money and had nothing he could do with it, spend it for, since he knew that alcohol would kill him like poison, who had no friends and had never known a woman'—in other words, he was the compendium of all the hateful qualities that Faulkner assigns to finance capitalism. *Sanctuary* is not the connected allegory that Mr. O'Donnell presents in outline (he doesn't approve of allegorical writing by novelists), but neither is it the accumulation of pointless horrors as which it has been dismissed by other critics. It is an example of the Freudian method turned backwards, being full of sexual nightmares that are in reality social symbols. In the author's mind, the novel is somehow connected with what he regards as the rape and corruption of the South.

And the descendants of the old ruling caste, in Faulkner's novels, have the wish but not the courage or the strength of will to prevent this new disaster. They are defeated by Popeye (like Horace Benbow), or they run away from him (like Gowan Stevens, who had gone to school at Virginia and learned to drink like a gentleman, but not to fight for his principles), or they are robbed and replaced in their positions of influence by the Snopeses (like old Bayard Sartoris, the president of the bank), or they drug themselves with eloquence and alcohol (like Mr. Compson), or they retire into the illusion of being inviolable Southern ladies (like Mrs. Compson, who says, 'It can't be simply to flout and hurt me. Whoever God is, He would not permit that. I'm a lady.'), or they dwell so much on the past that they are incapable of facing the present (like Reverend Hightower, of *Light in August*, who loses his wife and his church through living in a dream world), or they run from danger to danger (like young Bayard Sartoris) frantically seeking their own destruction. Faulkner's novels are full of well-meaning and even admirable people, not only the grandsons of the cotton aristocracy, but also pine-hill farmers and storekeepers and sewing-machine agents and Negro cooks and sharecroppers; but they are almost all of them defeated by circumstances and they carry with them a sense of their own doom.

They also carry, whether heroes or villains, a curious sense of submission to their fate. 'There is not one of Faulkner's characters,' says André Gide in his dialogue on 'The New American Novelists,' 'who, properly speaking, has a soul'; and I think he means that not one of them exercises the faculty of conscious choice between good and evil. They are haunted, obsessed, driven forward by some inner necessity. Like Miss Rosa Coldfield (in *Absalom, Absalom!*), they exist in 'that dream state in which you run without moving from a terror in which you cannot believe, toward a safety in which you have no faith.' Or, like the slaves freed by General Sherman's army (in *The Unvanquished*), they follow the roads toward any river, believing that it will be their Jordan:

They were singing, walking along the road singing, not even looking to either side. The dust didn't even settle for two days, because all that night they still passed; we sat up listening to them, and the next morning every few yards along the road would be the old ones who couldn't keep up any more, sitting or lying down and even crawling along, calling to the others to help them; and the others—the young ones—not stopping, not even looking at them. 'Going to Jordan,' they told me. 'Going to cross Jordan.'

All Faulkner's characters, black and white, are a little like that. They dig for gold frenziedly after they have lost their hope of finding it (like Henry Armstid in *The Hamlet* and Lucas Beauchamp in *Go Down, Moses*); or they battle against and survive a Mississippi flood for the one privilege of returning to the state prison farm (like the tall convict in *The Wild Palms*); or, a whole family together, they carry a body through flood and fire and corruption to bury it in the cemetery at Jefferson (like the Bundrens in *As I Lay Dying*); or they tramp the roads week after week in search of men who had promised to marry them (like Lena Grove, the pregnant woman of *Light in August*); or, pursued by a mob, they turn at the end to meet and accept death (like Joe Christmas in the same novel). Even when they seem to be guided by a conscious design, like Colonel Sutpen, it is not something they have chosen by an act of will, but something that has taken possession of them: '. . . not what he wanted to do but what he just had to do, had to do it whether he wanted to or not, because if he did not do it he knew that he could never live with himself for the rest of his life.' In the same way, Faulkner himself writes, not what he wants to, but what he just has to write whether he wants to or not. And the effect produced on us by all these haunted characters, described in hypnagogic prose, is that of myths or fairy tales or dreams, where again the people act under compulsion, toward fatally predetermined ends.

In addition to being a fatalist, Faulkner is also an idealist, more strongly so than any other American writer of our time. The idealism disguises itself as its own opposite, but that is because he is deeply impressed by and tends to exaggerate the contrast between the life around him and the ideal picture in his mind. No other American writer makes such a use of negative turns of speech: his stories abound in words like 'paintless,' 'lightless,' 'windowless,' 'not-feeling,' 'unvisioned.' He speaks of 'that *roadless* and even *pathless* waste of *unfenced* fallow and wilderness jungle—*no* barn, *no* stable, *not so much as* a hen-coop; just a log cabin built by hand and *no* clever hand either, a meagre pile of clumsily cut firewood sufficient for about one day and *not even* a gaunt hound to come bellowing out from under the house when he rode up.' In the same story ('The Bear'), he speaks of '. . . the empty fields without plow or seed to work them, fenceless against the stock which did not exist within or without the walled stable which likewise was not there.' He speaks of faces watching 'without alarm, without recognition, without hope,' and he speaks of the South under Reconstruction as 'a lightless and gutted and empty land.' Always in his mind he has an ideal picture of how the land and the people should be—a picture of painted, many-windowed houses, fenced fields, overflowing barns, eyes lighting up with recognition; and always, being honest, he measures that picture against the land and people he has seen. And both pictures are not only physical but moral; for always in the background of his novels is a sense of moral standards and a feeling of outrage at their being violated or simply pushed aside. Seeing little hope in the future, he turns to the past, where he hopes to discover a legendary and recurrent pattern that will illuminate and lend dignity to the world about him. So it is that Reverend Hightower, dying in the dingy ruin of his plans, sees a vision of Bedford Forrest's troopers, who lived without question by a single and universally accepted code:

> He hears above his heart the thunder increase, myriad and drumming. Like a long sighing of wind in trees it begins, then they sweep into sight, borne now upon a cloud of phantom dust. They rush past, forwardleaning in the saddles, with brandished arms, beneath whipping ribbons from slanted and eager lances; with tumult and soundless yelling they sweep past like a tide whose crest is jagged with the wild heads of horses and the brandished arms of men like the crater of the world in explosion. They rush past, are gone; the dust swirls skyward sucking, fades away into the night which has fully come. Yet, leaning forward in the window . . . it seems to him that he still hears them: the wild bugles and the clashing sabres and the dying thunder of hooves.

83. Robert Penn Warren, 'Cowley's Faulkner'

August 1946

New Republic (12 August and 26 August 1946), cxv, 176–80, 234–7.

An essay-review of *The Portable Faulkner*, this was printed in two parts. *All the King's Men*, Warren's popular novel, came out the same year.

Malcolm Cowley's editing of *The Portable Faulkner* is remarkable on two counts. First, the selection from Faulkner's work is made not merely to give a cross-section or a group of good examples but to demonstrate one of the principles of integration in the work. Second, the introductory essay is one of the few things ever written on Faulkner which is not hagridden by prejudice or preconception and which really sheds some light on the subject.

The selections here are made to describe the place, Yoknapatawpha County, Mississippi, which is, as Cowley puts it, 'Faulkner's mythical kingdom,' and to give the history of that kingdom. The place is the locale of most of Faulkner's work. Its 2,400 square miles lie between the hills of north Mississippi and the rich, black bottom lands. It has a population of 15,611 persons, composing a society with characters as different as the Bundrens, the Snopeses, Ike McCaslin, Percy Grimm, Temple Drake, the Compsons, Christmas, Dilsey, and the tall convict of *The Wild Palms*. No land in all fiction lives more vividly in its physical presence than this mythical county—the 'pine-winey' afternoons, the nights with 'a thin sickle of moon like the heel print of a boot in wet sand,' the tremendous reach of the big river in flood, 'yellow and sleepy in the afternoon,' and the 'little piddling creeks, that run backward one day and forward the next and come busting down on a man full of dead mules and hen houses,' the ruined plantation which was Popeye's hangout, the swamps and fields and hot, dusty roads of the Frenchman's Bend section, and the remnants of the great original forests, 'green with gloom' in summer, 'if anything actually dimmer than they had been in November's gray dissolution, where even at noon the sun fell only in windless dappling upon the earth which never completely dried.'

And no land in all fiction is more painstakingly analyzed from the sociological standpoint. The descendants of the old families, the descendants of bushwhackers and carpetbaggers, the swamp rats, the Negro cooks and farm hands, bootleggers and gangsters, peddlers, college boys, tenant farmers, country storekeepers, county-seat lawyers are all here. The marks of class, occupation, and history are fully rendered and we know completely their speech, dress, food, houses, manners, and attitudes. Nature and sociology, geography and human geography, are scrupulously though effortlessly presented in Faulkner's work, and their significance for his work is very great; but the significance is of a conditioning order. They are, as it were, aspects of man's 'doom'—a word of which Faulkner is very fond—but his manhood in the face of that doom is what is important.

Cowley's selections are made to give the description of the mythical kingdom, but more important, they are made to give its history. Most critics, even those who have most naïvely or deliberately misread the meaning of the fact, have been aware that the sense of the past is crucial in Faulkner's work. Cowley has here set up selections running in date of action from 1820 to 1940. . . .

[summarizes Cowley's selections and the argument of his introduction]

This is, in brief, Cowley's interpretation of the legend, and it provides an excellent way into Faulkner; it exactly serves the purpose which an introduction should serve. The interpretation is indebted, no doubt, to that of George Marion O'Donnell (the first and still an indispensable study of Faulkner's theme), but it modifies O'Donnell's tendency to read Faulkner with an allegorical rigidity and with a kind of doctrinal single-mindedness.

It is possible that the present view, however, should be somewhat modified, at least in emphasis. Although no writer is more deeply committed to a locality than Faulkner, the emphasis on the Southern elements may blind us to other elements, or at least other applications, of deep significance. And this is especially true in so far as the work is interpreted merely as Southern apologetics or, as it is by Maxwell Geismar, as the 'extreme hallucinations' of a 'cultural psychosis.'

It is important, I think, that Faulkner's work be regarded not in terms of the South against the North, but in terms of issues which are common to our modern world. The legend is not merely a legend of the South, but is also a legend of our general plight and problem. The modern world is in moral confusion. It does suffer from a lack of discipline, of sanctions, of community of values, of a sense of a mission. It is a world in which self-interest, workableness, success, provide the standards. It is a world which is the victim of abstraction and of mechanism, or at least, at moments, feels itself to be. It can look back nostalgically upon the old world of traditional values and feel loss and perhaps despair—upon the world in which, as one of Faulkner's characters puts it, men 'had the gift of living once or dying once instead of being diffused and scattered creatures drawn blindly from a grab bag and assembled'—a world in which men were, 'integer for integer,' more simple and complete.

If it be objected that Faulkner's view is unrealistic, that had the old order satisfied human needs it would have survived, and that it is sentimental to hold that it was killed from the outside, the answer is clear in the work: the old order did not satisfy human needs—the Southern old order or any other—for it, not being founded on justice, was 'accursed' and held the seeds of its own ruin in itself. But even in terms of the curse the old order, as opposed to the new order (in so far as the new is to be equated with Snopesism), allowed the traditional man to define himself as human by setting up codes, concepts of virtue, obligations, and by accepting the risks of his humanity. Within the traditional order was a notion of truth, even if man in the flow of things did not succeed in realizing that truth. Take, for instance, the passage from 'The Bear':

> 'All right,' he said. 'Listen,' and read again, but only one stanza this time and closed the book and laid it on the table. 'She cannot fade, though thou hast not thy bliss,' McCaslin said: 'Forever wilt thou love, and she be fair.'
>
> 'He's talking about a girl,' he said.
>
> 'He had to talk about something,' McCaslin said. Then he said, 'He was talking about truth. Truth is one. It doesn't change. It covers all things which touch the heart—honor and pride and pity and justice and courage and love. Do you see now?'

The human effort is what is important, the capacity to make the effort to rise above the mechanical process of life, the pride to endure, for in endurance there is a kind of self-conquest.

When it is said, as it is often said, that Faulkner's work is 'backward-looking,' the answer is that the constant ethical center is to be found in the glorification of the human effort and of human endurance, which are not in time, even though in modernity they seem to persist most surely among the despised and rejected. It is true that Faulkner's work contains a savage attack on modernity, but it is to be remembered that Elizabethan tragedy, for instance, contained just such an attack on its own special 'modernity.' (Ambition is the most constant tragic crime, and ambition is the attitude special to an opening society; all villains are rationalists and appeal to 'nature' beyond traditional morality for justification, and rationalism is, in the sense implied here, the attitude special to the rise of a secular and scientific order before a new morality can be formulated.)

It is not ultimately important whether the traditional order (Southern or other) as depicted by Faulkner fits exactly the picture which critical historical method provides. Let it be granted, for the sake of discussion, that Faulkner does oversimplify the matter. What is ultimately important, both ethically and artistically, is the symbolic function of that order in relation to the world which is set in opposition to it. The opposition between the old order and the new does not, however, exhaust the picture. What of the order to come? 'We will have to wait,' old Ike McCaslin says to the mulatto girl who is in love with a white man. A curse may work itself out in time; and in such glimpses, which occur now and then, we get the notion of a grudging meliorism, a practical supplement to the idealism, like Ike McCaslin's, which finds compensation in the human effort and the contemplation of 'truth.'

The discussion, even at a larger scope and with more satisfactory analysis, of the central theme of Faulkner would not exhaust the interest of his work. In fact, the discussion of this question always runs the risk of making his work appear too schematic, too dry and too complacent when in actual fact it is full of rich detail, of shadings and complexities of attitudes, of ironies and ambivalences. Cowley's introduction cautions the reader on this point and suggests various fruitful topics for investigation and thought. But I shall make bold—and in the general barrenness of criticism on Faulkner it does not require excessive boldness—to list and comment on certain topics which seem to me to demand further critical study.

Nature. The vividness of the natural background is one of the impressive features of Faulkner's work. It is accurately observed, but observation only provides the stuff from which the characteristic effects are gained. It is the atmosphere which counts, the poetry, the infusion of feeling, the symbolic weight. Nature provides a backdrop—of lyric beauty (the meadow in the cow episode of *The Hamlet*), of homely charm (the trial scene of the 'Spotted Horses' story from the same book), of sinister, brooding force (the river in 'Old Man' from *The Wild Palms*), of massive dignity (the forest in 'The Bear')—for the human action and passion. The indestructible beauty is there: 'God created man,' Ike McCaslin says in 'Delta Autumn,' 'and He created the world for him to live in and I reckon He created the kind of world He would have wanted to live in if He had been a man.'

Ideally, if man were like God, as Ike McCaslin puts it, man's attitude toward nature would be one of pure contemplation, pure participation in its great forms and appearances; the appropriate attitude is love, for with Ike McCaslin the moment of love is equated with godhood. But since man 'wasn't quite God himself,' since he lives in the world of flesh, he must be a hunter, user, and violator. To return to McCaslin: God 'put them both here: man and the game he would follow and kill, foreknowing it. I believe He said, "So be it." I reckon He even foreknew the end. But He said, "I will give him his chance. I will give him warning and foreknowledge too, along with the desire to follow and the power to slay. The woods and the fields he ravages and the game he devastates will be the consequence and signature of his crime and guilt, and his punishment." '

There is, then, a contamination implicit in the human condition—a kind of Original Sin, as it were—but it is possible, even in the contaminating act, the violation, for man to achieve some measure of redemption, a redemption through love. For instance, in 'The Bear,' the great legendary beast which is pursued for years to the death is also an object of love and veneration, and the symbol of virtue, and the deer hunt of 'Delta Autumn' is for Ike McCaslin a ritual of renewal. Those who have learned the right relationship to nature—'the pride and humility' which young Ike McCaslin learns from the half-Negro, half-Indian Sam Fathers—are set over against those who have not. In 'The Bear,' General Compson speaks up to Cass McCaslin to defend the wish of the boy Ike McCaslin to stay an extra week in the woods: 'You got one foot straddled into a farm and the other foot straddled into a bank; you ain't even got a good hand-hold where this boy was already an old man long before you damned Sartorises and Edmondses invented farms and banks to keep yourselves from having to find out what this boy was born knowing and fearing too maybe, but without being afraid, that could go ten miles on a compass because he wanted to look at a bear none of us had ever got near enough to put a bullet in and looked at the bear and came the ten miles back on the compass in the dark; maybe by God that's the why and the wherefore of farms and banks.'

Those who have the wrong attitude toward nature are the pure exploiters, the apostles of abstractionism, the truly evil men. For instance, the very opening of *Sanctuary* presents a distinction on this ground between Benbow and Popeye. While the threat of Popeye keeps Benbow crouching by the spring, he hears a Carolina wren sing, and even under these circumstances tries to recall the local name for it. And he says to Popeye: 'And of course you don't know the name of it. I don't suppose you'd know a bird at all, without it was singing in a cage in a hotel lounge, or cost four dollars on a plate.' Popeye, as we may remember, spits in the spring (he hates nature and must foul it), is afraid to go through the woods ('Through all them trees?' he demands when Benbow points out the short cut), and when an owl whisks past them in the twilight, claws at Benbow's coat with almost hysterical fear ('It's just an owl,' Benbow says. 'It's nothing but an owl.').

The pure exploiters, though they may gain ownership and use of a thing, never really have it; like Popeye, they are impotent. For instance, Flem Snopes, the central character and villain of *The Hamlet*, who brings the exploiter's mentality to Frenchman's Bend, finally marries Eula Varner, a kind of fertility goddess or earth goddess; but his ownership is meaningless, for she always refers to him as 'that man' (she does not even have a name for him), and he has only got her after she has given herself willingly to one of the bold, hotblooded boys of the neighborhood. In fact, nature can't, in one sense, be 'owned.' Ike McCaslin, in 'The Bear,' says of the land which has come down to him: 'It was never Father's and Uncle Buddy's to bequeath me to repudiate, because it was never Grandfather's to bequeath them to bequeath me to repudiate, because it was never old Ikkemotubbe's to sell to Grandfather for bequeathment and repudiation. Because it was never Ikkemotubbe's father's father's to bequeath Ikkemotubbe to sell to Grandfather or any man because on the instant when Ikkemotubbe discovered, realized, that he could sell it for money, on that instant it ceased ever to have been his forever, father to father, to father, and the man who bought it bought nothing.'

The right attitude toward nature is, as a matter of fact, associated with the right attitude toward man, and the mere lust for power over nature is associated with the lust for power over other men, for God gave the earth to man, we read in 'The Bear,' not 'to hold for himself and his descendants inviolable title forever, generation after generation, to the oblongs and squares of the earth, but to hold the earth mutual and intact in the communal anonymity of brotherhood, and all the fee He asked was pity and humility and sufferance and endurance and the sweat of his face for bread.' It is the failure of this pity which curses the earth (the land in Faulkner's particular country is 'accursed' by chattel slavery, but slavery is simply one of the possible forms of the failure). But the rape of nature and the crime against man are always avenged. The rape of nature, the mere exploitation of it without love, is always avenged because the attitude which commits that crime also commits the crime against men which in turn exacts vengeance, so that man finally punishes himself. It is only by this line of reasoning that one can, I think, read the last page of 'Delta Autumn':

> This land which man has deswamped and denuded and derivered in two generations so that white men can own plantations and commute every night to Memphis and black men own plantations and ride in jim crow cars to Chicago to live in millionaires' mansions on Lake Shore Drive; where white men rent farms and live like niggers and niggers crop on shares and live like animals; where cotton is planted and grows man-tall in the very cracks of the sidewalks, and usury and mortgage and bankruptcy and measureless wealth, Chinese and African and Aryan and Jew, all breed and spawn together until no man has time to say which one is which nor cares. . . . No wonder the ruined woods I used to know don't cry for retribution! he thought: The people who have destroyed it will accomplish its revenge.

The attitude toward nature in Faulkner's work, however, does not involve a sinking into nature. In Faulkner's mythology man has 'suzerainty over the earth,' he is not of the earth, and it is the human virtues which count—'pity and humility and sufferance and endurance.' If we take even the extreme case of the idiot Snopes and his fixation on the cow in *The Hamlet* (a scene whose function in the total order of the book is to show that even the idiot pervert is superior to Flem), a scene which shows the human being as close as possible to the 'natural' level, we find that the scene is the most lyrical in Faulkner's work: even the idiot is human and not animal, for only human desires, not animal, clothe themselves in poetry. I think that George Marion O'Donnell is right in pointing to the humanism–naturalism opposition in Faulkner's work, and over and over again we find that the point of some novel or story has to do with the human effort to find or create values in the mechanical round of experience—'not just to eat and evacuate and sleep warm,' as Charlotte Rittenmeyer says in *The Wild Palms*, 'so we can get up and eat and evacuate in order to sleep warm again,' or not just to raise cotton to buy niggers to raise cotton to buy niggers, as it is put in another place. Even when a character seems to be caught in the iron ring of some compulsion, of some mechanical process (the hunted Negro of 'Red Leaves,' the tall convict of *The Wild Palms*, Christmas of *Light in August*), the effort may be discernible. And in Quentin's attempt, in *The Sound and the Fury*, to persuade his sister Caddy, who is pregnant by one of the boys of Jefferson, to confess that she has committed incest with him, we find among other things the idea that 'the horror' and 'the clean flame' would be preferable to the meaninglessness of the 'loud world.'

Humor. One of the most important remarks in Cowley's introduction is that concerning humor. There is, especially in the later books, 'a sort of homely and sober-sided frontier humor that is seldom achieved in contemporary writing.' Cowley continues: 'In a curious way, Faulkner combines two of the principal traditions in American letters: the tradition of psychological horror, often close to symbolism, that begins with Charles Brockden Brown, our first professional novelist, and extends through Poe, Melville, Henry James (in his later stories), Stephen Crane and Hemingway; and the other tradition of frontier humor and realism, beginning with Augustus Longstreet's *Georgia Scenes* and having Mark Twain as its best example.' The observation is an acute one, for the distortions of humor and the distortions of horror in Faulkner's work are closely akin and frequently, in a given instance, can scarcely be disentangled.

It is true that the most important strain of humor in Faulkner's work is derived from the tradition of frontier humor (though it is probable that he got it from the porches of country stores and the courthouse yards of county-seat towns and not from any book), and it is true that the most spectacular displays of Faulkner's humor are of this order—for example, the 'Spotted Horses' episode from *The Hamlet* or the story 'Was.' But there are other strains which might be distinguished and investigated. For example, there is a kind of Dickensian humor; the scene in the Memphis brothel from *Sanctuary*, which is reprinted here under the title 'Uncle Bud and the Three Madams,' is certainly more Dickensian than frontier. There is a subdued humor, sometimes shading into pathos, in the treatment of some of the Negro characters and in their dialogue. And there is an irony ranging from that in the scene in *Sanctuary* where Miss Reba, the madam, in offended decency keeps telling Temple, 'Lie down and cover up your nekkidness,' while the girl talks with Benbow, to that in the magnificently sustained monologue of Jason at the end of *The Sound and the Fury*.

In any case, humor in Faulkner's work is never exploited for its own sake. It is regularly used as an index, as a lead, to other effects. The humor in itself may be striking, but Faulkner is not a humorist in the sense, say, that Mark Twain is. His humor is but one perspective on the material and it is never a final perspective, as we can see from such an example as the episode of 'Spotted Horses.' Nothing could be more wide of the point than the remark in Maxwell Geismar's essay on Faulkner to the effect that Faulkner in *The Hamlet* 'seems now to accept the antics of his provincial morons, to enjoy the chronicle of their low-grade behavior; he submerges himself in their clownish degradation.' All the critic seems to find in Mink Snopes' victim with his lifelong devotion to the memory of his dead wife, and in Ratliff with his good heart and ironical mind and quiet wisdom, is comic 'descendants of the gangling and giggling Wash Jones.'

The Poor White. The above remark leads us to the not uncommon misconception about the role of the poor white in Faulkner's work. It is true that the Snopeses are poor whites, descendants of bushwhackers (and therefore outside society, as the bushwhacker was outside society, had no 'side' in the Civil War but tried to make a good thing of it), and it is true that Snopesism represents a special kind of villainy and degradation, the form that the pure doctrine of exploitation and degradation takes in the society of which Faulkner writes, but any careful reader realizes that a Snopes is not to be equated with a poor white. For instance, the book most fully about the poor white, *As I Lay Dying*, is full of sympathy and poetry. There are a hundred touches like that in Cash's soliloquy about the phonograph: 'I reckon it's a good thing we ain't got ere a one of them. I reckon I wouldn't never get no work done a-tall for listening to it. I don't know if a little music ain't about the nicest thing a fellow can have. Seems like when he comes in tired of a night, it ain't nothing could rest him like having a little music played and him resting.' Or like the long section toward the middle of the book devoted to Addie Bundren, a section which is full of eloquence like that of this paragraph: 'And then he died. He did not know he was dead. I would lie by him in the dark, hearing the dark land talking of God's love and His beauty and His sin; hearing the dark voicelessness in which the words are the deeds, and the other words that are not deeds, that are just the gaps in people's lacks, coming down like the cries of geese out of the wild darkness in the old terrible nights, fumbling at the deeds like orphans to whom are pointed out in a crowd two faces and told, That is your father, your mother.' Do these passages indicate a relish in the 'antics of his provincial morons'?

The whole *As I Lay Dying* is based on the heroic effort of the Bundren family to fulfill the promise to the dead mother, to take her body to Jefferson; and the fact that Anse Bundren, after the heroic effort has been completed, immediately gets him a new wife, the 'duck-shaped woman' with the 'hard-looking pop-eyes,' does not negate the heroism of the effort nor the poetry and feeling which give flesh to the book. We are told by one critic that 'what should have been the drama of the Bundrens thus becomes in the end a sort of brutal farce,' and that we are 'unable to feel the tragedy because the author has refused to accept the Bundrens, as he did accept the Compsons, as tragic.' Rather, I should say, the Bundrens may come off a little better than the latter-day Compsons, the whining mother, the promiscuous Caddy, the ineffectual Quentin, and the rest. The Bundrens, at least, are capable of the heroic effort, and the promise is fulfilled. What the conclusion indicates is that even such a fellow as Anse Bundren (who is not typical of his family, by the way), in the grip of an idea, in terms of promise or code, is capable of rising out of his ordinary level; Anse falls back at the end, but only after the prop of the idea and obligation have been removed. And we may recall that even the 'gangling and giggling Wash Jones' has always been capable of some kind of obscure dream and aspiration (his very attachment to Sutpen indicates that), and that in the end he achieves dignity and manhood.

The final and incontrovertible evidence that Snopes is not to be equated with poor white comes in *The Hamlet* (though actually most of the characters in the book, though they may be poor, are not, strictly speaking, 'poor whites' at all, but rather what uninstructed reviewers choose to call by that label). The point of the book is the assault made on a solid community of plain, hard-working small farmers by Snopeses and Snopesism. Ratliff is not rich, but he is not Flem Snopes. And if the corruption of Snopesism does penetrate into the community, there is no one here who can be compared in degradation and vileness to Jason of *The Sound and the Fury*, the Compson who has embraced Snopesism. In fact, Popeye and Flem, Faulkner's best advertised villains, cannot, for vileness and ultimate meanness, touch Jason.

The Negro. In one of Faulkner's books it is said that every white child is born crucified on a black cross. Remarks like this have led to a gross misconception of the place of the Negro in Faulkner's work, to the notion that Faulkner 'hates' Negroes. For instance, we find Maxwell Geismar exclaiming what a 'strange inversion' it is to take the Negro, who is the 'tragic consequence,' and to exhibit him as the 'evil cause' of the failure of the old order in the South.

This is a misreading of the text. It is slavery, not the Negro, which is defined, quite flatly, as the curse, over and over again, and the Negro is the black cross in so far as he is the embodiment of the curse, the reminder of the guilt, the incarnation of the problem. That is the basic point. But now and then, as a kind of tangential irony, we have the notion, not of the burden of the white on the black, but of the burden of the black on the white, the weight of obligation, inefficiency, and so on, as well as the weight of guilt (the notion we find in the old story of the plantation mistress who, after the Civil War, said: 'Mr. Lincoln thought he was emancipating those slaves, but he was really emancipating me').

For instance, we get hints of this notion in 'Red Leaves': one of the Indians, sweating in the chase of the runaway Negro who is to be killed for the Man's funeral, says, 'Damn that Negro,' and the other Indian replies, 'Yao. When have they ever been anything but a trial and a care to us?' But the black cross is, fundamentally, the weight of the white man's guilt, the white man who now sells salves and potions to 'bleach the pigment and straighten the hair of negroes that they might resemble the very race which for two hundred years had held them in bondage and from which for another hundred years not even a bloody civil war would have set them completely free.' The curse is still operative, as the crime is still compounded.

The actual role of the Negro in Faulkner's fiction is consistently one of pathos or heroism. It is not merely, as has been suggested more than once, that Faulkner condescends to the good and faithful servant, the 'white folks' nigger.' There are figures like Dilsey, but they are not as impressive as the Negro in 'Red Leaves' or Sam Fathers, who, with the bear, is the hero of 'The Bear.' The fugitive, who gains in the course of the former story a shadowy symbolic significance, is told in the end by one of the Indians who overtake him, 'You ran well. Do not be ashamed,' and when he walks among the Indians, he is 'the tallest there, his high, close, mud-caked head looming above them all.' And Sam Fathers is the fountainhead of wisdom which Ike McCaslin finally gains, and the repository of the virtues which are central for Faulkner —'an old man, son of a Negro slave and an Indian king, inheritor on the one hand of the long chronicle of a people who had learned humility through suffering and learned pride through the endurance which survived suffering, and on the other side the chronicle of a people even longer in the land than the first, yet who now existed there only in the solitary brotherhood of an old and childless Negro's alien blood and the wild and invincible spirit of an old bear.'

Even Christmas, in *Light in August*, though he is sometimes spoken of as a villain, is a mixture of heroism and pathos. He is the lost, suffering, enduring creature (the figure like Sam Fathers, the tall convict of *The Wild Palms*, or Dilsey in *The Sound and the Fury*), and even the murder he commits at the end is a fumbling attempt to define his manhood, to lift himself out of 'nature,' for the woman whom he kills has become a figure of the horror of the human which has surrendered the human attributes. (We may compare Christmas to Mink Snopes in *The Hamlet* in this respect: Mink, mean and vicious as he is, kills out of a kind of warped and confused pride, and by this affirmation is set off against his kinsman Flem, whose only values are those of pure Snopesism.)

Even such a brief comment on the Negro in Faulkner's work cannot close without this passage from 'The Bear':

'Because they will endure. They are better than we are. Stronger than we are. Their vices are vices aped from white men or that white men and bondage have taught them: improvidence and intemperance and evasion—not laziness: evasion: of what white men had set them to, not for their aggrandizement or even comfort but his own—' and McCaslin

'All right. Go on: Promiscuity. Violence, Instability and lack of control. Inability to distinguish between mine and thine—' and he

'How distinguish when for two hundred years mine did not even exist for them?' and McCaslin

'All right. Go on. And their virtues—' and he

'Yes. Their own. Endurance—' and McCaslin

'So have mules:' and he

'—and pity and tolerance and forbearance and fidelity and love of children —' and McCaslin

'So have dogs:' and he

'—whether their own or not or black or not. And more: what they got not only from white people but not even despite white people because they had it already from the old free fathers a longer time free than us because we have never been free—'

And there is the single comment under Dilsey's name in the annotated genealogy of the Compsons which Faulkner has prepared for the present volume: 'They endured.'

Technique. There are excellent comments on this subject by Cowley, Conrad Aiken, Warren Beck, Joseph Warren Beach, and Alfred Kazin, but the subject has not been fully explored. One difficulty is that Faulkner is an incorrigible and restless experimenter, is peculiarly sensitive to the expressive possibilities of shifts in technique and has not developed (like Hemingway or Katherine Anne Porter—lyric rather than dramatic writers, artists with a great deal of self-certainty) in a straight line.

Provisionally, we may distinguish in Faulkner's work three basic methods of handling a narrative. One is best typified in *Sanctuary*, where there is a tightly organized plot, a crisp, laconic style, an objective presentation of character—an impersonal method. Another is best typified by *As I Lay Dying* or *The Sound and the Fury*, where each character unfolds in his own language or flow of being before us—a dramatic method in that the author does not obtrude, but a method which makes the subjective reference of character the medium of presentation. Another is best typified by 'Was,' 'The Bear,' or the story of the tall convict in *The Wild Palms*, where the organization of the narrative is episodic and the sense of a voice, a narrator's presence (though not necessarily a narrator in the formal sense), is almost constantly felt—a method in which the medium is ultimately a 'voice' as index to sensibility. The assumptions underlying these methods, and the relations among them, would provide a study.

Cowley's emphasis on the unity of Faulkner's work, the fact that all the novels and stories are to be taken as aspects of a single, large design, is very important. It is important, for one thing, in regard to the handling of character. A character, Sutpen, for instance, may appear in various perspectives, so that from book to book we move toward a final definition much as in actual life we move toward the definition of a person. The same principle applies to event, as Conrad Aiken has pointed out, the principle of the spiral method which takes the reader over and over the same event from a different altitude, as it were, and a different angle. In relation to both character and event this method, once it is understood by the reader, makes for a kind of realism and a kind of suspense (in the formal not the factual sense) not common in fiction.

The emphasis on the unity of Faulkner's work may, however, lead to an underrating of the degree of organization within individual works. Cowley is right in pointing out the structural defect in *Light in August*, but he may be putting too much emphasis on the over-all unity and not enough on the organization of the individual work when he says that *The Hamlet* tends to resolve into a 'series of episodes resembling beads on a string.' I think that in that novel we have a type of organization in which the thematic rather than the narrative emphasis is the basic principle, and once we grasp that fact the unity of the individual work may come clear. In fact, the whole subject of the principle of thematic organization in the novels and long stories, 'The Bear,' for instance, needs investigation. In pieces which seem disjointed, or which seem to have the mere tale-teller's improvisations, we may sometimes discover the true unity if we think of the line of meaning, the symbolic ordering, and surrender ourselves to the tale-teller's 'voice.' And it may be useful at times to recall the distinction between the formal, forensic realism of Ibsen as opposed to the fluid, suggestive realism of Chekhov.

Symbol and Image. Cowley and O'Donnell have given acute readings of the main symbolic outline of Faulkner's fiction, but no one has yet devoted himself to the study of symbolic motifs which, though not major, are nevertheless extremely instructive. For instance, the images of the hunt, the flight, the pursuit, such as we have in 'Red Leaves,' *The Wild Palms*, the episode of 'Percy Grimm' in *Light in August*, 'The Bear,' 'Delta Autumn,' 'Was,' and (especially in the hordes of moving Negroes) in *The Unvanquished*. Or there is the important symbolic relationship between man and earth. Or there is the contrast between images of compulsion and images of will or freedom. Or there is the device of what we might call the frozen moment, the arrested action which becomes symbolic, as in the moment when, in 'An Odor of Verbena' (from *The Unvanquished*), Drusilla offers the pistols to the hero.

Polarity. To what extent does Faulkner work in terms of polarities, oppositions, paradoxes, inversions of roles? How much does he employ a line of concealed (or open) dialectic progression as a principle for his fiction? The study of these questions may lead to the discovery of principles of organization in his work not yet defined by criticism.

The study of Faulkner is the most challenging single task in contemporary American literature for criticism to undertake. Here is a novelist who, in mass of work, in scope of material, in range of effect, in reportorial accuracy and symbolic subtlety, in philosophical weight can be put beside the masters of our own past literature. Yet this ment has been effected in what almost amounts to critical d silence, and when the silence has been broken it has usually n by someone (sometimes one of our better critics) whose been hasty, whose analysis unscholarly and whose judgments superficial. The picture of Faulkner presented to the public by such criticism is a combination of Thomas Nelson Page, a fascist and a psychopath, gnawing his nails. Of course, this picture is usually accompanied by a grudging remark about genius.

Cowley's book, for its intelligence, sensitivity, and sobriety in the introduction, and for the ingenuity and judgment exhibited in the selections, would be valuable at any time. But it is especially valuable at this time. Perhaps it can mark a turning point in Faulkner's reputation. That will be of slight service to Faulkner, who, as much as any writer of our place and time, can rest in confidence. He can afford to wait. But can we?

84. Ralph Ellison on Faulkner and the Negro

1946

From 'Twentieth-Century Fiction and the Black Mask of Humanity,' *Confluence*, December 1953, ii, 3–21. Though not printed until 1953, this was written in 1946. It was reprinted in *Shadow and Act* (New York, Random House, 1964).

Ellison (b. 1914) published *Invisible Man* in 1952.

I see no value either in presenting a catalogue of Negro characters appearing in twentieth-century fiction or in charting the racial attitudes of white writers. We are interested not in quantities but in qualities. And since it is impossible here to discuss the entire body of this writing, the next best thing is to select a framework in which the relationships with which we are concerned may be clearly seen. For brevity let us take three representative writers: Mark Twain, Hemingway and Faulkner. Twain for historical perspective and as an example of how a great nineteenth-century writer handled the Negro; Hemingway as the prime example of the artist who ignored the dramatic and symbolic possibilities presented by this theme; and Faulkner as an example of a writer who has confronted Negroes with such mixed motives that he has presented them in terms of both the 'good nigger' and the 'bad nigger' stereotypes, and who yet has explored perhaps more successfully than anyone else, either white or black, certain forms of Negro humanity.

[Ellison covers Twain and Hemingway]

Hard-boiled writing is said to appeal through its presentation of sheer fact, rather than through rhetoric. The writer puts nothing down but what he pragmatically 'knows.' But actually one 'fact' itself—which in literature must be presented simultaneously as image and as event—became a rhetorical unit. And the symbolic ritual which has set off the 'fact'—that is, the fact unorganized by vital social myths (which might incorporate the findings of science and still contain elements of mystery)—is the rite of superstition. The superstitious individual responds to the capricious event, the fact that seems to explode in his face through blind fatality. For it is the creative function of myth to protect the individual from the irrational, and since it is here in the realm of the irrational that, impervious to science, the stereotype grows, we see that the Negro stereotype is really an image of the unorganized, irrational forces of American life, forces through which, by projecting them in forms of images of an easily dominated minority, the white individual seeks to be at home in the vast unknown world of America. Perhaps the object of the stereotype is not so much to crush the Negro as to console the white man.

Certainly there is justification for this view when we consider the work of William Faulkner. In Faulkner most of the relationships which we have pointed out between the Negro and contemporary writing come to focus: the social and the personal, the moral and the technical, the nineteenth-century emphasis upon morality and the modern accent upon the personal myth. And on the strictly literary level he is prolific and complex enough to speak for those Southern writers who are aggressively anti-Negro and for those younger writers who appear most sincerely interested in depicting the Negro as a rounded human at is more, he is the greatest artist the South has produced. complex to be given more than a glance in these notes, even more revealing of what lies back of the distortion of the nodern writing than any attempt at a group survey might be.

's attitude is mixed. Taking his cue from the Southern mentality in which the Negro is often dissociated into a malignant stereotype (the bad nigger) on the one hand and a benign stereotype (the good nigger) on the other, most often Faulkner presents characters embodying both. The dual function of this dissociation seems to be that of avoiding moral pain and thus to justify the South's racial code. But since such a social order harms whites no less than blacks, the sensitive Southerner, the artist, is apt to feel its effects acutely—and within the deepest levels of his personality. For not only is the social division forced upon the Negro by the ritualized ethic of discrimination, but upon the white man by the strictly enforced set of anti-Negro taboos. The conflict is always with him. Indeed, so rigidly has the recognition of Negro humanity been tabooed that the white Southerner is apt to associate any form of personal rebellion with the Negro. So that for the Southern artist the Negro becomes a symbol of his personal rebellion, his guilt and his repression of it. The Negro is thus a compelling object of fascination, and this we see very clearly in Faulkner.

Sometimes in Faulkner the Negro is simply a villain, but by an unconsciously ironic transvaluation his villainy consists, as with Loosh in *The Unvanquished*, of desiring his freedom. Or again the Negro appears benign, as with Ringo, of the same novel, who uses his talent not to seek personal freedom but to remain the loyal and resourceful retainer. Not that I criticize loyalty in itself, but that loyalty given where one's humanity is unrecognized seems a bit obscene. And yet in Faulkner's story, 'The Bear,' he brings us as close to the moral implication of the Negro as Twain or Melville. In the famous 'difficult' fourth section, which Malcolm Cowley advises us to skip very much as Hemingway would have us skip the end of *Huckleberry Finn*, we find an argument in progress in which one voice (that of a Southern abolitionist) seeks to define Negro humanity against the other's enumeration of those stereotypes which many Southerners believe to be the Negro's basic traits. Significantly the mentor of the young hero of this story, a man of great moral stature, is socially a Negro.

Indeed, through his many novels and short stories, Faulkner fights out the moral problem which was repressed after the nineteenth century, and it was shocking for some to discover that for all his concern with the South, Faulkner was actually seeking out the nature of man. Thus we must turn to him for that continuity of moral purpose which made for the greatness of our classics. As for the Negro minority, he has been more willing perhaps than any other artist to start with the stereotype, accept it as true, and then seek out the human truth which it hides. Perhaps his is the example for our writers to follow, for in his work technique has been put once more to the task of creating value.

Which leaves these final things to be said. First, that this is meant as no plea for white writers to define Negro humanity, but to recognize the broader aspects of their own. Secondly, Negro writers and those of the other minorities have their own task of contributing to the total image of the American by depicting the experience of their own groups. Certainly theirs is the task of defining Negro humanity, as this can no more be accomplished by others than freedom, which must be won again and again each day, can be conferred upon another. A people must define itself, and minorities have the responsibility of having their ideals and images recognized as part of the composite image which is that of the still forming American people.

The other thing to be said is that while it is unlikely that American writing will ever retrace the way to the nineteenth century, it might be worth while to point out that for all its technical experimentation it is nevertheless an ethical instrument, and as such it might well exercise some choice in the kind of ethic it prefers to support. The artist is no freer than the society in which he lives, and in the United States the writers who stereotype or ignore the Negro and other minorities in the final analysis stereotype and distort their own humanity. Mark Twain knew that in *his* America humanity masked its face with blackness.

NTRUDER IN THE DUST

New York, September 1948
London, September 1949

85. Edmund Wilson, 'William Faulkner's Reply to the Civil-Rights Program'

October 1948

New Yorker, 23 October 1948, 106–13.

Wilson (1895–1972) was one of the best examples of his generation of the Man of Letters. Scholar, critic, editor, and creative writer, he combined a broad reading in and concern for social and political matters with the careful reading of text demanded by the New Critics. Perhaps surprisingly he wrote hardly at all on Faulkner before the late 1940s.

William Faulkner's new novel, *Intruder in the Dust*, is the story of a Negro with white blood who refuses to behave with the submissiveness demanded of his color in the South and has developed so rigid a pride that, even when wrongfully charged with the murder of a white man, he can hardly bring himself to stoop to defend himself against his race enemy. The narrative deals with the adventures of the handful of people in the community (the Jefferson, Mississippi, which is the locale of most of Faulkner's fiction) who, having come to respect Lucas' independence, interest themselves in his case and exert themselves to save him from lynching. These champions include a boy of sixteen, who had once been rescued by Lucas when he had fallen through the ice; the boy's uncle, a local lawyer, who has lived abroad and has, to some degree, been able to surmount provincial prejudices; and an old lady of the best local quality, who had grown up with the accused man's dead wife in the relation of mistress and maid. All the happenings are presented from the point of view of the boy. It is his loyalty to the old Negro that leads to the discovery of evidence that the crime has been committed by someone else; and his emergence, under the stimulus of events, out of boyhood into comparative maturity is as much the subject of the book as the predicament of the Negro. The real theme is the relation between the two.

The novel has the suspense and excitement that Faulkner can nearly always create and the disturbing emotional power that he can generate at his best. The earlier Faulkner of *Sanctuary* was often accused of misanthropy and despair, but the truth is that, from *Pylon*, at any rate, one of the most striking features of his work, and one that sets it off from that of many of his contemporaries, has been a kind of romantic morality that allows you the thrills of melodrama without making you ashamed, as a rule, of the values which have been exploited to produce them. I do not sympathize with the line of criticism which deplores Faulkner's obstinate persistence in submerging himself in the mentality of the community where he was born, for his chivalry, which constitutes his morality, is a part of his Southern heritage, and it appears in Faulkner's work as a force more humane and more positive than almost anything one can find in the work of even those writers of our more mechanized society who have set out to defend human rights. *Intruder in the Dust* is one of the most ardent demonstrations of this reconditioned Southern chivalry; and the question that arises in connection with it is not whether it paints too hopeless a picture but, on the contrary, whether it is not *too* positive, too optimistic—whether the author has not yielded too much to the temptations of the novelist's power to summon for innocence in difficulties the equivalents of the United States Marines.

I shall return to this aspect of *Intruder in the Dust*. In the meantime, it ought to be said that, from the point of view of the writing, this is one of the more snarled-up of Faulkner's books. It is not so bad as 'The Bear,' which has pages that are almost opaque. But in his attempt to record the perceptions—the instinctive sensations and the half-formed thoughts—of his adolescent boy, in aiming at prisms of prose which will concentrate the infrared as well as the ultraviolet, he leaves these rays sometimes still invisible, and only tosses into our hands some rather clumsy and badly cut polygons. It would require a good deal of very diligent work and very nice calculation always to turn out the combinations of words that would do what Faulkner wants. His energy, his image-making genius get him where he wants to go about seventy per cent of the time, but when he misses it, he lands in a mess. One cannot object in principle to any of Faulkner's practices: to his shifting his syntax in the middle of a sentence, to his stringing long sequences of clauses together with practically no syntax at all, to his inserting in parenthesis in the middle of a scene (in one case, in the middle of a sentence) a long episode that took place at some other time, to his invention of the punctuation (( )) to indicate a parenthesis within a parenthesis, or to his creation of non-dictionary words. He has, at one time or another, justified all these devices. But what is the excuse for writing 'the old grunt and groan with some long familiar minor stiffness so used and accustomed as to be no longer even an ache and which if they were ever actually cured of it, they would be bereft and lost'?—a mismanagement of relatives quite common in the Faulkner of the latest books. One is willing to give the benefit of the doubt to 'regurg,' 'abnegant,' 'dismatchment,' 'divinant,' 'perspicuant,' until one runs into a dictionary word used out of its real meaning, as in 'it's only men who burk at facts'—when once realizes that Faulkner is not merely coining but groping. It is true that his new way of writing has enabled him to render impressions more accurately than he did before; but the passages that become unintelligible on account of a confusion of pronouns or that have to be read twice for lack of proper punctuation are not really the results of an effort to express the hardly expressible but the casualties of an indolent taste and a negligent workmanship that did not appear to the same degree in the prose—for the most part so steady and clear as well as so tense and telling—of such a book as *Light in August*.

One finds here both the vigor of a tradition and the signs of its current decay. For the writing of Faulkner, too, has a noble and ancient lineage. Though he echoed, in his earlier novels, Hemingway and Sherwood Anderson, he really belongs not to their school but to the full-dress post-Flaubert group of Conrad, Joyce, and Proust, whom he has sometimes echoed since. To their kind of highly complex novel, he has brought the rich and lively resources, reappearing with amazing freshness, of English lyric verse and romantic prose (as distinguished from what we now call American). This is an advantage that the Southerners often have—a contact with the language of Shakespeare which, if they sidestep the oratorical Southern verbiage, they may get from their old-fashioned education. And Faulkner, it must be said, often succeeds as Shakespeare does—by plunging into the dramatic scene and flinging down the words and images that flow to the ends of his fingers. This book, like all his books, is full of passages that could not have been written if he had sat down and contemplated the object—as Flaubert is said to have done the cabbage garden by moonlight—instead of allowing himself to be possessed by it. Minor but admirable examples in *Intruder in the Dust* are the renderings of the impression on the white boy of the smell of a Negro cabin, with all its social implications, and of the effect of a little frame church that, though lacking a steeple and shabbily patched, speaks to him with the spirit of the Calvinism that its Scotch–Irish congregation have given a degenerate shrine there. He has described so many things so well!—got out of them so much human meaning. No other of our contemporary novelists, perhaps, can compete with him in this department—for most of the best of them were bred in a world that is based on abstract assumptions, and they cannot help sharing these; whereas, for William Faulkner, everything that man has made wears the aspect of the human agent, and its impact is that of a human meeting.

To be thus out of date, as a Southerner, in feeling and in language and in human relations, is, for a novelist, a source of strength. But Faulkner's weakness has also its origin in the antiquated community he inhabits, for it consists in his not having mastered—I speak of the design of his books as wholes as well as that of his sentences and paragraphs—the discipline of the Joyces, Prousts, and Conrads (though Proust had his solecisms and what the ancients called anacolutha). If you are going to do embroidery, you have to watch every stitch; if you are going to construct a complex machine, you have to have every part tested. The technique of the modern novel, with its ideal of technical efficiency, its specialization of means for ends, has grown up in the industrial age, and it has a good deal in common with the other manifestations of that age. In practicing it so far from such cities as produced the Flauberts, Joyces, and Jameses, Faulkner's provinciality, stubbornly cherished and turned into an asset, inevitably tempts him to be slipshod and has apparently made it impossible for him to acquire complete expertness in an art that demands of the artist the closest attention and care.

But *Intruder in the Dust* does not come to us merely as a novel: it also involves a tract. The story is evidently supposed to take place sometime this year or last, and it seems to have, at any rate partly, been stimulated by the crisis at the time of the war in the relations between Negroes and whites and by the recently proposed legislation for guaranteeing Negro rights. The book contains a kind of counterblast to the anti-lynching bill and to the civil-rights plank in the Democratic platform. The author's ideas on this subject are apparently conveyed, in their explicit form, by the intellectual uncle, who, more and more as the story goes on, gives vent to long disquisitions that seem to become so 'editorial' in character that it is impossible to take them merely as part of the presentation of the furniture of the uncle's personality. The series may be pieced together as something in the nature of a public message delivered by the author himself. The first difficulty about this message is the way in which it is expressed. Faulkner, who has shown himself a master at making every possible type of Mississippian talk in his natural idiom, has chosen to couch the uncle's conversations with the boy in a literary prose like his own at its most complicated and non-colloquial—so that it is difficult to reduce what is said to definite propositions. I shall, however, make an attempt to do so.

The point of view, then, seems to be as follows (interpolated comment by the reviewer):

'The people named Sambo' [the uncle's way of designating the Negroes] have survived the ordeal of slavery and they may survive the ordeal of dictatorship. The capacity for endurance of the Negro is a recurrent theme of Faulkner's, and his respect for their humble persistence is unconsciously but strikingly contrasted here with his attitude toward 'the coastal spew of Europe, which this country quarantined unrootable into the rootless ephemeral cities' [as if the Italians, Greeks, Hungarians, Poles, and Czechs had not shown as much tenacity as the Negroes, and as if the Southern Negroes had not been kept alive—that is, encouraged to persist—by the people who had an interest in employing them, just as the immigrants from Europe were].

The Southerners in the United States are the only 'homogeneous people.' (The New Englander, in his pure and respectable form, crowded back by the coastal spew of Europe, is no longer of real importance.) 'We are defending not actually our politics or beliefs or even our way of life, but simply our homogeneity, from a federal government to which, in simple desperation, the rest of this country has had to surrender voluntarily more and more of its personal and private liberty in order to continue to afford the United States.' The Negro is homogeneous, too, 'except that part of him which is trying to escape not even into the best of the white race but into the second best.' The saving remnant of Southerners, such as the characters in the story who rescue old Lucas Beauchamp, should combine with the non-second-rate Negro—the second-rate variety being, by the author's definition, the Negro who demands 'not an automobile nor flash clothes nor his picture in the paper, but a little of music (his own), a hearth, not his child but any child [back to Uncle Tom and Uncle Remus!], a God, a heaven which a man may avail himself a little of at any time without having to wait to die [Oh, dem golden slippers!], a little earth for his own sweat to fall on among his own green shoots and plant [no large-scale agriculture for Sambo!].' Let the white man give the Negro his rights, and the Negro teach the white man his endurance, and 'together we would dominate the United States; we would present a front not only impregnable but not even to be threatened by a mass of people who no longer have anything in common save a frantic greed for money and a basic fear of a failure of national character which they hide from one another behind a loud lipservice to a flag.' [The Mississippian may have hold of something here.]

Lucas-Sambo must be defended 'from the North and East and West—the outlanders who will fling him decades back not merely into injustice but into grief and agony, and violence, too, by forcing on us laws based on the idea that man's injustice to man can be abolished overnight by police.' Any other course of conduct toward the Negro is to risk dividing the country. Attempts on the part of the people in other sections of the United States to strengthen the hand of the Negro amount to nothing more than 'a paper alliance of theorists and fanatics and private and personal avengers plus a number of others' [including a good many Negroes] against 'a concorded [i.e., solid] South,' which is now full of 'ignorant people' from other parts of the country, 'who fear the color of any skin or shape of nose save their own.' Such action will force the many Southerners 'who do begrieve Lucas' shameful condition and would improve it,' and will eventually abolish it, to ally themselves with all those objectionable elements 'with whom we have no kinship whatever, in defense of a principle [the inalienable right to keep the Negro down] which we ourselves begrieve and abhor.' They will thus be forced into 'the position of the German after 1933, who had no other alternative between being either a Nazi or a Jew, or the present Russian (European, too, for that matter), who hasn't even that, but must be either a Communist or dead.' So they must be allowed themselves, without intervention or advice from others, to grant the Negro his citizenship. Otherwise—

Otherwise, what? I have been able, I think, up to now, to make Faulkner's argument clear by quoting or paraphrasing his own words, with the addition of a little punctuation; but here I must present you with a chunk of his text without any elucidation, for I cannot be sure what it means: Otherwise, 'Lucas' equality' cannot 'be anything more than its own prisoner inside an impregnable barricade of the direct heirs of the victory of 1861–1865 which probably did more than even John Brown to stalemate Lucas' freedom which still seems to be in check going on a hundred years after Lee surrendered.' But, the other side may object: The South will never get around to doing anything for the Negro. Your policy, the South retorts, is dangerous, in any case: it will give rise to 'a people divided [Faulkner thus seems to take it for granted that if Washington tries to back the Negroes, it will arouse the whole South to resistance] at a time when history is still showing us that the anteroom to dissolution is division.'

But is pressure from outside worth nothing? Has it had no moral effect on the South? It seems to me that this book itself, which rejects outside interference, is a conspicuous sign that it has. The champions of Lucas Beauchamp are shown as rather reluctant, as even, at moments, resentful, in recognizing his rectitude and dignity, but they do rally energetically to clear him—all of them of the best old stock—in a way that I do not remember the inhabitants of Jefferson behaving in any other of Faulkner's books. Young Charles and his young Negro pal become regular Boy Scouts. Miss Habersham proves herself a dear, gallant old thoroughbred. The uncle is as ironic and delightful as the uncle of the boy next door in E. Nesbit's books about the Bastable children. And when this wonderful posse is on the march, they have hairbreadth escapes but get all the breaks. And, in the end, the vulgar people who wanted to see Lucas lynched get into their vulgar cars and turn tail and run away. There has been nothing so exhilarating in its way since the triumphs of the Communist-led workers in the early Soviet films; we are thrilled with the same kind of emotion that one got from some of the better dramatizations of the career of Abraham Lincoln.

This is a new note to come from the South; and it may really represent something more than Faulkner's own courageous and generous spirit, some new stirring of public conscience. In the meantime, in harping on this message, I do not want to divert attention from the excellence and interest of the book, which sustains the polymorphous vitality, the poetic truth to experience, of Faulkner's Balzacian chronicle of Yoknapatawpha County. Old Lucas and certain of the other characters have already appeared in *Go Down, Moses*, to which *Intruder in the Dust* is, indeed, more or less of a sequel, and the later adventures of Lucas are more interesting if you know his past history as recounted in the earlier volume, and understand his role in the tangle of black-and-white relationships which Faulkner has presented there. This subject of the complicated consequences of the mixture of white with Negro blood has been explored by Faulkner with remarkable intelligence and subtlety and variety of dramatic imagination; and Lucas himself, the black man who embarrasses a set of white relatives by having inherited the strongest traits of a common white ancestor, is one of the author's most impressive creations. Even when the prose goes to pieces, the man and his milieu live.

86. Eudora Welty, review, *Hudson Review*

Winter 1949, i, 596–8

Eudora Welty (b. 1909) published her first six books of fiction in the 1940s, the best of it consisting of tales and short novels of rural and small-town Mississippi life. Like Faulkner's it thrives on a mythic method, a comic vision, and the fusion of the ordinary and realistic with the grotesque and non-realistic.

What goes on here? Grave digging. 'Digging and undiggin.' What's in the grave? One body or maybe another, maybe nothing at all—except human shame, something we've done to ourselves. Who digs? Who but the innocent, the young—and the old and female, their burning-up energy generating a radiance over Yoknapatawpha County and its concerns? Not forgetting the Gowrie twins—like the vaudeville team that follows behind the beautiful stars with its hilarious, mechanical parody, the Gowries from the hills dig too.

Intruder in the Dust is a story of the proving of innocence, this proof a maddening physical labor and a horrendous, well-nigh impossible undertaking, full of riddles and always starting over. The real innocents are the provers, the technical innocent is old, black Lucas Beauchamp in danger of lynching for murder of a white man—and Lucas is a lightless character, high-and-mighty and gorgeously irritating, who would be so temptingly guilty if he weren't so irrevocably innocent, just the kind of man to get in just this kind of fix, who has been building up to it all his life, and now, by hints, condescends to be saved, offering cash fees, and requiring a receipt. The provers, exhumers that they have to be, are Miss Eunice Habersham, 'a practical woman' in her seventies, who 'hadn't taken long . . . to decide that the way to get a dead body up out of a grave was to go out to the grave and dig it up,' and the sixteen-year-olds, Charles Mallison, white, Aleck Sander, colored, who end up dog-tired and a step along in man's wisdom. Gavin Stevens, the articulate uncle who by his character partly forecasts and foretells for Charles, and the sighing mother—wonderfully done—are near at hand, summoned or pushed back, and beyond and dipping down is the menacing fringe of the Gowries from the ridges of the wild Beat Four. Out of the digging comes a solution and an indictment, defining a hope, prayer, that we should one day reach that point where it will be *Thou shalt not kill at all*, where Lucas Beauchamp's life will be secure not despite the fact that he is Lucas Beauchamp but because he is.

The action of *Intruder* is frantic—and meditative, not missing a minute. The more-than-possible failure of the task overhangs it like a big cliff. The suspense is of the chase—sometimes slow-motion, sometimes double-time; leg-work, horses, mules ('unspookable' for this business), pickup trucks, on up to a fast Sheriff's auto, bear the characters toward their grave-digging with greater and greater urgency. The setting is the open country at night lighted by 'a thin distillation of starlight,' and a few dusky interiors, smelly. (How Faulkner can show us that making things out in the dark is a quality of perception as well as a quantity!) In counterpoint is the Square, back in Jefferson, with the Face of its crowd, the immobile, inflexible crowd around which sentience strives and threads and skirts, until the crowd's final whizzing away like a battery of witches on brooms. Even when old man Gowrie gets his Vinson back, brushes the quicksand off and takes him home to bury again tomorrow, is this story going to stop? 'This time Hampton and his uncle could go out there tomorrow night and dig him up' is the boy's sleepy valediction that night.

Intruder is marvelously funny. Faulkner's veracity and accuracy about the world around keeps the comic thread from ever being lost or fouled, but that's a simple part of the matter. The complicated and intricate thing is that his stories aren't decked out in humor, but the humor is born in them, as much their blood and bones as the passion and poetry. Put one of his stories into a single factual statement and it's pure outrage—so would life be—too terrifying, too probable and too symbolic too, too funny to bear. There has to be the story, to bear it—wherein that statement, conjured up and implied and demonstrated, not said or the sky would fall on our heads, is yet the living source of his comedy—and a good part of that comedy's adjoining terror, of course.

It doesn't follow that *Intruder*, short, funny, of simple outline, with its detective-story casing, is one of the less difficult of Faulkner's novels. Offering side-by-side variations of numerous words, daringly long, building ever-working sentences (longer than *The Bear's*, maybe, if anybody is counting), moods and moments arrested, pulled up to peaks, wilfully crowned with beauty and terror and surprise and comedy, Faulkner has at once re-explored his world with his marvelous style that can always search in new ways, and also appeared to use from beginning to end the prerogatives of an impromptu piece of work. It could be that to seem impromptu is an illusion great art can always give as long as profundities of theme, organization, and passionate content can come at a calling, but the art of what other has these cadenzas? Even the witty turns and the perfect neatness of plot look like the marks of a flash inspiration. If *Intruder* did come intruding in a literal way, shaped from the dust into life before the eyes, then we have a special wonder here; but it's none of our business, and the important thing is the wonder, special or not.

Time shifts its particles over a scene now and then, past and future like seasoning from a shaker, and Yoknapatawpha County we know now too, while the new story in its year, month, and ticking hour of day and night, emerges in that illumination and shading which Faulkner supplies to the last inch and the ultimate moment. The political views in *Intruder*, delivered outright as a speech, are made, rightly enough, another such shading to the story.

As in all Faulkner's work, the separate scenes leap up on their own, we progress as if by bonfires lighted on the way, and the essence of each scene takes form before the eyes, a shape in the fire. We see in matchless, 'substituteless' (Faulkner's word for swearing) actuality and also by its contained vision: 'Miss Habersham's round hat on the exact top of her head such as few people had seen in fifty years and probably no one at any time looking up out of a halfway rifled grave.' Every aspect of vision is unique, springs absolute out of the material and the moment, only nominally out of 'character' or 'point of view,' and so we see hats and happenings and every other thing, if not upwards from a half rifled grave, then down the road of the dark shuttered cabins, or up a jail stair, from the lonely ridge where Gowries come; or see in accompaniment with the smell of quicksand (a horse is there to get the smell and rear up), by the light even of impending conflagrations. Old Man Gowrie turning over a body that's the wrong body, not his son's, becomes 'only an old man for whom grief was not even a component of his own but merely a temporary phenomenon of his slain son, jerking a strange corpse over onto its back not in appeasement to its one mute indicting cry not for pity not for vengeance not for justice but just to be sure he had the wrong one, crying cheery abashless and loud, "Yep it's that damned Montgomery damned if it ain't!" ' The boy's feverish dream of Miss Habersham trying to drive around the mob to get back to her own house, a vision of How the Old Woman Got Home, is this writer's imagination soaring like the lark.

Of course it's a feat, this novel—a double and delightful feat, because the mystery of the detective-story plot is being ravelled out while the mystery of Faulkner's prose is being spun and woven before our eyes. And with his first novel in eight years, the foremost critics are all giving cries as if (to change the image) to tree it. It's likely that Faulkner's prose can't be satisfactorily analyzed and accounted for, until it can be predicted, God save the day. Faulkner's prose, let's suspect, is intolerantly and intolerably unanalyzable and quite pure, something more than a possum in a tree—with its motes bright-pure and dark-pure falling on us, critics and non-critics alike.

87. Charles Glicksberg, review, *Arizona Quarterly*

Spring 1949, 85–8

Glicksberg (b. 1900) was teaching at this time at Brooklyn College. More recently his most important work has been in comparative modern literature.

If a newcomer to fiction had submitted the manuscript of this novel for consideration by a publisher, it would most likely have been rejected as promptly and decisively as *Sanctuary* was before Faulkner achieved recognition. It has all the glaring faults that would disqualify a beginner: a pretentious vocabulary, a baroque style, a thesis which, though skillfully integrated within the context of the story, is ridden hard for all it is worth. Even so, the most memorable feature of this novel is not the story but the 'moral' which stands out sharply and challengingly; the entire plot is so constructed as to elaborate and emphasize the author's central convictions about the Negro problem in the South.

The story itself does not amount to much, but, as is usual with Faulkner, his method of presentation is so subtle, so powerful, and so complex that he carries the reader along with him, in spite of the purple patches and the rather pretentious theorizing. Lucas Beauchamp, a Negro, is accused of having shot a white man in the back. The rest of the plot is taken up with the attempt to prove his innocence and to frustrate the milling mob, many of them kinsmen of the murdered man, from lynching the Negro. The grave of the murdered man is dug up in the thick of night by a white lad, helped by a Negro boy and an elderly lady. When the news finally gets around that Lucas Beauchamp did not commit the deed, the lynching mob quickly disperses. The Negroes come out of hiding; the town resumes its normal life.

A bare outline such as this is totally inadequate to suggest the nightmarish intensity with which each incident is developed, nor can it suggest the vibrant metaphysical overtones of the novel. *Intruder in the Dust* is of special importance in that it demonstrates unmistakably that Faulkner's rigorous naturalistic method in the past was but a mask worn for the occasion. Here the disguise is thrown off and his views on the vexed Negro problem are revealed in all their reactionary violence. Faulkner, like some other Southern writers, is still engaged in fighting the Civil War. In effect, he is telling Northerners and Westerners who suffer from the reformer's itch (and anyone who wishes to raise the condition of the Negro is, by definition, a 'reformer'), to mind their own business, since they have no comprehension of the complexity of the problem and how it must be solved gradually, if it is to be solved at all. The South, we are given to understand, will clean house in its own scrupulous, fair-minded, traditional way. Though this will take time it will eventually be done—but not by the ineffectual methods of legal compulsion or force recommended so urgently by humanitarians and liberals up North.

Yet Faulkner is fundamentally too honest and too conscientious a novelist to gloss over the truth. Lucas Beauchamp is drawn as a singularly compelling character, self-composed, sure of himself, a man not to be contradicted. The South is pictured as hagridden by a guilty, paranoiac awareness of the Negro's presence. The youngster, Charles, the peg on which the story is made to hang, makes the exciting discovery that even Negroes can grieve for the dead, that Negroes have their integrity and incorruptible pride. But much, too much, is made of the penetrating odor of Negroes. Most Southerners, according to Faulkner, accept the smell as irrefutable proof of ingrained racial differences. They cannot imagine an existence in which that disturbing 'racial' odor would be missing. In addition, Lucas is portrayed as being too independent in spirit, too indomitable, for the comfort of the whites in that region. He must be humbled, taught a lesson, made to act the part of a 'nigger.'

Faulkner is at best in describing the psychology of the mob waiting for the inciting word of command, the mob morbidly drawn to this scene of purgation by blood, this apotheosis by fire. Yet Faulkner, strangely enough, endeavors to exonerate these people of guilt. The code requires that all such violations by Negroes be punished by lynching the offender; then the slate is wiped clean, and it is possible to begin all over again. These are the rules according to which 'the game' is played in the South. Indeed, that is what the Negroes themselves count on. The Negroes must behave like Negroes and the whites like white folk. When this happens—once the blood-fury is appeased—there is no hard feeling on either side.

Still the instinct for justice is not to be denied; Charles is determined that Lucas shall not die simply because his skin is black. He digs up a grave to save a reputed Negro murderer from the wild vengeance of the community. The uncle, another Faulknerian mouthpiece, philosophizes at some length on the capacity of the Negro to endure all sorts of suffering, and still survive. Now all this may be defended as the dramatic projection of a character in the story, representative of a certain point of view to be found in the South, but it is repeated too often and given too much space, to be accidental. What Faulkner is doing (if he is present all the time behind his creation) is to reject the postulate on which the concept of democracy rests: namely, the assumption that just as people, black or white, cannot endure slavery, so all men yearn to achieve genuine freedom, the recognition of their fundamental humanity. The amazing thing is that the youngster Charles, really the protagonist in the story (if it can be said to have any protagonist), the spokesman for the author's point of view, is made to agree with the uncle. He discovers a mystical identity between man and the soul of his forebears, an identity which the alien, forever cut off from this blood-communion, cannot hope to understand. The North is incapable of comprehending the condition of the South, the problem it must work out for itself, without aid or interference from the outside. The North is the plague to be resisted and defied. It is intolerable that the North, filled with alien, gullible masses, should pass outrageous, slanderous judgments on the South.

It is the uncle who articulates the thought of the presumably enlightened members of the South. The South, he feels, is the only community which still has a homogeneous population, and this is sufficient reason for resisting the colossus of the North. Faulkner, speaking through the medium of the uncle, is willing to concede that the reforms the Northerners are clamoring for are desirable and indeed inevitable, but it cannot be done, he insists, by legislation or constitutional amendments or dint of force. It must be a slow evolutionary process, the outgrowth of folk-accommodation. The uncle is willing to accept even Lucas Beauchamp (or Sambo, as he calls him) as a homogeneous man. What he deplores is 'Sambo's' efforts to imitate not the best but the second-best of the white race, its flashy vulgarity, its mediocrity, its political corruption, its passion for wealth. He believes in the 'Sambo' who has rooted himself firmly and lovingly in the Southland, the 'Sambo' who can endure because he is sustained by patience, even when he is without hope, because he is in love with simple elemental things: his mule, his land, his hearth, his children, his religion.

Yet the uncle is perceptive enough to recognize the tyrannical influence Lucas Beauchamp and his brethren exercise over the conscience of the white community. However vindictive in temper, the community knows that this is so. It is a feeling which cannot be beaten down, a feeling for justice, a sense of conscience, and even of pity. In fact, the uncle maintains that he is defending the cause of Lucas Beauchamp against the North and East and West, against those who seem to believe that man's injustice to man can be abolished overnight by the police. He admits the injustice frankly and the need for expiation, but this expiation must take place without help or advice. At the end, Charles, too, comes to the realization that he is one with his people, bearing their shame and need for expiation. He understands at last what his mission is: to defend not only the South but also the United States against the meddling North and East and West, for their aim is to divide the nation. All Southerners would band together with unanimous solidarity against the use of force or any interference on the part of outsiders, especially theorists and do-gooders who are miles removed from the scene and do not understand the situation in the South. After all, in the North are to be found irrational hatreds and discriminations and forms of vengeance against foreigners and racial minorities even more cruel than those operative in the South.

It is unfair, of course, to tear all this out of context, but if it is meant as Faulkner's intransigent message to the North and the West, his apologia for the condition of the Negro in the South, then it is deplorable and appalling. No amount of genius can disguise the propagandist character of these fulminations. The South, convinced of its own righteousness, determined to keep the Negro in caste-bondage until such time as it sees fit to release him from this state—the South is again threatening to secede from the Union.

Intruder in the Dust represents dangerous doctrine. It marks a regression from the fine objectivity and naturalistic insight of the author who had composed *Light in August* and *Absalom, Absalom!* An angry, embittered tendentious novel, it is by no means Faulkner at his best. The psychological analyses are crude and amateurish; dog-eared dogmas are offered as profound revelations of the human soul; stale metaphysical reflections and inept anthropological lore are trotted out to vindicate the backward and oppressive tribal code of the South. If Faulkner is maintaining that the South harbors some noble and exalted spirits, men of tender conscience, high sense of honor, and profound humanity who would deny it? If he is asking that the South, because of its rich past, racial homogeneity, and historic traditions, be granted a special dispensation, exempt from the laws of democracy that are supposed to apply to all men, black as well as white, then he is guilty of darkening counsel.

88. Walter Allen, review, *New Statesman and Nation*

15 October 1949, 428–30

Allen (b. 1911) is an English critic and scholar best known for his surveys of the English and the modern novel. Surprisingly *Intruder in the Dust*, only six years after a most unfavorable British response to *Go Down, Moses*, received almost no negative comments in Britain.

No author can conceive of the difficulty of writing a romance about a country where there is no shadow, no antiquity, no mystery, no picturesque and gloomy wrong, nor anything but a commonplace prosperity, as is happily the case with my dear native land.

Hawthorne need not have worried: it did not remain happily the case with his dear native land for long. He died while the Civil War was still in progress, and for the South, at any rate, the War and the Reconstruction were to provide quite as much shadow, mystery, picturesque and gloomy wrong as any literary man could reasonably demand; and if there was no antiquity in the European sense there were plenty of ruins, without which, according to Hawthorne, romance and poetry could not grow. And to-day, if we wish to find in contemporary writing the fullest reflection of the qualities Hawthorne desired in a country, where do we go to if not to the literature of the South and, in particular, to the obsessed, doom-drenched fiction of Mr. Faulkner? There have been times when one has felt that Mr. Faulkner's exceedingly romantic imagination has got the better of him, when he has seemed to be revelling in spiritual melodrama for its own sake and busy parodying himself, as in *Absalom, Absalom!* with its nimiety of lunatics. Yet it would be impossible, I think, for even the most resolute hater of Mr. Faulkner's art to say this of *Intruder in the Dust*; it is much more likely that the austerer critics will find it too full of meaning, its message too plain.

Certainly it is the most explicit of his novels since *Soldiers' Pay* and, I would say, the most disciplined. The tortuous yet always carefully controlled style still makes its demands on the reader; there are still sentences four pages long, with a minimum of punctuation, and parentheses within parentheses. Yet the technical and stylistic devices are all subordinated to a thesis; the ancient wrongs—and what must be done about them—are stated quite clearly. And perhaps because of its very explicitness, it is considerably lighter in tone than most of Mr. Faulkner's work. For once he has deliberately refrained from attempting tragedy. He has written a novel which in form is a thriller—and a very good thriller, too—but this without detracting from its profundity: and he has also gone back to one of the most compelling and enduring archetypes of American fiction.

Fundamental to Mr. Faulkner's vision is his conception of time. As he writes in *Intruder in the Dust*:

> It's all now you see. Yesterday won't be over until tomorrow and tomorrow began ten thousand years ago. For every Southern boy fourteen years old, not once but whenever he wants it, there is the instant when it's still not two o'clock on that July afternoon in 1863, the brigades are in position behind the rail fence, the guns are laid and ready in the woods and the furled flags are already loosened to break out and Pickett himself with his long oiled ringlets and his hat in one hand probably and his sword in the other looking up the hill waiting for Longstreet to give the word and it's all in the balance, it hasn't happened yet, it hasn't even begun yet, it not only hasn't begun yet but there is still time for it not to begin against that position. . . .

It is this conception of time that explains much that is eccentric (though never arbitrary) in his style; it also makes him a traditionalist: he is still fighting the Civil War, is still living in the old Southern civilisation that the War destroyed, is still repudiating in proud poverty the domination of the Yankees. No less important, it gives him a special relation to the Negro. This relation is the theme of the novel, which is, in my view, the most satisfying study of the colour problem in the South that we have yet had in fiction.

[summarizes story and 'Mr. Faulkner's creed,' the words of Gavin beginning, 'We alone in the United States are a homogeneous people. . . .']

What Mr. Faulkner does in *Intruder in the Dust* is to show us a community suddenly aware of guilt in itself: 'Lucas Beauchamp, once the slave of any white man within range of whose notice he happened to come, now tyrant over the whole country's white conscience.' Mr. Faulkner evokes the community of Jefferson with all his old skill, which is more than skill. The sense of mobs, not waiting to lynch but waiting passively to watch a lynching, is superbly rendered. And Mr. Faulkner has the art of seeing his characters with, as it were, a double vision, in both their temporal and their enduring aspects, as in this shapshot of a Negro ploughing: 'the man and the mule and the wooden plow which coupled them furious and solitary, fixed and without progress in the earth, leaning terrifically against nothing.' So Chick is at once a sixteen-year-old boy of the present decade, a boy of the Confederate Army of 1862, even a British officer of the first world war. While completely retaining his individuality, he becomes an image of all who can say:

> Some things you must always be unable to bear. Some things you must never stop refusing to bear. Injustice and outrage and dishonor and shame.

Similarly with Lucas Beauchamp: out of date in fine rags, refusing to make distinctions between white and black, refusing to be beholden to anybody, he is both a most satisfying comic creation and an image of human integrity. What is striking in this novel, beyond the great gifts that we take for granted in Mr. Faulkner, is its humanity. In the past he has seemed to be gravelled by his sense of picturesque and gloomy wrongs. He is not in this new novel. In *Intruder in the Dust* he has written a book that is positively inspiriting; which is scarcely the adjective one would have applied to his work in the past.

89. Richard Chase on *Light in August*

Autumn 1948

'The Stone and the Crucifixion: Faulkner's *Light in August*,' *Kenyon Review*, x, 539–51. This issue also included an article by Lawrence Bowling on *The Sound and the Fury*.

Chase (1914–62) the following year wrote an important book on Melville. In the 1950s he published studies of Whitman and Dickinson as well as the influential *The American Novel and Its Tradition*. Though eclectic in his criticism, he frequently emphasizes patterns of symbol or myth.

1.

WITHOUT MUCH ADO I wish to direct attention to the symbolic texture of *Light in August*. This texture is very much a matter of mechanics and dynamics—a poetry of physics. Repeatedly Faulkner presents appearance, event, and even character in the images of stasis, motion, velocity, weight, lightness, mass, line, relative position, circle, sphere, emptiness, fullness, light, and dark. The phrase 'light in August' has at least two meanings. As Mr. Malcolm Cowley informs us in his *Portable Faulkner*, the phrase means 'light' as opposed to 'heavy' and refers to a pregnant woman who will give birth in August. And it also means 'light' as opposed to 'dark'—an affirmation of life and human spirit. *Light in August* may be described, in Faulkner's own words (though he is describing something else), as 'the mechanics, the theatring of evil.' This is not a complete or fully fair description of Faulkner's novel, but it is complete and fair enough to demand that we look at the novel from this point of view—and that we finally ask, How successful is the author in extending his account of the mechanics and theatring of evil into an account of the human situation?

The reader of *Light in August* will be puzzled in the first few pages by what may be called 'the string of beads image.' We read that the wagon in which Lena Grove rides through the August afternoon is like 'a shabby bead upon a mild red string of road' and that the village beside the railroad, from which she begins her long journey, is like 'a forgotten bead from a broken string.' Later our attention is called to the row of iron bars in the fence which surrounds the orphanage of Joe Christmas' childhood, to the identical windows of a street car, to a picket fence, and to the rows of identical white houses in which the lower-middle-class whites live. To these images of linear discreteness Faulkner opposes images of the curve. Lena Grove—searching for Lucas Burch, the father of her unborn child—passes through 'a long monotonous succession of peaceful and undeviating changes from day to dark and dark to day'; but her mode of action and of consciousness is not of the order of the 'string of beads.' She is 'like something moving forever and without progress across an urn.' For her the road is not linear but like a string 'being rewound onto a spool.' These images of linear discreteness and curve are extended into one of the central images of the book: flight and pursuit.

We have already encountered the symbolic representation of two realms of being which are counterposed throughout the novel. The linear discrete image stands for 'modernism': abstraction, rationalism, applied science, capitalism, progressivism, emasculation, the atomized consciousness and its pathological extensions. The curve image stands for holistic consciousness, a containing culture and tradition, the cyclical life and death of all the creatures of earth. Throughout the novel, Lena retains her holistic consciousness and she is strong, enduring, hopeful. All the other characters in one way or another are victims of the linear delusion. For Joe Christmas, in whom the linear consciousness becomes pathological, the curve image is a 'cage' or a 'prison' to be broken out of. Or it is something to be gashed from the outside so that whatever it contains will be spilled meaninglessly out. Joe gashes the whiskey tins he and Burch have buried in the woods as he has a vision of trees in the moonlight, standing like 'a row of suavely shaped urns,' each one cracked and extruding 'something liquid, deathcolored, and foul.' At the end, when Joe can no longer perform this symbolic act of even smashing, the curve image becomes the fateful circle of repetition which he has never really either escaped or broken and which is the only path to the only kind of holism he will ever find: death. 'I have never got outside that circle. I have never broken out of the ring of what I have already done and cannot ever undo.' The tragic irony of the linear consciousness, Faulkner seems to say, is that it is an illusion; all consciousness is holistic, but it may be the holism of life (Lena) or of death (Joe). The remarkable symbol of the wheel in the passage describing the final madness of the Reverend Mr. Hightower presumably coincides with Joe's circle of doom, though here it may symbolize the completion in death of a cycle of legendary family history.

Faulkner's counterposing of motionlessness and motion seems to imply a fairly consistent deploying of polarity of character. Lena, Joe, and Hightower each has a certain kind of motionlessness. Lena, 'her voice quite grave now, quite quiet,' sitting 'quite still, her hands motionless upon her lap,' has the inner quiet of the wheel's axle, a stillness within movement. The stillness behind Joe's cold, contemptuous mask is the abstract stillness of separation, a schizoid disengagement from outer action. The motionlessness of Hightower, sitting 'rigidly' behind his desk, his 'forearms parallel upon the armrests of the chair,' is the negation of the will and action by fear, 'denial,' and impotence.

The quality of Joe's action is simply a willed translation of his separateness. Whenever he is in motion, in fantasy or actuality, he is in flight; and this is true even of his many connections with women—these also he must turn into the pattern of flight whenever they threaten to bring him too close to the kind of central and holistic place represented by Lena. Although Burch is throughout the book in a sense in flight from Lena, Byron Bunch, or the sheriff, his movements entirely lack Joe's willed abstract control. He is pure aimless motion, a rural poor white uprooted and cast adrift in an industrial-urban society. 'He puts me in mind,' says Byron Bunch, 'of one of these cars running along the street with a radio in it. You can't make out what it is saying and the car ain't going anywhere in particular and when you look at it close you see that there ain't even anybody in it.' A friend of Bunch's replies, 'Yes, he puts me in mind of a horse. Not a mean horse. Just a worthless horse.' This rude progression of metaphors will serve to indicate that Faulkner's imagination very frequently approaches the level of human character and consciousness beginning with the mechanical, and proceeding to the animal level through an intermediate level of dynamics.

The denouement of the novel can be conceived as the final resolution of several kinds of motion. Byron Bunch separates himself from his spiritual kinship with Hightower and his hitherto meaningless life finds its repose in Lena. Burch moves away from Lena, dooming himself, as it were, to aimless perpetual motion. The final flight of Joe to Hightower's house may seem too little explained as part of the plot. But it has a symbolic significance, since Joe, turning away for the last time from the realm of being which is represented by Lena and which he has tried to find in his various women, finds his ultimate refuge in the castration and death vouchsafed to him by Percy Grimm (only the last of all the symbolic castrations and deaths he has first sought and then endured). Hightower himself had turned away from the Lena-holism when years earlier he had in effect pursued his wife out of existence by believing in his fantasy that his 'seed' had died with his grandfather in the Civil War.

2.

MR. ROBERT PENN WARREN suggests that Faulkner's objection to the modern world is that it lacks the ability to set up 'codes, concepts of virtue, obligations' by which man can 'define himself as human' and 'accept the risks of his humanity.' In *Light in August*, Faulkner seems to be concerned with showing that the codes modern man *does* set up do *not* allow him to define himself as human—that codes have become compulsive patterns which man clings to in fear and trembling while the pattern emasculates him. Byron Bunch, wondering why he lives to the split second by his big silver watch and works alone in the planing mill every Saturday afternoon and why the Reverend Mr. Hightower has refused to leave Jefferson, the scene of his ruin and disgrace, reflects, 'It is because a fellow is more afraid of the trouble he might have than he ever is of the trouble he's already got. He'll cling to trouble he's used to before he'll risk a change.' Byron and Hightower have for years been sustaining one another in their 'patterns.' Their relationship ends over the question of Bunch's aiding and courting Lena, pregnant with another man's child. The dilemma for each is whether to stick to a pattern of behavior which prohibits accepting 'the risks of his humanity' or to become involved responsibly in a human situation. Byron chooses to break the pattern and accept the consequences of intervention. Hightower remains in the pattern (though he makes certain senile excursions from it), choosing to conspire in closing the circle of his destiny, choosing separation and madness. It is not true, as has been said, that all of Faulkner's characters are rigidly controlled by fate: Byron, for one, is left free to choose his own fate.

Joe Christmas is in many ways a masterful portrait of a man whose earliest years have been spent in an institution—an experience, as the psychiatrists show, which definitively affects not only the emotional centers of the victim but also the character of his conceptual thinking.

In the forbidding orphanage (a true symbol of the conditions of modern life) Joe finds a surrogate mother—a cynical, suspicious and indeed almost paranoiac dietitian, a mockery of the Nursing Mother of the myths. His surrogate father is an obscenely fanatical inquisitor and peeping tom who functions as the janitor of the orphanage and who later turns out to be Joe's grandfather. The pattern of Joe's life is inexorably formed when the dietitian finds that he has been hiding in her closet eating tooth paste while she has been entertaining an interne on her bed (the tube of tooth paste is another urn symbol). The definitive event is not that Joe has seen the dietitian in the act but that she fails to punish him and instead offers him money not to tell. Having felt terribly guilty, having expected and even wanted to be punished, and having had no idea of giving away the secret, he is irretrievably shocked when she offers him the money. He had wanted the woman to engross him in her life, if only by beating him. Instead she denies him this engrossment and gives him a silver dollar, whose shining circumference forms a circle Joe will never break through. Joe's homosexualism is another theme symbolized by the 'string of beads' image. The relationship between Joe and his guardian, McEachern, a fanatical apostle of a parochial and degenerate Presbyterianism who beats Joe with the impersonal violence of a machine, has for both McEachern and Joe the uneasy satisfaction of an abnormal but vehemently pure sexual alliance. McEachern has succeeded with Joe where the dietitian failed. Joe finds the relationship 'perfectly logical and reasonable and inescapable,' and he quickly learns to hate Mrs. McEachern because her proffered feminine kindnesses always threaten to taint an abstract and predictable relationship—just as the food she offers him makes him sick (all the women in Joe's life try to feed him; one of them is a waitress in a restaurant).

Joe's many adventures with women are attempts to escape the abstract quality of a latently homosexual life. As Joe pauses outside Miss Burden's house before keeping a tryst with her, Faulkner says, 'The dark was filled with the voices, myriad, out of all time that he had known, as though all the past was a flat pattern. And going on: tomorrow night, all the tomorrows, to be part of the flat pattern, going on.' 'Then,' says Faulkner, 'it was time'—which seems to be a pun (the same one occurs in *The Sound and the Fury*) meaning that now Joe's existence can be measured by time (the urn consciousness) rather than by the abstraction of eternity. But the connection with Miss Burden, like all of Joe's connections with women, turns into a ritual reaffirmation that no such connection is possible, a circular path back to the compulsive pattern—as we see when after various ingenious phases of sexual flight and pursuit, Miss Burden, before Joe kills her, is transmuted in appearance and behavior into a mocking likeness of McEachern. The sexual dilemma of Joe's life is nicely symbolized in the episode where he lolls in the woods (and gashes the whiskey tins) reading a magazine 'of that type whose covers bear either pictures of young women in underclothes or pictures of men shooting one another with pistols.' He reads as a man 'walking along the street might count the cracks in the pavement, to the last final page, the last and final word.' He goes through life with this same attachment to his pattern, hating the women in underclothes, longing for a purely masculine annihilation.

In symbolic polarity to the compulsive pattern we have Lena, who does not need to flee from involvement in human life, and Lucas Burch. Distantly adumbrating all the polarities of *Light in August*, the gay, irresponsible, aimless Burch symbolizes pure Chaos. Perhaps through the child in Lena's womb, Burch symbolizes the undetermined possibility of a future the direction of which will be decided by the final resolution of forces among the other characters. If so, we may say that *Light in August* is a 'hopeful' book. For the future is in the hands of Lena and Byron Bunch—a woman who endures and loves and a man who has decided to 'accept the risks of his humanity.'

3.

MR. WARREN suggests that we ought not to think of Faulkner as an exclusively Southern writer but as a writer concerned with modern times in general. To this, one might add that Faulkner has many affinities with both Hawthorne and Melville. As Malcolm Cowley has said, the myth of a Southern society which emerges from Faulkner's work as a whole can be compared with Hawthorne's myth of New England. One might add that the dilemma with which Faulkner confronts Bunch and Hightower—whether to take the responsibility of moral intervention in human affairs—is the same dilemma which confronts many of Hawthorne's characters (for example, the painter in 'Prophetic Pictures'). Joe Christmas would be recognized by Hawthorne; for he is frightened and obsessed by the inescapable stain on every human life. There is never any real proof that Joe is part Negro, but Joe's gratuitous assumption that he is tainted is at the root of all his actions. He becomes as obsessed with his stain as does Aylmer with the blemish on his wife's face in Hawthorne's 'The Birthmark' and with a purpose as relentless and immoral as Aylmer's he goes about removing the stain—an impulse which arises in the central figures of both 'The Birthmark' and *Light in August* from what is, in the final moral terms, simply their inability to bear the burden of being human. (The word 'burden,' by the way, seems to have the same significance for the Southern writers as the pack of the peddler had for Hawthorne and Melville: the 'burden' of one's history or of one's continually self-annihilating humanity. Miss Burden, in *Light in August*, is not the only character in Southern fiction so named.)

Faulkner and Melville share a liking for physical, dynamic, and animal images. Both abound in images of light and dark. In Faulkner's novel there is a persistent reference to white 'blood' and black 'blood,' and Joe's ambiguous character is symbolized by the dark serge trousers and white shirt he invariably wears. Both Ahab and Joe Christmas are seeking an elusive *purity*, symbolized by whiteness. Both shape their doom by their sharp rejections of their own humanity. Both are 'unmanned,' to use Melville's word, by fate or by their own moral acts. Faulkner's manner of handling symbols and themes is like Melville's. His downright spiritual vehemence often produces a wonderful lyric or epic sense of life; but sometimes the symbols are crudely imagined or imperfectly assimilated in context. For example, the uneasy connection of Joe Christmas with Christ: several of Joe's acts take place on Friday, or 'on the third day'; Mrs. McEachern washes his feet; Burch betrays him for a thousand pieces of silver; Hines, his grandfather and the only father Joe knows, imagines that he is God. Faulkner seems not to sense exactly how the Christ theme should be handled, sometimes making it too overt and sometimes not overt enough. His attempts to enlarge Joe's character by adducing a willed mythology remind one of Melville's similar attempts in *Pierre*. It may finally seem to us that Faulkner and Melville are most in control of their work when they approach the epic form, as in *As I Lay Dying* and *Moby-Dick*; but that when they try novels of complex symbolic human relationships, their effort suffers from their uncertain power of grouping symbols into a close coherent statement.

4.

IT HAS BEEN SAID of Faulkner that his rhetoric and the actions it expresses are so terrific that they annihilate his characters, that his characters become mere targets for violent emotive bombardments. The measure of truth in this criticism does not destroy Faulkner as an artist. It simply indicates that he is one kind of artist—surely he is not a novelist of manners in quite the way that such a phrase as 'the Balzac of the South' would imply. As if in self-criticism, Faulkner writes of Hines and his fanatical sermons: 'So they believed that he was a little crazy. . . . It was not that he was trying to conceal one thing by telling another. It was that his words, his telling, just did not synchronize with what his hearers believed would (and must) be the scope of a single individual.' Yet in one of the utterances of the Reverend Mr. Hightower we find this idea translated into a true definition of tragedy: 'Too much happens. That's it. Man performs, engenders, more than he can or should have to bear. That's how he finds that he can bear anything. That's it. That's what is so terrible.' In such a statement as this Faulkner begins to justify the overplus of superhuman and subhuman violence in his novels. Nevertheless there remains a discrepancy between the theoretical justification and the artistic practice. We cannot avoid phrasing the aesthetic implication of Hightower's words in some such way as this: 'Faulkner attributes more action and emotion to his characters than can meaningfully be attributed to them.'

The alienation of man *via* language is a common theme in *Light in August*. The people who have beaten and robbed Joe and left him on the floor of a cheap boarding house, speak 'in a language which he did not understand.' The sermons of Hightower seem to have been expressly contrived to separate him from his congregation. As for Lena, her separation-by-language is always maintained only to the degree necessary to her total purpose. When she asks along the road for Burch, people direct her to 'Bunch,' but to her they always seem to say 'Burch.' She is purposefully separated from irrelevance and relaxed in her vision of reality. Separation by language is surely a fact of human life. But is Faulkner entirely in control of this theme? In the orphanage the dietitian and Hines meet 'calm and quiet and terse as two conspirators' and then proceed to discourse in some pseudo-Old Testament language which is anything but calm, quiet, or terse. But perhaps it is another form of dissociation which makes this putatively powerful situation seem defective. Perhaps—in order that the dissociation might be in *his* mind, for it needs to be in *someone's* mind—the five-year-old Joe should have been present, watching and listening in awe to the terrible creatures, his mythical father and mother. It is simply a novelist's mistake to present us with a sharp dislocation between his characters and what they say, without accounting in context for the dislocation. One feels that Faulkner has missed a chance in this scene to form a profound associative human situation.

This leads us to a general question: What is the quality of consciousness displayed in *Light in August*? Surely, it is not a consciousness which broods over the whole range of action, associating people with each other or with a culture, establishing their manners and morals in a whole containment. It is a consciousness in flight and pursuit, wonderfully aware of fact, the physical and animal fact, wonderfully in possession of extreme emotions and the ecstasy of violence, cognizant too of the tender humorousness of love, and in general wonderfully fantastic and magical. *Par excellence*, it is the American folk-literary consciousness. When it seeks to interpret or enlighten the human situation, when Faulkner breaks off the humorous-tragical flow of rhetorical poetry and ventures an observation on human manners, he is likely to sound naive. He will speak in the manner of the folk proverb: 'Yes, sir. You just let one of them get married or get into trouble without being married, and right then and there is where she secedes from the woman race and spends the balance of her life trying to get joined up with the man race. That's why they dip snuff and smoke and want to vote.' Or he will attempt a more intellectually formulated observation, with the following unhappy result: 'the faces of the old men lined by that sheer accumulation of frustration and doubt which is so often the other side of the picture of hale and respected full years'—What a piece of philosophy! One can hardly help sensing an uncomfortable hiatus between Faulkner's poetic portrayal of manners and his explicit consciousness of them.*

Probably the episodes of family and cultural history which accompany Faulkner's account of Miss Burden and Hightower would mean more to a Southerner than they do to me. But especially in the case of Hightower there seems to be a failure of consciousness precisely at the point where we should understand the quality of the association between Hightower and his own history. Hightower has projected his sexual and spiritual impotence back upon a myth of his grandfather. Faulkner goes along with Hightower on this point, assuming too much that a fantasy projected from some center of real causation is the cause itself. He nearly allows Hightower to determine the quality of his

* But the observations I have made in this paragraph would be substantially less true if applied to *The Sound and the Fury*.

(Faulkner's) consciousness. On the other hand, he is capable of involving Burch in a situation which calls for a degree of consciousness far above what seems possible, and then arbitrarily giving him the necessary consciousness; so that we have a dull country lout whose 'rage and impotence is now almost ecstatic. He seems to muse now upon a sort of timeless and beautiful infallibility in his unpredictable frustrations' (the qualifiers 'almost,' 'seems to,' 'a sort of' are significant). And a moment later we find Burch (so it seems) reflecting that a Negro he is talking with 'does not appear to have enough ratiocinative power to find the town.' In *Anna Karenina* a dog conducts a humorous and anxious conversation with himself. But unlike the Burch episode, this does not seem in the least out of place, because Tolstoy with his great associative consciousness always gives one the feeling that he knows exactly when and how much to withdraw or extend his mind in the universe of his novel. I do not mean to imply that Faulkner's novel *lacks* consciousness, but only that the consciousness it displays is sometimes unhappily biassed, bardic, parochial, and, in the societal or cultural sense, unmannered. Davy Crockett still screams in the Southern wilderness.

But of course any discussion which compares Faulkner unfavorably with a writer like Tolstoy must not be guilty of the assumption that Faulkner's Southern culture is as cohesive and knowable as Tolstoy's Russian culture was; obviously it is not. And Faulkner's claim to be the novelist of a culture (if that is his claim) must be judged on the basis of his whole work. Nevertheless the evidence of *Light in August*, though it shows that Faulkner is capable of very fine and very extensive and complex fictional constructions, also seems to indicate that he can fail us exactly at that level of existence where the subtle complications of human behavior have to be established. Faulkner works inward from the extremities, from the mechanics and the ecstasy of life. And this relentless, bardic-American bias often makes us wish he would reverse the procedure, that his consciousness would work through human manners into the human character and then outward toward the extremities it can contain or fail to contain. Human life submits itself to die at the hands of the artist so that it may be reborn in art, somewhat as Joe Christmas submits himself to the beatings of McEachern: 'The boy's body might have been wood or stone; a post or a tower upon which the sentient part of him mused like a hermit, contemplative and remote with ecstasy and selfcrucifixion.' One wants to know finally, What manner of man is this *between* the stone and the crucifixion?

5.

BUT IT IS ONLY one's high estimation of Faulkner which raises these questions at all. Like the author of *Moby-Dick* Faulkner might say of himself, 'I try everything; I achieve what I can.' In these bad times, a serious venturesomeness must count heavily with us. But it is also a sense of Faulkner's achievement which makes me think him the equal of any American novelist of his generation. Perhaps *The Great Gatsby* is the only novel of the time which can be defended as superior to Faulkner's best work.

In the nineteen-thirties the liberal-progressive culture turned away from Faulkner for many of the same bad reasons which caused it, eighty years before, to turn away from Melville. If our liberal thought now begins to return from its disastrous wanderings of the last decades—that era of the great rejections—and to recover its vitality, it is because it grows capable of coming to terms with Faulkner, as it already learns again to come to terms with Hawthorne and Melville.

90. Charles Glicksberg, 'The World of William Faulkner'

Spring 1949

Arizona Quarterly, v, 46–58.

This was one of the last pieces of serious criticism to emphasize the element of naturalism in Faulkner's fiction. Later critics stressed on the one hand the symbolic and mythic dimensions that separated his technique from that of the naturalists and on the other the humanism that distinguished his point of view from that of a purer naturalism. They have frequently blurred the characteristics Glicksberg described in this article.

Practically all of Faulkner's novels are bathed in an atmosphere of, and culminate in, implacable tragedy. Though there are occasional touches of tenderness, there is no intrusion of irony, no attempt at metaphysical or religious consolation and certainly none at justifying the actions of the characters, nearly all of whom are at the mercy of their biological impulses or caught in a web of circumstance from which they cannot possibly escape. Faulkner has never, so far as I know, sought to defend his uncompromising treatment by depending, as does Farrell for example, on the thought contained in the bitter lines of A. E. Housman:

> And how am I to face the odds
> Of man's bedevilment and God's?
> I, a stranger and afraid
> In a world I never made.

Yet this outlook is implicit in his naturalistic method. For with an imagination as nightmarish and nihilistic as Celine's, he carries to a logical extreme the definition of naturalism as pessimistic realism and portrays man as the victim of his environment and conditioning. Faulkner is no moralist. Holding no brief for any ethical standard, he refuses to sit in judgment on the life of man. Yet there can be no doubt that a judgment is involved in his selection of material, his predilection for characters, frustrated, violent, abnormal, who carry within the seed of their own doom. Even his creative aim, namely, to record objectively the fate of all those trapped by deterministic forces stronger than their individual will, presupposes a philosophical bias, a verdict rendered. As in a Greek tragedy, the conclusion is known as soon as the drama opens. With flaming nostrils and terrible, fire-glaring eyes, the four horses of the Apocalypse ride through Faulkner's pages. His naturalism rises to a crescendo of pessimism more intransigent than any that has hitherto found expression in American fiction, more absolute, more horrifying even, than the vision of evil in *Moby Dick*.

Civilization, stripped to its essence, is interpreted as a hideous, dust-swept arena, a place of agonized violence, filled with horrible cries of cruelty and pain, the scent of blood, disease, and death. Since there is no illusion about any ultimate meaning that would justify these tragedies, there is no interpolation of pity; all one hears is the accent of tolerance which reveals everything without condemnation, without irony, and without surprise. This *ne plus ultra* of naturalistic pessimism is all the more poignant because it is not communicated overtly as doctrine; there is no propaganda and no preachment. The philosophy emerges out of the struggles and speech of the characters in moments of passionate experience, out of the furious pace and pattern of the action. These Faulknerian creatures who sin and suffer, who couple like demented animals and kill like murderers and are henceforth pursued by the furies of conscience, blindly seeking their own destruction, are pictured as victims, but they are to be neither pitied nor admired, for there is no particular triumph in their failure, no significance in their dying. Their tragedy is full of sound and fury, signifying nothing.

After a work like *Sanctuary* (1931), the reader is prepared to expect almost anything of a novelist like Faulkner: the morbid, the macabre, the psychopathological. He has recorded in vivid imaginative terms all the symptoms contained in Krafft-Ebing's *Psychopathia Sexualis*. One of the primary qualities of his characters is their addiction to lust, the enormity and irresistible compulsion of their sex instinct. It is not, however, the physical act that he dwells upon with circumstantially documented details but its repercussions in the mind of the characters, their lacerating introspections, their agonies of remorse and expiation. The horror mounts cumulatively and there is no break in the skillfully contrived structure of suspense. That is so not only because Faulkner is a consummate craftsman who squeezes the last drop of dramatic significance out of a scene or withheld secret but also because, as a general rule, he has no fortifying philosophy to offer the reader—nothing but a tale of terror and degradation, with evil triumphant riding hard for perdition. These lust-driven biological organisms explode in a moment of violent death and the rest is silence. As the father explains to his son, Quentin, when he has given him Grandfather's watch: 'I give it to you not that you may remember time, but that you might forget it now and then for a moment and not spend all your breath trying to conquer it. Because no battle is ever won,' he said. 'They are not even fought. The field only reveals to man his own folly and despair, and victory is an illusion of philosophers and fools.' As Quentin later puts it, in *The Sound and the Fury*, one carries the symbol of his frustration into eternity.

The Sound and the Fury (1929), a story about a tragically doomed family, is a striking example of Faulkner's use of violence and horror as a fictional device. The story unrolls in spiral fashion, going backward and forward at the same time, past and present confounded, the world of action being beheld through the suffering, guilt-tormented minds of the characters. As Quentin cries out: 'theres a curse on us its not our fault is it our fault.' In this run-on, incoherent prose, we get the discontinuities of the dream-state, the erratic yet unbroken flow of the stream-of-consciousness, all rendered vivid by the luminous and precise hypnagogic images. The total effect, however, is one of unrelieved confusion and despair. There are incursions of stark pessimism, as when the father, who later drinks himself to death, teaches his young ones 'that all men are just accumulations dolls stuffed with sawdust swept up from the trash heaps where all previous dolls had been thrown away. . . .' One must be patient and see evil done on earth for a little while, for every man is under the dominion of necessity. The father who in this novel seems to sum up Faulkner's philosophy, declares:

> . . . and the strange thing is that a man who is conceived by accident and whose every breath is a fresh cast with dice already loaded against him will not face that final main which he knows before hand he has assuredly to face without essaying expedients ranging all the way from violence to petty chicanery that would not deceive a child until someday in very disgust he risks everything on a single blind turn of a card no man ever does that under the first fury of despair or remorse or bereavement he does it only when he has realized that even the despair or remorse or bereavement is not particularly important to the dark diceman.

The gods, in short, have us in their power, and every experience, every passion, every action, leads us inevitably to consequences of which we have no prevision.

The discontinuity revealed by science, the inexplicable leap of the electron, finds its reflection in modern fiction. The rationally ordered universe of the nineteenth-century mind has been supplanted by a multiverse, a pandemonium of conflicting, incompatible selves. The personality is revealed to be pluralistic, unpredictable in its complexity, full of treacherous, libidinal depths, dangerous emotional rapids, terrific downsucking whirlpools of passion. There is the dynamic flow of the unconscious, the uprush of repressed instinctual impulses, the counter-action of the superego trying to keep the irrepressible *id* within bounds. All this is treated at great length in a number of modern psycho-analytic novels: the ebb and flow of the unconscious tide of the mind, the conflict between the conventional, ideal self and the lower self. Some novelists portray these turbulent conflicts in a straightforward narrative pattern, following a regular time sequence, using recognized methods of transition and development. Others, however, try to suggest the discontinuity of feeling, and thought, memory and desire, by breaking up the pattern into discrete particles, a flying welter of impressions, yet they cannot in the end shuffle off the responsibility of assembling the pieces into some sort of intelligible unity of design. Faulkner does this, on the whole, with remarkable effectiveness in *The Sound and the Fury* and in *Absalom, Absalom!* The story is pieced out bit by bit, the secret coming out in artfully disclosed fragments, growing more horrible with each partial disclosure, until the worst is known and the curtain rings down.

It is understandable why Faulkner regarded *As I Lay Dying*, a triumph of the psychological method over the disruptive complexities of form, as his masterpiece. A few bare incidents on a stricken land, in a poor Southern household, are spun out, it would seem, to interminable length: like a film run over and over again but seen each time from different perspectives. That in reality constitutes the essence of the method: the same slice of life is viewed through the eyes of the different characters involved in the course of the action. This approximates in fiction what mass observation attempts to do in sociological reporting.

The woman of the house is dying and her son Cash, an expert carpenter, is doing his best to finish the coffin while she lies near the window, silent, immobile, but watching his labor all the time. The sound of the saw can be heard distinctly throughout the house, and we get the reactions, told sensitively, discerningly, but with remorseless objectivity and dispassionateness, of the various characters, none of whom is more important than the other. Just as in the dust each particle is of equal significance and value, so among human beings there are, fundamentally, no hierarchies of rank but each one, anguished with fear and love, hate and grief, must bear his own cross and walk alone the journey to the end of night. There is the brooding, tempestuous, wild-tempered Jewel who thinks: 'if there is a God what the hell is He for.' There is Darl, the queer one, musing on the mystery of birth, on how the world is going to end. Each character is burdened with his own private obsession, his own portion of suffering, and describes the same scene as he sees it refracted through the glass of his temperament. There is throughout no taking of sides, no show of partiality or partisanship. That is how these simple people are constituted, that is how they react when confronted with the crisis of death. Each one has his pride, his bitterness, his dream. This, indeed, marks Faulkner's greatest triumph as a novelist: the realization that to the eye of the Olympian observer all is significant, everything makes ineluctably for tragedy; each soul has its own incommunicable longings and frustrations and woes; each one blindly follows his own star, and all end equally in the obliterating darkness of death. There is, then, no need for pity or judgment, only understanding.

Of all contemporary novelists, Faulkner is probably the least involved in the passions and agonized struggles of his characters. At least, by not obtruding his presence or passing any comments on the course of the action, he makes it seem that they enact their own destiny. His is the all-beholding eye of God, but a God without anthropomorphic qualities, without concern for the tragicomedy that is taking place on earth, utterly devoid of love, kindness, compassion. Faulkner is an American Dostoyevski who exhibits the Golgothean progression of the lost souls of the damned, the injured, the psychopathic, the doomed, but without ever introducing the catharsis of Christian faith. There is no redemption by prayer or penitence, no providential salvation through the merciful mediation of God. His supreme task as a novelist is to focus his lens properly, to portray the truth of the precarious human situation as objectively as possible, undistracted by human, all-too-human shibboleths and illusions. It is not a photographic copy, however, that he gives us but something that is more like an X-ray portrait of the working of the inner psyche, a study of morbidity and violence, cruelty and evil and madness, rising to a final climax of tragedy. All this is set against the background of a decadent South.

Not that there is no trace at all of compassion in the warp and woof of Faulkner's compassion; like the deterministic thesis, it is there implicit in the presentation and development of the characters, the fate they undergo: the betrayals, adulteries, suicides, seductions, incests, death. No matter how grotesque or terrible the outcome of their lives, somewhere in it there is an unfolding pattern of causation—events of childhood, the pressure of environment, the cruelty of people or the laws of society—which accounts for their behavior, their downfall. It is, then, not a question of compassion but of understanding, for the understanding is the only sort of compassion Faulkner can offer us.

Light in August (1932) is a good illustration of this point. We read of Lena Burch, pregnant, wandering along the sun-streaked roads from Alabama to Jefferson, Mississippi, in search of the man she had naively trusted; there is Hightower, the tormented pastor, who has had to resign from his church because of the adultery committed by his wife; there is Byron Bunch, working hard to escape the strangling clutch of evil; and there is Joe Christmas, the protagonist, the evil one incarnate, Satan in human form, always walking alone, bootlegging whiskey, living with a queer, elderly white woman two miles from town. Then the art of motivation, the implicit 'compassion,' steps in: flashbacks to scenes of the past reveal the concatenation of malign influences—cruel blows, the fiendish malice of adults, the impact of a hostile, hate-charged environment—that made Christmas a criminal, an outcast, an enemy of mankind. There is the suspicion that he has Negro blood in his veins. Constantly he broods on the knowledge that he is infected with 'black' blood, for that is the unpardonable sin in the South. Until gradually the reader begins to perceive the creative intention of this novel. As in *The Sound and the Fury*, not the least of God's creatures, not the most wicked and damned, are without their sustaining spark of humanity: their irrationality, their crises of conscience, their troubled dreams. Even a Christmas has his restless moments, his sleepless nights. His vicious hatred of the world, his outbursts of cruelty, are the expression of his warped upbringing. This is what the world has made of him, and this is the only way he knows of fighting the malevolent persecution of society, its hatred masked as righteousness, its lust parading as Christian love. Throughout his life all he has received is deprivation, harshness, ostracism, hatred, enmity, and his only defense is to remain outwardly calloused, indifferent, rebellious, repaying blow for blow, contemptuous of God's law and defiant of man's compulsion. All this is drawn against the background of a sun-scorched, pietistic South, a land of superstition and ignorance, vindictiveness and violence, sadistic passion and horror.

Here, then, is a novelist who beholds the actions of his world with an eye of complete objectivity. Nothing is insignificant or unimportant. Everything has its place in the grand design. If his prose is successful in presenting with artistic fidelity the sensuous concreteness and immediacy of external reality, he is even more successful in penetrating the haunted corridors of the mind, the recesses of psychic conflict, so that we are enabled to comprehend the complex network of causes that makes these people act as they do. As Faulkner phrases it: 'Man knows so little about his fellows. In his eyes all men or women act upon what he believes would motivate him if he were mad enough to do what the other man or woman is doing.' Faulkner's object is to remedy the deficiency caused by our myopic, ego-bound ignorance of the true motives of human action. *Light in August* draws to a close: Christmas, accused of an atrocious murder, escapes from his captors and is killed. Hightower dies, recapitulating his whole past, his life of wasted effort, frustration, and failure, coming to the bitter conclusion that 'there are more things in heaven and earth too than truth.' For there are intolerable crises in which man's only stay and support is his power of guarding himself against the truth. He dies with the knowledge that all heaven is 'filled with the lost and unheeding cry of all the living who ever lived, wailing still like lost children among the cold and terrible stars.'

Absalom, Absalom! has the quality of a continuous nightmare. There is no relief from the slow but relentless unwinding of the spool of evil, the sense of impending tragedy. And the method of narration, retrospective, crablike, presenting the central events of the plot bit by bit as seen by different characters and from different points of vantage and perspectives of time, adds cumulatively to the mounting horror. In this novel interest is centered not so much on the action itself as on the tangled skein of motives that led up to the tragic culmination. Which means that concern with the dynamics of character transcends the importance of the logic of plot. Not that Faulkner fails to skirt the edge of melodrama with his detailed account of shooting, fighting, sinister crimes, seductions, violated codes of honor, but he avoids it by seeking to probe, in each instance, beneath the passion and violence to the psychological forces that made these men and women behave in this eccentric, abnormal manner. Since the background of the story is

Mississippi, this means that attention is concentrated on the environment, the soil and place, the mores of the plantation, the influence of slavery, the disturbing presence of the Negro.

The style of narration is adapted to the needs of the plot, which spins itself endlessly, uncoiling, winding up again and then unrolling with a new insight, a new revelation. What lends a touch of the nightmarish, of Laocoönic violence, to these scenes and incidents is that they deal with a proud, gracious, picturesque past. Beneath its pomp and circumstance, however, beneath the traditional façade of elegance and chivalric dignity, we can see the working out of tameless, abysmal passions, frustrations that are rooted in the cells of the blood, in the germ plasm. Through the eyes of his characters Faulkner draws a composite picture of life in the South, a picture lighted from multiple angles. The sentences pour out copiously, in a stream that overflows its banks, in a language of the night, a curiously involved language of reminiscence, introspection, and retrospection, the past taking on sinister hues of foreboding and disaster, until the town of Mississippi, the people, the landscape are bathed in a lowering, crepuscular atmosphere, as scenes of the past, emerging in no strictly ordered succession, confused, repetitious, but tied together at the end to form a unified tale, enact their doom-decreed destiny. This is a Greek drama, but without the intercession of the gods, of evil and retribution in a Southern environment.

In *Absalom, Absalom!* the style is mannered, baroque, turgid, even pretentious, but it must be considered effective as a whole in light of the special atmosphere and mood it seeks to produce. Joyce, in *Ulysses* and *Finnegans Wake*, was a pioneer in the field of composing 'night language.' One recalls in particular his masterly use of nocturnal dream-monologue in the last section of *Ulysses*, the earth-sensual stream of imagery and association of ideas flowing through the relaxed, sleep-encompassed mind of Molly Bloom, the fecund mother, mistress, and wife, without periods or commas or pauses of any kind. Molly Bloom, however, possesses an unconscious that is representative in its promiscuous lubricity, its frank yielding to the appetites of the flesh, while Faulkner is bent on suggesting the increment of horror, the ghostliness and ghastliness, connected with the romantic shell of a past that is the South. Therefore, it is not so much dream-sequences that he relates but remembrances of things past, recollections filtered through the memory of lingering ghosts who have long brooded on the wrongs of the past, the passions, the murder, the revenge, recognizing at last the continuity of life, the fatality of events, the working out of the law of Karma.

As in his other novels, only gradually does the full force of the creative design strike us: the complexity of the plot, the repetitive cyclical pattern, something new revealed with each forward and backward movement of the story—the motives for which we have been searching at last brought forth into the light of day, though even then obscured and tangled, as all motives are bound to be in the human soul. Piece by piece the jigsaw puzzle falls into place and a clear-cut pattern finally emerges, but the suggestion of horror and doom is maintained throughout. The secret that is finally disclosed, the secret on which the resolution of the plot hinges, is the discovery that Charles Bon has part Negro blood in his veins; he is the illegitimate son of Colonel Sutpen, but the boy's mother, when she finds herself rejected by the Colonel, devotes herself with paranoiac energy to the pursuit of revenge, with her son as the chosen instrument to wreak ruin on the man who has cast her aside. The father refuses to acknowledge this product of miscegenation. When the knowledge of this dreadful secret is finally brought home to the legitimate son, Henry, he kills Charles Bon rather than allow him to marry his sister, who is thus condemned to widowhood.

It is the mark of Faulkner's genius that he has seized upon this theme —the race problem and all that it involves—as the central problem of his novel and the dominant problem of the South, and handled it with scrupulous honesty and objectivity. If Faulkner is the Dostoyevski of the South, this land and its people, haunted by ghosts of the past, tormented by a crushing sense of guilt, burdened with an antiquated and iniquitous caste system, present a handicap and a complication. There is Charles Bon, with his dreadful 'secret,' pleading with Henry the justification for incest. There is also the realization that our illusions are as integral a part of us as our flesh and bone. But it is the miscegenation, not the incest, which is the insuperable barrier. Shreve, the listener in the novel, the Canadian outsider, confesses that his people are not afflicted in this manner. 'We don't live among defeated grandfathers and freed slaves. . . .' The air breathed by the natives of the South is 'a kind of vacuum filled with wraithlike and indomitable anger and pride and glory at and in happenings that occurred and ceased fifty years ago. . . .'

From a consideration of these selected novels by Faulkner we can see that his strength is also the source of his central weakness. It is not a question of truth or falsity, romanticism or realism, but of emphasis, selectivity, proportion. The revelations that Faulkner made had to be made: the exploration of the abysses of the unconscious, the abnormality present in varying degrees in each of us, ready to leap out as soon as the pressure of adverse circumstances becomes strong enough, the unmitigated horror of life in the South, the savagery of lust that slumbers fitfully beneath the outward surface of easy-going gentility and slothful ignorance, the backwash of perversion and homicidal impulses churned up by the forces of repression. No Faulkner novel is complete without its compounded plot of horror, its ingredients of rape, seduction, prostitution, illegitimate children, incest, perversion, miscegenation, and *Sanctuary* is in this respect his best, or worst, novel. Overriding all these elements of plot, of course, is the theme of the Negro: 'black' blood as an abomination, a source of defilement, an inexpiable curse. It is an obsession that is present not only in the horror-haunted mind of Faulkner but also in the collective psyche of the South.

But horror, cumulative and intense, is only part of the picture. Though these scenes of tragic violence take place against the peaceful, somnolent background, the fields shimmering gold beneath the hot sun, the crickets sounding musically at night, Faulkner's object is to make it clear that these seemingly self-contained, God-fearing men and women of Mississippi are subject to gusts of murderous passion, bestial lusts, destructive impulses. In *Light in August*, the farmer who adopts Christmas is a monster of hate who masks his sadism under the guise of Christian righteousness. *Absalom, Absalom!* is the story of a family doomed by the fatal admixture of Negro blood. Now in all these tales of miscegenation, rape, seduction, degeneration, and crime, there is no implication, no hint even, that life can fulfill its appointed rounds graciously, 'normally,' without morbid complications and inevitably tragic outcomes. If Faulkner is the Dostoyevski of the South, he is without the Russian's universality of vision, his saving grace of compassion. What Faulkner is doing is to impose a romantic psychopathological point of view on starkly realistic material, with the result that what he produces is a Freudian nightmare. There is sin without any hope of redemption, struggle without the possibility of victory, suffering without meaning or purpose, sex without love, life without fulfillment. It is all a tale told by an idiot and, as in parts of *The Sound and the Fury*, in the idiot's own words and impressions. Faulkner does not succeed—he does not attempt to do so—in holding steadily before our gaze the knowledge that other patterns of life exist, that other perspectives are possible.

The critic is perhaps not justified in demanding of an author that which he is not prepared to give. Faulkner is not understandable if we seek to impose a sociological or metaphysical gloss on his work, least of all if we judge him by Marxist standards. He is neither a philosopher nor a socialist but a writer of fiction. If he dwells on the slow stages of decadence in the South, he is not concerned about pointing a moral but in presenting the process dramatically and objectively in terms of human suffering. The stream-of-consciousness method he employs is more profound and subtle and varied, certainly more passionate, than its counterpart in the novels of Virginia Woolf. This stream is colored and turbulent, responsive to the complex emotions—the memories and lusts, the desires and guilt and remorse—that agitate the minds of various characters. Through it all Faulkner remains practically invisible, a medium of communication but never a participant in the course of the action, venturing no commentary of praise or blame. The people in his fiction are stricken with fatal desires, moved by impulses they cannot control, driven to compulsive actions of guilt and fantastic rituals of expiation and flight. The mind, as Faulkner sees it, cannot cease its gyrations, memory will not die. In the end, these victims must go under and meet defeat. Having no philosophy of life to offer except one of absolute nihilism, Faulkner creates characters who reflect his baffled uncertainty, the torment of his unknowing.

William Faulkner has been criticized severely for a number of reasons, but for none more sharply than for his morbidity and nihilism. What is reprehensible, it seems, is that his work is overshadowed by a sense of utter futility. When this is combined with the theme of decadence, developed brilliantly with a plethora of naturalistic details, the humanistic critic has had more than he can stomach. He cannot be led to believe that the decadence of the South after the Civil War was as vicious and depraved as it is made out to be in the lurid pages of Faulkner. Such objections on moralistic grounds will not, however, carry weight. Faulkner is primarily concerned to tell the truth as objectively and effectively as he can within the limits of fiction, without compromising his integrity of vision. If he finds cruelty and obscenity, incest and perversion and horror in the South, characters that are abnormal, spiritually lost and doomed, it is because such things exist; he has seen them happen, and his conscience as a writer forbids him to gloss them over. The reader must decide for himself whether he is to reject a novelist because he finds his outlook on life unpleasant, but how, if he is to be fair in his judgment, can he reject him without at least giving his work a trial?

COLLECTED STORIES OF WILLIAM FAULKNER

New York, August 1950
London, October 1951

91. Horace Gregory, review, *New York Herald Tribune Weekly Book Review*

20 August 1950, 1, 12

Gregory (b. 1898), poet, translator of the classics, critic, and biographer, had already written favorable reviews of *Go Down, Moses* and *Intruder in the Dust. Collected Stories* came out less than three months before the announcement that Faulkner had been selected for the Nobel Prize.

In the early years of the present century when undergraduates in colleges made their first discovery of Chekhov, every one who dreamed of writing a book some day felt the sudden impulse to write, if nothing else, the perfect short story. It seemed so easy: if almost any one on a fortunate occasion could tell a story, then it followed naturally that any one could write it, and with the slightest effort could become both rich and famous. And today when more short stories than ever are being written, the perfect story, or if less than that, the story worthy to be remembered, is just as rare as ever. In contemporary literature a number of the stories and short novels of William Faulkner seem to possess an immortality; some few of them have haunted the imagination of their readers, including other writers, for nearly twenty years. Are the stories perfect works of art? Not many, for William Faulkner is not that kind of artist: some of the stories, no matter how highly we may regard them, contain blurred passages of prose, or if read for themselves alone, seem willfully obscure. Why is it then that Faulkner's writing has the sign of genius and the promise of an enduring life?

One answer to this question is that Faulkner always has something to say, but beyond that answer there is the likeness that he bears (which does not mitigate in the least his individual qualities) to certain writers who have stirred and guided the sub-channels of fiction during the first half of the twentieth century—if one becomes literal, three of them are not of this century at all. I refer, of course, to Henry James, Herman Melville, Dostoevsky and Franz Kafka, James Joyce and D. H. Lawrence.

A generation ago most of these writers were considered too obscure in meaning, or too dark, too complex, too gloomy to read for pleasure, or to some readers, too dangerously modern. Today their names are the familiars of academic discourse and are among the clichés of reference in quarterly reviews. However in or out of fashion these writers are or may become, each carries within his prose the essentials of poetic insight and imagination; beyond the rules of art, of critical taste and controversy, each conveys an awareness of the mystery of being and of moral integrity. Within this company where the independent spirit is kept alive, in the company of the sometimes difficult and sometimes obscure, the writings of William Faulkner find their natural environment.

It is there that the laws of literary perfection are often broken, yet every writer I have named is well outside the dreary provinces, flat and suburban, of false intentions and mediocrity. Different as they are from one another (and I can think of no greater extremes than those represented by Henry James, Kafka and D. H. Lawrence) all meet, including Faulkner, in the singular likeness of illuminating, better than any of their critics, the direction and meanings of their major works within the concentrated areas of the short novel and the short story.

The present volume of Faulkner's stories—there are forty-two of them—has the almost literal appearance of an omnibus; it is a collection made from earlier volumes, now unobtainable, and it includes seventeen stories that have been published separately in magazines, but not between the covers of any of his books. It contains all the varieties of Faulkner's writings, rearranged for this occasion in something that approximates a topographical order: The Country, The Village, The Wilderness, The Wasteland, The Middle Ground, Beyond.

The first impression that the book conveys is one of an Elizabethan richness: here is the variety of life itself, its humors, its ironies, its ancient tempers, its latest fashions, its masks of horror, its violence, its comedy, its pathos. It is gratuitous to say that the stories are uneven in depth, quality and interest. After a closer view, what emerges from the casting of this wide net, is Faulkner's extended chronicle of Mississippi, a country in which his novels, *Sanctuary*, *Light in August*, *Absalom, Absalom!*, *The Hamlet*, and *The Unvanquished* have their being. The stories that venture beyond that particular topography are less convincing; only one, 'Mistral,' with its scene in post-World War I Italy, is the exception to the rule. Faulkner's Mississippi is of the same authority as scenes in Joyce's Dublin and Kafka's Prague; and in Faulkner's stories, as in stories of Joyce's 'Dubliners' and Kafka's 'The Penal Colony,' the writer draws upon the sources of universal truth when he is most at home.

For the last fifteen years it has been obvious enough that Faulkner is a regional novelist; he is of Mississippi and of a country that fought the Yankees during the Civil War and many of the long, difficult years that followed it, but it is also clear that he is a regional novelist with a difference; whenever he raises the ghostly image of the Confederate flag, it is in memory of those who fought a losing cause with honor—honor and pride and a not unconscious sense of irony. The idea of honor, however thinly worn, however gray it may appear, floats behind the panorama of Faulkner's writings; his people, rich or poor, red-skinned, or black or white, carry that idea as though it were an unnamed element of blood within their veins.

D. H. Lawrence once remarked that America was haunted by the Indians; something very like that conviction and that feeling enters into Faulkner's tales of The Wilderness, particularly his 'Red Leaves,' one of the memorable stories reprinted in the present volume. Surely no one has written of a deeper South than Faulkner's wilderness where Chickasaw Indian, Negro and white American conquered the land and lost it to one another. In another story, 'The Bear' (which is part of *Go Down, Moses*, and is not included in *The Collected Stories*), and in the speech of one of its characters, another aspect of 'Red Leaves' is shown:

> Don't you see? This whole land, the whole South is cursed, and all of us who derive from it, whom it ever suckled, white and black both, lie under the curse?

It is by this kind of penetration into the psyche of the South and of America that Faulkner retains his kinship to Melville, for like the elder writer, Faulkner looks downward and inward to the causes of guilt (which is also the subjective, inward look of Dostoevsky) before the sense of sin can start its long journey toward expiation.

Of the South that is now America there are three stories of World War II in *The Collected Stories*: 'The Tall Men,' 'Two Soldiers,' and 'Shall Not Perish,' in which the gods of family honor and devotion are invoked; there the emotions aroused by the interweaving of pathos and irony are resolved in the ancient truth that patriotism has its deepest roots at home. The closing paragraph of 'Shall Not Perish' ends in a statement that has an air of particular timeliness today:

> . . . The men and the women who did the deeds, who listed and endured and fought the battles and lost them and fought again because they didn't even know they had been whipped, and tamed the wilderness and overpassed the mountains and deserts and died and still went on as the shape of the United States grew and went on. I knew them too: the men and women still powerful seventy-five years and twice that and twice that again afterward, still powerful and still dangerous and still coming, North and South and East and West, until the name of what they did and what they died for became just one single word, louder than any thunder. It was America, and it covered all the western earth.

So much then for one aspect of what Faulkner has to say. What of the less known side of Faulkner in which serious, half grotesque farce and comedy are in the foreground of his scenes and in which the themes of honor, devotion and personal integrity are woven into the fabric of the story? It is important, I think, that at least two of these stories, 'Uncle Willy' and 'That Will Be Fine,' are told in the person of an all-seeing, shrewd, half-innocent, adolescent boy, a boy who seems to be the direct descendant of Melville's Ishmael through Mark Twain's Huckleberry Finn and Sherwood Anderson's George Willard of *Winesburg, Ohio*.

This line of heritage is of no discredit to Faulkner, and it shows how well he adjusted the character of his own gifts to the example set before him by Anderson. Uncle Willy, who was all too fond of drugs and drink and who resisted reform through the commands of well meaning relatives and ladies of the church, is one of the memorable characters of American fiction, and another is Uncle Rodney in 'That Will Be Fine.' These figures are of the romantic but no less real American who will never be fenced in, whose independence is inviolate, whose ingenuity almost, but not quite, circumvents the laws of ethical behavior and social propriety.

Among the best of *The Collected Stories* is also 'Hair,' which is a comedy of the first order; nor is there a better story anywhere of the barber and the peculiar delicacy of his craft. The story teeters on the verges of the ridiculous, the absurd, the sentimental: the precisely mild, neat, shabby figure of the barber reminds one of Venus' victims in Lucretius's treatise on the nature of love; it is the nature of his devotion to the images of beauty and honor held in his mind's eye which lends him dignity even in his devotion to an angular little girl of easy virtue and rescues him from oblivion in bathos.

Of the stories reprinted in the present collection, 'A Rose for Emily' is the best known, and it is also among the best of its kind in a genre which includes Walter de la Mare's 'Seaton's Aunt,' Henry James's 'Last of the Valerii' and Edgar Poe's 'Fall of the House of Usher.' It has, I fear, provided an inspiration for large bales of creeping moss, magnolia fiction from the South, and which has now, even as I write, grown into giant, mushroom-like proportions, has escaped the modest bindings of several books (not by William Faulkner) and is heard weeping behind adolescent smiles or drunken laughter upon the Broadway stage. This is, of course, dubious flattery to Faulkner's gifts and insights, and it is the price that every writer pays for writing supremely well.

The least fortunate side of Faulkner's gift in drawing upon the wells of memory are in his stories of airplane pilots—'all the dead pilots' of World War I; the stories have all the pathos of personal tributes paid to unworthy friends: but are they heroes? They were once young, and possessed of physical beauty in skill and action; they are cursed by the passage of time, but not by the deeper forces that are at work in Faulkner's tales of the South; nor do Faulkner's pilots hold so clearly and with almost religious fervor to the codes of honor and loyalty possessed by his other characters, the codes by which they expiate their sins of violence, their taint of madness.

To the general reader perhaps the greatest difficulty in reading a Faulkner short story is the experience of coming upon one that seems meaningless or incomplete. Unfortunately the true answer to the reader's question must be sought for in *Go Down, Moses*, or in *Light in August*, or another one of Faulkner's books. For at least twenty years, Faulkner has kept in mind, as though they moved upon a turning wheel, the fabulae, part family legend and part history, of Mississippi; yet he is seldom provincial in the sense that many regional writers feel compelled to be. His South with its mingling of races, with its remains of Baroque horror and decay, with its bartering of lands and birthrights, with its interludes of the shrewd, half-innocent eye of half-grown children, with its Puritanical hold upon the rights of individual being, action and thought is, as Faulkner would say it, of the America that covers all the Western earth.

If Faulkner's extraordinary rhetoric is at times obscure, and is at times as baroque as the plot and substance of some of his stories, he has also written more passages of unmistakable lucidity than any writer of his generation. He is more distinctly the master of a style than any writer of fiction living in America today. Surely few writers of the short story can withstand the test so well as he in having a story read aloud; more than half the art of Faulkner's prose is in the meaning and the pleasure it conveys to the reader's inner ear. To keep the rhythms of his prose within the ranges of the human voice is one of the reasons, I think, that Faulkner, in the writing of a story, so often employs the use of the monologue; it is the tone of voice in which the words are spoken that gives color to the meaning of the story.

Above, beyond all questions of Faulkner's style rises the evidence of his ability to haunt the imagination of those who read his stories. Even when his stories are not at their best, the conviction of encountering a moment of human action and reality remains. One finds it difficult to forget the little melodrama of Elly, the self-obsessed young woman, the all-too-obvious victim of self-pity. 'The Brooch,' the story of the son dominated by his mother, is another part of the same glimpse into reality, and the black-out of resolving self-love through violent injury and death. Faulkner's solution is, of course, too easy, but he has caught within a very few pages the moral horror of self-destruction and the too-often sentimental motives of suicide.

The secret of Faulkner's hold upon the imagination is that he moves always to the unseen, unliterary and essential springs of human action; and on occasion he destroys a few of his more profound revelations of evil by an impatient thrust of counter-violence. His great accomplishment is of one who is never blind to the conflicting forces of evil, of honor, of loyalty, of spiritual death and earthly love, and if, like some of the Elizabethan dramatists, he is regional and of the American South in the same sense that they were island Englishmen; if, like them, he leaves his dead sprawled across the footlights of the stage, like them he has succeeded in giving the public of his time a vision of the quickness, the romantic mutability of life which survives the subtle passion of decay.

92. Leslie A. Fiedler, 'William Faulkner: An American Dickens'

October 1950

Commentary, x, 384–7.

Fiedler (b. 1917), one of America's most fertilely imaginative critics, was at this time at the University of Montana. Insisting on the need to go beyond the impersonal formalism of the New Criticism, he combines Freudian and archetypal insights with historical and biographical background. *Love and Death in the American Novel* includes a discussion of *Sanctuary*.

No one can write about William Faulkner without committing himself to the weary task of trying to disengage the author and his work from the misconceptions that surround them. It has taken me ten years of wary reading to distinguish the actual writer of *The Sound and the Fury* from a synthetic Faulkner, compounded of sub-Marxian stereotypes (Negro-hater, nostalgic and pessimistic proto-fascist, etc.); and I am aware that there is yet another pseudo-Faulkner, derived mostly from the potboiling *Sanctuary*, a more elaborate and chaotic Erskine Caldwell, revealing a world of barnyard sex and violence through a fog of highbrow rhetoric. The grain of regrettable truth in both these views is lost in their misleading emphases; and equally confusing are the less hysterical academic partial glimpses which make Faulkner primarily a historian of Southern culture, or a canny technician whose evocations of terror are secondary to Jamesian experiments with 'point of view.' Faulkner, also distorting Faulkner, once told a class of young writers that he never considers form at all! I am moved by the newest collection of Faulkner's short stories (*Collected Stories of William Faulkner*) to propose another partial view as a counterweight to the others.

There have been in the last weeks predictions from various quarters that Faulkner, now that his latest novel was chosen by the Book of the

Month Club, will shortly win a wider audience. But he has been, though the fact has been astonishingly overlooked, for nearly twenty years the most widely read American writer of whom any respectable critic has been tempted to use the word 'great.'

In Dixon Wecter's recent history of American life during the years of the Great Depression, the name of Faulkner is not even mentioned; yet in the years covered by Mr. Wecter's book, Faulkner published not only his two greatest novels, but also some sixty stories, nearly twenty of them in the *Saturday Evening Post*, which is, I suppose, the magazine most likely to be picked up by the common man when he has seen all the movies in town. One must make certain qualifications, of course; neither *The Sound and the Fury* nor *Light in August*, his most eminent novels, have had a wide sale. But as a short story writer, he has sold consistently to the mass circulation magazines, apparently pleasing the widest of our reading publics.

It is a strange experience for those of us to whom Faulkner's name is associated with the critical journals in which his fiction almost never appears, to find his stories, dressed up with the obvious pictures of the weekly family magazine, flanked not by a Kafka or Joyce, but by the dismal hacks whose names I cannot even now (though I have just looked) remember. Sometimes Faulkner writes for *Harper's*, but never for anything even as pretentious as the *New Yorker*. The only 'little magazine' which has printed any of the present stories is *Sewanee Review*, in which first appeared the charming but utterly slick 'A Courtship.'

If Faulkner's stories were the work of his left hand, their appearance in popular magazines would be of little consequence (a man has to live!), but Faulkner is essentially a short story writer. He has no special talent for sustained narrative, though twice he has brought off a *tour de force* in long fiction. The forty-three stories in the present collection are by no means his total achievement. In it are included most of the stories from two earlier collections now out of print, *These Thirteen* and *Dr. Martino*; but the seven stories of *Go Down, Moses* are not included, nor those loosely worked together in *The Unvanquished*, nor the four magazine tales woven into the text of *The Hamlet*, nor the Gavin Stevens detective stories (*Saturday Evening Post* favorites) which were gathered together last year in a pseudo-long narrative called *Knight's Gambit*.

Faulkner as a storyteller is apparently short-breathed by nature, and his years of writing for the stringent space limits of the magazines has confirmed his tendency to write in gasps. What look like novels at first glimpse, *The Hamlet* or *The Unvanquished*, for instance, come apart into loosely linked short narratives; *Light in August* achieves substance by intertwining two separate stories, and *Sanctuary*, slim enough in finished form, consists of various sub-plots out of the Sartoris–Snopes background, tacked onto the original money-making shocker. Only in *Absalom, Absalom!* and *The Sound and the Fury* has Faulkner worked out genuine full-length narratives by extension rather than patchwork; and even in these two books, he attains novelistic thickness not by inventing a long, complex fable, but by revealing in a series of strict 'point of view' accounts of the same experience the amount of narrative material proper to a short story. It is this experiment with 'point of view,' a virtue made of a short-breathed necessity, that has concealed somewhat the essentially popular nature of Faulkner's work, and has suggested to his critics comparisons with Proust or Joyce or James, rather than Dickens, whom he so strikingly resembles. The inventor of Popeye and the creator of Quilp have a great deal in common besides an obsession with the grotesque, and especially they have a demonic richness of invention (typified by their equal skill at evoking names that are already myths before the characters are drawn) and a contempt for the platitudes of everyday experience.

Like Dickens, Faulkner is primarily, despite his intellectual *obiter dicta*, a sentimental writer; not a writer with the occasional vice of sentimentality, but one whose basic mode of experience is sentimental, in an age when the serious 'alienated' writer emblazons anti-sentimentality on his coat of arms. In a writer whose very method is self-indulgence, that sentimentality becomes sometimes downright embarrassing, as in the stories of World War II in the present collection, 'Tall Men,' 'Two Soldiers,' etc., in which the soupiest clichés of self-sacrifice and endurance are shamelessly worked; he is not above the crassest 'happy endings,' stagemanaging creakily the fulfillments that we had hoped for against all logic and probability. Even in so good a story as 'Uncle Willy' the subtlety of tone and the ingenuity of development serve the conventional soft tale of the town lush opposed to the embattled forces of spinsterhood in a struggle for the old man's life and a boy's soul. Since Romanticism, the reservoir of the sentimental has been nostalgia, and in popular American literature this reservoir has been preeminently the nostalgia for boyhood and for our only home-grown Middle Ages, the ante-bellum South. The South conquered the popular imagination at the moment of its defeat, and the number of synthetic latterday supporters of the Confederacy is exceeded among us only by the synthetic rooters for Notre Dame. When the bloody corn-cobs are brushed aside, we can see there is a large area of popular commitment which Faulkner shares with the author of *Gone With the Wind*.

Faulkner is a Rousseauist at a time when scarcely a serious writer has not found a way to mock the Noble Savage. Recently, in a general recantation of his earlier bitterness, he has been telling us that all men are good, that is, better than their circumstances would lead us to expect. And the best men in Faulkner are small boys, peasants, Indians, and Negroes. The American extension of Rousseauism through James Fenimore Cooper leads directly to William Faulkner. The great un-popular novels of the twentieth century are urban, cosmopolite, but his writing has been non-urban, even anti-urban, as has the popular sub-literature produced largely for city-dwellers from fashionable suburbs. Faulkner is, without doubt, the last serious writer in the United States to attempt Noble Savage Indian stories ('The Courtship,' 'Lo!'), as well as tales of hunting, fishing, horsemanship, and aviation—stunt and combat flying, to be sure—where the matter-of-fact machine is triumphed over, as the plod and pull of the horse is romantically sublimated in jumping. What other novelist of first rank can write so directly to the average American?

The subject matter *par excellence* of the modern novel, the alienation of the artist, and the hero *par excellence*, a Dedalus wandering the city in the vain hope of embracing his father, the citizen, are alien to Faulkner. He has only one story and one early novel in which the artist is protagonist; and this, too, is fortunate for Faulkner. The occasional 'intellectual' whom he uses for a mouthpiece, Ratliffe, the sewing machine salesman, or Gavin Stevens, is an intellectual who can mingle unnoticed with the boys on the front porch, wearing the Phi Beta Kappa key which no one recognizes. This is Faulkner's sentimentalized image of himself, not even the writer but the peddler or the lawyer, accepted and admired by the whole people, for whom he adjusts his grammar and to whom he reveals the truth of their plight, not as a prophet but as a detective—the poor man's intellectual.

The detective story is the inevitable crown of Faulkner's work; in it (the six stories in *Knight's Gambit* and *Intruder in the Dust*) many strains of writing find fulfillment, not least his concern with the 'switcheroo' and the surprise ending. Such devices are generally regarded these days as old-fashioned and factitious, but Faulkner has always shared with the mass public a sneaking fondness for them. 'A Rose for Emily,' in some ways the best of his short stories, is marred by the last-minute use of such machinery, and many of his other pieces good or bad ('Hair,' 'A Courtship') employ that disreputable device, presumed to have died with O. Henry. In the sub-literature of the detective novel the 'switcheroo' has not only survived, but has become its very point; and it is therefore inevitable that Faulkner turn more and more to that form, as, indeed, Dickens was doing at the end of his career.

The final likeness of Dickens and Faulkner has been almost obliterated by opposite distortions; we are inclined to believe, if we accept the stereotypes, that the grotesque in Dickens is almost exclusively comic, while the same element in Faulkner is invariably horrible. But Dickens has won increasing recognition as a sober exploiter of irrational evil, and attempts have been made to establish Faulkner as a humorist. There are various kinds of humor in Faulkner, the most common 'pure' form being the bargaining story, with the climax of the trickster tricked. But precisely as in Dickens, there is no clear line between the horrible and the funny; it is all what we would call in our newest vocabulary 'the absurd.' The cast of most of Faulkner's humorous stories is drawn from the Snopeses, the perpetrators of his most revolting horrors. One of the best stories in the present collection, 'Barn Burning,' is a tale of unrelieved horror told through the eyes of a boy watching his father, the aboriginal Ab Snopes; and from the seed of that story is developed a large part of *The Hamlet*, which begins in terror and passes through the affair of the idiot and the cow to an ambivalent climax of horse-trading and treasure-hunting, by turns simply funny and absolutely horrible; and the final generation of Snopeses appears in the midst of Popeye's impotent ravages in *Sanctuary*, as two purely burlesque cornballs, mistaking a brothel for a hotel. The art of the grotesque, whether comical or horrible, has always a popular appeal, impelling each character toward becoming his own archetype, and thus making possible the playing out of moral conflicts as melodrama or farce.

There are, of course, obstacles between Faulkner and complete popular acceptance. His monstrously involved 'point of view' is a lion in the path, but it poses a problem in only three or four of his eighteen books, and is not troublesome at all in the short stories. Then, there is his prose style, whose sheer pretentious ineptitude often puts off all readers, popular or highbrow; but the pseudo-poetry of the author of bad verse is rather an attraction really for the common reader with his dim sense of rhetoric as desirable. If it were only easier to skip in Faulkner! It is necessary in simple self-defense; but his connecting links are so often lost within the double-parentheses of precisely the most unreadable passages, that one skips only at the price of confusion.

In general, the subject matter of Faulkner is congenial to popular taste, but he suffers in two respects, by an omission and an emphasis. His concern with sex at its most lurid, his monotonously nymphomaniac women, his lovers of beasts, his rapists and dreamers of incest, put off the ordinary reader, who tends to prefer his pornography pure. The average reader is no prude about sex, he merely insists that it be kept in its place, that is, in trash and not in literature, demanding a distinction much like that between the harlot and the honest woman he marries.

More important, I think, is Faulkner's avoidance of young love, his almost hysterical campaign against the myth of the pure girl, which joins him to most post-Flaubertian serious novelists, but cuts him off from the providers of popular entertainment. The purest passionate relations in Faulkner are between men in love with the same woman, who is usually quite unworthy of either; the tenderest feeling he evokes (barring the almost sickly-sweet idyll of Ike and the cow) are between brother and sister, or a boy and an old man, whether a white hophead, an Indian hunter, or a proud Negro. Even in *Knight's Gambit*, the most syrupy of Faulkner's works, he cannot quite bring himself to redeem the *ingénue* for love, but saves the final clinch for a middle-aged pair, to whom a nineteen-year-old boy says at the curtain, 'Bless you my children!'

But American literature, popular and serious, has a counter-tradition to the boy-girl-marriage routine, a pair of juvenile, sub-sexual myths of love, perhaps even more deeply rooted in our land: unconsummated brother–sister incest (from the very first American novel through Hawthorne, Poe, and Melville to a recent successful movie, *Miss Tatlock's Millions*), and the platonic passion of white boy and colored man, the dream of a love stronger than our strongest guilt (most splendidly expressed in *Huckleberry Finn*) that reaches a climax in *Go Down, Moses* and *Intruder in the Dust*.

That Faulkner is an uneven writer everyone knows; but the good and bad in his work cannot be equated with the popular and highbrow elements. The two distinctions cut through his achievement on different planes; he is neither a natural storyteller confusing his talent with forays into the 'literary,' nor a great artist prostituting his talents for a living.

His successes and failures are alike rooted in each level; and, indeed, he is often a 'bad' writer, both by purely slick standards and in light of the higher criticism.

Why he is such a super-eminently good 'bad' writer, surmounting excesses of maudlin feeling and absurd indulgences in overripe rhetoric alike, is a mystery. We can only cite the astonishing richness of invention and specification, the ability to realize characters and tensions with a power to coerce our credence that has nothing to do with a resemblance to 'real' life or the technical standards we had fondly supposed would be demanded of any first-rate fiction in our time. It is only the just and delightful final turn of the screw that so baffling a writer has pleased over twenty-five years two audiences, each unaware of the fact, much less the grounds, of the other's appreciation.

93. John Lydenberg, 'Nature Myth in Faulkner's "The Bear"'

March 1952

American Literature, xxiv, 62–72. This was the first article on Faulkner in *American Literature*.

Most of the early articles on mythic patterns in Faulkner's fiction were on 'The Bear'; usually they treated it as a discrete story rather than as a part of *Go Down, Moses.* Two of the best were this one and R. W. B. Lewis's 'The Hero in the Modern World,' *Kenyon Review*, Autumn 1951.

Lydenberg has taught for many years at Hobart College, Geneva, New York.

I

William Faulkner's power derives in large part from his myth-making and myth-using ability. The mythical aspects of this work are twofold. One type of Faulkner myth has been widely recognized and discussed. Probably the best exposition of this appears in the introduction to the Viking *Portable* selections, in which Malcolm Cowley shows how Faulkner's vision of a mythical South informs and gives unity to the bulk of his best work. His characters grow out of the dense, lush fabric of Southern society. But they are not realistic exemplars of aspects of the South. The most notable of them are larger than life and carry with them an obvious, if not always clear, allegorical significance. Men like Sutpen or Hightower or Joe Christmas or Popeye—to suggest only a few of the many—are more-than-human actors in the saga of the mythical kingdom of Yoknapatawpha, the Mississippi county that symbolizes Faulkner's South.

But of course his stories are not merely about the South; they are about men, or Man. Here appears the other type of myth: the primitive nature myth. Perhaps one should not say 'appears,' for the myth lies imbedded in Faulkner's feeling about human actions and seldom appears as a readily visible outcropping, as does his conception of the mythical kingdom. Faulkner feels man acting in an eternity, in a timeless confusion of past and future, acting not as a rational Deweyan creature but as a natural, unthinking (but always moral) animal. These men do not 'understand' themselves, and neither Faulkner nor the reader fully understands them in any naturalistic sense. Sometimes these creatures driven by instinct become simply grotesques; sometimes the inflated rhetoric gives the characters the specious portentousness of a gigantic gray balloon. But often the aura of something-more-ness casts a spell upon the reader, makes him sense where he does not exactly comprehend the eternal human significance of the ritual activities carried out by these suprahuman beings. They are acting out magical tales that portray man's plight in a world he cannot understand or control. They are Man, the primordial and immortal, the creator and protagonist of myth.

This dual myth-making can best be demonstrated in the short story 'The Bear.' 'The Bear' is by general agreement one of Faulkner's most exciting and rewarding stories. Malcolm Cowley and Robert Penn Warren have both shown its importance for an understanding of Faulkner's attitudes toward the land, the Negro, and the South. Warren referred to it as 'profoundly symbolic,' but refrained from examining its symbolism except as it relates to Faulkner's Southern mythology. No one—so far as I know—has sought to explain just what makes it so powerful and moving, what gives one the feeling that it is more than a superb hunting story and more than an allegory of man's relation to the land and to his fellow man.* The source of this power can be discerned if we see that beneath its other layers of meaning, the story is essentially a nature myth.

'The Bear,' in its final version, can be summarized briefly. When Ike McCaslin is ten, he is first taken with a group of men on their yearly hunting trip into the wilderness of Sutpen's hundred. He quickly learns to be a good hunter under the tutelage of the old half-Indian, half-Negro guide, Sam Fathers. The routine hunting has an added goal: the killing of Old Ben, a huge and sage, almost legendary bear, who always

* Since this was written an essay by R. W. B. Lewis, 'The Hero in the New World: William Faulkner's *The Bear*,' appeared in the *Kenyon Review*, Autumn, 1951. Mr. Lewis's essay makes a more elaborate analysis of the story, including Part IV, than I do here, and deals with the second type of myth. Although his interpretation is quite different from mine, it seems to me that the two readings are not so much contradictory as complementary.

defies capture. Sam Fathers maintains that none of their dogs can bring Old Ben to bay, and that they must find one stronger and braver. Finally he gets what he needs, a wild dog named Lion. When Ike is sixteen, the last chase occurs. Hunters shoot in vain, hounds are killed as they try to hold Ben. And then Lion rushes in, followed by Boon, the quarter-Indian retainer, who charges like the dog, directly upon the bear, to make the kill with his knife. Lion dies from his wounds the next day. Sam Fathers drops from exhaustion and dies shortly thereafter. The story proper is then interrupted by Part IV, a section as long again as the rest. Part V is a short epilogue, telling of Ike's sole return to the scene of his apprenticeship, his visit to the graves of Lion and Sam Fathers, and his meeting with Boon.

On one level the story is a symbolic representation of man's relation to the land, and particularly the Southerner's conquest of his native land. In attempting to kill Old Ben, the men are contending with the wilderness itself. In one sense, as men, they have a perfect right to do this, as long as they act with dignity and propriety, maintaining their humility while they demonstrate the ability of human beings to master the brute forces of nature. The hunters from Jefferson are gentlemen and sportsmen, representing the ideals of the old order at its best, the honor, dignity, and courage of the South. In their rapport with nature and their contest with Old Ben, they regain the purity they have lost in their workaday world, and abjure the petty conventions with which they ordinarily mar their lives. But as Southerners they are part of 'that whole edifice intricate and complex and founded upon injustice'; they are part of that South that has bought and sold land and has held men as slaves. Their original sins have alienated them irrevocably from nature. Thus their conquest of Old Ben becomes a rape. What might in other circumstances have been right, is now a violation of the wilderness and the Southern land.

Part IV makes explicit the social comment implied in the drama of Old Ben. It consists of a long and complicated account of the McCaslin family, white and mulatto, and a series of pronunciamentos by Ike upon the South, the land, truth, man's frailties and God's will. It is in effect Ike's spiritual autobiography given as explanation of his reasons for relinquishing and repudiating, for refusing to own land or participate actively in the life of the South. Ike discovers that he can do nothing to lift or lighten the curse the Southerners have brought on themselves, the monstrous, offspring of their God-given free will. The price of purity, Ike finds, is non-involvement, and he chooses purity.

Thus Part IV carries us far beyond the confines of the story of the hunt. It creates a McCaslin myth that fits into the broad saga of Faulkner's mythical kingdom, and it includes in nondramatic form a good deal of direct social comment. The rest of 'The Bear' cannot be regarded as *simply* a dramatic symbolization of Ike's conscientious repudiation. Its symbolism cannot fully be interpreted in terms of this social myth. One responds emotionally to the bear hunt as to a separate unit, an indivisible and self-sufficient whole. Part IV and Old Ben's story resemble the components of a binary star. They revolve about each other and even cast light upon each other. But each contains the source of its own light.*

II

It is the mythical quality of the bear hunt proper that gives the story its haunting power. Beneath its other meanings and symbolisms lies the magical tale enacted by superhuman characters. Here religion and magic are combined in a ritual demonstration of the eternal struggle between Man and Nature. A statement of the legend recounting their partial reconciliation would run somewhat as follows:

Every fall members of the tribe make a pilgrimage to the domain of the Great Beast, the bear that is more than a bear, the preternatural animal that symbolizes for them their relation to Nature and thus to life. They maintain, of course, the forms of routine hunts. But beneath the conventional ritual lies the religious rite: the hunting of the tribal god, whom they dare not, and cannot, touch, but whom they are impelled to challenge. In this rite the established social relations dissolve; the artificial ranks of Jefferson give way to more natural relations as Sam Fathers is automatically given the lead. The bear and Sam are both taboo. Like a totem animal, Old Ben is at the same time sacred, and dangerous or forbidden (though in no sense unclean). Also he is truly animistic, possessing a soul of his own, initiating action, not inert like other creatures of nature. And Sam, the high priest, although alone admitted to the arcana and trusted with the tutelage of the young neophyte, is yet outside the pale, living by himself, irrevocably differentiated from the others by his Negro blood, and yet kept pure and attuned to nature by his royal Indian blood.

This particular legend of man and the Nature God relates the

* Two early versions of 'The Bear' appeared in magazines; little of Part IV is to be found in either version.

induction of Ike, the natural and pure boy, into the mysteries of manhood. Guided by Sam Fathers, Ike learns how to retain his purity and bring himself into harmony with the forces of Nature. He learns human woodlore and the human codes and techniques of the hunt. And he learns their limitations. Old Ben, always concerned with the doings of his mortals, comes to gaze upon Ike as he stands alone and unprepared in a clearing. Ike 'knew that the bear was looking at him. He never saw it. He did not know whether it was facing him from the cane or behind him.' His apprehension does not depend on human senses. Awareness of his coming relation to the bear grows not from rational processes, but from intuition: 'he knew now that he would never fire at it.'

Yet he must see, must meet, Old Ben. He will be vouchsafed the vision, but only when he divests himself of man-made signs of fear and vanity. '*The gun*, the boy thought. *The gun*. "You will have to choose," Sam said.' So one day, before light, he starts out unarmed on his pilgrimage, alone and helpless, with courage and humility, guided by his newly acquired woodlore, and by compass and watch, traveling till past noon, past the time at which he should have turned back to regain camp in safety. He has not yet found the bear. Then he realizes that divesting himself of the gun, necessary as that is, will not suffice if he wishes to come into the presence. 'He stood for a moment—a child, alien and lost in the green and soaring gloom of the markless wilderness. Then he relinquished completely to it. It was the watch and the compass. He was still tainted.'

He takes off the two artifacts, hangs them from a bush, and continues farther into the woods. Now he is at last pure—and lost. Then the footprints, huge, misshapen, and unmistakable, appear, one by one, leading him back to the spot he could no longer have found unaided, to the watch and the compass in the sunlight of the glade.

> Then he saw the bear. It did not emerge, appear; it was just there, immobile, fixed in the green and windless noon's hot dappling, not as big as he had dreamed it but as big as he had expected, bigger, dimensionless against the dappled obscurity, looking at him. Then it moved. It crossed the glade without haste, walking for an instant into the sun's full glare and out of it, and stopped again and looked back at him across one shoulder. Then it was gone. It didn't walk into the woods. It faded, sank back into the wilderness without motion as he had watched a fish, a huge old bass, sink back into the dark depths of its pool and vanish without even any movements of its fins.

Ike has seen the vision. That is his goal, but it is not the goal for the tribe, nor for Sam Fathers who as priest must prepare the kill for them. They are under a compulsion to carry out their annual ritual at the time of 'the year's death,' to strive to conquer the Nature God whose very presence challenges them and raises doubts as to their power.

The priest has first to make the proper medicine; he has to find the right dog. Out of the wilds it comes, as if sent by higher powers, untamable, silent, like no other dog. Then Sam, magician as well as priest, shapes him into the force, the instrument, that alone can master Old Ben. Lion is almost literally bewitched—broken maybe, but not tamed or civilized or 'humanized.' He is removed from the order of nature, but not allowed to partake of the order of civilization or humanity.

Sam Fathers fashions the instrument; that is his duty as it has been his duty to train the neophyte, to induct him into the mysteries, and thus to prepare, in effect, his own successor. But it is not for the priest to perform the impious and necessary deed. Because he belongs to the order of nature as well as of man—as Ike does now—neither of them can do more than assist at the rites. Nor can Major de Spain or General Compson or other human hunters pair with Lion. That is for Boon, who has never hit any animal bigger than a squirrel with his shotgun, who is like Lion in his imperturbable nonhumanity. Boon is part Indian; 'he had neither profession job nor trade'; he has 'the mind of a child, the heart of a horse, and little hard shoe-button eyes without depth or meanness or generosity or viciousness or gentleness or anything else.' So he takes Lion into his bed, makes Lion a part of him. Divorced from nature and from man—'the big, grave, sleepy-seeming dog which, as Sam Fathers said, cared about no man and no thing; and the violent, insensitive, hard-faced man with his touch of remote Indian blood and the mind almost of a child'—the two mavericks live their own lives, dedicated and fated.

The 'yearly pageant-rite' continues for six years. Then out of the swamps come the rest of the tribe, knowing the climax is approaching, accepted by the Jefferson aristocrats as proper participants in the final rites. Ike, the young priest, is given the post of honor on the one-eyed mule which alone among the mules and horses will not shy at the smell of blood. Beside him stands the dog who 'loved no man and no thing.' Lion 'looked at him. It moved its head and looked at him across the trivial uproar of the hounds, out of the yellow eyes as depthless as Boon's, as free as Boon's of meanness or generosity or gentleness or viciousness. They were just cold and sleepy. Then it blinked, and he knew it was not looking at him and never had been, without even bothering to turn its head away.'

The final hunt is short, for Old Ben can be downed only when his time has come, not by the contrived machinations of men, but by the destined ordering of events and his own free will. The hounds run the bear; a swamper fires; Walter Ewell fires;* Boon cannot fire.† Then the bear turns and Lion drives in, is caught in the bear's two arms and falls with him. Ike draws back the hammers of his gun. And Boon, like Lion, drives in, jumps on Ben's back and thrusts his knife into the bear's throat. Again they fall. Then 'the bear surged erect, raising with it the man and the dog too, and turned and still carrying the man and the dog it took two or three steps towards the woods on its hind feet as a man would have walked and crashed down. It didn't collapse, crumple. It fell all of a piece, as a tree falls, so that all three of them, man dog and bear, seemed to bounce once.'

The tribe comes up, with wagon and mules, to carry back to camp the dead bear, Lion with his guts raked out, Boon bleeding, and Sam Fathers who dropped, unscathed but paralyzed, at the moment that Ben received his death wound. The doctor from the near-by sawmill pushes back Lion's entrails and sews him up. Sam lies quiet in his hut after talking in his old unknown tongue, and then pleading, 'Let me out, master. Let me go home.'

Next day the swampers and trappers gather again, sitting around Lion in the front yard, 'talking quietly of hunting, of the game and the dogs which ran it, of hounds and bear and deer and men of yesterday vanished from the earth, while from time to time the great blue dog would open his eyes, not as if he were listening to them but as though to look at the woods for a moment before closing his eyes again, to remember the woods or to see that they were still there. He died at sundown.' And in his hut Sam quietly goes after the bear whose death he was destined to prepare and upon whose life his own depended, leaving behind the de Spains and Compsons who will no longer hunt in this wilderness and the new priest who will keep himself pure to observe, always from the outside, the impious destruction of the remaining Nature by men who can no longer be taught the saving

* In 'The Old People,' the story preceding 'The Bear' in *Go Down, Moses*, Faulkner says that Walter Ewell never misses. Thus mention of his shooting and missing at this particular time takes on added significance.

† Boon explained that he could not fire because Lion was too close. That was, of course, not the 'real' reason; Boon could not kill Ben with a civilized gun (to say nothing of the fact that he couldn't hit anything with his gun anyway).

virtues of pride and humility. They have succeeded in doing what they felt they had to do, what they thought they wanted to do. But their act was essentially sacrilegious, however necessary and glorious it may have seemed. They have not gained the power and strength of their feared and reverenced god by conquering him. Indeed, as human beings will, they have mistaken their true relation to him. They tried to possess what they could not possess, and now they can no longer even share in it.

Boon remains, but he has violated the fundamental taboo. Permitted to do this by virtue of his nonhumanity, he is yet in part human. He has broken the law, killed with his own hand the bear, taken upon himself the mastery of that which was no man's to master. So when the chiefs withdraw, and the sawmills grind their way into the forests, Boon polices the new desecrations. When Ike returns to gaze once more upon the remnants of the wilderness, he finds Boon alone in the clearing where the squirrels can be trapped in the isolated tree. Boon, with the gun he could never aim successfully, frenziedly hammers the barrel against the breech of the dismembered weapon, shouting at the intruder, any intruder, 'Get out of here! Don't touch them! Don't touch a one of them! They're mine!' Having killed the bear, he now possesses all the creatures of nature, and will snarl jealously at the innocent who walks peacefully through the woods. The result of his impiety is, literally, madness.

III

That, of course, is not exactly Faulkner's 'Bear.' But it is part of it, an essential part. If a reading of the story as myth results in suppressions and distortions, as it does, any other reading leaves us unsatisfied. Only thus can we answer certain crucial questions that otherwise baffle us. The most important ones relate to the four central characters: Why can Ike or Sam not kill the bear? why can Boon? Why are Boon and Lion drawn precisely so? And why does Sam Fathers die along with Old Ben?

Ike has developed and retained the requisite purity. He has learned to face nature with pride and humility. He is not tainted like de Spain and Compson by having owned slaves. According to Faulkner's version of the huntsman's code, Ike should be the one who has the right to kill Old Ben, as General Compson feels when he assigns him the one mule that can approach the bear. Or it might be argued that Sam Fathers, with his unsurpassed knowledge, instinct, and dignity, rightly deserves the honor. If old Ben is merely the greatest of bears, it would seem fitting for either Ike or Sam to demonstrate his impeccable relationship to nature by accomplishing the task. But Faulkner rules differently.

Lion and Boon do it. At first glance that may seem explicable if we consider Old Ben's death as symbolizing man's destruction of the wilderness. Then the deed cannot be performed by Ike or Sam, for it would be essentially vicious, done in violation of the rules by men ignorant or disrespectful of the rules. Thus one may think it could be assigned to Boon, 'the plebeian,' and that strange, wild dog. But actually neither of them is 'bad,' neither belongs to a mean order of hunters. Boon and Lion are creatures set apart, dehumanized, possessing neither virtues nor vices. In their actions and in his words describing them, Faulkner takes great pains to link them together and to remove from them all human traits.*

Thus the killing of the bear cannot be explained by a naturalistic interpretation of the symbolism. Old Ben is not merely an extraordinary bear representing the wilderness and impervious to all but the most skilful or improper attacks. He is the totem animal, the god who can never be bested by men with their hounds and guns, but only by a nonhuman Boon with Lion, the instrument fashioned by the priest.

Sam Fathers' death can likewise be explained only by the nature myth. If the conquest of Old Ben is the triumphant culmination of the boy's induction into the hunting clan, Sam, his mentor, would presumably be allowed a share in the triumph. If the bear's death symbolizes the destruction of the wild, Sam's demise can be seen as paralleling that of the nature of which he is so completely a part. But then the whole affair would be immoral, and Sam could not manage and lead the case so willingly, nor would he die placid and satisfied. Only as part of a nature rite does his death become fully understandable. It is as if the priest and the god are possessed of the same soul. The priest fulfils his function; his magic makes the god vulnerable to the men. He has to do it; and according to human standards he wins a victory for his tribe. But it is a victory for which the only fit reward is the death he is content to accept. The actors act out their ordained roles. And in the end the deed brings neither jubilation nor mourning—only retribution, tragic in the high sense, right as the things which are inevitable are right.

A further paradox, a seeming contradiction, appears in the conjunction of the two words which are repeated so often that they clearly

* In 'The Old People,' Boon is referred to as 'a mastiff.'

constitute a major theme. Pride and humility. Here conjoined are two apparently polar concepts: the quintessence of Christianity in the virtue of humility; and the greatest of sins, the sin of Satan. Though at first the words puzzle one, or else slip by as merely a pleasant conceit, they soon gather up into themselves the entire 'meaning' of the story. This meaning can be read in purely naturalistic terms: Faulkner gives these two qualities as the huntsman's necessary virtues. But they take on additional connotations. Humility becomes the proper attitude to the nature gods, with whom man can merely bring himself into harmony as Sam teaches Ike to do. The pride arises out of the individual's realization of his manhood: his acquisition of the self-control which permits him to perform the rituals as he should. Actually it is humanly impossible to possess these two qualities fully at the same time. Sam alone truly has them, and as the priest he has partly escaped from his humanity. Ike apparently believes he has developed them, finally; and Faulkner seems to agree with him. But Ike cannot quite become Sam's successor, for in acquiring the necessary humility—and insight—he loses the ability to act with the full pride of a man, and can only be an onlooker, indeed in his later life, as told in Part IV and 'Delta Autumn,' a sort of Ishmael.

In conclusion, then, 'The Bear' is first of all a magnificent story. The inclusion of Part IV gives us specific insights into Faulkner's attitudes toward his Southern society and adds another legend to the saga of his mythical kingdom. The tale of Old Ben by itself has a different sort of effect. Our response is not intellectual but emotional. The relatively simple story of the hunting of a wise old bear suggests the mysteries of life, which we feel subconsciously and cannot consider in the rationalistic terms we use to analyze the 'how' of ordinary life. Thus it appears as a nature myth, embodying the ambivalences that lie at the heart of primitive taboos, rituals, and religions, and the awe we feel toward that which we are unable to comprehend or master. From strata buried deep under our rationalistic understanding, it dredges up our feeling that the simple and the primitive—the solid dignity and the superstitions of Sam Fathers—are the true. It evokes our terrible and fatal attraction toward the imperturbable, the powerful, the great—as symbolized in the immortal Old Ben. And it expresses our knowledge that as men we have to conquer and overcome, and our knowledge that it is beyond our human power to do so—that it is necessary and sacrilegious.

94. R. W. Flint, 'Faulkner as Elegist'

Summer 1954

Hudson Review, vii, 246–57.

Robert W. Flint (b. 1921) is an American critic. Recently he has published translations of the Italian writers Pavese and Marinetti. Several months after this article he wrote an unfavorable review of *A Fable*, which he described as 'an embarrassingly *literary* experiment.'

It is a good thing in general to complement the several excellent studies of individual works of Faulkner's that have appeared recently with fresh overall treatment of his themes, to extend and deepen the principles of Faulkner criticism worked out by Robert Penn Warren in his indispensable essay.* Mr. Howe's book-length study is by no means exhaustive in that regard, nor without what seems to me a certain schematic insensitivity to Faulkner's intentions.† I approach Faulkner with a theory which I hope will go a certain way toward answering the objections of critics like Mr. Howe who often appear to be judging him by the standards of the novelists he suggests (or those, like James and George Eliot, against whom he stands in the most glaring contrast) rather than by his own standards. Briefly, I want to consider him as a poetic novelist.

That the novel has moved toward the condition of poetry as poetry itself has declined in prestige is by now a fairly widely recognized critical axiom. To apply it, however, to so robustly concrete a writer as Faulkner, himself an indifferent poet in conventional metres, may seem a particularly foolhardy venture. Criticism has come to think of

* Review of Malcolm Cowley's Introduction to *The Portable Faulkner*, in *Faulkner: Two Decades of Criticism*, edited by Frederick W. Hoffman and Olga Vickery. Michigan State College Press, 1951. The essays by William Poirier, Richard Chase and George Marion O'Donnell mentioned at points in my essay are also included in this valuable anthology which is unfortunately already seriously out of date.

† *William Faulkner: A Critical Study*, by Irving Howe, Random House, 1951.

poetry in fiction as, so to speak, the earned increment of the usual novelistic virtues, not as an added grace-note (in the best instances) nor as a sort of obbligato woven around the more solid and interesting material, but rather as something integral to it, its most precious essence. So, if one defines Faulkner as a poetic novelist in the tradition of Flaubert, Joyce and Lawrence, rather than Maeterlinck, Virginia Woolf or Thomas Wolfe, it is not to shirk the usual tasks of the critic of fiction. On the contrary. This is what makes the job so difficult; many vital considerations must be met before one can reach such a definition.

At the same time, I think my view of Faulkner can help to clarify many of the problems which bother critics who treat him only as a 'pure' novelist in the great moral tradition of English fiction, or, as one fashionable theory would have it, as only a brilliant episodic writer, a sort of 'American Dickens' who derives his power from a species of pre-conscious collaboration with the destructive forces of his time. The 'poetry' I want to demonstrate in my quoted touchstones should, if acknowledged as such, substantially justify many of the digressions which readers have found troublesome in his novels. It would do this by establishing a stylistic perspective, a hierarchy of styles, in fact, of varying weight and authority. But to proceed in terms of style alone would be to defeat my purpose; the great moments must be seen as a sublimation into affirmative statement of *everything* the fiction does, of every tone and theme it adopts.

Faulkner has been one of the most prolific adapters of style in modern literature. The height of his achievement, however, is like nothing else in fiction, a unique transformation of his special literary heritage as an American Southerner. No other novelist, in the act of reaching fairly austere heights of vision, has so often *seemed* to be floundering. His public poses of the coy amateur or the canny, folksy professional hack have kept his most serious audience at a distance; he is delighted to mislead whoever wants to be misled. And the tone of his public speeches, though appropriate enough in terms of the Yoknapatawpha chronicle, must strike anyone who does not know and love his work as somehow queer. I don't mean to imply by this that his Nobel Prize speech may not be inspiriting to other novelists and laymen alike, but I am sceptical of its authority for the non-Faulknerian. Faulkner speaks mostly for himself, hardly at all for 'us'. He cannot help sounding like a 'Faulkner character,' a voice out of that world which rises like a volcanic island from beneath our usual plane of vision. Gavin Stevens notwithstanding, to extract any one philosophical formulation from this world as its essential message is no more than to bring back a flower or rare bird on the supposition that it adequately represents the island. This, I believe, is due to the superior weight of dramatic and poetic over merely intellectual realization in his work. He has a broad working philosophy of life but nowhere distills it out so that it can be examined apart from the fiction itself.

Faulkner's bardic tone is of the essence and no mere affectation: it is only superficially naive or neo-primitive. His elegiac tragi-comedy embraces what he chooses to regard as the decay of the institutionalized middle class wisdom on which James and George Eliot drew so heavily, towards which they had a more sanguine attitude (though James, I think, is also essentially an elegist of the international upper-middle class). We may perhaps not initially sympathize with Faulkner's attitude, especially in a writer himself from the middle class, but we will be the better readers for recognizing it as such.

It is no longer possible, therefore, to treat him as a fabulous *naif*. On the contrary, the worst faults of his writing derive from a deliberate writing down, a mixing of tones and genres under too little pressure of vision. Then we can complain of his vulgarity and note his uncanny adroitness in meeting the *Saturday Evening Post* on its own ground, or his nervous asides to a false ideal of sophistication; for example, when he tells us that Eula Varner, in *The Hamlet*, is a 'kaleidoscopic convolution of mammalian ellipses.' This sort of thing belongs in the novels where verbal fanaticism and vulgarity are evoked only to be ironically reflected upon. But to describe vulgar, inarticulate people in a comic spirit, as he does in *The Hamlet*, one need not be vulgar oneself. I have more to say about this later. My point here is that Faulkner, in fact, is immensely professional and fairly careful to match the spirit of what his people say to their exact social status in Yoknapatawpha. His true naïveté is ambition in the most honorable sense.

The first thing one notices in Faulkner is the high proportion of mere activity to the small amount of decisive moral action. One can be easily fooled by this into supposing that there is no full-blooded moral action at all, that Faulkner is offering some final vision of nihilism, alienation and disaster. How preposterous this theory really is has already been several times demonstrated, most concretely by Cleanth Brooks* and William Poirier in their convincing analyses of

* '*Absalom, Absalom!:* The Definition of Innocence', by Cleanth Brooks, in the *Sewanee Review* for Autumn, 1951.

Absalom, Absalom! As a Southerner, writing at the moment when a regional culture is passing into legend but still available as such, Faulkner can be prodigiously inventive and a firm moral realist in the act of writing poetic novels which are elegiac in the larger perspective. Everything in his background and literary conditioning works towards this end. His genius, then, has been to define his *spirit* in the light of the tradition, to experiment freely, even to play the fool at times, without violating this spirit.

To come down to cases, I want to plunge *in medias res* with a discussion of the vexed question of the meaning of *Light in August*. Mr. Howe's analysis of this book seems to come a cropper over one or two small but crucial points. He feels that Hightower should somehow have saved Christmas from the crude justice inevitably due him as the part-negro murderer of Joanna Burden. The final form of this justice is excruciatingly painful, to be sure; but it *is* inevitable as Faulkner sees the world in this book. If you think of Hightower as really failing at this juncture, then the book does fall apart and is indeed inexplicable as a whole. Malcolm Cowley has called Christmas a 'villain' and Richard Rovere has found him a focus of experience with no clear identity of his own. Both critics are certainly right in detail, but both miss the novel's rationale by a considerable margin. Whether or not Faulkner has read *The Idiot*, his practice in this book is similar to Dostoievsky's. Christmas's ordeal—sexual, racial, moral—is the action which unifies the story, the fundamental, unbreakable rhythm which draws the other people into a common act of judgment by which their world is clarified. The town of Jefferson is appreciably wiser and better when the ordeal is over, and Byron Bunch can marry Lena in a comic pastoral coda matching the lyric prelude of Lena's overland journey. The various Yoknapatawpherian fanaticisms of Hightower, the McEacherns, the Hineses, Joanna Burden and Percy Grimm are absorbed into the grimly successful effort of society to keep itself upright, ironically counterpointed against the greater, more inevitable suffering of Christmas.

Christmas and Hightower must be thought of together; their respective impoverishments are complementary views of a world in which action is radically divorced from thought. Hightower is the radically imperfect clergyman as Christmas is the radically imperfect 'savior' and 'martyr'. Together, they sit in judgment, not on Christianity itself (Faulkner is too profound a realist for that), but on the smug parochial certainties of organized religion. Both, on occasion, are driven from beyond themselves to deliver in the pulpit blasphemous parodies of the Gospel. But Hightower, on the other hand, in the mere act of recognizing Christmas's plight and sheltering him for as long as he could, and by helping Lena as a result of the crisis thereby brought to a head, sees his human duty towards society at large for the first time and gladly performs it at the risk of further disgrace. Far from relapsing into senile indifference, as Mr. Howe claims, he has emerged from romantic confusion, public disgrace and a botched marriage to the point where he can act according to his professed principles. I need hardly add that for him to have sacrificed himself to stop the lynching, which even the upright sheriff was unwilling to attempt, would have made *Light in August* a quite different novel. That would be Ike McCaslin's sort of heroism, not Hightower's, and would demand a quite different mythical context. On the mythical level, *Light in August* is uniquely a 'passion', but any ultimate analogy with Christ ends there. Christmas, as criminal and scapegoat, is clearly meant to atone for all the sins practiced against him, not, indeed, as a 'saint of the underworld' nor as a scapegoat alone, but as a warning memory for future times, 'of itself alone serene, of itself alone triumphant.' We can assent to Faulkner's faith in the value of this example: 'They are not to lose it in whatever peaceful valleys, beside whatever placid and reassuring streams of old age, in the mirroring faces of whatever children they will contemplate old disasters and newer hopes.' In this impeccably firm rhetoric, Faulkner is surely the very opposite of hopeless; its tone implies that everyone has experienced some sort of catharsis. As a matter of fact, as Mr. Howe admits, the novel is full of a radiant sense of human possibility, of an imaginative gusto even in the extremes of Doc Hines's crazy evangelism, and of a lyric feeling for nature. Christmas is returned to the justice of Yoknapatawpha as Myshkin is returned to the bosom of nineteenth-century Russia. Hightower, in the meantime, recognizes his obsession with the past for what it is, and in so doing, is granted an elegiac vision that is one of the chief splendors of Faulkner's art.

From here I must return to some further generalizations about the fiction at large. Suffering is protean and universal in Faulkner, the possibilities of intellectual or spiritual heroism relatively few. From beginning to end, his people are radically defeated in their efforts to reach some safe intellectual vantage-point outside the action. One could even claim that it is 'mind' itself, in the Aristotelian or Jamesian definitions, which plays the role of tragic hero. Faulkner's defeated heroes are an analogue to the integrity of his fiction as elegiac vision.

They remain upright in the reader's mind. We honor Quentin Compson's tenacity if we don't grant him the dignity of a Hamlet. None of them are Hamlets or Christs or Captain Veres or Chillingworths or even Marcels or Stephen Dedaluses. Something more than their respective wisdoms is required to account for Faulkner's sanity; and this, I believe, is the incantatory meditation which emerges from the great moments of action. At the highest level, this is the 'mind' which the fiction itself makes. It is weighted with overtones of florid Southern speechmaking, of Cicero, Byron and Sir Walter Scott, but it is also thoroughly original and unromantic, stiffened by Faulkner's classic sense of affairs, his tragic view of life. Loose, rolling, bardic, it is also a gathering into 'poetry' of the novel's main concerns, a tender celebration of the values released in the action. Faulkner's vision is a sort of improvised Platonism, a world in which certain, not ideas in the antithetical Hegelian sense but ideals in the Kantian sense, subsistent *realities*, such as honor, courtesy, fidelity, integrity and love, are embodied and recognized only in action.

Unless, therefore, one is referring to this 'poetry', I think one must admit that action in Faulkner is always more finished and compelling, more acceptable as a large version of reality, than the opinions of his people about the meaning of their lives. His profusion of folkish apothegms is part of his fiction's secondary texture, a means whereby his people keep themselves going. Even the garrulous Gavin is no more than *primus inter pares* in point of authority. The voice of 'Faulkner himself' whipping up a froth of epithets, forcing home an emphasis, overloading something or other with symbolic weight, is usually an ironic feature, the extension of some quirk in his characters, often serving to reflect ironically on the slow, calm gathering of the main crisis. As Mr. Warren has observed, Faulkner is not primarily a humorist, though humor is part of his given material; in a subdued way (compared to Twain or Dickens) he is highly proficient at it. But in *The Hamlet*, his nearest approach to pure humor, he cannot restrain himself from attributing a metaphysical superabundance of evil to his characters which gives the humor a bitter edge. The Varners and Snopeses, like Miss Reba and her crew in *Sanctuary*, are believable only in the long Faulknerian perspective. But when he relieves the epic tone of *Go Down, Moses* with the misadventures of Uncle Buck and Buddy, or Lucas Beauchamp's quiet fleecing of the Northern salesman, proportion is kept. For Faulkner's vision to condense itself out, he needs to make extensive excursions 'downward' into humor and vulgarity, outward into epic action, and 'upward' into legend. One can also discover subsidiary plays of pure physical quality, as Richard Chase has traced the play of 'round' and 'straight' ideas in *Light in August*, and a rough metaphysic of culture, as George Marion O'Donnell has broken the fiction down into a 'Snopes world' and a 'Sartoris World'. The lesser novels, like *The Unvanquished* or *Sartoris*, set too exclusively in the past, or like *Pylon*, *The Wild Palms*, *Soldiers' Pay*, *Intruder in the Dust*, or *Sanctuary* too exclusively in the present, hamper Faulkner's contrapuntal play of legend and fact. Critics are always finding neglected interest in these books, and rightly so, for nothing Faulkner has written is without touches of his genius. But they are set on too shallow a stage and the action is correspondingly shallow. (*As I Lay Dying*, I think, is the one clear exception to this rule.) Popeye's ghastly corn-shuck or the details of Charlotte's abortion are too violently forced outward, as symbols, against the modern world at large. (The books about the past are relatively temperate and delightful, but minor Faulkner nonetheless.)

Within Yoknapatawpha's boundaries, most of the classic themes of Western fiction are rehearsed: rites of initiation and passage, the quest, the curse, bloodguilt, incest and parricide, the comic journey, hubris and nemesis, sacrifice and atonement, the idyll and the vendetta, crime and punishment. Having said as much, one reflects, after all, how cool and small the world remains, clustered about its court-house square, presided over by the great court-house clock which begins to haunt the novels as far back as *Soldiers' Pay*.

It is immensely shock-absorbent in its warm-blooded lyric negroes, its salty, shiftless poor-whites, its sturdy farmers, lawyers and sheriffs. One can enjoy the novels without responding to their mythical overtones at all. The only element they obviously lack is Jamesian lovemaking and the Jamesian heroine. Faulkner handled it tentatively in *Soldiers' Pay* but soon recognized its uselessness for his fiction except as legend. In *Absalom, Absalom!* he invokes the glamor of the legend in the act of cutting it down to size. Sutpen is a warped realist but his son Henry, born into money but without family status, like Miss Rosa the minister's daughter, is a puritanical romantic, glamorizing what he cannot possess. Charles Bon and the parties at Sutpen's Hundred have a specious glamor for Henry and Miss Rosa, an illusion for which they suffer bitterly.

Faulkner's vision can rise to poetry because it is both aware of the principal modern ideologies and able to make good use of them for what they are worth. His portrait of Sutpen, the human analogue to Old Ben the bear as Melville's Ahab is the human analogue to Moby Dick, has a massive reality which puts it beyond the reach of the clichés of literary Marxism. Sutpen is certainly a prime exploiter of the masses, but in so far as he reenacts the American ideal of the self-made man in its innocence, the masses gladly cooperate with him. He is finally defeated by his arrogant inhumanity. If Marxists wish to draw a lesson from that, they are welcome, but it is proletarian only in the sense that all great art is proletarian. Arrogance is no monopoly of a class. As James deals tragically with the ironies of progressive reformism in Olive Chancellor of *The Bostonians*, so Faulkner deals with it in the meeting of Joe Christmas with Miss Burden, the transplanted New England 'nigger-lover'. That Christmas's ordeal should work itself out in specifically sexual terms is another instance of Faulkner's fruitful awareness of a powerful modern ideology. Sex, in Faulkner as in James, is a great coercive force, not in itself either good or evil.

I have been far from exhaustive in relating my leading ideas to the fiction in detail, but I must get on to some closer definitions of his method. A critic has suggested that Ike McCaslin of 'The Bear' be taken as the spokesman of a new note of hope in Faulkner, a 'new testament' to relieve the gloom of the old. Partial as I am to new testaments, I must agree with W. R. Moses* that this is a rather special-pleading theory. To be sure, Ike survives his rites of the wilderness a wiser and better man, but his life, his spiritual growth, stops exactly there. It would be highly patronizing to assume that Faulkner's does also. In the rest of *Go Down, Moses*, Ike is no more than an amiably cranky offshoot of a clan dominated by old Carothers McCaslin in the past and by Lucas Beauchamp, the mulatto, in the present. Ike breaks off, after the end of the hunting, into a visionary world of his own, no more and no less 'hopeful' than Faulkner's other visionary worlds. But the passage in 'Delta Autumn' in which Ike summons up the past ought to be quoted:

[quotes passage, 'He seemed to see the two of them . . . ,' ending 'phoenix-like to the soundless guns.']

It is altogether splendid,—controlled, firm and affirmative, without allowing us to forget, after all, that McCaslin is something of a crank.

* W. R. Moses, a note on 'The Bear' in *Accent* for Winter, 1953.

My second such touchstone is spoken by Miss Rosa in the middle of *Absalom, Absalom!*:

[quotes passage, 'That was I, I was there; something of me walked . . . ,' ending, 'Then he was. Then he was not.']

Again we have the rolling, fulsome periods towards a moment of strong emphasis, the single occasion when Miss Rosa willingly gives herself up to a larger interest and sees the world as it is. 'Measured cadence', 'sombre gloom', 'awkward and unmanageable', 'firm untrembling', 'gashy', 'knell' and 'sojourn' betray the spinster contributor of odes and elegies to the local newspapers. As an isolated piece of prose, it could hardly be offered as the model of anything except Faulkner's uniquely poignant Virgilian rhetoric (Virgilian in its tone rather than its form). The romantic dream is gone: winter, work, loyalty, competence and order remain.

If these are the most memorable episodes in Faulkner, his other styles need not compete with them for authority. Nor do they. Either they are plainly narrative, distorted to suggest some distortion of spirit (the famous 'fallacy of expressive form' which is, needless to say, very far from fallacious when not overdone) or they are elliptical and allusive, as in the well-known and perhaps overestimated Benjy monologue in *The Sound and the Fury* (whose incoherence stands in lyric-ironic contrast to the heightened prose of the superb Easter scene in the middle of the book). Faulkner will often establish a familiar fictional tone and then go on to undermine it: 'Not this, nor this, nor this, nor even this, but *that!*' thus cutting his way down through layers of conventional expectations, making fun of them as he demolishes them (a device which goes to seed in some later novels when he has nothing very important to reveal and no strong expectations to baffle). In *Absalom, Absalom!* as he successively undermines Miss Rosa's romantic egotism, Jason's romantic amoralism, Bon's truculent fatalism, Shreve's callow distaste and even Quentin's bitter tenacity, to mention only the principal 'voices' of the novel, the prose makes a steady circling motion, chipping away at the expectations his characters arouse. *Then*, indeed, after many excursions and ambushes, when we have finally arrived at the tragic gate which Judith symbolically holds open and Henry closes and the novel's main action is completed, it ceases to be pseudo-gothic and becomes gothic in earnest, in the long closing coda. This, I think, is what makes it such a haunting study of a particular ethos. Life has a way of imitating bad fiction, Faulkner implies. You can have your romantic embroidery and your gothic coda if you take the story seriously. Otherwise both will be intolerable.

I should mention one further feature of his method; his scrambling of time-sequences to provide a closer play of suggestion and analogy, a feature on which modern criticism, with its Joyce-Eliot-and-Pound-begotten avidity for puzzles, has perhaps too exclusively pounced. (Conrad Aiken's pioneering essay makes too much of a jocular mystery out of Faulkner's style, missing its Virgilian center.) Faulkner has nowhere suggested so radical a cyclical view of history as *Finnegans Wake*; but one remembers the turning wheel in Hightower's meditation, the cycles of the hunt, of planting and harvest, the ceaseless journeys of his people back and forth in time and space. Sometimes the analogy prepares us for the rest of the story, as in the following:

[quotes the first sentence of *Absalom, Absalom!*]

This threatening sense of festering energy sets the ground-rhythm of the book. One can claim, I think that the novel takes place between 'two o'clock' and 'sundown' in the history of Faulkner's world, that the house is Miss Rosa herself, that the steadily beating sun is Sutpen's growing interest in her (Mr. Poirier has admirably demonstrated how Sutpen and Miss Rosa complement each other) and the motes are glints of truth from the past which the 'wind' of her passion blows into sight from the 'scaling blinds' of her vision as she approaches the disinterestedness of death. Faulkner's fiction, made up as it is of a great many interrelated styles and techniques, deserves to be called thoroughly composed, *durchkomponiert*, as the Germans say of music, not only in what it presents but in what it suggests.* Each of the four or five great novels is radically different from the others on the surface, but in each he is doing the same kind of thing. It is neither romance nor allegory nor symbolic drama in the traditional meaning of those terms, but plain novelistic fiction with a poetic dimension, a distinguished episode of high tragi-comedy in Western art.

* From the large body of critical writing on Faulkner published after the Hoffman-Vickery anthology, I would single out essays by Cleanth Brooks, Carvel Collins, and Lawrance Thompson on various aspects of *The Sound and the Fury* (*English Institute Essays—1952*, Columbia University Press, 1954) as particularly lucid and illuminating. William Van O'Connor's *The Tangled Fire of William Faulkner* (University of Minnesota Press, 1954) I found rich in information but somewhat timid and conventional in judgment. Irving Howe's book, in spite of its habit of ragging Faulkner for not being more of an Arnoldian liberal, remains the best general introduction, as Robert Penn Warren's essay is the most solid and penetrating critique.

BIBLIOGRAPHY

A selected list of additional articles on Faulkner, 1931–50

In selecting articles for this volume I applied the following criteria: representativeness in Faulkner criticism and in critical attitudes of the period, significance depending on the importance of the reviewer or critic, quality and value of insight. The articles by O'Donnell, Aiken, Cowley, and Warren are much anthologized but indispensable in this historically oriented volume. Olga Vickery's excellent article on *As I Lay Dying* (*Perspective,* 1950) is readily available in her *The Novels of William Faulkner*, as the early articles by Cleanth Brooks and Irving Howe are in their books. With the exception of two articles from the early 1950s, one of the first mythic interpretations of Faulkner (Lydenberg) and an insightful but never reprinted study of Faulkner as elegist (Flint), the collection terminates in 1950, the year Faulkner received the Nobel Prize.

What follows here is a selected list of additional commentaries in English on Faulkner, excluding book reviews, prior to the awarding of the Nobel Prize to him, that is prior to the flourishing and proliferation of Faulkner studies. A checklist of reviews and other materials can be found in my *William Faulkner: An Annotated Checklist of Criticism* (New York, 1972).

1931

JUNIUS JUNIOR, *The Pseudo-Realists* (New York, Outsider Press), pamphlet on *Sanctuary*.

1932

ALAN R. THOMPSON, 'The Cult of Cruelty,' *Bookman*.

A. WIGFALL GREEN, 'William Faulkner at Home,' *Sewanee Review*; reprinted in F. J. Hoffman and O. W. Vickery, ed., *William Faulkner: Two Decades of Criticism* (East Lansing, Michigan, 1951).

JOHN RIDDELL [COREY FORD], *In the Worst Possible Taste* (New York, Scribner's), parody of *Sanctuary*.

LOUIS COCHRAN, article in Memphis *Commercial Appeal*, reprinted in *Mississippi Quarterly*, 1964.

1933

ROBERT LINN, 'Robinson Jeffers and William Faulkner,' *American Spectator*, reprinted in *A. S. Yearbook* (New York, Stokes, 1934), derogatory article.

1934

PHIL STONE, articles in *Oxford Magazine*, reprinted in *Mississippi Quarterly*, 1964.

WYNDHAM LEWIS, 'The Moralist with a Corn-cob,' in *Men Without Art* (London, Cassell), sardonic towards Faulkner.

HARRY HARTWICK, 'The Cult of Cruelty,' in *The Foreground of American Fiction* (New York, American Book Co.).

LAWRENCE S. KUBIE, 'William Faulkner's *Sanctuary:* An Analysis,' *Saturday Review of Literature*, 20 October 1934, 218, 224–26; reprinted in R. P. Warren, ed., *Faulkner* (Englewood Cliffs, New Jersey, 1966); a Freudian analysis of the novel as an example of the 'literature of horror' so prevalent at the time.

1935

JAMES W. LINN and H. W. TAYLOR, 'Counterpoint: *Light in August*,' in *A Foreword to Fiction* (New York, Appleton-Century).

BILL HUDSON, 'Faulkner Before *Sanctuary*,' *Carolina Magazine*, April.

CAMILLE J. MCCOLE, 'The Nightmare Literature of William Faulkner,' *Catholic World*, included in *Lucifer at Large* (New York, Longmans, 1937).

1937

HERBERT J. MULLER, *Modern Fiction* (New York, Funk & Wagnalls).

1940

PERCY BOYNTON, *America in Contemporary Fiction* (University of Chicago Press).

1941

WARREN BECK, 'Faulkner and the South,' *Antioch Review*.

JOSEPH WARREN BEACH, *American Fiction*, 1920–1940 (New York, Macmillan), two entire chapters, one on themes and one on methods.

OSCAR CARGILL, 'The Primitivists,' in *Intellectual America* (New York, Macmillan).

WARREN BECK, 'William Faulkner's Style,' *American Prefaces*; reprinted in F. J. Hoffman and O. W. Vickery, ed., *William Faulkner: Two Decades of Criticism*, also in their *William Faulkner: Three Decades of Criticism* (East Lansing, 1960), and in R. P. Warren, ed., *Faulkner*.

1942

ALFRED KAZIN, 'Faulkner: The Rhetoric and the Agony,' *Virginia Quarterly Review*, included in *On Native Grounds* (New York, Reynal & Hitchcock, 1942).

1943

NORMAN NICHOLSON, *Man and Literature* (London, SCM Press), on Faulkner as romantic and primitivist.

HARRY MODEAN CAMPBELL, 'Experiment and Achievement: *As I Lay Dying* and *The Sound and the Fury*,' *Sewanee Review*, an analysis of style and method.

1945

JOHN MACLACHLAN, 'William Faulkner and the Southern Folk,' *Southern Folklore Quarterly*, on his treatment of poor whites.

1946

NORMAN NICHOLSON, 'William Faulkner,' in *The New Spirit*, ed., E. W. Martin (London, Dobson).

JAMES TURNER JACKSON, 'Delta Cycle: A Study of William Faulkner,' *Chimera*, an impressionistic summary bearing comparison with Cowley's article.

GEORGE SNELL, 'The Fury of William Faulkner,' *Western Review*, included in *The Shapers of American Fiction* (New York, Dutton, 1947).

1947

REED WHITTEMORE, 'Notes on Mr. Faulkner,' *Furioso*, on irrationality and fatalism.

VINCENT F. HOPPER, 'Faulkner's Paradise Lost,' *Virginia Quarterly Review*, on puritanism and despair.

EDWIN BERRY BURGUM, 'William Faulkner's Patterns of American Decadence,' in *The Novel and the World's Dilemma* (New York, Oxford University Press).

HUBERT D. SAAL, 'Faulkner: Chronicler and Prophet,' *Yale Literary Magazine*.

1948

JOHN ARTHOS, 'Ritual and Humor in the Writing of William Faulkner,' *Accent*; reprinted in F. J. Hoffman and O. W. Vickery, ed., *William Faulkner: Two Decades of Criticism*.

LAWRENCE E. BOWLING, 'Faulkner: Technique of *The Sound and the Fury*,' *Kenyon Review*; reprinted in F. J. Hoffman and O. W. Vickery, ed., *William Faulkner: Two Decades of Criticism*.

1949

ANDREW LYTLE, 'Regeneration for the Man,' *Sewanee Review*; reprinted in F. J. Hoffman and O. W. Vickery, ed., *William Faulkner: Two Decades of Criticism*, as well as in R. P. Warren, ed., *Faulkner*.

ROBERT BUNKER, 'Faulkner: A Case for Regionalism,' *New Mexico Quarterly*. This and Lytle's article are essay-reviews of *Intruder in the Dust*.

CHARLES I. GLICKSBERG, 'William Faulkner and the Negro Problem,' *Phylon*.

W. M. FROHOCK, 'William Faulkner: The Private versus the Public Vision,' *Southwest Review*; included in *The Novel of Violence in America* (Dallas, Southern Methodist University Press, 1950).

DAYTON KOHLER, 'William Faulkner and the Social Conscience,' *College English*.

Perspective: special issue (Summer) with Ruel E. Foster, 'Dream and Symbolic Act in Faulkner'; Phyllis Hirshleifer, 'As Whirlwinds in the South: *Light in August*'; Ray B. West, Jr, 'Atmosphere and Theme in Faulkner's "A Rose for Emily" '; Russell Roth, 'William Faulkner: The Pattern of Pilgrimage'; and Sumner C. Powell,

'William Faulkner Celebrates Easter, 1928' (on *The Sound and the Fury*). The Hirshleifer article is reprinted in L. W. Wagner, *William Faulkner: Four Decades of Criticism* (East Lansing, 1973); the West article in the *Two Decades* collection and in M. T. Inge, ed., *William Faulkner: A Rose for Emily* (Columbus, Ohio, 1970); the Foster article in the book he wrote with H. M. Campbell, *William Faulkner: A Critical Appraisal* (Norman, Oklahoma, 1951).

1950

BARBARA GILES, 'The South of William Faulkner,' *Masses and Mainstream*, a Marxist assessment.

KENNETH LaBUDDE, 'Cultural Primitivism in William Faulkner's *The Bear*,' *American Quarterly*.

TOM GREET, 'Toward the Light: The Thematic Unity of Faulkner's "Cycle",' *Carolina Quarterly*.

Perspective: special issue (Autumn) with Harry Modean Campbell, 'Structural Devices in the Works of Faulkner'; Edgar Whan, '*Absalom, Absalom!* as Gothic Myth'; Olga Westland [Vickery], '*As I Lay Dying*'; Tommy Hudson, 'William Faulkner: Mystic and Traditionalist'; and a checklist by J. L. Longley and Robert Daniel. The Vickery article has been reprinted in the *Two Decades* and *Three Decades* collections and, in a revised form, is in her *The Novels of William Faulkner* (Baton Rouge, Louisiana, 1959, rev. ed., 1964); the Campbell article is included in *William Faulkner: A Critical Appraisal*.

Index

The index is divided into three sections: I. William Faulkner's works; II. Characteristics and topics; III. General index (including critics, periodicals, etc.).

I WILLIAM FAULKNER'S WORKS

INDEX

II CHARACTERISTICS AND TOPICS

III GENERAL INDEX